www.wadsworth.com

wadsworth.com is the World Wide Web site for Wadsworth Publishing Company and is your direct source to dozens of online resources.

At wadsworth.com you can find out about supplements, demonstration software, and student resources. You can also send e-mail to many of our authors and preview new publications and exciting new technologies.

wadsworth.com
Changing the way the world learns®

The Religious Life in History Series

The Way of Torah

An Introduction to Judaism

Seventh Edition

JACOB NEUSNER

Bard College

THOMSON

™

WADSWORTH

Australia • Canada • Mexico • Singapore • Spain
United Kingdom • United States

THOMSON
━━★━━ ™
WADSWORTH

Religion Editor: Steve Wainwright
Assistant Editor: Lee McCracken
Editorial Assistant: Anna Lustig
Technology Project Manager: Susan DeVanna
Marketing Manager: Worth Hawes
Marketing Assistant: Kristi Bostock
Project Manager, Editorial Production: Paul Wells
Print/Media Buyer: Barbara Britton
Permissions Editor: Elizabeth Zuber

Production Service: Matrix Productions
Copy Editor: Victoria Nelson
Cover Designer: Margarite Reynolds
Cover Image: Corbis
Cover Printer: Webcom
Compositor: Carlisle Communications, Ltd.
Printer: Webcom

Printed in Canada
1 2 3 4 5 6 7 07 06 05 04 03

For more information about our products, contact us at:
Thomson Learning Academic Resource Center
1-800-423-0563

For permission to use material from this text, contact us by:
Phone: 1-800-730-2214 **Fax:** 1-800-730-2215
Web: http://www.thomsonrights.com

Library of Congress Control Number: 2002117039

ISBN 0-534-51603-3

Wadsworth/Thomson Learning
10 Davis Drive
Belmont, CA 94002-3098
USA

Asia
Thomson Learning
5 Shenton Way #01-01
UIC Building
Singapore 068808

Australia/New Zealand
Thomson Learning
102 Dodds Street
Southbank, Victoria 3006
Australia

Canada
Nelson
1120 Birchmount Road
Toronto, Ontario M1K 5G4
Canada

Europe/Middle East/Africa
Thomson Learning
High Holborn House
50/51 Bedford Row
London WC1R 4LR
United Kingdom

Latin America
Thomson Learning
Seneca, 53
Colonia Polanco
11560 Mexico D.F.
Mexico

Spain/Portugal
Paraninfo
Calle/Magallanes, 25
28015 Madrid, Spain

Contents

VII Classical Judaism in Modern Times: Reform, Orthodox, Conservative Judaisms and Zionism   195

VIII The Practice of Judaism in Contemporary North America 241

✣

Preface

The call for this seventh edition, completely revised, after six prior editions,[1] over more than three decades and in many reprintings, is heartening to me. It means that my descriptive, analytical approach to the academic study of religion exemplified by the case of Judaism will enjoy a hearing well into the twenty-first century. I aim at a coherent account of Judaism over time, with stress upon the large and stable motifs, Creation, Revelation, and Redemption. Through the retelling of a master narrative made actual in both theology and law these generative categories come to concrete expression. So I represent Judaism as the story of the human condition, the familiar tale that through generations of retelling makes a compelling and coherent statement.

While building on the sixth, this seventh edition effects fundamental changes. Some chapters in the sixth edition were dropped or replaced (same topic, new treatment), others were combined into a single chapter, and still other chapters of the seventh edition are altogether new. The changes derive partly from the experience of those who taught introductory courses using the book, beginning with my own experience.

---

[1] The initial publisher was Duxbury Press, but by the time the work was done Duxbury had been taken over by Dickenson. The book began, then, as *The Way of Torah. An Introduction to Judaism* (Encino, CA: Dickenson, 1970), in the *Living Religion of Man* series, edited by Frederick Streng. The second edition, revised, came out in 1973; the third edition, thoroughly revised, was published in 1979 by Wadsworth Publishing Co. The fourth edition, completely revised and rewritten, appeared in 1988; the fifth edition revised and augmented, in 1992. The sixth edition was once again in the *Living Religion of Man* series, revised by Wadsworth and edited this time by Charles Hallisey, in 1997.

On the negative side, in some of the topics I found that more energy than was commensurate with the results was required to teach certain distinctions and propositions. In retrospect, these points were important to me but not to beginning students. In all, I have aimed at a more precise focus for each topical exposition than previously.

On the positive side, the perspective on religion as story, announced in the new Chapter 1, has reshaped the presentation of everything else. The whole presentation now exhibits a narrative character. The course this textbook supports, therefore, forms an exercise in spinning out and illustrating a thesis concerning the character, as a religion, of Judaism. This thesis is, in the words of Father Andrew M. Greeley cited at the head of Chapter 1: "Religion is experience, image and story before it is anything else and after it is everything else. . . ." What I try to show is that the various Judaic religious systems have aimed at telling chapters of a single story, the one that is founded upon scripture read as a coherent statement. Chapter 1 shows how Judaism transforms Scripture's stories into the master-narrative of the human condition.

Let me now specify in detail what I have done to revise the sixth edition and produce a fresh introduction to Judaism.

Completely new, Chapter 1 starts with the definition of the religion, Judaism, within its own native categories. Chapter 2 then defines the history of Judaism viewed from the outside, in the categories of history. Chapter 2 completely revises its counterpart chapters in the sixth edition, some of which I dropped, others of which I combined into the present statement. Only revised from its previous version, Chapter 3 defines Judaism from the perspective of the competing religious tradition, Christianity. Chapter 3 has a new beginning, linking it more tightly to the task of the textbook as a whole. Compared with its counterpart in the sixth edition, this chapter has been heavily pruned. I aimed here at a more economical presentation of the problem.

Chapter 4 is new, providing a more ample introduction to the concept of "Torah" that encompasses the documents of the Oral Torah. I revised Chapters 5 through 7 both by pruning out discussions I found superfluous and also by discussing problems not treated earlier. I have shortened Chapter 8 and moved some of its more general discussions to Chapter 5, on the Mishnah's system of Israel's social order. Chapter 9 is pruned and clarified at a number of points. The concluding unit of Chapter 10 is new.

Chapter 11 combines two chapters of the sixth edition and considerably recasts them both in line with the approach set forth in Chapter 1. Chapter 12 is revised to introduce into the issue of individual and community relationships the motif of Judaism as the realization of the Torah's master narrative of the human condition. Chapters 13 and 14 have been reviewed and lightly revised.

The first four units of Chapter 15 are new. Chapters 16 and 17 are only lightly revised. The opening unit of Chapter 18 is completely new, the other sections merely revised. Chapters 19 through 22 are taken over with only ad hoc changes from the sixth edition. The presentation of the Zohar is fresh; the rest is only glossed and polished. Why include this unit from the earliest editions onward? The reason is that throughout my academic teaching about Judaism I have aimed at translating into the concrete life situation of ideal types of Judaic personalities the narrative theology and law of Judaism—thus, the philosopher, the mystic, the ordinary man, and two extraordinary women. In this way I am able to show how the Judaic system of the Rabbinic sages, set forth in the first five parts of the textbook, through the centuries from the seventh to the nineteenth, was articulated and amplified, developed and revised, while remaining, if not intact, forever unimpaired.

I simplified Chapter 23 removing problems and topics that I treated in the counterpart chapter in the sixth edition. My teaching experience has told me that some of the problems I earlier addressed were not so productive as I had originally supposed. I also reorganized the discussion and, in line with the new Chapter 27, added a discussion of the place of Zionism in the modern period of the history of Judaism. Chapter 24 is pruned, reorganized and tightened. Chapter 25 is reorganized, augmented with the discussion of Samson R. Hirsch, and considerably pruned, relieved of some excessively theoretical discussions. I added to Chapter 26 the concluding unit and cut out what struck me as redundant in the opening units. Chapter 27 is entirely new.

Forming the bridge from the nineteenth to the twentieth centuries, Chapter 28 is entirely new. Chapter 29 is revised and pruned, with some new ideas. But it is now placed into a different context by Chapter 28. Chapter 30 is revised, rewritten in places, and heavily pruned. Chapter 31 is lightly polished and pruned. Chapter 32 is new.

The changes from the sixth edition, therefore, prove formidable. Throughout, I have aimed at a more narrative presentation, treating Judaism as the story the faithful take personally and representing the practices of Judaism as realizations of chapters of that story. From the first chapter to the last, I linked the theology and law of Judaism to its generative story. That meant I had systematically to recast the intervening chapters in light of the new opening.

But there is another source of revision—experience in teaching from this book. Specifically, I read the sixth edition after some years of teaching from it, and consequently I deleted passages and entire chapters that struck me as needlessly complex, focused as they were on problems of special interest to me, not to the students. A comparison between chapters reproduced, with revisions, in the seventh edition with their counterparts in the sixth will show that I have aimed to simplify the presentation and focus more precisely on basic facts, in proper context. I hope that the seventh edition is clearer and more accessible than the prior one(s).

Let me place the ongoing project into its personal context, my own academic autobiography. I got my Ph. D. in 1960, at the age of twenty-eight, and *The Way of Torah*'s successive editions cover nearly the whole of my scholarly life, reflecting its intellectual twists and scholarly turns.

My first effort to think through how to teach the religion, Judaism, in a secular, nonsectarian, and academic framework commenced in 1964, when, after some postdoctoral studies, I began my teaching career at Dartmouth College (1964–1968). This book, in its first edition, written in 1969 and published in 1970, emerged from conversations with my colleagues and experience with my students at Dartmouth. The textbook has formed a companion to my personal and professional life. At that time I had a young family and was just completing the first decade of my teaching career. Life unfolded as later editions were called for. The third edition coincided with the celebration of the bar mitzvah of my firstborn, in 1978. The fourth edition went to press as he entered his senior year of college and went on to his service as an ensign in the U.S. Navy, as his two brothers wended their way through college, and as his sister proceeded through high school. When I reached a happy home at the University of South Florida, the fifth edition went to press as my third son, Noam, began his marriage. The sixth edition coincided with the birth of my wife's and my first grandchild, Emma Rose. So as my children, Samuel, Eli, Noam, and Margalit, to whom, to our great joy, are now added Jill, Samuel's wife, Andrea, Noam's wife, and Poly, Eli's wife, have grown and changed in the quarter-century since this textbook began its life, so have my wife, Suzanne, and I—she in her art, I in my labor of learning.

This seventh edition, realized at Bard College, another happy home indeed, coincides with my seventieth birthday and comes shortly after the birth of our sixth grandchild, with the seventh and eighth on the way. So life continues to unfold. I claim to remain always a learner, seeking to improve my understanding of matters and my presentation of what I understand. The fact that this book takes up a fresh perspective on a subject on which I have worked so long testifies to my goal: to remain always a beginner, seeing everything new and fresh every morning.

I call attention to the anthology of readings that I edited to enrich this textbook, *Signposts on the Way of Torah: A Reader for The Way of Torah,* also published by Wadsworth. These readings correlate with the expositions of this book, both amplifying them and also encompassing entirely new subjects. The textbook and anthology are meant to work together to shape productive class discussions of problems of general interest in the study of religion, illustrated by the data of Judaism.

Signposts on the Way of Torah[2] correlates with the seventh edition of *The Way of Torah* in the following way:

<table>
<tr><td>

Way of Torah, 7th edition

I Defining Judaism, the Religion and Its History

II Classical Judaism
The Oral Part of the Torah

III Classical Judaism
Three Important Doctrines:
Ethics, Ethos, and Ethnos

IV Classical Judaism
The Torah's Theology

V Classical Judaism
The Torah's Way of Life

VI Four Types of Judaic Piety

VII Classical Judaism in Modern Times: Reform, Orthodox, Conservative
Judaisms and Zionism

VIII The Practice of Judaism in Contemporary North America

</td><td>

Signposts on the Way of Torah

Prologue: Defining Judaism, pp. 1–6

I Classical Judaism, pp. 7–96

II Classical Judaism in Modern Times pp. 97–182

III The Practice of Judaism in Contemporary North America, pp. 183–238

IV Zionism and Judaism in the State of Israel, pp. 249–304

V What of the Future, pp. 305–343

</td></tr>
</table>

The first three parts of *Signposts* augment the counterpart units of *The Way of Torah,* seventh edition, and the last two parts introduce topics and discussions that are new.

In addition, for the comparative study of religions I have edited a five-part anthology of essays on important theological topics and a three-part anthology of essays for the comparative study of religious ethics with special reference to family, work, and virtue:

---

[2]Belmont, CA: Wadsworth, 1998.

The Pilgrim Library of World Religions, I. *Christianity, Judaism, Islam, Buddhism, and Hinduism on God.* Cleveland, OH: Pilgrim Press, 1997.

The Pilgrim Library of World Religions, II. *Judaism, Islam, Buddhism, Hinduism and Christianity on Sacred Texts and Authority.* Cleveland, OH: Pilgrim Press, 1998.

The Pilgrim Library of World Religions, III. *Buddhism, Hinduism, Christianity, Judaism, and Islam, on Evil and Suffering.* Cleveland, OH: Pilgrim Press, 1999.

The Pilgrim Library of World Religions, IV. *Islam, Buddhism, Hinduism, Christianity, and Judaism on Woman and the Family.* Cleveland, OH: Pilgrim Press, 1999.

The Pilgrim Library of World Religions, V. *Hinduism, Christianity, Judaism, Islam, and Buddhism on the Afterlife.* Cleveland, OH: Pilgrim Press, 1999.

Comparing Religious Traditions, I. *Judaism, Christianity, Islam, Hinduism, and Buddhism on the Ethics of Family Life: What Do We Owe One Another?* Belmont, CA: Wadsworth, 2000.

Comparing Religious Traditions, II. *Judaism, Christianity, Islam, Hinduism, and Buddhism on Making an Honest Living: What Do We Owe the Community?* Belmont, CA: Wadsworth, 2000.

Comparing Religious Traditions, III. *Judaism, Christianity, Islam, Hinduism, and Buddhism on Virtue: What Do We Owe Ourselves?* Belmont, CA: Wadsworth, 2000.

Comparing Religions Through Law: Judaism and Islam. [With Tamara Sonn] London: Routledge, 1999. E-book edition, London: Taylor and Francis, 2001.

Judaism and Islam in Practice: A Source Book of the Classical Age. [With Tamara Sonn & Jonathan Brockopp] London: Routledge, 2000. E-book edition, London: Taylor and Francis, 2001.

World Religions in America: An Introduction. Louisville, KY: Westminster/John Knox Press, 1994. Second edition: 1999. Third edition: 2002.

God's Rule: The Politics of World Religions. Washington, D.C.: Georgetown University Press, 2003.

Three Faiths, One God. The Formative Faith and Practice of Judaism, Christianity, and Islam [With Bruce D. Chilton & William A. Graham] Leiden and Boston: E. J. Brill, 2002.

In these textbooks and anthologies I make my contribution to the development of the academic study of religion in service of the moral intellect.

Jacob Neusner
Research Professor of Religion and Theology
Bard College
Annandale-on-Hudson, New York
July 28, 2002, My Seventieth Birthday

Introduction

This introduction to Judaism is addressed to students of religions without regard to their personal religious convictions and commitments, if any. People study religion in the neutral setting of the history and comparison of religions such as that presented here because they have decided they cannot understand the world in which they live without grasping the secular facts that concern what religions are and do. The history and comparative study of religion work from the specific religions to religion in general. The case of Judaism represents one important example of what religion is and does.

Why do people inquire? The reason is self-evident in today's world. Religions form principal components of society, culture, and politics in most of the countries of the world, as the conflicts within and between religions prove. The newspapers report daily on conflict between Hindu and Muslim in India, Hindu and Buddhist and Muslim in Sri Lanka, Catholic and Muslim in the Philippines, Judaist and Muslim in the Middle East, Orthodox Christian and Muslim in the Balkans, Evangelical Christian and Roman Catholic Christian in Latin America, Orthodox and Baptist in Russia, or Islamist Muslim and centrist Muslim in many Muslim countries and communities, Turkey, Egypt, and Malaysia, for example—not to mention the war, in the name of Islam, against the United States and the West that captured America's attention on September 11, 2001. So religion takes its place as a principal factor in defining the this-worldly issues of politics, culture, and the social order. That is why we cannot make sense of the world we share with others without some theory of what religion is and does.

So to whom is the case of Judaism introduced? To those that take up the study of world religions in their this-worldly traits and claims, Judaism supplies a useful example. It is both like religion in general and also different from religion in general. It is like other religions because in particular ways it exemplifies traits of religion in general. It conforms to the analytical categories that serve overall: for example, how this religion defines its social entity, how it nurtures a particular corpus of virtue, how it frames its convictions in terms of a logic common to religion in general. It also differs from other religions in striking ways. These differences will emerge when Judaism and other religions are asked to address a topic common to them all.

What exactly constitutes the focus of an introduction to a religion: belief or behavior, individual preferences or communal traits? In general, people define their religions by saying what they believe: for instance, reciting a creed. A definition of Judaism, therefore, could begin with the statement that Judaism believes God is one, unique, just and merciful, and concerned for us and our actions—thus, it is "ethical monotheism." But belief is too small a conception of what a religion is and accomplishes. Religion transcends matters of belief because it shapes behavior. It is rarely a matter of individual predilection but commonly a social construction. Religion makes a difference when it accounts for the life of the social group that professes that religion. So much for defining a religion only in terms of its worldview, its truth claims, its theological structure and system. Such a definition is necessary but insufficient.

But defining religion mainly in terms of what people do also provides only part of the definition. For rites and rituals require explanation—often, as we will see in Chapter 1, in the form of a story. Religions do take positions on theological questions; they do set forth explanations of things and do not merely require actions. So if theology is necessary but insufficient, so too religious practice demands reasoned explanation within the larger intellectual system that sustains a religion.

And a definition of a religion in terms of belief and practice still leaves out a third essential component of that definition. That concerns exactly who practices the faith and affirms its propositions, where we find the believers, and in what context within the larger social order their belief takes place. Religions are public, communal, and social; the faithful do things together; individuals join religious communities. And forming communities takes place over time, so the historical unfolding of a religious tradition enters in.

It is the social dimension that makes religion something we can study. If the individual reports what he or she believes, that is a subjective fact not susceptible of cultural analysis. Then when we study people's personal religions, we accumulate facts that remain inert, not subject to analysis and generalization. When a group of people form a community defined by a common belief, that is an objective fact of the social order, subject to study and analysis.

So a definition of propositions and practices without close attention to their social context in the everyday world proves necessary but insufficient. Where religion makes a difference in the world, such that we can study and analyze concrete facts, it is in the social reality—in the history, community, the here-

and-now of public action associated with specific religions. So, in this context of objective learning, religion matters for several reasons.

First, religion is public; it is social, something people do together; and what people believe tells us only about what individuals think or are supposed to think.

Second, religion governs what we do, telling us who we are and how we should live, whereas what people believe tells us only about attitudes. Religion therefore encompasses not only beliefs or attitudes—matters of mind and intellect—but also actions and conduct.

And third, religion forms the foundation of communities of the faithful and presents the world with objective facts. The ethnos is formed by people otherwise unrelated to one another but who see one another as an extended family, brothers and sisters for example.

TAKE JUDAISM, FOR EXAMPLE

This introduction to Judaism tells the story of how scripture's laws, narratives, and exhortations defined a cogent religious system for holy Israel's[1] social order. It provides a history of the principal system of that religion, the Rabbinic Judaism that took shape in the first six centuries of the Common Era (c.e. = a.d.) became normative. It encompasses an account of how the religion flourishes in the world today, with special emphasis on North America and the English-speaking world. That is where this textbook finds its readers.

This history of the religion Judaism sorts out through time how various religious formulations of that religion's practices and beliefs took shape. It identifies the major periods in the life of the paramount religious system and proposes to show how what happened to that religious system correlates what happened to the religious community—important events that demanded explanation, urgent issues that required attention—with the ongoing unfolding of the system.

In the case of Judaism, as of Christianity and Islam, which are equally complex, a major problem concerns the very definition of the faith: What do we mean by "Judaism"? For, over time, various Judaic religious systems have taken shape, and diverse communities of the faithful, all of them calling themselves "Israel," have defined Judaism for themselves. Christianity in its orthodox, catholic formulation was only one of these. From the inside, those definitions set forth not "our Judaism" or "a Judaism" but simply "Judaism." From the perspective of the observer, by contrast, each of the definitions, examined in the

---

[1] *Israel* in Judaism refers to the holy community brought into existence at Mount Sinai when God gave the Torah to a mixed multitude of Egyptian slaves and formed of them the kingdom of God. That is "Israel" in the context of Judaism, the religion. It is not to be confused with the contemporary Jewish state of Israel. In these pages, when reference is made to the state of Israel, in the context of Zionism or the practice of Judaism today, it is always explicitly *the state of. . . .* Otherwise, "Israel" on its own means the Jewish people. But, as will rapidly become clear, who belongs to "the Jewish people/Israel" and who does not forms a perennial issue of debate.

context of the life of the group that formulated it, tells us about a Judaism. Then what a history of Judaism will organize and explain is the picture of diverse Judaisms that competed in a given span of time and space. That is what I present in this seventh edition of my principal textbook.

Table of Dates

ca. 1200 B.C.	Exodus from Egypt under Moses; conquest of Canaan under Joshua
1200–1050	Period of the Judges
ca. 1050	Samuel
ca. 1013–973	David, king of Judah and then of Israel as well
973–933	Solomon
ca. 930	Kingdom divided
ca. 750	Amos
ca. 735	Hosea
ca. 725	Isaiah
722	Assyrians take Samaria; exile of the ten northern tribes; only Judah and Benjamin survive, in the South.
639–609	Josiah
620	Deuteronomic reforms
ca. 600	Jeremiah
586	Jerusalem temple destroyed; Judeans exiled to Babylonia
ca. 590	Ezekiel
ca. 550	Second Isaiah
538	First return to Zion under Sheshbazzar

520	Zerubbabel, Haggai lay foundation for Temple
515	Temple completed
ca. 444	The priest Ezra comes from Babylonia, then under Persian rule, with the task assigned to him by the Persian government of taking over Jerusalem and establishing the Torah as the governing document for the Jews of Jerusalem and surrounding Judea.
331	Alexander takes Palestine
168	Judaism prohibited by Antiochus IV; Maccabees revolt
165	Temple regained, purified by Maccabees
ca. 100	Community founded at Dead Sea, produces scrolls
63	Romans conquer Jerusalem, which becomes part of the Roman system
37–4	Herod rules as Roman ally
ca. 1 C.E.	Hillel, founder of a school of opinion within the Pharisaic sect.
ca. 40	Gamaliel I heads Pharisees
70	Destruction of Jerusalem by Romans
	Yohanan ben Zakkai founds center for legal study and judicial and administrative rule at Yavneh
ca. 80–110	Gamaliel heads academy at Yavneh
	Final canonization of Hebrew scriptures
	Promulgation of Order of Prayer by rabbis
115–117	Diaspora Jewries revolt against Trajan
120	Aqiba leads rabbinical movement
132–135	Bar Kokhba leads messianic war against Rome
	Southern Palestine devastated
140	Rabbis reassemble in Galilee, restore Jewish government
ca. 200	Judah the Prince, head of Palestinian Jewish community, promulgates Mishnah
ca. 220	Babylonian academy founded at Sura by Rab
ca. 250	Pact between Jews and Persian King, Shapur I: Jews to keep state law; Persians to permit Jews to govern selves, live by own religion
297	Founding of school at Pumbedita, in Babylonia, by Judah ben Ezekiel
ca. 330	Pumbedita school headed by Abbaye, then Raba, lays foundation of Babylonian Talmud
ca. 400	Talmud of the Land of Israel completed

ca. 450	Genesis Rabbah, commentary out of Genesis on the meaning of Israel's history, and Leviticus Rabbah, historical laws of Israel's society developed out of the book of Leviticus, are completed
ca. 475–500	Pesiqta deRav Kahana, set of essays on the salvation of Israel in the Messianic time, expected fairly soon, worked out
ca. 400	Rabbi Ashi begins to shape Babylonian Talmud; completed by 600.
ca. 700	Saboraim complete the final editing of Babylonian Talmud
630–640	Moslem conquest of Middle East
ca. 750	*Problems* of Ahai Gaon; compilation of legal discourses
ca. 780	Death of Anan ben David, leader of Karaite revolt against Rabbinic Judaism
882	Birth of Saadya, leading theologian, author of *Doctrines and Beliefs*
ca. 950	*Book of Creation,* mystical work, brief statement on how phenomena of world evolved from God
1040	Birth of Rashi, greatest medieval Bible and Talmud commentator
1096	First Crusade; Jews massacred in Rhineland by Crusader armies
1138	Birth of Moses Maimonides
1141	Death of Judah Halevi
1179	Third Lateran Council issues anti-Semitic decrees
1180	Maimonides completes code of Jewish law
1187	Saladin recaptures Jerusalem from crusaders
1190	Riots at Lynn; massacre of Jews at York, England
1233	Inquisition at Aragon
1244	Ritual burning of Talmuds at Paris by church authorities
1247	Papal bull against ritual murder libel
1264	Charter of Boleslav the Pious
1298–1299	Riots against Jews of Germany in Rhindfleisch; 1320–1321, Pastoureaux; 1336–1337, Armleder
1283–1287	Riots against Jews in Rhineland
1290	Expulsion of Jews from England
1306, 1311, 1322, 1349, 1394	Expulsions of Jews from France
1328	Massacres in Navarre

1348–1350	Black death; Jews massacred; migration to Poland begins en masse
1385	Spanish Jews forbidden to live in Christian neighborhoods
1391	Massacres of Spanish Jewry, forced conversions to Christianity
1492	Jews expelled from Spain
1496	Jews expelled from Portugal; mass conversions to Christianity
1506	Secret Jews (*Maranos/Conversos/New Christians*) killed in Lisbon
1516	Ghetto introduced at Venice; Jews forced to live in separate neighborhood
1520	First printed edition of Babylonian Talmud
1521	Jewish migrations to Palestine
1542–43, 1546	Martin Luther preaches against Jews
1553	Talmud burned in Italy
1567	Publication of *Shulhan Arukh,* code of Jewish law, by Joseph Karo
1624	Ghetto law instituted at Ferrara, Italy
1648	Massacres of Polish and Ukrainian Jews
1654	Jewish community founded in New Amsterdam (New York)
1655	Jews readmitted to England by Oliver Cromwell
1658	Newport, Rhode Island, Jewish community founded
1665	Shabbetai Zevi proclaimed Messiah in Smyrna, Turkey
1670	Jews expelled from Vienna
1712	First public synagogue in Berlin
1760	Death of Baal Shem Tov, founder of Hasidism
1772	Rabbis of Vilna oppose Hasidism
1786	Death of Moses Mendelssohn, philosopher of the Jewish Enlightenment
1789	U.S. Constitution guarantees freedom of religion
1791	Jews receive full citizenship in France
1796	Jews receive full citizenship in Batavia (Holland)
1807	Sanhedrin called by Napoleon
1812	Jews receive partial citizenship in Prussia
1815	Polish Constitution omits Jewish rights
1825	Jews granted full citizenship in state of Maryland
1832	Jews receive full rights in Canada

1847	Birth of Solomon Schechter, leader of Conservative Judaism in the United States
1866	Emancipation of Jews in Switzerland
1868	Emancipation of Jews in Austria-Hungary
1870	Unification of Italy; ghettos abolished
1873	Founding of Union of American Hebrew Congregations (Reform)
1874	Death of Abraham Geiger, founder of German Reform
1881	Beginning of mass immigration of Eastern European Jews to the United States, Britain, Canada, Australia, South Africa, Argentina
1882	Bilu movement—beginning of Jewish immigration into Palestine
1885	Pittsburgh Platform of Reform Rabbis renounces hope to return to Zion; affirms reason, progress
1886	Jewish Theological Seminary founded to train conservative rabbis
1888	Death of Samson R. Hirsch, leader of German Orthodoxy
1892	Anti-Semites elected to German Reichstag
1896	Herzl publishes *The Jewish State,* urging the creation of a Jewish state as the solution to the problem of the anti-Semitic politics developing in Europe
1897	Zionist movement founded at Basel, Switzerland
1897	The Bund, a Jewish Workers' Union, founded in Poland as the Jewish section of the international workers' movement; identifies the Yiddish language as its principal instrument of culture
1909	Tel Aviv founded, first Hebrew-speaking city in the world since ancient times
1917	Balfour Declaration favors founding of Jewish national home in Palestine
1933	Hitler becomes chancellor of Germany; Jews begin to lose rights
1935	Nuremberg Laws in Germany; Jews lose all rights
1937	Columbus Platform of Reform Rabbis reaffirms Zionism, Jewish peoplehood
1938	Every synagogue in Germany burned down, 9 November
1939–1945	Deportation to death camps and mass starvation, massacres of Jews of Europe
1942	"Final Solution" adopted by German government, systematically to exterminate all Jews in German-occupied

Acknowledgments

I f this revision of what has become the standard textbook on Judaism in the field of religious studies shows merit and attracts a still larger readership than the six prior editions, credit belongs to my colleagues at Bard College, in particular Professor Bruce D. Chilton, and to my co-workers on all projects, especially Professor William Scott Green, University of Rochester, among many. On particular topics I had the generous comments of Rabbi Avi Shafran, Agudath Israel; Allan Nadler, Drew University; and David Berger, Brooklyn College, among many.

Among the valuable suggestions that were made to me for this seventh edition, the most important came from Aaron Catz, my student at Bard College, who made two important suggestions upon which I acted. First, he wanted to know more about Hasidic Judaism in contemporary Judaic life, with special reference to the most prominent Hasidic Judaic system, Habad. This request resulted in the addition of Chapter 28. Second and more important, he asked the fundamental question that I had missed in all six prior editions and their numerous reprintings: What about scripture? I had left out an explicit account of the role of scripture's narrative in defining Judaism. This question yielded the new Chapter 1.

Writing this new chapter also required a rereading and revision of all the later chapters. It demanded an account of how Judaism translates the narratives, laws, and prophecies of the Torah, that is, of the Hebrew scripture, into a religious system for the social order. Judaism is represented here as the structure of belief and behavior that realizes in the everyday life of the holy community the Torah scripture's story of God's imperatives. Taking Judaism at its word, the world regards Judaism as the religion of the "Old Testament" or ancient Israelite scripture. Here we follow the main lines of structure and system, individual and corporate, that the scripture's narratives, prophecies, and laws sustain. That requires linking the living faith to its foundations in scriptural narrative, which I have done in revising the sixth edition for this seventh one.

Unacknowledged translations are the author's own. He gratefully acknowledges permission to reprint the following copyrighted material:

From Judah Goldin, trans., *The Grace After Meals* (New York: Jewish Theological Seminary of America, 1955), pp. 9, 15ff.

From Philip Birnbaum, trans. and ed., *Daily Prayerbook* (New York: Hebrew Publishing Co., 1949), p. 424.

From Maurice Samuel, trans., *Haggadah of Passover* (New York: Hebrew Publishing Co., 1949), pp. 9, 13, 26, 27.

From Israel Abrahams, *Hebrew Ethical Wills,* (Philadelphia: Jewish Publication Society, 1948), pp. 207–218.

From *Weekday Prayer Book,* ed. Rabbinical Assembly of America Prayerbook Committee, Rabbi Gershon Hadas, Chairman, and Rabbi Jules Harlow, Secretary (New York: Rabbinical Assembly of America, 1962), pp. 42, 45–46, 50–54, 97–98.

From *A Rabbi's Manual,* ed. Rabbi Jules Harlow (New York: Rabbinical Assembly of America, 1965), pp. 45, 96.

From A. S. Halkin, "The Judeo-Islamic Age," in *Great Ages and Ideas of the Jewish People,* ed. Leo Schwarz (New York: Random House, 1956).

From Isaak Heinemann, *Judah Halevi, Kuzari* (London: East & West Library, 1957).

From Franz Kobler, *Letters of Jews Through the Ages* (London: East & West Library, 1952), pp. 565–567. © Horovitz Publishing Co. Ltd., 1952.

From Bernard Martin, *Prayer in Judaism,* pp. 84–85, © 1968 Basic Books, Inc., Publishers, New York.

From Sholom Alchanan Singer, trans., *Medieval Jewish Mysticism: The Book of the Pious* (Northbrook, IL: Whitehall Company, 1971), pp. 37–38.

From Abraham J. Heschel, "The Mystical Elements of Judaism," in *The Jews: Their History, Culture, and Religion,* Louis Finkelstein, vol. 2, pp. 932–951. © 1949, 1955, 1960, 1971 Louis Finkelstein. By permission of Harper & Row, Publishers, Inc.

PART I

Defining Judaism:
The Religion and its History

1

Judaism and the "Old Testament"

*Religion is experience, image and story before it is anything else
and after it is everything else....*

ANDREW M. GREELEY[1]

RELIGION AS STORY

We start with the known, what most people know about Judaism, if
they know anything at all. Judaism is a religion, and it is the "religion of the Old Testament." To see the religion, Judaism, whole and
complete, we require a definition of religion. The great sociologist of religion,
Father Andrew Greeley, defines religion as story; accordingly, to define the religion, Judaism, we ask what story Judaism tells. The answer is: Judaism retells
the story of what Christianity knows as the "Old Testament," and, in neutral language, that is the story of scripture.

By *scripture* is meant the privileged collection of books that, taken together,
Judaism calls the *Torah,* or Teaching, and that Christianity calls the *Old Testament*
or the *Pentateuch.* For Judaism, the Torah, a.k.a. the Old Testament, sets forth
the master narrative of the human condition: God's story of who we are. Judaism holds that God's perspective upon the story of humanity prevails. And as
a religious system Judaism turns scripture's cases into rules and examples, its
story into a pattern. That is how Judaism is the "religion of the Old Testament":
It transforms scripture's narrative into religion—that is, the design for the social order, the theology, and the law that are embodied in the tale. Judaism
therefore claims to be—uniquely—the religion that translates into norms of
conduct and conviction, deed and deliberation, the narratives of the Hebrew
scripture.

To practice Judaism, then, means to act out in behavior and belief the key
stories that are told in the Torah. Judaism stakes its claim to knowledge of God
upon that scripture. It systematically treats as exemplary the narratives of scripture, the laws, prophecies, and admonitions that accompany those stories. These

---

[1]Andrew M. Greeley, "Why Do Catholics Stay in the Church? Because of the Stories," *New York Times,* reprinted
in Greeley, *White Smoke* (New York: 1996), pp. 448–458. Father Greeley proceeds: "Catholics like their heritage
because it has great stories.... [T]he heritage for most people most of the time was almost entirely story, ritual,
ceremony, and eventually art. ... Catholicism has great stories because at the center of its heritage is 'sacramentalism,'
the conviction that God discloses himself in the objects and events and persons of ordinary life."

it forms into its account of the social order that God has designed: the law and theology of the religious community of Judaism.

JUDAISM AND THE "OLD TESTAMENT"

Although Judaism is the religion of the "Old Testament," there is an important qualification. It emerges when we frame that sentence—"Judaism is the religion of the Old Testament"—in the language and native categories of Judaism itself. In the language of Judaism, the writings Christianity calls the Old Testament are called the Torah. Thus Judaism is "the religion of the Torah revealed by God to Moses at Mount Sinai." And that formulation carries us to the qualification at hand: Of what, precisely, does this revealed Torah consist?

The answer is that the Torah consists of revelation formulated and passed on in two media, writing and memory. So we define Judaism in more precise language:

Judaism is the religion of the Torah, which is comprised of the Written Torah (a.k.a. the Old Testament) and the Oral or Memorized Torah.

In due course we shall encounter some of the documents that preserve, in writing, this originally memorized Torah. At this point it is enough to recognize that Judaism encompasses as revelation a formidable corpus of traditions in addition to those preserved in scripture.

Judaism, accordingly, claims as God's revelation not only the "Old Testament" which it knows as the "Written Torah," but the corpus of oral or memorized, not-written-down, tradition revealed as part of the Torah, or Teaching, of Sinai, that interprets and mediates scripture and forms of it a religious structure and system. The Written Torah comes first, for scripture forms the foundation and tells the story. (We later on shall meet the documents that record the originally oral Torah.)

What do we find in the Hebrew scripture or Old Testament or Written Torah? To begin with, three large collections of writings. The Hebrew scripture is divided into three components: the Torah, which to begin with refers to the Five Books of Moses; the Prophets; and the Writings. (The Hebrew is *Torah, Nebi'im, Ketubim,* and it yields T/N/K, or TaNaK.)

Torah: The Five Books of Moses cover the beginnings of the people of Israel as sojourners in-the-Land of Israel and as slaves in the Land of Egypt freed by God through Moses and led by him to the border of the Land of Israel.

Prophets: The former prophets, Joshua, Judges, Samuel, and Kings, tell the story of how Israel got the Land and lost it, but later got it back. The latter prophets, Isaiah, Jeremiah, Ezekiel, and the twelve minor prophets, go over the same ground.

Writings: The Writings are a diverse group of stories that do not fit into the sequential history of Israel but contain much important information.

And where, among the Torah, Prophets, and Writings, do we find the stories of which we spoke just now? If Judaism sets forth the master narrative of the human condition, what tale does it tell? The first two, the Torah and the Prophets, tell a continuous story. It concerns the formation of the holy people, Israel,[2] how it got the Land of Israel, how it lost the Land of Israel, how it recovered the Land of Israel, and how by adhering to the imperatives of the Torah it could continue to possess the Land.

Thus Hebrew scripture tells the story of Israel and the Holy Land: its possession of the Land and the conditions for its continued settlement there, its loss of the Land, and the beginnings of its recovery thereof.

Which books of scripture tell the story? Let us rapidly consider the specific scriptural books that, read as a continuous unfolding account, tell the story.

The Torah: The first book of the Torah/Five Books of Moses is *Genesis,* the story of creation and the formation of the holy family, Abraham and Sarah, Isaac and Rebecca, Jacob and Leah and Rachel, yielding the children of Jacob, also called Israel. It ends with the children of Jacob/Israel going down to Egypt to sojourn there in a time of famine in the Land of Israel that God had given to Abraham and Sarah and their descendants. The second book of the Torah, *Exodus,* tells how the Egyptians enslaved the Israelites, but how God heard their cry and sent Moses, the prophet, to gather them out of Egypt and lead them back to the promised land. The third book of the Torah, *Leviticus,* records the laws of the sacrificial service that God afforded to Israel as a means of atonement for sin, covering the priesthood that would preside over the offerings. The fourth book of the Torah, *Numbers,* tells the story of Israel's forty years of wandering in the wilderness, prevented from entering the promised land. The fifth book of the Torah, *Deuteronomy,* retells the story of Israel in its redemption from Egyptian slavery and its wandering in the wilderness, ending with the vision of Moses for Israel's future in the Land.

The Prophets: The Prophets is divided into the *Former Prophets* and the *Latter Prophets.* The scriptural books of Joshua, Judges, Samuel, and Kings are the Former Prophets. Isaiah, Jeremiah, Ezekiel, and the twelve minor (because of the brevity of the writings) prophets: Hosea, Joel, Amos, Obadiah, Jonah, Micah, Nahum, Habakkuk, Zephaniah, Haggai, Zecharian, and Malachi are the Latter Prophets.

The principal writings of the Former Prophets, Joshua through Kings, tell the story of Israel in the Land of Israel, from the conquest and settlement led by Joshua through the progressive decline of Israel in the Land by reason of its disloyalty to God and its "straying after false gods." First the people asked for a monarch to replace the prophetic rulership of judges divinely inspired, the last of whom was Samuel. The result was King Saul, replaced by King David,

---

[2]In Judaism, "Israel" refers to the holy people, the family of Abraham and Sarah, of whom Scripture speaks from Genesis 12 forward, who assembled at Sinai and accepted God's Torah, or teaching, as the foundation of their life. This holy people forms a religious construct, not a fact of secular history and sociology; "holy Israel" is not to be confused with the state of Israel, the Jewish state, founded in 1948. "Israel" in these pages refers to the holy people, the people of God, defined by the laws of the Torah. To keep things clear, "state of Israel" is used to refer to the Jewish state of modern times.

succeeded by King Solomon. Then, after the united monarchy of Saul, David, and Solomon, the people broke into northern and southern wings, Israel on the north, Judea on the south.

The northern kingdom, called Israel, was conquered by the Assyrians in 701 B.C.E. and the ten tribes that comprised Israel were taken into exile, never to return. The southern kingdom, made up of the tribes of Judah and Benjamin and called Judea, centered around Jerusalem and its Temple, persisted for another century but then was conquered in 586 B.C.E. by the Babylonians, who destroyed the Temple on Mount Zion in Jerusalem and exiled the Judeans to Babylonia. When the Babylonians were conquered by the Persians, however, the Judeans were allowed to return to Zion, and some did. Led by Ezra, the scribe, and Nehemiah, the viceroy of the Persians, they rebuilt the Temple and restored its offerings.

So much for what is called the "authorized history," which emerges from a continuous reading of Joshua-Judges-Samuel-Kings.

The Latter Prophets comprises *Isaiah, Jeremiah, Ezekiel,* and the *twelve minor prophets.* The book of Isaiah contains prophecies that pertain to several periods, the first thirty-nine chapters focusing on the events that culminated in 701 B.C.E. in the conquest by the Assyrians of the northern kingdom, but their failure to pursue the siege of Jerusalem; the next group, chapters 40 to 56, address the period of the return to Zion in the sixth century B.C.E. The book of Jeremiah focuses upon the final decades of the southern kingdom, from about 620 to 586. The prophet warns the Judeans to submit to Babylonia and also prophesies, at the time of the siege, the ultimate restoration of Israel to its Land. The book of Ezekiel addresses the same period from the perspective of the Babylonian exile.

The Writings are *Psalms, Proverbs, Job, Song of Songs, Ruth, Lamentations, Ecclesiastes* (Hebrew: *Qoheleth*), *Esther, Daniel, Ezra, Nehemiah,* and *Chronicles.* These diverse pieces do not fit into the continuous official history of how Israel got, lost, and was restored to, the Land. Of the group, Chronicles recapitulates the stories of Samuel and Kings, and Ezra and Nehemiah tell about the return to Zion under Persian sovereignty. So at the foundations of scripture's many stories in the Torah and the Prophets, Genesis through Kings, Judaism identifies a single pattern, a governing motif: possession and loss of the Land. And, finding in Genesis 1–3 the story of humanity in the persons of Adam and Eve, Judaism compares the experience of Adam and Eve and the experience of Israel, drawing the lessons common to them both.

Given the formidable volume, diversity, and complexity of the books of Genesis through Kings, we must ask: How are these complex, diverse writings, with numerous stories covering centuries of narratives, turned into a coherent and systematic account of the human condition? How are the prophets' admonitions and revelations in God's name transformed into a cogent and concrete theology message? What vision of the whole imparts to the details of Scripture's many laws the cogency of a legal structure and system?

The answer derives from the Rabbinic sages of the Torah who flourished in the first centuries of the Common Era. In dialogue with the oral tradition of Sinai, they framed a vision of scripture's stories, laws, and prophecies as a coherent, cogent conception of holy Israel's condition and calling. We shall now see their basic point and how it is formulated out of the facts of scripture. Here is how they discern the patterns that the narratives yield and how they define the meanings of those patterns. From talking about Judaism, we now encounter Judaism in its own voice and language: how Judaism tells scripture's tale, a fine case of what it means for Judaism to be the "religion of the Old Testament."

ADAM, EVE, AND EDEN; ISRAEL AND THE LAND: SCRIPTURE'S MASTER NARRATIVE OF THE HUMAN CONDITION

The Rabbinic sages who flourished in the early centuries of the Common Era compare the story of Israel's possession and loss of the Land with the story of Creation and Adam's and Eve's possession and loss of Eden. The key is their quest for patterns, and in scripture they find a huge pattern. From their perspective, the entire narrative of scripture from Genesis through Kings shows how Israel recapitulates the story of Adam and Eve, but it is a pattern with a difference: Adam and Eve lost Paradise, never to return. Israel, however, went into exile but then got back to the Land and, with the Torah for guidance, would endure there.

In this reading, the books of Genesis through Kings tell a simple story. First, the prologue sets forth the human condition, Genesis 1–11, on how Adam and Eve were given Paradise but sinned and brought pain, suffering, and death to the world. Then God tried again with Noah and this time succeeded in finding, in Abraham and Sarah, the beginnings of a humanity worthy of being designated "in our image, after our likeness"—that is, humanity in the model of God. Then, from Genesis 12 through the end of the book of Kings, the story shows how Israel, like Adam, was given Eden, now the Land of Israel, but lost it, like Adam, through sin in the form of rebellion against God's will. But there is an essential difference between Adam, without the Torah, and Israel, with the Torah. Whereas Israel, like Adam, sinned and lost the Land, Israel also breaks out of the pattern. Guided by the Torah, Israel could recover and now hold the Land by loyalty to God's will expressed in the Torah.

The Rabbinic sages thus took scripture to form not a one-time narrative but a model and a pattern, in the theory that—in the case of the book of Genesis, for example—the deeds of the founding generations, Abraham and Sarah, Isaac and Rebecca, Jacob and Leah and Rachel, defined a paradigm for their descendants. So they went in quest of the patterns implicit in the narratives.

Adam and Israel: The Parallel Stories Now to the centerpiece of the Rabbinic sages' reading of scripture. In the case at hand, they found intelligible markers in parallel details of two stories, Adam's and Israel's. And everything follows from that discovery. The text before us derives from Genesis Rabbah, the reading of the book of Genesis by Rabbinic sages in the fifth century of the Common Era. Seeking patterns in abundant data like natural historians in a tropical forest, the Rabbinic sages constantly cite verses of scripture to provide the facts at hand. But with those verses they construct a pattern that permits the comparison they have in mind. Notice how various books of scripture, the Torah and the Prophets and the Writings alike, contribute to the exposition. Scripture is now turned into a vast corpus of facts, and the task of the faithful sage is to discern out of those facts the patterns and regularities that signal the workings of laws, just as in natural history the philosopher turns the facts of nature into natural laws. This text compares Israel to "a man," that is, Adam:

Genesis Rabbah XIX:IX.1–2

2. A. R. Abbahu in the name of R. Yosé bar Haninah: "It is written, 'But they [Israel] are like a man [Adam], they have transgressed the covenant' (Hos. 6:7).

   B. " 'They are like a man,' specifically, like the first man." [We shall now compare the story of the first man in Eden with the story of Israel in its land.]

Now the sage identifies God's action in regard to Adam with a counterpart action in regard to Israel, in each case matching verse for verse, beginning with Eden and Adam. Adam is brought to Eden as Israel is brought to the Land, with comparable outcomes:

> C. " 'In the case of the first man, I brought him into the garden of Eden, I commanded him, he violated my commandment, I judged him to be sent away and driven out, but I mourned for him, saying "How…" ' " [which begins the book of Lamentations, hence stands for a lament, but which, as we just saw, also is written with the consonants that also yield 'Where are you.']
>
> D. " 'I brought him into the garden of Eden,' as it is written, 'And the Lord God took the man and put him into the garden of Eden' (Gen. 2:15).
>
> E. " 'I commanded him,' as it is written, 'And the Lord God commanded. …' (Gen. 2:16).
>
> F. " 'And he violated my commandment,' as it is written, 'Did you eat from the tree concerning which I commanded you' (Gen. 3:11).
>
> G. " 'I judged him to be sent away,' as it is written, 'And the Lord God sent him from the garden of Eden' (Gen. 3:23).

H. " 'And I judged him to be driven out.' 'And he drove out the man' (Gen. 3:24).

I. " 'But I mourned for him, saying, "How. ...." ' 'And he said to him, "Where are you" ' (Gen. 3:9), and the word for 'where are you' is written, 'How. ....' "

Now comes the systematic comparison of Adam and Eden with Israel and the Land of Israel:

J. " 'So too in the case of his descendants [God continues to speak], I brought them [Israel] into the Land of Israel, I commanded them, they violated my commandment, I judged them to be sent out and driven away but I mourned for them, saying, "How. ...." '

K. " 'I brought them into the Land of Israel.' 'And I brought you into the Land of Carmel' (Jer. 2:7).

L. " 'I commanded them.' 'And you, command the children of Israel' (Ex. 27:20). 'Command the children of Israel' (Lev. 24:2).

M. " 'They violated my commandment.' 'And all Israel have violated your Torah' (Dan. 9:11).

N. " 'I judged them to be sent out.' 'Send them away, out of my sight and let them go forth' (Jer 15:1).

O. " '....and driven away.' 'From my house I shall drive them' (Hos. 9:15).

P. " 'But I mourned for them, saying, "How. ...." ' 'How has the city sat solitary, that was full of people' (Lam. 1:1)."

We end with Lamentations, the writing of mourning produced after the destruction of the Temple in Jerusalem in 586 by the Babylonians. Here we end where we began, Israel in exile from the Land, like Adam in exile from Eden. But the Torah is clear that there is a difference, which we shall address in its proper place: Israel can repent.

These persons, Israel and Adam, form not individual and particular, one-time characters, but exemplary categories. Israel is Adam's counterpart, Israel is the other model for the human, the one being without the Torah, the other possessing, and possessed by, the Torah. Adam's failure defined Israel's task, marked the occasion for the formation of Israel. Israel came into existence in the aftermath of the failure of Creation with the fall of Man and his ultimate near-extinction; in the restoration that followed the Flood, God identified Abraham to found in the Land, the new Eden, a supernatural social entity to realize his will in creating the world. Called, variously, a family, a community, a nation, a people, Israel above all embodies God's abode in humanity, his resting place on earth. I hardly need repeat that this definition of "Israel" cannot be confused with any secular meanings attributed to the same word—that is, as a nation or ethnic entity, counterpart to other nations or ethnic groups.

FROM NARRATIVE TO SOCIAL NORMS: HOW JUDAISM LINKS THE COMMANDMENTS TO SCRIPTURE'S STORY OF HUMANITY

Scripture in the hands of the Rabbinic sages yields an account of what God wants of the community formed by the Torah, which is to form the kingdom of Heaven: "You shall be holy, for I the Lord your God am holy" (Lev. 19:2). What, precisely does Judaism conceive to constitute the kingdom of Heaven—the state of Israel under God's rule? The answer is given, once more, in the form of a narrative, involving Adam, Noah, Abraham, and Israel at Sinai—another case of how, in Father Greeley's words, "religion is story."

By "the kingdom of Heaven" Judaism means the realm that God rules. This above all was realized in the ordinary world in which Israel performed the commandments. When an Israelite carried out a positive commandment or, more important, in obedience to Heaven refrained from a deed prohibited by a negative commandment, that act of omission or commission formed the moment of ultimate realization of God's rule on earth. Then Israel, through the submission to God's will of Israelites, may bring about God's rule on earth.

In the language of Judaism, when the Israelite recites the *Shema,* "Hear O Israel, the Lord is our God, the Lord is one," he or she accepts "the yoke of the kingdom of Heaven," and when he or she recites the blessing immediately following that sentence, which is, "Blessed be the name of his glorious kingdom forever and ever," he or she accepts "the yoke of the Torah," thus, the commandments. In the recitation of the *Shema,* which we shall meet again in its liturgical and theological setting, Judaism affords the religious experience of entering into God's kingdom.

The commandments, originally emerging in small groups, mark the appearance of God's kingdom on earth. But alone among nations Israel finally got all of them, 248 positive ones, matching the bones of the body, 365 negative ones, matching the days of the solar year. So Israel alone within humanity has the possibility, and the power, to bring about God's rule. Here the story of the gradual delivery of the commandments is spelled out by a Rabbinic document of scriptural exegesis and theology produced around 500 C.E.

Pesiqta deRab Kahana XII:I.1ff

1. A. R. Judah bar Simon commenced discourse by citing the following verse: "Many daughters show how capable they are, but you excel them all. [Charm is a delusion and beauty fleeting; it is the God-fearing woman who is honored. Extol her for the fruit of her toil and let her labors bring her honor in the city gate]' (Prov. 31:29–31).

We start with the six commandments assigned to Adam, as the facts of scripture indicate. Here we revert to the transformation of scripture's narrative into the law and theology that comprise Judaism. So the narrative now takes over:

B. "The first man was assigned six religious duties, and they are: not worshipping idols, not blaspheming, setting up courts of justice, not murdering, not practicing fornication, not stealing.

C. "And all of them derive from a single verse of Scripture: 'And the Lord God commanded the man, saying, 'You may freely eat of every tree of the garden, [but of the tree of the knowledge of good and evil you shall not eat, for in the day that you eat of it you shall die]' (Gen. 2:16).

D. " 'And the Lord God commanded the man, saying': this refers to idolatry, as it is said, 'For Ephraim was happy to walk after the command' (Hos. 5:11).

E. " 'The Lord': this refers to blasphemy, as it is said, 'Whoever curses the name of the Lord will surely die' (Lev. 24:16).

F. "God: this refers to setting up courts of justice, as it is said, 'God [in context, the judges] you shall not curse' (Ex. 22:27).

G. "The man: this refers to murder, as it is said, 'He who sheds the blood of man by man his blood shall be shed' (Gen. 9:6).

H. "Saying: this refers to fornication, as it is said, 'Saying, will a man divorce his wife' (Jer. 3:1).

I. " 'You may freely eat of every tree of the garden: 'this refers to the prohibition of stealing, as you say, 'but of the tree of the knowledge of good and evil you shall not eat.' "

Following the story of Scripture carries us from Adam ten generations later to Noam. Noah inherited those six commandments and was given another:

J. "Noah was commanded, in addition, not to cut a limb from a living beast, as it is said, 'But as to meat with its soul—its blood you shall not eat' (Gen. 9:4)."

Another ten generations passed, then Abraham got the seven obligatory for Noah, meaning, all humanity after the Flood, and an eighth (though, elsewhere, it is alleged that Abraham in any event observed all of the commandments):

K. "Abraham was commanded, in addition, concerning circumcision, as it is said, 'And as to you, my covenant you shall keep' (Gen. 17:9).

L. "Isaac was circumcised on the eighth day, as it is said, 'And Abraham circumcised Isaac, his son, on the eighth day'(Gen. 21:4)."

Jacob got a ninth, his son Judah a tenth:

M. "Jacob was commanded not to eat the sciatic nerve, as it is said, 'On that account the children of Israel will not eat the sciatic nerve' (Gen. 32:33).

N. "Judah was commanded concerning marrying the childless brother's widow, as it is said, 'And Judah said to Onen, Go to the wife of your childless brother and exercise the duties of a levir with her' (Gen. 38:8)."

But in the revelation of the Torah at Sinai, Israel got them all, matching the bones of the body to the days of the year, the whole of life through all time:

> O. "But as to you, at Sinai you received six hundred thirteen religious duties, two hundred forty-eight religious duties of commission [acts to be done], three hundred sixty-five religious duties of omission [acts not to be done].
>
> P. "The former matching the two hundred forty-eight limbs that a human being has.
>
> Q. "Each limb says to a person, 'By your leave, with me do this religious duty.'
>
> R. "Three hundred sixty-five religious duties of omission [acts not to be done] matching the days of the solar calendar.
>
> S. "Each day says to a person, 'By your leave, on me do not carry out that transgression.' "

That Israel got them all is what requires explanation, and the explanation has to do with the union of the days of the solar year with the bones of man: At all time, with all one's being, one obeys God's commandments. The mode of explanation here does not require the introduction of proof texts, appealing rather to the state of nature—the solar calendar, the bone structure of man—to account for the facts. The kingdom of Heaven, then, encompasses every day of the year and the components of the human body. The amplification at R–S cannot be improved upon. So the Rabbinic sages taught how Eden—the kingdom of Heaven, the Garden of Eden, Paradise—is to be recovered. In the humble details of Israel's ordinary life is embodied the simple story of the world: unflawed creation, spoiled by man's act of will, restored by Israel's act of repentance.

"THIS IS THE TORAH THAT MOSES SET BEFORE THE CHILDREN OF ISRAEL ON THE INSTRUCTION OF THE LORD— AT THE HAND OF MOSES"

Can we identify Judaism's moment? Where do we locate precisely when and how the story turns into religion—the climactic experience of experience, of rite, the palpable imagery of music, dance, gesture, proclamation—"before it is anything else, after it is everything else," in Father Greeley's language? The answer for Judaism comes in the liturgy of the synagogue, with the recapitulation, the acting out, of Sinai. The climax of Judaic worship for sabbaths and festivals and holy days, specifically, comes at the declamation of the Torah, and that defines Judaism's moment. It marks the realization of the faith in action. Specifically, Judaism is embodied in the rite of displaying and declaiming the Torah in the community of Holy Israel.

That takes place when the Torah, meaning in this context the scrolls on which the Five Books of Moses are incised and from which, at the center of synagogue worship, passages are read in sequence, start to finish, is set forth. Then the choreography of worship embodies in the music and dance of worship the meaning and message of the faith.

Then the scroll of the Torah, containing the Five Books of Moses, is removed from the ark where it is kept safe and held up for viewing by the assembly of Israel gathered in that place. The congregation of holy Israel sings out the proclamation of faith:

"This [scroll] is the Torah that Moses set before the children of Israel on the instruction of the Lord—at the hand of Moses."

How does the story figure in this declaration of faith? What are invoked are not abstract creedal principles but the concrete story of the actors and their action: Israel at Sinai, God and Moses. And the Torah then is celebrated in dance and gesture and song and word. Not only referred to, the story becomes a religious action. Then comes the dance: The scroll is carried in a procession through the congregation, where each Israelite pays respect to it. The congregation sings as the Torah is carried in procession: "Yours, O Lord, are the greatness and the power and the glory. Yours are triumph and majesty over all heaven and earth. Yours, O Lord, is supreme sovereignty."[3]

Then, having been carried through worshipping Israel, the Torah scroll is set forth on a table, opened, and with appropriate benedictions, the lection of the week is declaimed in a chant that derives from ages past. The song and dance have set the stage for the declamation of the Torah: God's teaching to Israel at the hand of Moses. The weekly lection, in sequence from Genesis through Deuteronomy, matched by a reading from the Prophets to set the Torah into context and underscore its main point, imparts specificity to the encounter with the Torah. That is where the story fits, chapter by chapter.

In this way, in the rite of displaying and declaiming the Torah, Judaism's story is acted out in all its chapters: Torah, Moses, children of Israel, the act of revelation, God made known in words of law and admonition. To know the meaning of the rite, one has to retell the story. To grasp the implications of the story for the social order of the faithful, one has to engage in the rite. In the encounter with the sacred scroll and its narratives, admonitions, and laws, holy Israel realizes the story of scripture in the living community of the faithful. That is because these humble people find in the story God's account of who they are and what they mean together. Holy Israel is the community of those who take the story of the Torah personally.

So much for the story Judaism tells whole and complete. How did the story take shape over time, in a this-worldly framework? To answer that question, we take up the main lines of the history of Judaism. That history takes place from the moment in which scripture took shape to the day before yesterday. Four stages, five events, capture the whole.

---

[3]Gershon Hadas, ed., *Weekday Prayerbook* (New York: Rabbinical Assembly, 1966), p. 82.

2

The History of Judaism

RELIGION AS A CULTURAL SYSTEM:
ETHOS, ETHICS, ETHNOS

Seeing itself and seen by its faithful as unique, from the perspective of others—outsiders—Judaism is a religion bearing traits in common with any other religion. In what secular, historical circumstance did it take shape? Let us begin with a this-worldly definition of religion, then of Judaism: the Judaism whose history we trace here.

In a social perspective, religion forms a cultural system that is comprised of three components: its worldview, its way of life, and its definition in social context of the believing and practicing community of the faithful. *Ethos* refers to the worldview, *ethics* to its way of life and definition of virtue, and *ethnos* to the social entity that takes shape among the believers and practitioners of the faith. The social dimension of religion, the community that it forms, coalesces with the intellectual dimension (the worldview), and the cultural dimension (the way of life). So religion combines these three components of a cultural system:

1. **Belief** or attitude, worldview, which we may call *ethos*
2. **Behavior** or way of life or right action, which we may call in a broad and loose sense *ethics.*
3. **Community,** a social entity ("group") that explains itself by appeal to beliefs and realizes itself in common conduct, which, for the sake of an easy mnemonic, we may call *ethnos,* the group.

In combination, ethos, ethnos, and ethics cohere in the conviction that God (or supernatural counterpart) favors that ethnos, approves that ethos, and values that ethics.

What marks such a system of the social order as religious? The introduction of the divine dimension is what distinguishes a religious from a secular system of the social order and its culture. Theology is to religion what ideology, such as communism or Nazism—to name two once-competitive accounts of the human condition—is to a secular system.

Why the stress on the social and cultural and communal? These are things that we can study, subject to reasoned analysis. If people tell you what they believe, you can only accept the information; you cannot argue about what is utterly subjective and personal. But when people do things together, you can ask questions about their shared and public activity and attitude. Only when we understand that religion studied in the academy is not only personal but public and does its work in the social world can we begin our academic work. And that is, to grasp why religion is the single most powerful social force in the life and politics of most of the world today, as it was in nearly the whole of recorded history.

That definition of religion as public and communal serves especially well when we come to Judaism, which, as we shall see, frames its entire message in the setting of the life of a group that calls itself "Israel," meaning those who take personally scripture's stories. "Israel" is comprised of those who tell about themselves and their group, today, those tales of long-ago times and far-off places that the Torah sets forth.

JUDAISM: THE SOCIAL ENTITY, WAY OF LIFE, WORLDVIEW

What if we wanted to identify a Judaic religious community—what are the components we should look for? The elements of Judaism, the religion, are defined in these specific terms:

Social Group/Israel The first requirement is to find a group of Jews who see themselves as "Israel"—that is, the Jewish people who form the family and children of Abraham, Isaac, Jacob, Sarah, Rebecca, Leah, and Rachel, the founding fathers and mothers. That same group must tell us that it uniquely constitutes "Israel," not *an* Israel, the descriptive term we use. So an "Israel" is comprised of a group of Jews (children of a Jewish mother[1] or converts to Judaism) who take personally, as the account of who they are, the story told by the Torah.

Worldview/Torah The second requirement is to identify the forms through which that distinct group expresses its worldview. Ordinarily, we find that expression in writing, so we turn to the authoritative holy books that the group studies and deems God given, that is, the group's Torah or statement of God's revelation to Israel. In Chapter 1 we have met the Torah that embodies Judaism's worldview. We have seen how the normative Judaism defined by the Rabbinic sages of the first six centuries of the Common Era interpreted the Torah: the pattern of all patterns that they discerned therein.

Way of Life/Commandments A group expresses its worldview in many ways, through music (singing the Torah and the prayers, for example) dance, drama, rite and ritual; through art and symbol; through politics and through the ongoing institutions of society; through where it lives, what it eats, what it

---

[1]In contemporary Reform and Reconstructionist Judaisms, a Jew is a person who has one Jewish parent, either father or mother. In the Law of Return of the state of Israel, a single Jewish grandparent suffices to confer Israeli citizenship. Consequently, a sizable population of Russian immigrants who practice Christianity or no religion but possess Jewish ancestors have taken up Israeli citizenship as Jews.

wears, what language it speaks, and the opposites of all these: what it will not eat, where it will not live. Synagogue architecture and art bear profound and powerful visible messages. The life cycle, from birth through death, the definition of time and the rhythm of the day, the week, the month and the year—all of these elements define the worldview and the way of life of the social group that, all together, all at once, constitutes a Judaism.

Urgent Question, Self-Evidently Valid Answer How does religion work, and what holds the whole together? A religious system—way of life, worldview, theory of the social entity that lives by the one and believes in the other—identifies an urgent and ongoing question facing a given social group. Repeating its answer to that urgent question in the context of countless details, the system responds. It provides an answer that for the faithful is self-evidently valid and everywhere transparent. In the case of the Jews as a social group, for example, one urgent question that such a small and dissenting community, living as a minority among various political and cultural majorities and adapting itself to the life of the majority, must answer is: Why be different? Judaism transforms difference into destiny. It explains—for example, by appeal to the sanctification of Israel through its everyday way of life—just why that "Israel" of which it speaks must preserve its unique way of life and worldview to realize God's purposes. That is the power of the Judaic telling of the story set forth in scripture. It is the capacity to answer, in small details, in a repetitious manner, the urgent question facing the Jews as a group wherever over time and space they have found themselves: why the group persists and should continue to do so. God's plan and expectation for the Israel the tale of which the Torah tells.

To study any vital religion is to address a striking example of how groups of people explain to themselves, by appeal to God's will or word or works, who they are as a social entity—such as "the body of Christ," "the abode of Islam." Religion as a powerful force in human society and culture is realized not only or mainly in theology but in society; religion works through the social entity that embodies that religion. Religions form social entities—"churches" or "peoples" or "holy nations" or monasteries or communities—that, in the concrete, constitute the "us," as against "the nations" or merely "them." And religions carefully explain, in deeds and in words, who that "us" is—and they do it every day. To see religion in this way is to take religion seriously as a way of realizing, in classic documents, a large conception of the world.

THE FOUR PERIODS
IN THE HISTORY OF JUDAISM

But religious systems take place in historical time, and patterns, in their own setting viewed as enduring and eternal, in fact begin in some one place and respond to some distinctive circumstance. The pattern persists when it shows the power to reproduce itself: to replicate the urgent question that gives rise to the system, to restate the self-evidently valid answer that has responded to that question. Judaism as the story of Paradise/the Land, sin and the loss of Paradise/the Land, but repentance and restoration of Paradise/the Land—that Judaism, embodied in the Torah's story as the Rabbinic sages read it, took shape at a particular moment. When was that?

Although the Torah tells the tale of humanity from Creation to Sinai and points toward the ultimate redemption of humanity through the Torah of Sinai, much of biblical scholarship concurs, in fact, that the Torah took shape out of received traditions after the destruction of the Temple in 586 B.C.E. So let us start the history of Judaism not with the creation of the world nor with Abraham's response to God's call (Genesis 12), not with Sinai, but in historical time: in 586 B.C.E.

The First Age of Diversity, ca. 500 B.C.E. to 70 C.E.

The history of Judaism begins in 586 B.C.E., with the destruction of the Temple of Jerusalem built centuries earlier by King Solomon. In Chapter 1 we have already met that event. It precipitated reflection on the traditions of ancient Israel, such as Scripture presents, in quest for the explanation of the calamity.

The destruction of Jerusalem in 586 B.C.E. produced a crisis of faith because ordinary folk supposed that the god of the conquerors had conquered the God of Israel. Israelite prophets represented by Jeremiah saw matters otherwise. Israel had been punished for her sins, and it was God who had carried out the punishment. God was not conquered but vindicated; the pagans were merely his instruments. Even in exile in Babylonia, God could moreover be served, not only in the holy and promised land of Israel. Israel in Babylonian exile continued the cult of the Lord through worship, psalms, and festivals; the synagogue, a place where God was worshipped without sacrifice, would take shape. The Sabbath became Israel's sanctuary, the seventh day of rest and sanctification for God. When, for political reasons, the Persians chose to restore Jewry to Palestine and many returned (ca. 500 B.C.E.), the Jews were not surprised, for they had been led by prophecy to expect that with the expiation of sin through suffering and atonement, God would once more show mercy and bring them homeward. The prophets' message was authenticated by historical events.

In the early years of the Second Temple (ca. 450 B.C.E.), Ezra, the priest-scribe, came from Babylonia to Palestine and brought with him the Torah book, the collection of ancient scrolls of law, prophecy, and narrative. Jews resolved to make the Torah the basis of national life. The Torah was publicly read on New Year's Day in 444 B.C.E., and those assembled pledged to keep it. Along with the canonical scripture, oral traditions, explanations, instructions on how to keep the law, and exegeses of scripture were needed to apply the law to changing conditions of everyday life. A period of creative interpretation of the Written Torah began, one that has yet to come to conclusion in the history of Judaism. For that time forward, the history of Judaism became the history of the interpretation of Torah and its message for each successive age. Naturally, different Judaic systems would read scripture each in its own way.

Of what did the diversity consist? It involved more than arguments over scripture. At issue were distinct readings of what God wanted of Israel. There were three main components of the religious life of the Jews in the last two centuries B.C.E. and the first century C.E. to which we must pay attention. These components, not mutually exclusive, were: the priests, with their commitment to the Temple of Jerusalem and its sacred offerings and to governance of the people of Israel in accord with the orderly world created by and flowing out of the Temple; the scribes, with their commitment to the ancient scripture and their capacity to interpret and apply this scripture to the diverse conditions of the life of the people (later on, the heirs of the scribes would gain the honorific title of *rabbi,* which was not distinctive to their group of Jews or even to the Jews); and the messianic Zealots, who believed that God would rule the Jews when foreign rulers had been driven out of the Holy Land. Obviously, these three components were talking about different things to different people.

Of these three groups, one predominated in the shaping of events in the first century C.E., and the other two fused thereafter. The messianic Zealots until the destruction of the Temple of Jerusalem in 70 C.E. were the most powerful force in the history of the Jews. For they precipitated the single most important event of the time: The war fought against Rome from 66 to 73 C.E., climaxed by the fall of Jerusalem in 70 C.E.. And the messianic Zealots must have remained paramount for another three generations, since the next major event in the history of the Jews was yet a second, and still more disastrous, holy and messianic war against Rome fought under the leadership of Ben Kosiba (also called *Bar Kokhba,* the Star's Son) from 132 to 135 C.E.. That war surely was a mass uprising, which tells us that a large part of the population was attracted to the Zealot way of thinking.

The other two groups—the priests and the scribes—with their interest in continuity, order, and regularity lost out both times. The priests of the Temple saw the destruction of their sanctuary in 70 C.E. and realized after 135 C.E. that it would not be rebuilt for a long time. The scribes who taught scripture and administered their law witnessed the upheavals of society and the destruction of the social order that war inevitably brings in its aftermath. While both groups doubtless shared in the messianic hopes, they most certainly could not have sympathized with the policies and disastrous programs of the messianic Zealots.

So the first age of diversity begins with the writing down, in more or less their present form, of the scripture of ancient Israel, beginning with the Five Books of Moses. Drawing upon writings and oral traditions of the period before the destruction of the first Temple of Jerusalem, in 586 B.C.E., the authorship of the surviving leadership of that Temple and court, the priests, produced most of the books we now know as the Hebrew Bible ("Old Testament," or "Tanakh"), specifically, the Pentateuch or Five Books of Moses; the prophetic writings from Joshua and Judges through Samuel and Kings and Isaiah, Jeremiah, Ezekiel, and the twelve smaller books of prophetic writings; and some of the other scripture as well. During this same period a number of diverse groups of Jews, living in the Land of Israel as well as in Babylonia, to the east, and in Alexandria, Egypt, to the west, took over these writings and interpreted them in diverse ways. Hence during the period from the formation of the Torah book to the destruction of the second Temple, there were many Judaisms. The competition between and among these systems to define what and who "Israel" is and what would happen to that "Israel" produced that diversity.

The Age of Definition, ca. 70 C.E. to 640 C.E.

The next great event in the history of the Jews was the destruction of the Second Temple in 70 C.E.. A political and military event, its religious consequences were drawn by Yohanan ben Zakkai and other great rabbis of the age. These rabbis, heirs of the tradition of oral interpretation and instruction in Torah and the continuators of the prophets of old, taught that the God of Israel could still be served by the Jewish people, who had not been abandoned by God but once more chastised. The rabbis in the following Talmudic story—told not after the year 70 but after a deep disappointment three hundred years later—taught that by obedience to Torah through acts of gratuitous mercy and altruism Israel would again be restored to its land:

> When a disciple of Yohanan ben Zakkai wept at seeing the Temple mount in ruins, Yohanan asked him, "Why do you weep, my son?"
>
> "This place where the sins of Israel were atoned, is in ruins, and should I not weep?" the disciple replied.
>
> "Let it not be grievous to your eyes, my son," Yohanan replied, "For we have another means of atonement, as effective as Temple sacrifice. It is deeds of loving-kindness, as it is said [Hosea 6:6], *For I desire mercy and not sacrifice.*"

Once again, as in 586, a historical event produced a major religious revolution in the life of Judaism. After the event of 586 was repeated in 70, the Rabbinic sages began to seek the patterns that events yielded, the rules and laws signaled by the teachings of the Torah, as we recall from Chapter 1.

That revolution in thinking, from episodic and one-time to the systematic quest for patterns, did produce patterns, everywhere valid, for Judaism. Once and for all, the rabbis defined "being Jewish" in terms of laws universally applicable, laws that might be kept by Jews living in every civilization. Wherever Jews might go, they could serve God through prayer, study of Torah, practice of the commandments, and acts of loving kindness. All Jews were able to study. No clerical class was required—only learned men. So rabbis took the priests' place as teachers of the people. The Jews thus formed a commonwealth within an empire, a religious nation within other nations, living in conformity with the laws of alien governments, but in addition carrying out their own Torah. It was a commonwealth founded on religious belief, a holy community whose membership was defined by obedience to laws believed given at Sinai and interpreted and applied by Rabbinical sages to each circumstance of daily life.

We see, therefore, that the first age of diversity, the age from the formation of the Pentateuch ca. 500, down to before the first century C.E., was a period in which religious experiences and beliefs of various kinds, among diverse groups, took shape among the Jewish people, the people of ancient (and modern) Israel. One principal development in that long period was the Hebrew scripture, called by Christians the Old Testament and by Jews *Tanakh,* which we met in Chapter 1.

The age of definition, beginning with the destruction of the Second Temple in 70, saw the diverse Judaisms of the preceding period give way, over a long period of time, to a single Judaism. That was the system worked out by the sages who, after 70, developed a system of Judaism linked to scripture but enriched by an autonomous corpus of holy writings in addition. This Judaism is marked by its doctrine of the dual media by which the Torah was formulated and transmitted—in writing on one side, in formulation and transmission by memory, hence, orally, on the other. The doctrine of the dual Torah, written and oral, then defined the canon of Judaism.

The Oral Torah added the writings of the sages, beginning with the Mishnah, a philosophical law code produced ca. 200 C.E.; two massive commentaries on the Mishnah; the two Talmuds, one produced in the Land of Israel and called the *Yerushalmi,* or Jerusalem Talmud, ca. 400 C.E., the other in Babylonian and called the *Bavli,* or Talmud of Babylonia, ca. 600 C.E. In that same age, alongside Mishnah commentary, systematic work on scripture yielded works organized around particular books of the Written Torah, parallel to works organized around particular tractates of the Mishnah. These encompassed *Sifra,* to the book of Leviticus; *Sifré,* to Numbers; another *Sifré,* to Deuteronomy; works containing statements attributed to the same authorities who stand behind the Mishnah, to be dated sometime between 200 and 400; as well as *Genesis Rabbah* and *Leviticus Rabbah,* discursive works on themes in Genesis and Leviticus, edited between 400 and 450; *Pesiqta deRav Kahana,* a profoundly eschatological treatment of topics in Pentateuchal writings, from about 450; and similar works. These writings all together, organized around first the Mishnah and then, Scripture, comprised the first works of the Oral Torah. The teachings of the sages, originally formulated and transmitted in memory, were the written-down contents of the Oral Torah that God had revealed—so the system maintained—to Moses at Sinai. During the age of definition, that Judaism of the dual Torah reached its literary statement and authoritative expression.

The Age of Cogency, ca. 640 C.E. to ca. 1800

The age of cogency ran from Late Antiquity, with the formation of its authoritative statement in the Talmud of Babylonia, into the nineteenth century. That does not mean there were no other Judaic systems. It means that the Judaism of the dual Torah set the standard. A heresy selected its "false doctrine" by defining in a way different from the Judaism of the dual Torah a category emerging in that Judaism of the dual Torah. Such a group was the Karaites, who believed that the Torah of Sinai encompassed only the written part and rejected the authority of the books that Rabbinic Judaism called the Oral Torah, which we shall meet in due course. There were shifts and changes of all sorts. But the Judaism of the dual Torah absorbed into itself and its structure powerful movements, such as philosophy, on the one side, and mysticism (called Kabbalah), on the other, and found strength in both of them. The philosopher defended the way of life and worldview of the Judaism of the dual Torah. The mystic observed the faith defined by that same way of life as the vehicle for gaining his or her mystical experience.

So when we say that the Judaism of the dual Torah was cogent for nineteen centuries, it is not because the system remained intact and unchanged, but because it was unimpaired—forever able to take within itself, treat as part of its system of values and beliefs, a wide variety of new concepts and customs. This is an amazingly long time for something so volatile as a religion to have remained essentially stable and to have endured without profound shifts in symbolic structure, ritual life, or modes of social organization for the religious community. The Judaism that predominated during that long period and that has continued to flourish in the nineteenth and twentieth centuries bears a number of names: *Rabbinic* because of the nature of its principal authorities, who are rabbis; *Talmudic* because of the name of its chief authoritative document after the Hebrew scripture, which is the Talmud; *classical* because of its basic quality of endurance and prominence; or, simply, *Judaism* because no other important alternative was explored by Jews.

What proved the stability and essential cogency of Rabbinic Judaism during the long period of its predominance was its capacity—its modes of thought, its definitions of faith, worship, and the right way to live life—to take into itself and to turn into a support and a buttress for its own system a wide variety of separate and distinct modes of belief and thought. Of importance were, first, the philosophical movement, and, second, the mystical one. Both put forward modes of thought quite distinct from those of Rabbinic Judaism.

Philosophers of Judaism raised a range of questions and dealt with those questions in ways essentially separate from the established and accepted Rabbinic ways of thinking about religious issues. But all of the philosophers of Judaism not only lived in accord with the Rabbinic way of life; all of them were entirely literate in the Talmud and related literature, and many of the greatest philosophers were also great Talmudists. The same is to be said of the mystics. Their ideas about the inner character of God, their quest for a fully realized experience of union with the presence of God in the world, their particular doctrines, with no basis in the Talmudic literature produced by the early rabbis, and their intense spirituality, were all thoroughly "rabbinized"—that is, brought into conformity with the lessons and way of life taught by the Talmud. In the end, Rabbinic Judaism received extraordinary reinforcement from the spiritual resources generated by the mystic quest. Both philosophy and mysticism found their way into the center of Rabbinic Judaism. Both of them were shaped by minds that, to begin with, were infused with the content and spirit of Rabbinic Judaism.

The age of cogency is characterized by the predominance, from the far West in Morocco, to Middle East in Iran and South Asia in India, and from Egypt to England, of the Judaism of the dual Torah. During this long period, the principal question facing Jews was how to explain the success of the successor religions,

Christianity and Islam, which claimed to replace the Judaism of Sinai with a new testament on one side or a final and perfect prophecy on the other. Both religions affirmed but then claimed to succeed Judaism, and the Judaism of the dual Torah enjoyed success, among Jews, in making sense of the then-subordinated status of the enduring people and faith of Sinai. While during this long period heresies took shape, the beliefs of the new systems responded to the structure of the established one, so that a principal doctrine—for example, the doctrine of the dual Torah, Written and Oral—or of the Messiah as a faithful sage, would take shape in opposition to the authoritative doctrines of the Judaism of the dual Torah.

The Second Age of Diversity, ca. 1800 to the Present

It is only in modern times that other than religious consequences have been drawn from cataclysmic historical events. Because Judaism had developed prophecy and Rabbinic leadership, it was able to overcome the disasters of 586 B.C.E. and 70 C.E. The challenge of modern times comes not only from the outside but also from within: the nurture of new religious leadership for Jews facing a world of new values and ideals. Religion provides a particularly subtle problem for students of the process of modernization. Whereas in such other areas as politics and economics, that which is "modern" may meaningfully be set apart and against that which is "traditional," in religion the complexities of the process of social change become most evident, the certainties less sure.

What happened in modern times is that new questions arose, which Rabbinic Judaism did not address. In the nineteenth century, continuator Judaisms, referring to the same authoritative books as Rabbinic Judaism but finding in them answers to questions not previously addressed, came to the fore. They did not replace Rabbinic Judaism in its historical forms, they simply took shape as other Judaisms alongside that Judaism and related to it in fundamental ways. The new Judaisms of the nineteenth century all wanted to know how people could be both "Israel"—God's holy people—and also other things, citizens of the nation-state in which they lived, for example. All of them differentiated a religious from a secular part of everyday life, making space in that secular corner for Jews' other commitments and concerns besides the religion one. Reform, integrationist Orthodox, and Conservative Judaisms all responded to the critical issues Jews in Western countries wished to address.

In the twentieth century, essentially secular systems responded to yet another set of questions. These questions derived not from the challenges of other religions, but rather from the political crisis represented by the rise of racist anti-Semitism, which identified the Jews as the source of all evil and denied them the right to live at all. Zionism in the first half of the twentieth century and the Judaism of Holocaust and Redemption in the second half responded to that crisis by explaining the conditions under which Jews could endure.

From the last third of the nineteenth century onward, many Jews began to understand that the promises of Enlightenment and of emancipation would never be kept; indeed, were false to begin with. There was no place in Western civilization for the Jews, who had to build their own state as a refuge from the storms that were coming upon them. These Jews rejected that fundamental teleological optimism, rationalism, yielding patience, and quietism with which classical Judaism had viewed the world. They did not believe that the world was so orderly and reliable as Judaism had supposed. They regarded Judaism as a misleading and politically unwise view of the Jewish people and their worldly context. What was needed was not prayer, study of Torah, and a life of compassion and good deeds.

What the hour demanded was renewed action, a reentry into politics, and the repoliticization of the Jewish people. Zionism was the movement that redefined the Jewish people into a nation and revived the ancient political status of the Jews. So far as Zionism saw the world as essentially irrational and unreliable, unable to proceed in the orderly, calm, reasonable fashion in which Judaism assumed the world would always do its business, Zionism marked an end to Judaism as it had been known. The fact that, in time to come, Zionism would, as we shall see, take up the old messianic language and symbolism of Judaism and make over these ancient vessels into utensils bearing new meaning is not to be ignored. But at its beginning, Zionism marked a break from Judaism, not because of Zionism's messianic fervor, but because of its rejection of the quiet confidence, rationalism, and optimism of Rabbinic Judaism.

Thus, these two things—the promise of emancipation and the advent of racist and political anti-Semitism—fell so far outside the worldview of Rabbinic Judaism that they could not be satisfactorily interpreted and explained within the established system. The result, as we shall observe later on, is the breakdown of the Judaic system for many, many Jews. The system of Judaism was not overturned; for these people, it simply had become implausible. It had lost the trait of self-evidence. To state matters very simply: Rabbinic Judaism was and is a system of balance between cosmic, teleological optimism and short-term skepticism—a system of moderation and restraint, of rationalism and moderated feeling. Just as it came into being in response to the collapse of unrestrained Messianism, feelings unleashed and hopes unbounded by doubt, so it came to an end, where and when it did come to an end, in a renewed clash with those very emotions and aspirations that, in the beginning, it had overcome: passionate hope and unrestrained, total despair. A system of optimistic skepticism and skeptical optimism, a world grasped with open arms and loved with a breaking heart, could never survive those reaches toward the extremes, those violations of the rules and frontiers of moderate and balanced being, that characterize modern times.

The second age of diversity is marked not by the breaking apart of the received system, but by the development of competing systems of Judaism. In this period new Judaisms came into being that entirely ignored the categories and doctrines of the received system, not responding to its concerns but to other issues altogether. Now the principal question addressed by new systems concerned matters other than those found urgent by the received Judaism of the dual Torah, with its powerful explanation of the Jews' status in the divine economy. The particular points of stress, the self-evident answers to urgent questions, came at the interstices of individual life. Specifically, Jews needed to explain to themselves how as individuals, able to make free choices on their own, they found a place, also, within the commanded realm of the holy way of life and worldview of the Torah of Judaism. The issue again was political, but it concerned not the group but the individual. Judaisms produced in modern times answered the urgent question of individual citizenship, just as the Judaism of the long period of Christian and Muslim hegemony in Europe, Africa, and western Asia had taken up the (then equally pressing) question of a subordinated, but in its own view, holy society's standing and status as Israel in Islam or in Christendom.

SUMMARY: THE FIVE FACTS THAT DEFINE THE HISTORY OF JUDAISM

One paramount fact imposes structure on the history of Judaism. For a long time, from Late Antiquity (the early centuries of the Common Era) to modern times (the nineteenth century), a single Judaic system, Rabbinic Judaism, has predominated. Its success in defining for nearly the whole Jewish world the normative faith is marked in two ways. First, that Judaism absorbed into its own system new modes of thought and piety—philosophy and mysticism being the main ones. Second, that same Judaism defined the terms by which its competition—"heresies"—defined themselves. That is, the competition adopted doctrines antithetical to those of Rabbinic Judaism rather than building fresh and freestanding systems of its own. To define the issues of debate means to dominate, and Rabbinic Judaism dominated, specifically, from ancient times to nearly our own day, for close to 1800 years. When we speak of competing Judaic systems or Judaisms, both in ancient and in modern times, we must not lose sight of the fact that through most of the history of Judaism into contemporary times Rabbinic Judaism defined the norm. And for the larger number of Jews who practice Judaism, it still does.

That fact is the key to the history of Judaism. It is the story of how diverse Judaisms before 70 gave way to that single Judaism, the Rabbinic kind, that predominated from 70 onward, and of how, in the modern age, Rabbinic Judaism broke up into derivative Judaisms and also lost its commanding position as the single, defining force in the life of the Jews as a social group. Here we consider the history of Judaism as a whole. In later units we return to important chapters in that history, examined in detail, though our emphasis is on modern times. Seen whole, the history of Judaism the religion divides into the four principal periods we have examined in this chapter.

The first age of diversity	ca. 586 B.C.E. to 70 C.E.
The age of definition	ca. 70 C.E. to 640 C.E.
The age of cogency	ca. 640 C.E. to ca. 1800
The second age of diversity	ca. 1800 to the present

The history of Judaism is punctuated by five facts of political history that mark off everything else. With these dates in mind, everything holds together.

1. 586 B.C.E.: The Destruction of the First Temple
in Jerusalem by the Babylonians

The ancient Israelites, living in what they called the Land of Israel, produced scripture that reached its present form in the aftermath of the destruction of their capital city and Temple. Whatever happened before that time was reworked in the light of that event and the meaning imputed to it by authors who lived afterward. All Judaisms, from 586 forward, appeal to the writings produced in the aftermath of the destruction of the first Temple. These writings encompass the Five Books of Moses, or the Pentateuch—Genesis, Exodus, Leviticus, Numbers, and Deuteronomy—and important prophetic works as well. Therefore we must regard the destruction of that Temple as the date that marks the beginning of the formation of Judaism.

2. 70 C.E.: The Destruction of the Second Temple
in Jerusalem by the Romans

After 586, the Jews' leaders—the political classes and priesthood—were taken to Babylonia, the homeland of their conquerors, where they settled down. A generation later, Babylonia fell under the rule of the Persians, who permitted Jews to return to their ancient homeland. A small number did so, where they rebuilt the Temple and produced the Hebrew scripture. The Second Temple of Jerusalem lasted from about 500 B.C.E. to 70 C.E., when the Romans—by that time ruling the entire Middle East, including the Land of Israel, mainly through their own friends and allies, put down a Jewish rebellion and destroyed Jerusalem again. The second destruction proved final and marked the beginning of the Jews' history as a political entity defined in social and religious terms but not in territorial ones. That is, the Jews formed a distinct religious-social group, but all of them did not live in any one place, and some of them lived nearly everywhere in the West, within the lands of Christendom and Islam alike.

3. 640 C.E.: The Conquest of the Near and Middle East
and North Africa by the Muslims

The definition of the world in which the Jews would live was completed when the main outlines of Western civilization had been worked out. These encompassed Christendom, in Western and Eastern Europe, inclusive of the world west of the Ural Mountains in Russia, and Islam, in command of North Africa and the Near and Middle East, and, in later times, destined to conquer India and much of the Far East, Malaysia and Indonesia in particular, as well as sub-Saharan Africa. During this long period of time, the Jews in Christendom and Islam alike ordinarily enjoyed the status of a tolerated but subordinated minority and were free to practice their religion and sustain their separate group existence. Of still greater importance, both Christianity and Islam affirmed the divine origin of the Jews' holy book, the Torah. Christianity acknowledged the special status among the nations of Israel, the Jewish people, and Islam recognized both Judaism and Christianity as religions of the Book, the revealed scripture that culminated in the prophet Muhammad, the seal of prophecy. Each for its own theological reasons ordinarily, but not always, tolerated Judaism and those who practiced that religion.

4. 1787 or 1789: The American Constitution or the French Revolution

The American Constitution in the United States and the French Revolution in Western Europe marked the beginning of an age in which political change reshaped the world in which the West, including Western Jewries, lived. Politics became essentially secular, and political institutions no longer acknowledged supernatural claims of special status accorded either to a church or to a religious community. The individual person, rather than the social group, formed the focus of politics. In the case of the Jews, the turning meant that the Jews would be received as individuals and given rights equal to those of all others at the same time that "Israel" as a holy people and community no longer would enjoy special status and recognition. The French Revolution proclaimed, "To the Jews as citizens, everything; to the Jews as a nation, nothing." The American Constitution and Bill of Rights would afford to Jews the status of equality before the law but would accord to Judaism (among all religions) no recognition whatever.

5. 1933–1948: The Destruction of the Jews in Europe (the "Holocaust") and the Creation of the State of Israel

In 1933, Germany chose the National Socialist Party to govern. A principal doctrine of that party was that various groups among humanity, called races, possess traits, dubbed racial characteristics, that are inherent in the genes and that are passed on through time. Some races have good traits, others bad, and the worst of all of these "races" are the Jews. To save humanity from this dreadful "curse," all of the Jews of the world have to be murdered, and this will constitute the "final solution of the Jewish problem." This racist doctrine, broadly held in Europe and elsewhere during World War II (1939–1945), led to the murder of nearly 6 million European Jews. In the aftermath of the war, seeking a home for the remnants who had survived, the United Nations voted in 1947 to create a Jewish and an Arab state in what was then the territory of Palestine. The Jewish state came into being on May 15, 1948, as the state of Israel. These events defined an entirely new ecology for Judaism. On one side, the problem of evil was restated with great intensity. On the other, the social and political life of the Jews was entirely redefined. The issue of "exile and return," paramount at the outset, was framed with fresh urgency but with a new resolution. The formation of the state of Israel in the aftermath of the Holocaust opened a new chapter in the history of Judaism, but the story that that chapter will tell is not yet clear to any observer.

So far we have followed two definitions, Judaism's definition of itself and the academic definition of that same Judaism's history. Both treat Judaism as a freestanding religious system, autonomous of other such systems. That is quite natural, for religions pretend to an autonomy that defies the facts of humanity's diversity. But they take shape in constant competition with one another, for religions that address the whole of humanity, world religions, must explain not only why but why not: Why this religion and not that, competing one. So we now ask: How is Judaism defined by its competition?

3

Defining Judaism in the
Context of Christianity

"TO SEE OURSELVES AS OTHERS SEE US"

Nearly every Christian reader brings to this book a question of definition: Why is there Judaism at all? So if the issue is, how does Christianity define Judaism? the answer is, the dominant trait of Judaism imputed by Christianity is that it is *not-Christianity.* Let me explain.

Judaism has now been defined twice: First, in Chapter 1, we have seen how Judaism has defined itself, in its own canon or official documents, as comprising the Torah. That definition required seeing Judaism from within its own perspective. Second, in Chapter 2, we have followed how academic scholarship has defined Judaism in the context of secular history. Now we take up the third perspective, that of a competing religion sharing the same scripture as God's self-revelation. That exercise is necessary because religions in reality are not solitary but compete and define one another in their interaction in the everyday world. Christianity defines itself against Judaism, which in its view it supersedes, and Islam defines itself against Judaism and Christianity, both of which it affirms and in its view also completes.

In the case of Judaism, that third dimension—the competition's definition—dictates how much of the world has seen and still sees Judaism. That is because Christianity and Islam affirm that God revealed himself to Israel, so that Christianity's Old Testament, and Islam's "book"—the Bible—encompass Judaism's Written Torah. Christianity then added the New Testament, and the prophet Muhammad affirmed the prior revelations of God to Moses and Jesus, finding both of them necessary but insufficient, with the Quran then the final and perfect revelation. So Christianity and Islam contributed to the world's view of Judaism.

In today's world, the view of Judaism set forth by Christianity takes priority over that put forth by Islam. That is because Judaism flourishes in countries where Christianity is the dominant religion, but from 1948, with the creation of the state of Israel, and from 1956, with the expulsion of the Jews from Egypt and other Muslim countries, Judaism is scarcely represented in any numbers in the Muslim world where it once flourished. The conflict in the Middle East has made difficult any sort of religious and intellectual dialogue between Judaism and Islam such as flourished in medieval Spain, for example. But Judaism is practiced in Europe, and the European Diaspora, in flourishing communities in

North and Latin America, sustains a vivid religious dialogue indeed with Christianity in those territories.

From the beginning, particularly from the fourth Christian century onward, when Emperor Constantine afforded Christianity legal status and when his successors made Christianity the official religion of the Roman empire and thus of the West, Judaism responded to a world defined by Christianity. Not only so, but most of those who are introduced to Judaism in the pages of this book practice some other religion (or no religion at all), and, in the North American setting, they are more likely to practice Christianity than any other religion. That is serendipitous, for among religions, Christianity tells the story of its origins in a narrative that intersects with that of Judaism, appealing to scriptures held in common, Christianity's Old Testament that is Judaism's Written Torah.

THE JUDAEO-CHRISTIAN
CONFLICT OVER SCRIPTURE

To answer the Christian question very simply: The Jews who practice Judaism do not believe in Jesus as Christ because they believe in the Torah of Moses. They have a religion, too, and it is not Christianity but Judaism. They do not practice Christianity because they practice Judaism. That's why not. As to why: The Judaic faithful do not meet God Incarnate in Jesus Christ because they meet God in the Torah as expounded by "our sages of blessed memory." They have a religion of their own, which they believe to be true.

The earliest Christians were Jews who saw their religion as normative and authoritative: namely, Judaism, based on Judaic prophecy and on the Torah. A natural question troubling believing Christians, therefore, is why Judaism as a whole remains a religion that believes other things, or, as Christians commonly ask, "Why did the Jews not 'accept Christ'?" or "Why, after the resurrection of Jesus Christ, is there Judaism at all?" It is a constructive question, for it leads us deeper into an understanding not only of the differences between one religion and the other, but also of the traits of the religion under study. In other words, it is a question of comparison—even though the question is not properly framed.

THE ORAL TORAH AND THE
CHALLENGE OF CHRISTIANITY

Christianity, with its fully articulated Bible made up of the Old Testament and the New Testament, with its claim to succeed and replace the old Israel, with its proof for the kingship of Jesus as Christ in the Christian empire, and with its dismissal of Israel after the flesh as now rejected and set aside by God, presented a powerful challenge to Judaism as the Rabbinic sages defined matters. They countered with the dual Torah, with the reaffirmation of holy Israel as God's first love, and with the claim that the Messiah will come in the future and that the prophetic promises have not yet been fulfilled. Just as Christianity found in the Bible ample proof for its claim, so sages found in the Torah probative evidence in behalf of theirs. The issue became urgent in the fourth century, when Christianity could no longer be ignored by the sages, as, in general, it had been. That is because it was then that Christianity became first licit, then favored, and finally, the official religion of the Roman empire.

With the triumph of Christianity through Constantine and his successors in the West, from the legalization of Christianity in 312 to its establishment as state religion by the end of the fourth Century, Christianity's explicit claims, now validated in world-shaking events of the age, demanded a reply. The sages provided it. At those very specific points at which the Christian challenge met Israel's worldview head on, the Rabbinic sages' doctrines responded. What did Israel's sages have to present as their answer to the cross? It was the Torah, the definition of Judaism that therefore emerges in the encounter with Christianity.

This definition took three forms. The Torah was defined in the doctrine, first, of its status as oral and memorized revelation. That claim extended first of all to the Mishnah, which we shall meet in Chapter 5, and, by implication, of other rabbinical writings that flowed from it. The Torah, moreover, was presented as the encompassing symbol of Israel's salvation. The Torah, finally, was embodied in the person of the Messiah, who, of course, would be a rabbi. The Torah in all three modes confronted the cross, with its doctrine of the triumphant Christ, Messiah and king, ruler now of earth as of heaven. That is why the dual Torah formed the generative symbol for the Judaism that triumphed: It dealt with the urgent and critical question that had to be confronted, and it provided an answer that, to believers, was self-evidently valid, both necessary and sufficient. When we come to modern times, we shall see that when Christianity met competition from secular sources of truth, so did Judaism.

A FAMILY QUARREL,
AN ISRAELITE CIVIL WAR

Since both Christians and Judaists claim to inherit the ancient Israelite scripture and the promises God made to Israel of old, each party to the debate pointed to verses of scripture that proved its point and disproved the point of the other side. Both parties found it easy, moreover, to address the proof texts of the other side and dismiss them. The upshot is that each group talked to its adherents about its own points of urgent concern—that is, different people talked about different things to different people. Incomprehension marks relations between Judaism and Christianity in the first century as much as in the twenty-first, yet then as now the groups were two sectors of the same community of a shared revelation. Each addressed its own agenda, spoke to its own issues, and employed language distinctive to its adherents. Neither exhibited understanding of what was important to the other. Recognizing that fundamental inner-directedness may enable us to interpret the issues and the language used in framing them. For if each party perceived the other through a thick veil of incomprehension, the heat and abuse that characterized much of their writing about one another testifies to a truth different from that which conventional interpretations have yielded. If the enemy is within, if I see only the mote in the other's eye, it matters little whether there is a beam in my own.

THE PHARISEES

Who were the Pharisees, and why are they important in the definition of Judaism? First, the Pharisees are represented in some of the Gospels as leading critics of Jesus, and, second, the Pharisees also formed one of the principal groups that created the Mishnah and hence founded the Judaism of the dual Torah. The kind of Judaism that emerges from the first century—Rabbinic Judaism—thus draws heavily upon the methods and values imputed to the Pharisees in the later Rabbinic literature. Some of the same authorities identified in the New Testament or in Josephus as Pharisees occur in the Mishnah as sages— notably, the first-century figures Gamaliel and Simeon ben Gamaliel.

What was at issue between Jesus and the Pharisees? It was, in simple words, *salvation,* the focus of Jesus's message, versus *sanctification,* the principal concern of the Pharisees before 70 and of Rabbinic sages thereafter. Ultimately Judaism would unite the two foci of the faith, sanctification in the here and now, salvation at the end of days.

This requires spelling out. The Judaism defined by the system and method of the Pharisees, whom we met in Chapter 2 in the person of Yohanan ben Zakkai in connection with the destruction of the Second Temple by the Romans in 70, addressed the issue of the sanctification of Israel. Christianity, as defined by the evangelists, took up the question of the salvation of Israel. Both were expressions of Israel's religion. In retrospect, although they bear scripture in common, the two groups appear in no way comparable. Why not? The Gospels portray the first Christians as the family and followers of Jesus. So, as a social group, Christianity represented at its outset in a quite physical, familial, and genealogical way "the body of Christ." The Pharisees, by contrast, hardly formed a special group at all. It is easier to say what they were not than what they were. How so? Although the Pharisees appear as a political group by the first century in Josephus' writings about Maccabean politics, the Gospels and the Rabbinic traditions concur that what made an Israelite a Pharisee was not exclusively or even mainly his politics. The Pharisees were characterized by their adherence to certain cultic rules. They were not a member of a family in any natural or supernatural sense. Their social affiliations in no way proved homologous.

The Christians carried forward one aspect of scripture's doctrine of Israel, and the Pharisees another. The Hebrew scripture represents Israel as one very large family, descended from a single set of ancestors. The Christians adopted that theory of Israel by linking themselves, first of all, to the family of Jesus and his adopted sons, the disciples, and second, through him and them to his ancestry—to David, and on backward to Abraham, Isaac, and Jacob (hence the enormous power of the genealogies of Christ). The next step—the spiritualization of that familiar tie into the conception of the church as the body of Christ—need not detain us.

But scripture did not restrict itself to the idea of Israel as family; it also defined Israel as a kingdom of priests and a holy people. That is the way taken by the Pharisees. Their Israel found commonality in a shared, holy way of life required of all Israelites—so scripture held. The Mosaic Torah defined that way of life in both cultic and moral terms, and the prophets laid great stress on the latter. What made Israel holy—its way of life, its moral character—depended primarily on how people lived, not upon their shared genealogy.

Both Christians and Pharisees belonged to Israel but chose different definitions of the term. The Christians saw Israel as a family; the Pharisees saw it as a way of life. The Christians stressed their genealogy; the Pharisees their ethos and ethics. The Christian family held things in common; the holy people held in common a way of life that sanctified them. At issue in the argument between them are positions that scarcely intersect held by groups whose social self-definitions are incongruent.

Christians were a group comprised of the family of Israel, talking about salvation; Pharisees were a group shaped by the holy way of life of Israel, talking about sanctification. The two neither converse nor argue. Indeed, groups unlike one another in what, to begin with, defines and bonds them, groups devoid of a common program of debate, have no argument. They are different people talking about different things to different people. Yet, as is clear, neither group could avoid recognizing the other. What ensued was not a discussion, let alone a debate, but only a confrontation of people with nothing in common pursuing programs of discourse that do not in any way intersect. Not much of an argument.

PRIEST, SAGE, PROPHET: ANCIENT ISRAEL'S HERITAGE IN CHRISTIAN AND JUDAIC RECONSTRUCTION

Placing Christianity and Judaism into ancient Israel's heritage affords this perspective: Christianity emphasized the prophetic tradition, Judaism, that of the priests of the Torah and of the sages of the Wisdom books—Proverbs and Psalms, for example. Ancient Israel's heritage had yielded the cult with its priests, the Torah with its scribes and teachers, and the prophetic and apocalyptic hope for meaning in history and the eschaton—the end of history—mediated by Messiahs and generals. From these sources derive Temple, school, and (in the apocalyptic expectation) battlefield on earth and in heaven.

To seek a typology of the modes of Israelite piety, we must look for the generative symbol of each mode: an altar for the priestly ideal, a scroll of scripture for the scribal ideal of wisdom, a coin marked "Israel's freedom: year one" for the messianic modality. In each of these visual symbols we perceive things we cannot touch, hearts and minds we can only hope to evoke. The symbols under discussion—Temple altar, sacred scroll, victory wreath for the head of the King-Messiah—largely covered Jewish society. We need not reduce them to their merely social dimensions to recognize that on them was founded the organization of Israelite society and the interpretation of its history.

The priest viewed society as organized along structural lines emanating from the Temple. His caste stood at the top of a social scale in which all things were properly organized, each with its correct name and proper place. The inherent sanctity of the people of Israel, through the priests' genealogy, came to its richest embodiment in the high priest. Food set apart for the priests' rations, at God's command, possessed the same sanctity; so, too, did the table at which priests ate. To the priest, for the sacred society of Israel, history was an account of what happened in the Temple.

To the sage, the life of society demanded wise regulations. Relationships among people required guidance by the laws enshrined in the Torah and best interpreted by scribes; the task of Israel was to construct a way of life in accordance with the revealed rules of the Torah. The sage, master of the rules, stood at the head.

Prophecy insisted that the fate of the nation depended upon the faith and moral condition of society, a fact to which Israel's internal and external history testified. Both sage and priest saw Israel from the viewpoint of eternity, but the nation had to live out its life in this world, among other peoples coveting the very same land, and within the context of Roman imperial policies and politics. The Messiah's kingship would resolve the issue of Israel's subordinate relationship to other nations and empires, establishing once and for all the desirable, correct context for priest and sage alike.

Implicit in the messianic framework was a perspective on the world beyond Israel for which priest and sage cared not at all. The priest perceived the Temple as the center of the world; beyond it he saw in widening circles the less holy, then the unholy, and further still, the unclean. All lands outside the Land of Israel were unclean with corpse uncleanness; all other peoples were unclean just as corpses were unclean. In the world, accordingly, life abided within Israel; and in Israel, within the Temple. Outside, in the far distance, were vacant lands and dead peoples, comprising an undifferentiated wilderness of death—a world of uncleanness. From such a perspective, no teaching about Israel among the nations, no interest in the history of Israel and its meaning, was apt to emerge.

The wisdom of the sage pertained in general to the streets, marketplaces and domestic establishments (the household units) of Israel. What the sage said was wisdom as much for gentiles as for Israel. The universal wisdom proved international, moving easily across the boundaries of culture and language, from eastern to southern to western Asia. It focused, by definition, upon human experience common to all and undifferentiated by nation, essentially unaffected by the large movements of history. Wisdom spoke about fathers and sons, masters and disciples, families and villages, not about nations, armies, and destiny.

Because of their very diversity, these three principal modes of Israelite existence might easily cohere. Each focused on a particular aspect of the national life, and none essentially contradicted any other. One could worship at the Temple, study the Torah, and fight in the army of the Messiah—and some did all three. Yet we must see these modes of being—and their consequent forms of piety—as separate. Each contained its own potentiality to achieve full realization without reference to the others.

The symbolic system of cult, Torah, and Messiah demanded choices. If one thing was most important, others must have been less important. Either history matters, or it happens, without significance, "out there." Either the proper conduct of the cult determines the course of the seasons and the prosperity of the Land, or it is "merely ritual"—an unimportant external and not the critical heart. (We hear this judgment in, for example, the prophetic polemic against the cult.) Either the Messiah will save Israel, or he will ruin everything. Accordingly, though we take for granted that people could have lived within the multiple visions of priest, sage, and Messiah, we must also recognize that such a life was vertiginous. Narratives of the war of 66–73 emphasize that priests warned messianists not to endanger their Temple. Later Rabbinic sages paid slight regard to the messianic struggle led by Bar Kokhba, and after 70 claimed the right to tell priests what to do. To them, the Messiah would be a Rabbinic sage, not a great warrior.

THE PARTING OF THE WAYS

We may now return to our starting point, where Judaic and Christian religious life led in different directions. Judaic consciousness in the period under discussion had two competing but not yet contradictory symbol systems: the altar/scroll of the Pharisees and scribes, the wreath of the King-Messiah. What made one focus more compelling than the other? The answer emerges when we realize that each kind of piety addressed a distinctive concern; each spoke about different things to different people.

We may sort out the types of piety by returning to our earlier typology: priest, sage, Messiah. Priests and sages turned inward, toward the concrete everyday life of the community. They addressed the sanctification of Israel. Messianists and their prophetic and apocalyptic teachers turned outward, toward the affairs of states and nations. They spoke of the salvation of Israel. Priests saw the world of life in Israel, and death beyond. They knew what happened to Israel without concerning themselves with a theory about the place of Israel among the nations. For priests, the nations formed an undifferentiated realm of death.

Sages, all the more, spoke of home and hearth, fathers and sons, husbands and wives, the village and enduring patterns of life. What place was there in this domestic scheme for the realities of history—wars and threats of wars, the rise and fall of empires? The sages expressed the consciousness of a singular society amidst other societies. The issue for the priest/sage was being; for the prophet/messianist it was becoming.

The radical claims of the holiness sects, such as the Pharisees and Essenes as well as the community represented by the library of the Dead Sea scrolls, of professions such as the scribes, and of followers of Messiahs—all expressed aspects of Israel's common piety. Priest, scribe, Messiah—all stood together with the Jewish people along the same continuum of faith and culture. Each expressed in a particular and intense way one mode of the piety that the people as a whole understood and shared. That is why we can move from the particular to the general in our description of the common faith in first-century Israel. That common faith, we hardly need argue, distinguished Israel from all other peoples of the age, whatever the measure of "Hellenization" in the country's life; as far as Israel was concerned, there was no "common theology of the ancient Near East."

No wonder that the two new modes of defining Judaic piety that issued from the period before 70 and thrived long after that date—the Judaism framed by sages from before the first to the seventh century, and Christianity with its paradoxical King-Messiah—redefined that piety while remaining true to emphases of the inherited categories. Each took over the established classifications—priest, scribe, and Messiah—but infused them with new meaning. Though in categories nothing changed, in substance nothing remained what it had been. That is why both Christian and Judaic thinkers reread the received scripture—the Old Testament to the one, the Written Torah to the other—and produced, respectively, the New Testament and the Oral Torah. The common piety of the people of Israel in its land defined the program of religious life for both the Judaism and the Christianity that emerged after the caesura of the destruction of the Temple. The bridge to Sinai—worship, revelation, national and social eschatology—was open in both directions.

Thus, in the mind of the Church, Christ as perfect sacrifice, teacher, prophet, and King-Messiah brought together but radically recast the three foci of what had been the common piety of Israel in Temple times. Still later on, the figure of the Talmudic sage would encompass but redefine all three categories as well.

How so? After 70, study of Torah and obedience to it became a temporary substitute for the Temple and its sacrifice. The government of the sages in accord with "the one whole Torah of Moses, our rabbi," revealed by God at Sinai, carried forward the scribes' conception of Israel's proper government. The Messiah would come when all Israel, through mastery of the Torah and obedience to it, had formed that holy community that, to begin with, the Torah prescribed in the model of Heaven revealed to Moses at Sinai. Jesus as perfect priest, rabbi, and Messiah was a protean figure. So was the Talmudic rabbi as Torah incarnate, priest for the present age, and, in the model of (Rabbi) David, progenitor and paradigm of the Messiah. In both cases we find an unprecedented rereading of established symbols through the interpretation in fresh ways of the received scripture. And that brings us to the oral part of the Torah, which is what makes Judaism not simply the "religion of the Old Testament" or the "religion that is not Christianity," but very much a religion on its own: the religion of the dual Torah, the Written Torah as mediated by Oral or Memorized Torah of Sinai.

To answer the question with which we started: Judaism does not accept Christ as the Messiah because scripture for Judaism yields a different story from the one that Christians tell. But side by side, Christianity and Judaism in comparison and contrast do facilitate the work of defining each other. It is the Torah that makes all the difference. So let us now turn to the Torah and to the books that in response to scripture tell the Torah's story: Mishnah, Talmud, and Midrash. These form the first writing down of the Oral Torah of Sinai. We start with the question: How, exactly, does Judaism define the word *Torah*?

PART II

Classical Judaism:
The Oral Part of the Torah

4

What Does Judaism Mean by "Torah"?

We now know what *the* Torah is: It is a scroll, it is the revelation of God to Moses at Sinai. But the word *Torah* appears without the definite article, just *Torah,* and that fact alerts us to a complexity. So we take up the question: How does Judaism define the word *Torah* in the context of that oral tradition that, Judaism maintains, God revealed to Moses at Sinai along with the written one? The answer to that question takes two forms. First, what does Torah refer to in Judaism? Second, what particular books embody components of that oral part of the Torah? In this chapter we follow the definition of the word *Torah,* with and without the definite article, and in Chapters 5, 6, and 7 we examine some of the basic books of the Torah beyond those of scripture. At each point we find ourselves addressed by stories, just as in Chapter 1 we realized that Judaism is story "before it is anything else, after it is everything else."

"IT IS A MATTER OF TORAH, WHICH I NEED TO LEARN."

It is no surprise, in light of the power of the narrative pattern of Eden and the Land, exile and return, that we begin with three highly surprising stories. These now serve to embody the Torah's use of the word *Torah,* as the Talmud of Babylonia, ca. 600 C.E., uses the word:

Talmud of Babylonia Tractate Berakhot 62A

Said Rabbi Aqiba, "I once went after Rabbi Joshua to the privy and I learned the three things from him.

"I learned that people defecate not on an east-west axis but on a north-south axis.

"I learned that one urinates not standing but sitting.

"And I learned that one wipes not with the right hand but with the left."

Said Ben Azzai to him, "Do you behave so insolently toward your master?"

He said to him, "It is a matter of Torah, which I need to learn."

It has been taught on Tannaite authority:

Ben Azzai says, "I once followed Rabbi Aqiba into the privy, and I learned three things from him:

"I learned that people defecate not on an east–west axis but on a north–south axis.

"And I learned that one urinates not standing up but sitting down.

"And I learned that people wipe themselves not with the right hand but with the left."

Said Rabbi Judah to him, "Do you behave all that insolently toward your master?"

He said to him, "It is a matter of Torah, which I need to learn."

Rabbi Kahana went and hid under Rab's bed. He heard [Rab and his wife] "conversing" and laughing and doing what comes naturally. He said to him, "It appears that Abba's mouth has never before tasted 'the dish.'"

He said, "Kahana, are you here! Get out! That's disgraceful!"

He said to him, "It is a matter of Torah, which I need to learn."

In these stories from the Talmud, which capture the authentic use of the word *Torah,* the most important thing is that *Torah* does not refer to a particular book or set of books, let alone to a physical object, the scroll. It refers to the right way of doing things, in a context that is, to say the least, bizarre and jarring. But the main point emerges: Israel learns Torah not only in a book or in a statement of a sage but by observing how the models of Torah conduct themselves.

From the perspective of the sages of Rabbinic Judaism, the oral part of the Torah is transmitted from Sinai via master to disciple, from God to Moses and onward. So all learned persons, who have served as disciples and become masters themselves, have that capacity to embody and exemplify the teachings of the Torah. Learning in Torah, through discipleship, in community, through a process of learning the tradition that emphasizes the individual's own capacity for critical learning—that is what opens the way to everyone to know God and to embody the Torah.

We began with a set of three curious stories that make the same jarring point: Natural bodily processes, intimate chapters in the private life, both fall within the framework of Torah, which is to be taught by the sage and must be learned by the disciple. The details of the text need not detain us for long. The story presupposes that the storytellers are located east or west of Jerusalem, hence the matter of the north–south axis; the other two concern secular hygiene. Without apology I leave to the mature reader's imagination the interpretation of the euphemism of the third story.

Here the word *Torah* bears a meaning all its own. It clearly stands for more than the physical object, the Torah scroll containing the Five Books of Moses that is displayed and read Sabbath morning in synagogue worship. Here, by *Torah* the disciple means the proper way of doing things, the Godly way. And, it is clear, the disciple learns by imitating the master's deeds, not only by repeating his or words. The disciple takes for granted that how the master acts, not only what he says, conveys God's truth.

TORAH IN THE CHAIN
OF TRADITION FROM SINAI

That is what it means to take a place in a chain of tradition. A tradition encompasses not only sayings, sound advice, but gestures and patterns of relationship. That is why a tradition does not endure in only or mainly writing, why an oral, memorized and remembered Torah, as much as a written one, is required. If at stake is how people conduct themselves, then the Torah of Sinai can reach the living generation only through that chain of master and disciple that extends backward and forward through time. The master forms the model for the disciple, because the master has himself served as a disciple. The stakes then encompass the very basic conduct of affairs, the attitudes and the actions that all together define who and what the Israelite community is.

And that brings us to the center of matters: Whom do disciples imitate when disciples imitate the master, and whose disciple are they? The answer comes to mind when we recall who is the first master, who the original disciple. Tractate Abot opens, "Moses received Torah from Sinai," and that means, Moses was the first disciple, God the first master. This mythic account of matters, furthermore, reaches us in two statements, both of which underscore how, when Israelites study Torah, they strive to learn how to imitate God.

In the first of the two stories, we find a daring reading of Gen. 1:26–27, "Let us make man in our image, after our likeness. … And God created man in His image, in the image of God, He created him, male and female He created them." Now the Written Torah clearly wishes to say that humanity is made in the model of God. We need not find surprising, then, that the angels did not know the difference:

Genesis Rabbah 8:10

Said Rabbi Hoshaiah, "When the Holy One, blessed be he, came to create the first man, the ministering angels mistook him [for God, since man was in God's image] and wanted to say before him, 'Holy [holy, holy is the Lord of hosts].' "

"To what may the matter be compared? To the case of a king and a governor who were set in a chariot, and the provincials wanted to greet the king, 'Sovereign!' But they did not know which one of them was which. What did the king do? He turned the governor out and put him away from the chariot, so that people would know who was king.

"So too when the Holy One, blessed be he, created the first man, the angels mistook him [for God]. What did the Holy One, blessed be he, do? He put him to sleep, so everyone knew that he was a mere man. That is in line with the following verse of Scripture: 'Cease you from man, in whose nostrils is a breath, for how little is he to be accounted' (Isaiah 2:22)."

In humanity's mortality—"put him to sleep"—sages know that they are not God, and that suffices. But in the aspiration to imitate God, they fulfill the Creator's purpose.

WHAT GOD REVEALS,
WHAT GOD CONCEALS

Now to make sense of these matters, we must pay attention not only to what sages say, but to what they mean. And what they mean is to introduce a world of complexity, a world lacking in simple truths. So while, at first glance, the stories we have examined promise easy access to God's presence—just learn what the book says by studying with the right teaching, and lo, one hears God's own words, conjure up God's very person—other, equally vital accounts establish an altogether different context.

The Torah conceals more than it reveals, makes promises that somehow are not kept. That is how life is, and the Torah forms a commentary on the here and now—so the Rabbinic sages represent matters. It is only in that context that the following story makes sense:

Talmud of Babylonia Tractate Menahot 29 B

Said Rabbi Judah, "At the time that Moses went up on high, he found the Holy One in session, affixing crowns to the letters [of the words of the Torah]. He said to him, 'Lord of the universe, who is stopping you [from regarding the document as perfect without these additional crowns on the letters]?'

"He said to him, 'There is a man who is going to arrive at the end of many generations, and Aqiba b. Joseph is his name, who is going to interpret on the basis of each point of the crowns heaps and heaps of laws.'

"He said to him, 'Lord of the Universe, show him to me.'

"He said to him, 'Turn around.'

"He went and took a seat at the end of eight rows, but he could not grasp what the people were saying. He felt faint. But when the discourse reached a certain matter, and the disciples said, 'My lord, how do you know this?' and he answered, 'It is a law given to Moses from Sinai,' he regained his composure.

"He went and came before the Holy One. He said before him, 'Lord of the Universe, How come you have someone like that and yet you give the Torah through me?'

"He said to him, 'Silence! That is how the thought came to me.'

"He said to him, 'Lord of the Universe, you have shown me his Torah, now show me his reward.'

"He said to him, 'Turn around.'

"He turned around and saw his flesh being weighed out at the butcher-stalls in the market.

"He said to him, 'Lord of the Universe, "Such is Torah, such is the reward"?'

"He said to him, 'Silence! That is how the thought came to me.' "

Here again, the chosen medium of Judaic theology is narrative. God tells Moses less than Moses wants to know. Why has God chosen Moses, who practically stutters, rather than a man of eloquence such as Aaron—Moses, of limited intellect, rather than Aqiba, of incandescent mind? Because that is how God wanted things to be. What reward of Torah study has Aqiba gained? Martyrdom—some reward! Life does not always work out the way one hopes or wants. And the Torah for its part sets forth mysteries that people cannot always sort out or even fathom.

MEANINGS OF THE WORD *TORAH*

Clearly, it is time to give a systematic definition for the word *Torah,* which I have used in a variety of ways, both "Torah" and "the Torah," for example. To what do Rabbinic writings refer when they use that word?

In the context of Judaism Torah means "teaching" or instruction, as we saw in Chapter 1, and in scripture it refers to the teaching that God revealed to Moses at Mount Sinai. As we recall, the most familiar meaning of the word is "Torah = the five books of Moses, or Pentateuch" (Genesis, Exodus, Leviticus, Numbers, Deuteronomy). "The Torah" may also refer to the entirety of the Hebrew scripture. Since at Sinai, Judaism maintains, God revealed the Torah to Moses in two media, written and oral, with the written part corresponding to the Pentateuch, a further, oral part of the Torah is included in the meanings assigned to the word *Torah*. This oral part is held to encompass the teachings ultimately written down by the sages of the Torah in ancient times and is contained, in part, in the Mishnah, Talmud, and Midrash—compilations, which we shall meet in Chapters 5, 6, and 7.

But within Judaism, the word *Torah* has come to stand for what in secular language is called "Judaism." That is to say, what the world calls "Judaism" the faithful know as "the Torah" in the usage, "the Torah teaches." But that to which "Torah" makes reference proves far more encompassing than scripture and even transcends the limits of the whole Torah, Written and Oral, extending as it does to the teachings of the authoritative Rabbinic sages.

That is why the definitive ritual of the religion outsiders call Judaism consists in studying the Torah. The form of study is meant to be public, engaging all Israel, which is why the centerpiece of synagogue worship is meant to be the proclamation of the Torah. Study groups, in which people read sacred texts, discuss them, and relate what they read to the world they know, form the ideal setting for Torah study. In the classical tradition, moreover, study means discipleship, for study of Torah involves entering into a tradition that is preserved only in part in writing but in important measure also in memory, orally. Then Israel learns Torah from experienced teachers of the Torah, and, in time, disciples become teachers ourselves. So for the people of the Torah, study of the Torah requires a shared and public encounter.

One who studies Torah, according to the teachings thereof, becomes holy, like Moses, who is called *Moshe rabbenu,* "Moses, our lord" or "rabbi," and like

God, in whose image humanity was made and whose Torah provided the plan and the model for what God wanted of a humanity created in his image. As for Christians it was in Christ, God made flesh, so the framers of the system of Judaism at hand found in the Torah that image of God to which Israel should aspire, and to which the sage in fact conformed.

SEVEN MEANINGS OF *TORAH*

Clearly, the issues represented by the word *Torah* for the Rabbinic sages prove humble but weighty. In fact, we can identify seven ways in which the word occurs:

1. When *the Torah* refers to a particular thing, it is to a scroll containing divinely revealed words. Then the word always bears the definite article: *the Torah* means "the scroll of the Torah."

2. The Torah may further refer to revelation, not as an object but as a corpus of doctrine. "The Torah teaches" now refers not to the scroll but to Judaism, that is, the doctrines and dogmas of the faith, the rules of behavior and belief.

3. When one "does Torah," the disciple "studies" or "learns," and the master "teaches," Torah. Hence while the word *Torah* never appears as a verb, it does refer to an act. *Talmud Torah*—"study of the Torah"—covers that act.

4. The word also bears a quite separate sense, *torah* as category or classification or corpus of rules, e.g., "the torah of driving a car" is a usage entirely acceptable in some documents. This generic usage of the word does occur. In the context of the holy way of life, the "torah of driving a car" becomes "the Torah of proper conduct."

5. Obviously, no account of the meaning of the word *Torah* can ignore the distinction between the two Torahs, Written and Oral.

6. The word *Torah* refers to the source of salvation, often fully worked out in stories about how the individual and the nation will be "saved through Torah." In general, the sense of the word *salvation* is not complicated. It is simply salvation in the sense that, if Israel keeps the Torah, God will save Israel and redeem the people from the trials of this world and this age. In the canonical documents of the Oral Torah, knowledge of Torah bears a supernatural power: A person made holy by Torah learning has the power to do wonders.

7. The word *Torah* very commonly refers to a status, distinct from and above another status, as in "teachings of Torah" compared with "teachings of scribes."

But there is a further status to which reference is made. This matter of status requires amplification. For it points to the very center of matters: Knowledge of the Torah shapes conduct, and by one's conduct, a person shows precisely who he or she is. What difference does study of the Torah make within the community of holy Israel? The answer must surprise, even after having been asserted by Judaism for two thousand years: The person who masters the Torah enjoys the highest status, even overtaking the status conferred by birth, wealth, caste, or class. The Mishnah places a high value upon studying the Torah and upon the status of the sage.

Mishnah Tractate Horayyot 3:8

A priest takes precedence over a Levite, a Levite over an Israelite, an Israelite over a mamzer [one whose parents cannot legally marry by reason of consanguinity], a mamzer over a Netin [descendant of a Temple slave], a Netin over a proselyte, a proselyte over a freed slave.

Under what circumstances?
When all of them are equivalent.

But if the mamzer was a disciple of a sage and a high priest was an am ha'ares [lacking all knowledge of the Torah], the mamzer who is a disciple of a sage takes precedence over a high priest who is an am haares.

The stakes then prove very high, when we realize that the kind of knowledge afforded by Torah study—Talmud Torah—changes the status of the one who knows, moving that person from the lowest to the highest level of Israelite society. Only in the light of this account of the context in which the word *Torah* finds meaning will the strange tales cited at the head of this chapter make sense. But now they are easy to understand. The sage, learned in the Torah, is a living version of the Torah. What the sage does in private, not only what he says in public, constitutes a matter of Torah.

THE TORAH'S TRANSFORMATIVE POWER: THE MATTER OF STATUS

Torah transforms. That is the implicit message of the stories reviewed in Chapter 1, and here it becomes explicit. What Israelites learn, when they study Torah, not only informs but changes them, affecting not only mind but heart and soul and character. To state matters negatively, if Israelites are not changed, then they have not studied Torah, they have simply learned things. Here is a text that speaks of the change in supernatural terms, a change in the very meaning of family relationships for example:

Mishnah Tractate Baba Mesia 2:11

[If someone has to choose between seeking] what he has lost and what his father has lost,

his own takes precedence.

. . . what he has lost and what his master has lost,

his own takes precedence.

…what his father has lost and what his master has lost, that of his master takes precedence.

For his father brought him into this world.

But his master, who taught him wisdom, will bring him into the life of the world to come.

But if his father is a sage, that of his father takes precedence.

[If] his father and his master were carrying heavy burdens, he removes that of his master, and afterward removes that of his father.

[If] his father and his master were taken captive,

he ransoms his master, and afterward he ransoms his father.

But if his father is a sage, he ransoms his father, and afterward he ransoms his master.

Here is another surprising text, but one that spells out its own point: The natural father brings the child into this world, but the sage brings the disciple into the world beyond the natural, the world to come, life eternal. Once more, we confront a remarkable claim in behalf of study of the Torah.

FINDING GOD IN THE TORAH

What, then, are those matters of Torah that Israelites need to learn? They need in the Torah to find ways to God's presence.

Tractate Abot 3:6

Rabbi Halafta of Kefar Hananiah says, "Among ten who sit and work hard on Torah-study the Presence comes to rest, as it is said, 'God stands in the congregation of God' (Ps. 82:1) [and 'congregation' involves ten persons].

"And how do we know that the same is so even of five? For it is said, 'And he has founded his vault upon the earth' (Amos 9:6).

"And how do we know that this is so even of three? Since it is said, 'And he judges among the judges' [a court being made up of three judges] (Ps. 82:1).

And how do we know that this is so even of two? Because it is said, 'Then they that feared the Lord spoke with one another, and the Lord hearkened and heard' (Mal. 3:16).

"And how do we know that this is so even of one? Since it is said, 'In every place where I record my name I will come to you and I will bless you' (Ex. 20:24) [and it is in the Torah that God has recorded His name]."

Wherever else and however else the children of Israel meet God, the encounter takes place above all in the words of the Torah that God speaks to *Israel* in particular. The reason is that the Torah contains the record of God's self-manifestation to humanity through Israel. It is the permanent account of the encounter with God that the prophets of scripture and the sages of the Mishnah, Talmud, and Midrash record. In study of the Torah Israel relives the encounter and makes it its own. That is why they privilege the Torah, giving it the critical place in public worship and placing special emphasis upon its teachings. It is because, as we have seen over and over again in the normative texts of Judaism, holy Israel receives the Torah as God's revelation.

That view of the Torah comes to concrete expression every time an Israelite is called in public worship to the reading of the Torah and recites the blessing:

> Blessed are you, Lord, our God, ruler of the world, who has chosen us from all peoples by giving us the Torah. Blessed are you, who gives the Torah.

And at the end of the reading of the Torah, the blessing is recited:

> Blessed are you, Lord, our God, ruler of the world, who has given us an authentic Torah, planting in our midst life eternal. Blessed are you, who gives the Torah.

Here then is the affirmation of Israel at worship: The Torah marks Israel's election as God's first love, the Torah guarantees life eternal. These are the acts of grace that take place when believing Israel encounters God in the Torah.

The Torah is not the only place at which humanity and God come together. Some faithful of Judaism find God in history, as the prophets did, and others in nature, as the Psalmists did, for example, "The heavens declare the glory of God." For philosophers God serves as a postulate; for mystics, God takes place in an experience of immediate encounter. Some seek God in the depth of the soul, still others in the intersecting paths of human lives, through acts of love and service, where God lives. Many hear God's voice in humanity and find God's presence in the everyday. And none errs. But the specificities of the encounter—the *who* and the *what* and the *why*—evade definition.

In the Torah those who form holy Israel find the answers that the Torah sets forth to the questions, the *who* and the *what* and the *why,* of human existence. True, the Torah itself maintains that in the grandeur of nature—"the heavens declare the Glory of God"—or in the workings of history—"You have seen what I did at the Sea"—Israel meets God. The encounter takes place in the natural responses of intangible emotion and impalpable sentiment, and the personality of the God of mystic encounter or philosophical reflection likewise is difficult to pin down. But in the Torah Israel learns the particulars: "I am the Lord your God who brought you out of the land of Egypt, out of the house of bondage." It is in the Torah that not God, the divinity in general but the Lord God who commands and loves and yearns for humanity is made manifest. There Israel discovers what God has to say to holy Israel, in particular. In the Torah Israel finds out what God wants Israel to know about God, and what God wants them to do and to be. That is the theology that animates the books of the Oral Torah, in the manifest detail of the everyday and the here and now.

5

The Mishnah

THE ENIGMA OF THE MISHNAH

In Chapter 1 we saw how Judaism is a religious system in the form of a story. But beyond scripture, the Mishnah, the first document of Judaism, tells no story on the surface, and it does not in any way shape or form resemble the Torah. It contains little narrative, no prophecy, few admonitions, and it does not imitate the Hebrew of scripture. Rather, speaking to whom it may concern in objective, neutral, descriptive, generalizing language, it sets forth a philosophy in the form of a law code. Closed in ca. 200 C.E., deriving rulings from the Rabbinic sages of the Land of Israel who flourished in the early centuries before and after the beginning of the Common Era, the document does not claim to originate at Sinai. Its language in no way recalls that of scripture; it is a different kind of Hebrew altogether from biblical Hebrew. Here is how the Mishnah begins—no title, no preface, no contents, just rules that take for granted a vast corpus of ready-at-hand knowledge:

Mishnah Tractate Berakhot, I.1

From what time do they recite the *Shema* [the proclamation of the unity of God] in the evening?

From the hour that the priests enter [the status of purity, the sun having set completing their purification-rite] to eat their heave offering [priestly rations, which must be eaten in a state of cultic purity],

"until the end of the first watch," the words of R. Eliezer.
But sages say, "Until midnight."
Rabban Gamaliel says, "Until the rise of dawn."

There was the case in which his [Gamaliel's] sons returned from a banquet hall [after midnight].

They said to him, "We did not [yet] recite the Shema."
He said to them, "If the dawn has not yet risen, you are
obligated to recite [the Shema]."

And [this applies] not only [in] this [case]. Rather, [as regards] all [commandments] which sages said [may be performed] 'Until midnight," the obligation [to perform them persists] until the rise of dawn." [For example,] the offering of the fats and entrails—their obligation [persists] until the rise of dawn [(see Lev. 1:9, 3:3–5)].

And all [sacrifices] which must be eaten within one day, the obligation [to eat them persists] until the rise of dawn.

If so why did sages say [that these actions may be performed only] until midnight?

In order to protect man from sin.

So begins the Mishnah. Not a very promising start! Falling into the hands of someone who has never seen the writing before, the Mishnah must cause puzzlement. From the first line to the last, discourse takes up questions internal to a system that is never introduced. The Mishnah provides information without establishing context. It presents disputes about facts hardly urgent outside a circle of faceless disputants. Consequently, we start with the impression that we join a conversation already long under way about topics we can never grasp anyhow. Even though the language is our own, the substance is not. We shall feel as if we are in a transit lounge at a distant airport. We understand the words people say but are baffled by their meanings and concerns, above all, by the urgency in their voices

DEFINING THE MISHNAH: THE FIRST HOLY BOOK, AFTER THE HEBREW SCRIPTURES, IN RABBINIC JUDAISM

Defining the Mishnah presents difficulties because the Mishnah does not identify its authors. It permits only slight variations, if any, in its authorities' patterns of language and speech, so there is no place for individual characteristics of expression. It nowhere tells us when it speaks. It does not address a particular place or time and rarely speaks of events in its own day. It never identifies its prospective audience. There is scarcely a "you" in the entire mass of sayings and rules. As we just saw, the Mishnah begins nowhere. It ends abruptly. There is no predicting where it will commence or explaining why it is done.

Indeed, the Mishnah contains not a hint about what its authors conceive their work to be. Is it a law code? Is it a schoolbook? Because it makes statements describing what people should and should not do, or rather, do and do not do, we might suppose it is a law code. Because, as we shall see in a moment, it covers topics of both practical and theoretical interest, we might suppose it is a schoolbook. But the Mishnah never expresses a hint about its authors' intent. The reason is that the authors do what they must to efface all traces not only of individuality but even of their own participation in the formation of the document. So it is not only a letter from utopia to whom it may concern.

Nor should we fail to notice, even at the outset, that although the Mishnah clearly addresses Israel, the Jewish people, it is remarkably indifferent to Hebrew scripture. The Mishnah does not attribute its sayings to biblical heroes, prophets or holy men, as do the writings of the pseudepigraphs of Hebrew scripture. The Mishnah does not claim to emerge from a fresh encounter with God through revelation, as is not uncommon in Israelite writings of the preceding four hundred years. Indeed, the Holy Spirit is not alleged to speak here. So all the devices by which other Israelite writers gained credence for their messages are ignored. Perhaps the authority of the Mishnah was self-evident to its authors. But self-evident or not, they in no way take the trouble to explain to their document's audience why people should conform to the descriptive statements contained in their holy book.

If then we turn to the contents of the document, we are helped not at all in determining the place of the Mishnah's origination, the purpose of its formation, the reasons for its anonymous and collective plane of discourse and monotonous tone of voice. For the Mishnah covers a carefully defined program of topics. But the Mishnah never tells us why one topic is introduced and another is omitted, or what the agglutination of these particular topics is meant to accomplish in the formation of a system or imaginative construction. Nor is there any predicting how a given topic will be treated, why a given set of issues will be explored in close detail and why another set of possible issues ignored. Discourse on a theme begins and ends as if all things are self-evident, including the reason for beginning at one point and ending at some other.

In all, one might readily imagine, upon first glance at this strange and curious book, that what we have is a rulebook. It appears on the surface to be a book lacking all traces of eloquence and style, revealing no evidence of system and reflection, serving no important purpose. First glance indicates in hand is yet another shard from remote antiquity no different from the king lists inscribed on the ancient tablets, the random catalogue of (to us) useless, meaningless facts: a cookbook, a placard of posted tariffs, detritus of random information accidentally thrown up on the currents of historical time. Who would want to have made such a thing? Who would now want to refer to it?

The answer to that question is deceptively straightforward: The Mishnah is important because it is a principal component of the canon of Judaism. Indeed, that answer begs the question: Why should some of the ancient Jews of the Holy Land have brought together these particular facts and rules into a book and set them forth for the Israelite people? Why should the Mishnah have been received, as much later on it certainly was received, as a half of the "whole Torah of Moses at Sinai"? The Mishnah was represented, after it was compiled, as the part of the "whole Torah of Moses, our rabbi," which had been formulated and transmitted orally, so it bore the status of divine revelation right alongside the Pentateuch. That is why we take up the Mishnah as the first document of normative Judaism beyond scripture.

Yet it is already entirely obvious that little in the actual contents of the document evoked the character or the moral authority of the Written Torah of Moses. Indeed, since most of the authorities named in the Mishnah lived in the century and a half prior to the promulgation of the document, the claim that things said by men known to the very framers of the document in fact derived from Moses at Sinai through a long chain of oral tradition contradicted the well-known facts of the matter. So this claim presents a paradox even on the surface: How can the Mishnah be deemed a book of religion, a program for consecration, a mode of sanctification? Why should Jews from the end of the second century to our own day have deemed the study of the Mishnah to be a holy act, a deed of service to God through the study of an important constituent of God's Torah, God's will for Israel, the Jewish people?

In fact, the Mishnah is precisely that, after scripture a principal holy book of Judaism. The Mishnah has been and still is memorized in the circle of all those who participate in the religion, Judaism. Of still greater weight, the two great documents formed around the Mishnah and shaped as to serve as commentaries to the Mishnah, namely, the Talmuds of the Land of Israel (ca. 400 C.E.) and of Babylonia (ca. 600 C.E.), form the center of the curriculum of Judaism as a living religion. Consequently, the Mishnah is essential to the understanding of Judaism.

DESCRIBING THE MISHNAH: ITS CONTENTS AND CONTEXT

Let me now briefly describe the Mishnah. It is a six-part code of descriptive rules formed toward the end of the second century C.E. by a small number of Jewish sages and put forth as the constitution of Judaism under the sponsorship of Judah the Patriarch, the head of the Jewish community of the Land of Israel at the end of that century. The six divisions are: (1) agricultural rules; (2) laws governing appointed seasons, e.g., Sabbaths and festivals; (3) laws on the transfer of women and property along with women from one man (father) to another (husband); (4) the system of civil and criminal law (corresponding to what we today should regard as the "legal system"); (5) laws for the conduct of the Temple sacrificial cult and maintenance of the Temple buildings; and (6) laws on the preservation of cultic purity both in the Temple and under certain domestic circumstances, with special reference to the table and bed. These divisions define the range and realm of reality.

The world addressed by the Mishnah is hardly congruent to the worldview presented within the Mishnah. That fact becomes clear when we consider the time and context in which the document took shape. The Mishnah is made up of sayings bearing the names of authorities who lived, as I just said, in the later first and second centuries. These authorities generally fall into two groups, namely, three distinct sets of names, each set of names randomly appearing together, but rarely, if ever, with names of the other set. The former set of names is generally supposed to represent authorities who lived before the destruction of the Temple—for example, the famous authority Hillel, his opposite number Shammai, and their Houses; then comes the names of authorities who flourished between the destruction of the Temple in 70 and the advent of the second war against Rome, led by Simeon Bar Kokhba, in 132. The third set of names belongs to authorities who flourished between the end of that war,

ca. 135, and the end of the second century. The Mishnah itself is generally supposed to have come to closure at the end of the second century, and its date,
for conventional purposes only, is ca. C.E. 200. Now, of these groups of sages
from before 70 to about 70, from 70 to 130, and from 135 to 200, the last is
represented far more abundantly than the former sets. Approximately two-
thirds of the named sayings belong to mid-second century authorities. This is
not surprising, since these are the named authorities whose (mainly unnamed)
students collected, organized, and laid out the document as we now have it.
So, in all, the Mishnah represents the thinking of Jewish sages who flourished
in the middle of the second century. It is that group which took over whatever traditions they had in hand from the preceding century and from the
whole legacy of Israelite literature even before that time and revised and reshaped the whole into the Mishnah.

Let us briefly consider their world: the age beyond the loss of the Second
Revolt against Rome. To understand that world, we have to remember the context in which the war was fought and lost. Scripture told the story of exile and
return, and from the rebuilding of the Temple in the fifth century B.C.E.,
through the passage of five hundred years, people took for granted that the sequence of events, sin, punishment, repentance, reconciliation, represented by
the loss of Jerusalem and the Temple, the exile of the community of Israel to
foreign soil, and the return to Zion, made up a one-time lesson yielding all-
time security. But now the events of 586 to ca. 450 B.C.E. had happened once
more: History had yielded a pattern. One-time events no longer, the paradigm
of exile and return had taken their place. In that context, the issue of the
Torah—Genesis through Deuteronomy—renewed itself: Here is the covenant
that, when kept, promises permanent possession of Paradise, and that, when violated, brings about its loss. The pattern of history in mind, the framers of the
Mishnah set forth the counterpart of scripture: the pattern of restoration of Paradise. When the Mishnah's laws are fully realized, Israel will find itself restored
to Eden—now for the second and last time. The Mishnah then represents a
document of restoration, of return to Eden, a prescription for the formation of
a perfect Israelite society, all in balance, proportion, justice, purity, above all,
proper relationship, in the Land, with God.

At the outset I said the Mishnah sets forth no narrative. But the Mishnah is
best understood within the setting of that foundation story with which we began: a document responding to the memory and hope of Paradise. It is a law
code that holds together and makes sense in its catastrophic context only against
the background of the narrative patterns that place into juxtaposition and comparison Adam and Israel. As soon as the dimension of restoration defines the focus, the document makes sense, its narrative having been located within its laws,
at the foundations of its construction and structure.

The pattern of exile certainly is recapitulated—and responded to. In the aftermath of the war against Rome in 132–135, the Temple was declared perma-
nently prohibited to Jews, and Jerusalem was closed off to them as well. So there
was no cult, no Temple, no holy city, to which, at this time, the description of
the Mishnaic laws applied. We observe at the very outset, therefore, that a sizable proportion of the Mishnah deals with matters to which the sages had no

material access or practical knowledge at the time of their work. For we have seen that the Mishnah contains a division on the conduct of the cult, namely, the fifth, as well as one on the conduct of matters so as to preserve the cultic purity of the sacrificial system along the lines laid out in the book of Leviticus, the sixth division. In fact, a fair part of the second division, on appointed times, takes up the conduct of the cult on special days, such as the sacrifices offered on the Day of Atonement, Passover, and the like. Indeed, what the Mishnah wants to know about appointed seasons concerns the cult far more than it does the synagogue.

The fourth division, on civil law, for its part, presents an elaborate account of a political structure and system of Israelite self-government in tractates Sanhedrin and Makkot, not to mention Shebuot and Horayot. This system speaks of king, priest, Temple, and court. But it was not the Jews, their kings, priests, and judges, but the Romans who conducted the government of Israel in the Land of Israel in the time in which the second-century authorities did their work. So it would appear that well over half of the document before us speaks of cult, Temple, government, priesthood, for the Mishnah takes up a profoundly priestly and Levitical conception of sanctification. When we consider that in the very time in which the authorities before us did their work, the Temple lay in ruins, the city of Jerusalem was prohibited to all Israelites, and the Jewish government and administration that had centered on the Temple and based its authority on the holy life lived there were in ruins, the fantastic character of the Mishnah's address to its own catastrophic day becomes clear. Much of the Mishnah speaks of matters not even existing in the time in which the Mishnah was created, because the Mishnah wishes to make its statement on what really matters: the rules of the restoration.

In the age beyond catastrophe, the problem is to reorder a world off course and adrift, to gain reorientation for an age in which the sun has come out after the night and the fog. The Mishnah is a document of imagination and fantasy, describing how things "are" out of the shards and remnants of reality, but, in larger measure, building social being out of beams of hope. The Mishnah tells us something about how things were, but everything about how a small group of men wanted things to be. The document is orderly, repetitious, careful in both language and message. It is small minded, picayune, obvious, dull, routine—everything its age was not. The Mishnah stands in contrast with the world to which it speaks. Its message is one of small achievements and modest hope. It means to defy a world of large disorders and immodest demands. The heirs of heroes build an unheroic folk in the new and ordinary age. The Mishnah's message is that what a person wants matters in important ways. It states that message to an Israelite world that can shape affairs in no important ways and speaks to people who by no means will the way things now are. The Mishnah therefore lays down a practical judgment upon, and in favor of, the imagination and will to reshape reality, regain a system, reestablish that order upon which trustworthy existence is to be built.

Now the Judaism shaped by the Mishnah consists of a coherent worldview and comprehensive way of living. It is a worldview that speaks of transcendent things, a way of life in response to the supernatural meaning of what is done, a heightened and deepened perception of the sanctification of Israel in deed and in deliberation. Sanctification means two things: first, distinguishing Israel in all its dimensions from the world in all its ways; second, establishing the stability, order, regularity, predictability, and reliability of Israel at moments and in contexts of danger. Danger means instability, disorder, irregularity, uncertainty, and betrayal. Each topic of the system as a whole takes up a critical and indispensable moment or context of social being. Each orders what is disorderly and dangerous. Through what is said in regard to each of the Mishnah's principal topics, what the system as a whole wishes to declare is fully expressed. Yet if the parts severally and jointly give the message of the whole, the whole cannot exist without all of the parts, so well joined and carefully crafted are they all.

THE MISHNAH'S JUDAISM

Let me now describe and briefly interpret the six components of the Mishnah's system. The critical issue in the economic life, which means farming, is in two parts, revealed in the first division. First, Israel, as tenant on God's holy Land, maintains the property in the ways God requires, keeping the rules that mark the Land and its crops as holy. Next, the hour at which the sanctification of the Land comes to form a critical mass, namely, in the ripened crops, is the moment ponderous with danger and heightened holiness. Israel's will so affects the crops as to mark a part of them as holy, the rest of them as available for common use. The human will is determinative in the process of sanctification.

Second, in the second division, what happens in the Land at certain times, at Appointed Times, marks off spaces of the Land as holy in yet another way. The center of the Land and the focus of its sanctification is the Temple. There the produce of the Land is received and given back to God, the one who created and sanctified the Land. At these unusual moments of sanctification, the inhabitants of the Land in their social being in villages enter a state of spatial sanctification. That is to say, the village boundaries mark off holy space, within which one must remain during the holy time. This is expressed in two ways. First, the Temple itself observes and expresses the special, recurring holy time. Second, the villages of the Land are brought into alignment with the Temple, forming a complement and completion to the Temple's sacred being. The advent of the Appointed Times precipitates a spatial reordering of the Land, so that the boundaries of the sacred are matched and mirrored in village and in Temple. At the heightened holiness marked by these moments of Appointed Times, therefore, the occasion for an affective sanctification is worked out. Like the harvest, the advent of an Appointed Time, a pilgrim festival, also a sacred season, is made to express that regular, orderly, and predictable sort of sanctification for Israel which the system as a whole seeks.

If for a moment we now leap over the next two divisions, the third and fourth, we come to the counterpart of the divisions of agriculture and appointed times. These are the fifth and sixth divisions, namely, Holy Things and

Purities, those which deal with the everyday and the ordinary, as against the special moments of harvest, on the one side, and special time or season, on the other.

The fifth division is about the Temple on ordinary days. The Temple, the locus of sanctification, is conducted in a wholly routine and trustworthy, punctilious manner. The one thing that may unsettle matters is the intention and will of the human actor. This is subjected to carefully prescribed limitations and remedies. The division of Holy Things generates its companion, the sixth division, the one on cultic cleanness, Purities. The relationship between the two is like that between Agriculture and Appointed Times, the former locative, the latter utopian, the former dealing with the fields, the latter with the interplay between fields and altar.

Here, too, in the sixth division, once we speak of the one place of the Temple, we also address the cleanness that pertains to every place. A system of cleanness, taking into account what imparts uncleanness and how this is done, what is subject to uncleanness, and how that state is overcome, is fully expressed, once more, in response to the participation of the human will. Without the wish and act of a human being, the system does not function. It is inert. Sources of uncleanness, which come naturally and not by volition, and modes of purification, which work naturally and not by human intervention, remain inert until human will has imparted susceptibility to uncleanness—that is, introduced into the system that food and drink, bed, pot, chair, and pan that to begin with form the focus of the system. The movement from sanctification to uncleanness takes place when human will and work precipitate it.

Let us now return to the middle divisions, the third and fourth, on Women and Damages. They take their place in the structure of the whole by showing the congruence, within the larger framework of regularity and order, of human concerns of family and farm, politics and workaday transactions among ordinary people. For without attending to these matters, the Mishnah's system does not encompass what, at its foundations, it is meant to comprehend and order. So what is at issue is fully cogent with the rest.

In the case of Women, the third division, attention focuses upon the point of disorder marked by the transfer of that disordering anomaly, woman, from the regular status provided by one man, to the equally trustworthy status provided by another. That is the point at which the Mishnah's interests are aroused: once more, predictably, the moment of disorder.

In the case of Damages, the fourth division, there are two important concerns. First, there is the paramount interest in preventing, so far as possible, the disorderly rise of one person and fall of another, and in sustaining the status quo of the economy, the house and household, of Israel, the holy society in eternal stasis. Second, there is the necessary concomitant in the provision of a system of political institutions to carry out the laws that preserve the balance and steady state of persons.

The two divisions that take up topics of concrete and material concern— the formation and dissolution of families and the transfer of property in that connection, the transactions, both through torts and through commerce, which lead to exchanges of property and the potential dislocation of the state of families in society—are both locative and utopian. They deal with the concrete locations in which people make their lives, household and street and field, the sexual and commercial exchanges of a given village. But they pertain to the life of all Israel, both in the Land and otherwise. These two divisions, together with the household ones of Appointed Times, constitute the sole opening outward toward the life of utopian Israel, that Diaspora in the far reaches of the ancient world, in the endless span of time. From the Mishnah's perspective, this community is not only in exile but unaccounted for, outside the system, for the Mishnah declines to recognize and take it into account. Israelites who dwell in the land of (unclean) death instead of in the Holy Land simply fall outside of the range of (holy) life. Priests, who must remain cultically clean, may not leave the Land and neither may most of the Mishnah.

RESTORATION TO PARADISE: A STEADY-STATE WORLD OF PERMANENCE AND ORDER

What signals the restoration of Adam to Eden via Israel to the Land? Perfection, signified by a world at rest and in repose.

What the Mishnah really wants, therefore, is for nothing to happen. The Mishnah presents a tableau, a wax museum, a diorama. It portrays a world fully perfected and so fully at rest. The one thing the Mishnah does not want to tell us is about change, how things come to be what they are. That is why there can be no sustained attention to the priesthood and its rules, the scribal profession and its constitution, the class of householders and its interests. The Mishnah's pretense is that all of these have come to rest. They compose a world in stasis, perfect and complete, made holy because it is complete and perfect. It is an economy—again in the classic sense of the word—awaiting the divine act of sanctification that, as at the creation of the world, would set the seal of holy rest upon an again-complete creation, just as in the beginning. There is no place for the actors when what is besought is no action whatsoever but only perfection, which is unchanging. There is room only for a description of how things are: the present tense, the sequence of completed statements and static problems. All the action lies within, in how these statements are made.

Essentially, the Mishnah's authorship aimed at the fair adjudication of conflict, worked out in such a way that no party gained, none lost, in any transaction. The task of Israelite society, as they saw it, is to maintain perfect stasis, to preserve the prevailing situation, to secure the stability of not only relationships but status and standing. To this end, in the interchanges of buying and selling, giving and taking, borrowing and lending, transactions of the market and exchanges with artisans and craftsmen and laborers, it is important to preserve the essential equality, not merely equity, of exchange. Fairness alone does not suffice. *Status quo ante* forms the criterion of the true market, reflecting as it does the exchange of value for value, in perfect balance. That is the way that, in reference to the market, the systemic point of urgency, the steady-state of the polity, therefore also of the economy, is stated. The upshot of their economics is simple. No party in the end may have more than what he had at the outset, and none may emerge as the victim of a sizable shift in fortune and circumstance. All parties' rights to and in the stable and unchanging political economy are preserved. When, therefore, the condition of a person is violated, the law will secure the restoration of the antecedent status.

Critical to the social system of the Mishnah is its principal social entity, the village, imagined as a society that never changes in any important way, comprising households, and the model, from household to village to "all Israel," comprehensively describes whatever of "Israel" the authorship at hand has chosen to describe. We have therefore to identify as systemically indicative the centrality of political economy—"community, self-sufficiency, and justice"—within the system of the Mishnah. It is no surprise, either, that the point of originality of the Mishnah system's political economy is its focus upon the society organized in relationship to the control of the means of production—that is, the farm, for the household is always the agricultural unit.

In the context of a world of pervasive diversity, the Mishnah's authorship set forth a fantastic conception of a simple world of little blocks formed into big ones: households into villages, no empty spaces, but also no vast cities. In the conception of the authorship of the Mishnah, community, or village (*polis*), is made up of households, and the household (*bayit/oikos*) constituted the building block of both society or community and also economy. It follows that the household forms the fundamental, irreducible, and of course, representative unit of the economy, the means of production, the locus and the unit of production. We should not confuse the household with class status—for example, thinking of the householder as identical with the wealthy. The opposite is suggested on every page of the Mishnah, in which householders vie with craftsmen for ownership of the leavings of the loom and the chips left behind by the adz. The household, rather, forms an economic and a social classification, defined by function, specifically economic function. A poor household was still a household, and (in theory; the Mishnah's authorship knows none such in practice) a rich landholding that did not function as a center for a social and economic unit, such as a rural industrial farm, was not a household. The household constituted the center of the productive economic activities we now handle through the market. Within the household all local, as distinct from cultic, economic, therefore social, activities and functions were held together. For the unit of production comprised also the unit of social organization, and, of greater import still, the building block of all larger social, now also political, units with special reference to the village.

In its identification of the householder as the building block of society, to the neglect of the vast panoply of "others," "nonhouseholders," including, after all, that half of the whole of the Israelite society comprising women, the Mishnah's authorship reduced the dimensions of society to only a single component in it: the male landowner engaged in agriculture. But that is the sole option open to a system that, for reasons of its own, wished to identify productivity with agriculture, individuality in God's image with ownership of land, and social standing and status, consequently, with ownership and control of the land that constituted the sole systemically consequential means of production. Now if we were to list all the persons and professions who enjoy no role in the system, or who are treated as ancillary to the system, we have to encompass not only workers—the entire landless working class!—but also craftsmen and artisans, teachers and physicians, clerks and officials, traders and merchants, the whole of the commercial establishment, not to mention women as a caste.

Fair and just to all parties, the authorship of the Mishnah nonetheless speaks in particular for the Israelite landholding, proprietary person. The Mishnah's problems are the problems of the householder, its perspectives are his. Its sense of what is just and fair expresses his sense of the givenness and cosmic rightness of the present condition of society. These are men of substance and of means, however modest, aching for a stable and predictable world in which to tend their crops and herds, feed their families and dependents, keep to the natural rhythms of the seasons and lunar cycles, and, in all, live out their lives within strong and secure boundaries on earth and in heaven. This is why the sense of landed place and its limits, the sharp line drawn between village and world on one side, Israelite and gentile on the second, temple and world on the third, evoke metaphysical correspondences. Householder, which is Israel, in the village, and temple, beyond, form a correspondence. Only when we understand the systemic principle concerning God in relationship to Israel in its Land do we identify the fundamental and generative conception that reaches concrete expression in the here and now of the householder as the centerpiece of society.

So much for the Mishnah. What about its amplification and extension in the Mishnah commentary known as the Talmud?

6

The Mishnah and the Talmuds

A Talmud is a commentary on the Mishnah. When, in the world of classical Judaism, people "study Torah," this ordinarily means the Talmud and its commentaries and law codes. That defines the principal curriculum of the Rabbinical seminaries, or *Yeshivot,* in which people study Torah to know what God wants. Later on we shall find that contemporary systems of classical Judaism focus on Talmud study as a principal medium of piety.

In fact, there are two Talmuds, one produced in the Land of Israel and completed in about 400 C.E., called "the Talmud of the Land of Israel" (a.k.a. the *Yerushalmi* or Jerusalem Talmud); the other produced in Babylonia in the Iranian empire (present-day Iraq) and completed in about 600, called "the Talmud of Babylonia," or, in Hebrew, the *Bavli.*

Each of these extensive documents selected tractates—topical expositions—of the Mishnah for comment. The two Talmuds differ in their choices of tractates that require analysis, and their treatment of the tractates they do choose is quite distinct. The Talmud of the Land of Israel deals with thirty-nine tractates of the Mishnah's sixty-two, and the Talmud of Babylonia, thirty-seven of the same sixty-two. The former takes up the first four divisions of the Mishnah, the latter, the second through the fifth division of the Mishnah. Neither one works on the sixth division, Purities.

To sample the kind of religious writing we find in the Talmud's reading of the Mishnah, we consider the single most important statement of the Mishnah. It is the rule that defines who is, and who is not, a Jew—that is, "Israel, the holy people." It does so by explaining who belongs and who does not: "All Israel" will not die but will rise from the dead at the end of days; then those who do not "have a portion in the world to come" will not be part of Israel in the resurrection. Excluded are those who deny the resurrection of the dead, or deny that the Torah teaches that the dead will live that the Torah was given by God ("does not come from Heaven"), or a person who denies the principles of the faith ("an Epicurean").

Mishnah Tractate Sanhedrin 11:1–2

All Israelites have a share in the world to come,

as it is said, "your people also shall be all righteous, they shall inherit the land forever; the branch of my planting, the work of my hands, that I may be glorified" (Is. 60:21).

And these are the ones who have no portion in the world to come:

He who says, "The resurrection of the dead is a teaching which does not derive from the Torah," and "the Torah does not come from Heaven"; and an Epicurean.

The Babylonian Talmud to this passage begins with two questions in mind. First, is the rule of the Mishnah fair? Second, how, on the basis of the Written Torah, do we know the fact taken for granted by the Oral Torah—namely, that the resurrection of the dead will take place and that the Torah itself says so. First comes the justification of God's way:

Babylonian Talmud Tractate Sanhedrin
Folio Pages 90A–B

[With reference to the Mishnah's statement, And these are the ones who have no portion in the world to come:] Why all this [that is, why deny the world to come to those listed]?

On Tannaite authority [it was stated], "Such a one denied the resurrection of the dead, therefore he will not have a portion in the resurrection of the dead.

"For all the measures [meted out by] the Holy One, blessed be he, are in accord with the principle of measure for measure."

What someone denies shall be denied to that person; hence it is only fair that someone who does not believe in the resurrection will not live when the dead are raised up.

But where in scripture do we find that fact? The Talmud proceeds to many pages of proofs, among which the following provide a taste of the discussion:

It has been taught on Tannaite authority:

R. Simai says, "How on the basis of the Torah do we know about the resurrection of the dead?

"As it is said, 'And I also have established my covenant with [the patriarchs] to give them the land of Canaan' (Ex. 6:4)."

" 'With you' is not stated, but rather, 'with them,' indicating on the basis of the Torah that there is the resurrection of the dead."

"*Minim* [believers, sectarians, sometimes identified as Jews who believed in Jesus as the Messiah, hence, Christian Jews] asked Rabban Gamaliel, 'How do we know that the Holy One, blessed be he, will resurrect the dead?"

He said to them, "It is proved from the Torah, from the Prophets, and from the Writings." But they did not accept his proofs.

He said to them, "From the Torah: for it is written, 'And the Lord said to Moses, Behold, you shall sleep with your fathers and rise up' (Deut. 31:16)."

They said to him, "But perhaps the sense of the passage is, 'And the people will rise up' (Deut. 31:16)?"

He said to them, "From the Prophets: as it is written, 'Thy dead men shall live, together with my dead body they shall arise. Awake and sing, you that live in the dust, for your dew is as the dew of herbs, and the earth shall cast out its dead' (Is. 26:19)."

They said to him, "But perhaps that refers to the dead whom Ezekiel raised up."

He said to them, "From the Writings, as it is written, 'And the roof of your mouth, like the best wine of my beloved, that goes down sweetly, causing the lips of those who are asleep to speak' (Song 7:9)."...

[The *minim*—in this case, heretic Jews who did not believe in the resurrection of the dead—would not concur in Gamaliel's view] until he cited for them the following verse: " 'Which the Lord swore to your fathers to give to them' (Deut. 11:21)—to *them* and not to you, so proving from the Torah that the dead will live."

We see how the Talmud of Babylonia has faithfully expounded the Mishnah's teaching, so forming an expansion and explanation of the oral Torah's claim. When, in Chapter 1, I argued that "Judaism is the religion of the Old Testament," I did not exaggerate the centrality of the claim of normative Judaism to state no more, and no less, than is set forth in the Written Torah. The constant recourse to what people call "proof texts"—verses of scripture deemed to sustain a proposition distinct from those verses but relevant to them—shows how, in virtually every line, where the Rabbinic sages could demonstrate that theirs is the right reading of scripture, they took the opportunity to do so. The details just now reviewed lead us to the main point: situating the oral tradition set forth in the Mishnah and related Rabbinic documents into the encompassing Torah of Sinai.

THE TALMUD AND THE MISHNAH
AS PART OF THE ORAL TORAH

The most important statement concerning the Mishnah made by the two Talmuds is not set forth in so many words but is contained in every line of the two writings. It is that the Mishnah is part of the Torah, and in commenting on the Mishnah the authors of the two Talmuds were explaining the meaning of the Torah. As we just saw, this was expressed in a simple way. The framers of the two Talmuds tried to show how most of the rules of the Mishnah derive from statements in the scripture. So wherever possible, the Mishnah was shown to depend upon the Written Torah.

Not only so, but in the first important piece of writing after the Mishnah was closed, tractate Abot, the Fathers or the Founders, a collection of sayings attributed to sages of the Mishnah, the tradition of the Mishnah is shown to form part of the chain of tradition that began at Sinai. That is because the Rabbinic sages stand in a relationship of disciples of the prior generation and masters of the coming generation backward to Sinai and forward to the generation of masters following the closure of the Mishnah itself in ca. 250 C.E. So not only proof texts of scripture but a more generalized claim of tradition embodied in the Rabbinic sages and their teaching validated the standing of the Mishnah as Torah: revelation by God to Moses at Sinai.

This proposition is contained in a rather subtle exposition. It takes the form of a story, which is not surprising considering that Judaism is here represented as the story Israel tells about itself, its worldview, its way of life. Hence the propositions of a normative character, whether of conduct or conviction, will be conveyed in narrative. In the story that follows, first of all, it is alleged that when God gave the Torah at Sinai to Moses, he handed on a tradition that was to be memorized and repeated, master to disciple, for all time. This other medium by which the Torah was revealed was oral, hence the Oral Torah, referred to the part of the Torah formulated and handed on in memory:

Mishnah Tractate Abot 1:1–2

Moses received Torah at Sinai and handed it on to Joshua, Joshua to elders, and elders to prophets.

And prophets handed it on to the men of the great assembly. They said three things: "Be prudent in judgment. Raise up many disciples. Make a fence for the Torah."

Simeon the Righteous was one of the last survivors of the great assembly. He would say: "On three things does the world stand: On the Torah, and on the Temple service, and on deeds of loving kindness."

What is striking in this statement is three allegations. First, we find the claim that there is a tradition from God's revelation to Moses at Sinai that continues beyond the figures we know in the Written Torah, specifically, Joshua and the prophets. The men of the great assembly and Simeon the Righteous stand in the chain of tradition from Sinai. But they are not figures out of scripture. It follows that there is that other Torah, one not in writing, the orally formulated and orally transmitted part of the Torah.

The second claim is that this other Torah comes down through the relationship of master to disciple, who becomes a master later on.

The third striking fact is that what is stated is not a citation of scripture but a saying that stands on its own. Simeon's saying is part of that Torah from Sinai, for example, but it does not refer to or quote scripture.

By citing these figures within the chain of tradition from Sinai, the framer of the passage was able to show that the Mishnah contains part of the Torah of Sinai, the oral part.

Certainly the single most important figure in the chain of tradition from

Sinai onward to the sages who created the Mishnah itself is Hillel, a sage who flourished at about the same time as Jesus, and to whom is attributed a statement strikingly like the Golden Rule: "What is hateful to yourself, do not do to anybody else. That is the whole of the Torah. All the rest is commentary. Now go learn." Both the teaching of Hillel and that of Jesus in the Golden Rule—"Do unto others as you would have them do unto you"—state in other language the commandment of the Torah at Leviticus 19:18: "You shall love your neighbor as yourself," and many great sages of Judaism have maintained that that statement summarizes the whole of Judaism. A further statement in Hillel's name forms the foundation of the morality of Judaism:

> "If I am not for myself, who is for me? And when I am for myself, what am I? And if not now, when?"

The collection of sayings gathered in the Sayings of the Founders appears now as part of the most important holy book of Judaism after the Written Torah, and that is the Mishnah.

TORAH IN TWO MEDIA, WRITTEN AND ORAL

The conception of another form of the Torah, an oral, memorized form, is expressed by the Talmud of the Land of Israel in the following passage, in which we find the theory that there is a tradition separate from, and in addition to, the Written Torah. This tradition it knows as "the teachings of scribes." The Mishnah is not identified as the collection of those teachings.

Talmud of the Land of Israel Tractate Abodah Zarah 2:7–III.

Associates in the name of R. Yohanan: "The words of scribes are more beloved than the words of Torah and more cherished than words of Torah: 'Your palate is like the best wine' (Song 7:9)."

Simeon bar Ba in the name of R. Yohanan: "The words of scribes are more beloved than the words of Torah and more cherished than words of Torah: 'For your love is better than wine' (Song 1:2)."...

R. Ishmael repeated the following: "The words of Torah are subject to prohibition, and they are subject to remission; they are subject to lenient rulings, and they are subject to strict rulings. But words of scribes all are subject only to strict interpretation, for we have learned there: He who rules, 'There is no requirement to wear phylacteries,' in order to transgress the teachings of the Torah, is exempt. But if he said, 'There are five partitions in the phylactery, instead of four,' in order to add to what the scribes have taught, he is liable' (M. San.11:3)."

R. Haninah in the name of R. Idi in the name of R. Tanhum b. R. Hiyya: "More stringent are the words of the elders than the words of the prophets. For it is written, 'Do not preach'—thus they preach—one should not preach of such things' (Micah 2:6). And it is written, '[If a man should go about and utter wind and lies, saying,] "I will preach to you of wine and strong drink," he would be the preacher for this people!' (Micah 2:11).

"A prophet and an elder—to what are they comparable? To a king who sent two senators of his to a certain province. Concerning one of them he wrote, 'If he does not show you my seal and signet, do not believe him.' But concerning the other one he wrote, 'Even though he does not show you my seal and signet, believe him.' So in the case of the prophet, he has had to write, 'If a prophet arises among you...and gives you a sign or a wonder...' (Deut. 13:1). But here [with regard to an elder:] '...according to the instructions which they give you...' (Deut. 17:11) [without a sign or a wonder]."

What is important in the foregoing anthology is the distinction between teachings contained in the Torah and teachings in the name or authority of "scribes." These latter teachings are associated with quite specific details of the law and are indicated in the Mishnah's rule itself. Further, we have "elders" (that is, sages) rather than prophets. What happens to the Mishnah in the two Talmuds shows us how the later sages viewed the Mishnah.

That view may be stated very simply. The Mishnah rarely cites verses of scripture in support of its propositions. The two Talmuds routinely adduce scriptural bases for the Mishnah's laws. The Mishnah seldom undertakes the exegesis of verses of scripture for any purpose. The two Talmuds consistently investigate the meaning of verses of scripture and do so for a variety of purposes. Accordingly, the two Talmuds, subordinate as they are to the Mishnah, regard the Mishnah as subordinate to, and contingent upon, scripture. That is why, in the two Talmuds' view, the Mishnah requires the support of proof texts of scripture.

A broad shift was taking place in the generations that received the Mishnah, that is, over the third and fourth centuries. If the sages of the second century, who made the Mishnah as we know it, spoke in their own name and in the name of the logic of their own minds, those who followed, certainly the ones who flourished in the later fourth century and onward to the sixth and produced the two Talmuds, took a quite different view. Reverting to ancient authority like others of the age, they turned back to scripture, deeming it the source of certainty about truth.

7

The Midrash

WHAT IS MIDRASH?

In Chapter 1, with the systematic reading of the story of Israel in comparison with the story of Adam, we have already worked our way through a complex passage of Rabbinic Midrash: the reading of scripture by the Rabbinic sages of the formative age of normative Judaism. There we saw a process of analysis yielding a proposition, systematically pursued, with results compelling within the premises of the interpreters. Now let us generalize on the case: How, exactly, does Rabbinic Judaism read scripture?

The Rabbinic sages produced a commentary on the Mishnah, viewed as the foundation document of the originally Oral Torah in the form of the two Talmuds. Reading scripture as they read the Mishnah, they also produced commentaries to books privileged by Judaism of the Written Torah, the Pentateuch and those important in synagogue worship, the scrolls of Lamentations, Ruth, Song of Songs, and Esther. These took the form of scriptural explanation called Midrash.

By *Midrash,* the Hebrew word for investigation, people commonly mean one of three things. First comes the sense of Midrash as the *explanation,* by Judaic interpreters, of the meaning of individual verses of scripture. The result of the interpretation of a verse of scripture is called a *Midrash exegesis.* The result of the interpretation of scripture is formed into *collections,* second, in Midrash compilations, or what I call a *Midrash document.* Third, by Midrash people may also speak of the *process* of interpretation, for instance, the principles that guide the interpreter, and this is called *Midrash method.* So Midrash may refer to the result of investigation, or explanation; to the collection of such results, or compilation; and to the method of such inquiry, or process, thus Midrash interpretation, Midrash compilation, Midrash process or method.

Let us now proceed to a simple definition for the word *Midrash,* with close attention to the context, in literature and society, in which the writings of Midrash are produced, and to the techniques of Midrash exegesis. The best definition is provided by Gary G. Porton[1]:

Midrash is "a type of literature, oral or written, which has its starting point in a fixed, canonical text, considered the revealed word of God by

---

[1]Gary G. Porton, "Midrash: The Palestinian Jews and the Hebrew Bible in the Greco-Roman Period," in Hildegard Temporini and Wolfgang Haase, eds., *Aufstieg und Niedergang der römischen Welt* (Berlin & New York: De Gruyter, 1979), Vol. 2, 19.2, p. 104. See also his "Defining Midrash" in Jacob Neusner, ed., *The Study of Ancient Judaism I: Mishnah, Midrash, Siddur* (New York: Ktav, 1981), pp. 55–92, and *Understanding Rabbinic Midrash: Text and Commentary* (New York: Ktav, 1985).

the Midrashist and his audience, and in which this original verse is explicitly cited or clearly alluded to." ... For something to be considered Midrash it must have a clear relationship to the accepted canonical text of Revelation. Midrash is a term given to a Jewish activity which finds its locus in the religious life of the Jewish community. While others exegete their revelatory canons and while Jews exegete other texts, only Jews who explicitly tie their comments to the Bible engage in Midrash.

What is important in Porton's definition are three elements: (1) exegesis, (2) starting with scripture and (3) ending in community.

The Rabbinic sages who produced the Mishnah, Talmuds, and Midrash compilations represent the reading of scripture by Rabbinic Judaism. Other communities of Judaism set forth their approaches as well. In fact, Porton identifies five types of Midrashic activity pursued by one or another of the circles of diverse Judaisms of the formative age. These are the

1. Rabbinic Judaism, important here

2. The Midrash found in the Hebrew scripture itself, such as Deuteronomy's rewriting of Exodus, Numbers, and Leviticus or the reading of Samuel and Kings that is portrayed in the books of Chronicles

3. Translations of scripture into Aramaic (called *Targumim*), which by rendering a Hebrew passage into an Aramaic paraphrase impart a fresh perspective on the original Scripture

4. The rewriting of the biblical narrative through a retelling

5. The *Pesher* Midrash of an apocalyptic order, such as is found in the Dead Sea scrolls. In that community of Judaism that valued the books in the Qumran library, ancient prophecy was interpreted in light of events contemporary with the community itself, so that figures of scripture were identified with important persons in the time of the Midrash interpreters themselves.

Among the five kinds of Rabbinic Midrash he classifies, Porton writes as follows:

Rabbinic Midrash represents an independent phenomenon, for the rabbis are a distinct class within the Jewish community of Late Antiquity. The definitive characteristic of the ancient rabbi was his knowledge and how he attained it. What a rabbi knew distinguished him from the rest of the Jewish community, and the fact that he had gained his information by studying with another rabbi who participated in a chain of tradition which stretched back to God and Moses on Mount Sinai also set him apart in his larger environment. A rabbi's knowledge began with the Written Torah, the five books of Moses, the public record of the prefect revelation from the perfect God, and from there it moved into the Oral Torah, that part of revelation which had been handed down from God to Moses our Rabbi and from Moses our Rabbi, through an unbroken chain, to the rabbis of Late Antiquity. The Oral Torah is the record of

Rabbinic attempts to solve problems encountered in the Written Torah, for among other things it filled in the details, explained unclear matters and expanded upon enigmatic passages found in the Written Torah. The Oral Torah also offered the rules and methods according to which the Written Torah was to be interpreted and upon which an understanding of it should be based. In short, the Oral Torah provided the guidelines that made possible the understanding of and the application of Scripture's lessons in contemporary life. The Oral Torah was the key to unlocking the mysteries of the Written Torah, and the rabbis were the only ones who possessed this key. Rabbinic Midrash is the type of Midrash produced by this small segment of the Jewish population of Palestine and Babylonia during the first seven centuries of the common era.

Rabbinic Midrash is based on several presuppositions. The rabbis believed that the Written Torah was the accurate and complete public record of a direct revelation from the One, Unique, and Perfect God to His people; therefore, nothing in the Bible was unimportant or frivolous. Every letter, every verse, and every phrase contained in the Bible was important and written as it was for a specific reason. The Bible contained no needless expressions, no "mere" repetitions, and no superfluous words or phrases. The assumption that every element of the biblical text was written in a specific way in order to teach something underlies the Midrashic activity of the rabbis. Furthermore, the rabbis believed that everything contained in Scriptures was interrelated. Often, one verse is explained by reference to another verse. A section of the Prophets may be used to explain a verse from the Torah, or a portion of the Torah may explain a passage from the Writings.

These form some of the principal technical aspects of how sages read a verse of Scripture.

Let us now move to the theological side to matters—the Midrash analysis, compilation, and proposition of Rabbinic Judaism in particular. There are three types of compilations of Rabbinic Midrash: atomistic, constructive-analytical, and propositional-thematic.

Atomistic The first type of compilation focuses on individual verses of scripture and interpreting those verses, in the sequence in which they appear, forms the organizing principle of sustained discourse. The result is atomistic: This means this, that means that, but patterns do emerge out of the readings of individual verses from a particular perspective or with a determinate proposition in mind. This type is represented by *Sifra,* a commentary to Leviticus, *Sifré,* a commentary to Numbers, and another *Sifré,* this one a commentary to Deuteronomy.

Constructive-Analytical The second type of compilation tests and validates large-scale propositions that, through the reading of individual verses, an authorship wishes to test and validate. In that rather philosophical trend in Rabbinic Bible interpretation, the interpretation of individual verses takes a subordinated position, appealing to facts of scripture in the service of the syllogism at hand. Here the proposition is the dominant focus, the individual verses taking a diminished role. Examples are *Leviticus Rabbah,* a commentary to Leviticus, and *Pesiqta deRab Kahana,* a commentary to verses of scripture that comprise the synagogue lections for a given Sabbath, such as the verses important in the reading of the Torah for Passover or the New Year.

Propositional-Thematic   The third approach directs attention not to concrete statements of scripture, whether in sequences of verses or merely individual verses or even words or phrases, but to entire compositions of scripture: biblical themes, stories. This investigation of scripture's meaning generates Midrash as narrative: the imaginative recasting of scripture's stories in such a way as to make new and urgent points through the retelling. An example is *Lamentations Rabbati,* a commentary to the book of Lamentations, Jeremiah's lament for fallen Jerusalem.

Precisely how Rabbinic Midrash mediates scripture's lessons into patterns of meaning for the first centuries of the Common Era remains to be seen. Much of the power of Rabbinic Midrash makes itself felt when we are able to identify the contemporary issue and argument that have provoked reading scripture in one way rather than in another, with one set of emphases rather than another.

ONE EXAMPLE OF MIDRASH:
HOW THE SAGES OF JUDAISM READ
THE BOOK OF GENESIS AS A
PARABLE FOR THEIR OWN TIME

Our case in point is the book of Genesis, which is examined in the Midrash compilation, Genesis Rabbah, a document that took shape in the century beyond Constantine, ca. 400–450. The sages who composed Genesis Rabbah read the scripture account of creation and the beginnings of Israel, in which God set forth to Moses the entire scope and meaning of Israel's history among the nations and salvation at the end of days. Genesis drew their attention more than any other book of the Pentateuch, the five books of Moses. Sages read Genesis not as a set of individual verses, one by one, but as a single and coherent statement, whole and complete.

Sages further read scripture so that things were not what they seemed to be but meant something else altogether. For in general people read the book of Genesis as the story of how Israel saw the past, not the future: the beginning of the world and of Israel, humanity from Adam to Noah, then from Noah to Abraham, and the story first of the three patriarchs and four matriarchs of Israel—Abraham, Isaac, Jacob, Sarah, Rebecca, Leah and Rachel—and finally of Joseph and his brothers, from creation to the descent into Egypt. But to the rabbis who created Genesis Rabbah, the book of Genesis tells the story of Israel, the Jewish people, in the here and now. The principle was that what happened to the patriarchs and matriarchs signals what will happen to their descendants; the model of the ancestors sends a message for the children. So the importance of Genesis, as the sages of Genesis Rabbah read the book, derives not from its lessons about the past but its message for Israel's present—and, especially, its future.

In the way in which the sages of Genesis Rabbah dealt with this crisis, we follow in concrete terms what it means to see things as other than what they seem. Specifically, the sages conceded that Christian Rome required attention in a way in which pagan Rome had not. Furthermore, they appealed to their established theory of who Israel is in order to find a place for Rome. They saw Israel as one big family, children of Abraham, Isaac, Jacob. In order to fit Rome into the system, they had to locate for Rome a place in the family. Scripture—we now recognize—speaks of deeper truths. Hence when scripture told the story of certain members of the family, "we" who understand scripture know that what is meant is a member whom only we recognize. Specifically, Rome now is represented by Esau then: as Jacob's brother, Jacob's enemy. Or Rome may be Ishmael or Moab. "And we? We are Israel." Scripture therefore tells the story of Esau and Jacob, who are, in the world of Late Antiquity, Rome and Israel. Jacob supplants, Jacob wins the blessing and the patrimony and the birthright—and Jacob will again. Things are not what they seem, scripture speaks of other things than those on the surface, and Midrash exegesis, working out this mode of Midrash process collected in Midrash documents, tells that story.

That is an example of reading one thing in light of something else, and everything as though it meant something other than what it said. Identifying Rome as Esau is a fresh idea. In the Mishnah, two hundred years earlier, Rome appears as a place, not as a symbol. But in Genesis Rabbah Rome is symbolized by Esau. Why Esau in particular? Because Esau is sibling: relation, competitor, enemy, brother. In choosing Rome as the counterpart to Israel, sages simply opened Genesis and found there Israel, that is Jacob, and his brother, his enemy, who is Esau. Why not understand the obvious: Esau stands for Rome, Jacob for Israel, and their relationship represents, then, what Israel and Rome would work out even now, in the fourth century, the first century of Christian rule. Esau rules now, but Jacob possesses the birthright. Esau/Rome is the last of the four great empires (Persia, Media, Greece, Rome). On the other side of Rome? Israel's age of glory. And why is Rome now brother? Because, after all, the Christians do claim a common patrimony in the Hebrew scripture and do claim to form part of Israel. That claim was not ignored, it was answered: yes, part of Israel, the rejected part. Jacob bears the blessing and transmits the blessing to humanity, Esau does not.

That concession—Rome is a sibling, a close relative of Israel—represents an implicit recognition of Christianity's claim to share the patrimony of Judaism, to be descended from Abraham and Isaac. So how are we to deal with the glory and the power of our brother, Esau? And what are we to say about the claim of

Esau to enthrone Christ? And how are we to assess today the future history of Israel, the salvation of God's first, best love? It is not by denying Rome's claim but by evaluating it, not by turning our backs to the critical events of the hour but by confronting those events forcefully and authoritatively. In this instance we see how Rabbinic Midrash resorted to an allegorical or parabolic reading of scripture in order to bring to scripture the issues of the age and to discover God's judgment of those issues.

We now turn to a detailed examination of how sages spelled out what scripture really means. To sages, Genesis reported what really happened. But, as we see throughout, Genesis also spelled out the meanings and truth of what happened. In the following passage we have Esau in place of Rome. To highlight the relationship between the base verse of Genesis and the comments of the sages on the base verse, I put biblical verses in italics.

Genesis Rabbah LXI:VII

2.   "*[But to the sons of his concubines, Abraham gave gifts, and while he was still living,] he sent them away from his son Isaac, eastward to the east country]*' (Gen. 25:6):

He said to them, "Go as far to the east as you can, so as not to be burned by the flaming coal of Isaac."

But because Esau came to make war with Jacob, he took his appropriate share on his account: "*Is this your joyous city, whose feet in antiquity, in ancient days, carried her afar off to sojourn? Who has devised this against Tyre, the crowning city?*" (Is. 23:7)

Said R. Eleazar, "Whenever the name of Tyre is written in Scripture, if it is written out [with all of the letters], then it refers to the province of Tyre. Where it is written without all of its letters [and so appears identical to the word for enemy], the reference of Scripture is to Rome. [So the sense of the verse is that Rome will receive its appropriate reward.]"

This passage carries forward the eschatological reading of the incident. Israel's later history is prefigured in the gift to Isaac and the rejection of the other sons. The self-evidence that Esau's reward will recompense his evil indicates that the passage draws upon sarcasm to make its point. Sages essentially looked in the facts of history for the laws of history. We may compare them to social scientists or social philosophers, trying to turn anecdotes into insight and to demonstrate how we may know the difference between impressions and truths. Genesis provided facts. Careful sifting of those facts will yield the laws that dictated why things happened one way, rather than some other. The language, as much as the substance, of the narrative provided facts demanding careful study. We understand why sages thought so if we call to mind their basic understanding of the Torah. To them (as to many today, myself included), the Torah came from God and in every detail contained revelation of God's truth. Accordingly, just as we study nature and derive facts demanding explanation and yielding law, so we study scripture and find facts susceptible of explanation and yielding truth.

Let us consider an exemplary case of how sages discovered social laws of history in the facts of scripture. What Abraham did corresponds to what Balaam did, and the same law of social history derives proof from each of the two contrasting figures.

Genesis Rabbah LV:VIII

1. *"And Abraham rose early in the morning, [saddled his ass, and took two of his young men with him, and his son Isaac, and he cut the wood for the burnt offering and arose and went to the place which God had told him]"* (Gen. 22:3):

Said R. Simeon b. Yohai, "Love disrupts the natural order of things, and hatred disrupts the natural order of things.

"Love disrupts the natural order of things we learn from the case of Abraham: '... *he saddled his ass.*' But did he not have any number of servants? But that proves love disrupts the natural order of things.

"Hatred disrupts the natural order of things we learn from the case of Balaam:" *'And Balaam rose up early in the morning and saddled his ass'* (Num. 22:21). But did he not have any number of servants? But that proves hatred disrupts the natural order of things.

"Love disrupts the natural order of things we learn from the case of Joseph: *'And Joseph made his chariot ready'* (Gen. 46:29). But did he not have any number of servants? But that proves love disrupts the natural order of things.

'Hatred disrupts the natural order of things we learn from the case of Pharaoh: *'And he made his chariot ready'* (Ex. 14:6). But did he not have any number of servants? But that proves hatred disrupts the natural order of things."

The social law about the overriding effect of love or hatred is proven by diverse cases, as we see. Now we move from the laws of social history to the rules that govern Israel's history in particular.

2. Said R. Simeon b. Yohai, "Let one act of saddling an ass come and counteract another act of saddling the ass. May the act of saddling the ass done by our father Abraham, so as to go and carry out the will of him who speak and brought the world into being, counteract the act of saddling that was carried out by Balaam when he went to curse Israel.

"Let one act of preparing counteract another act of preparing. Let Joseph's act of preparing his chariot so as to meet his father serve to counteract Pharaoh's act of preparing to go and pursue Israel."

R. Ishmael taught on Tannaite authority, "Let the sword held in the hand serve to counteract the sword held in the hand.

"Let the sword held in the hand of Abraham, as it is said, *'Then Abraham put forth his hand and took the knife to slay his son'* (Gen. 22:10) serve to counteract the sword taken by Pharaoh in hand: *'I will draw my sword, my hand shall destroy them'* (Ex. 15:9)."

We see that the narrative is carefully culled for probative facts, yielding laws. One fact is that there are laws of history. The other is that laws may be set aside, by either love or hatred. Yet another law of history applies in particular to Israel, as distinct from the foregoing, deriving from the life of both Israel and the nations, Abraham and Balaam.

Here is an exercise in the recurrent proof of a single proposition that Abraham foresaw the future history of Israel, with special reference to the rule of the four monarchies, Babylonia, Media, Greece, then Rome—prior to the rule of Israel:

Genesis Rabbah XLIV:XVII

4. "*[And it came to pass, as the sun was going down,] lo, a deep sleep fell on Abram, and lo, a dread and great darkness fell upon him*" (Gen. 15:12):

" ... *lo, a dread*" refers to Babylonia, as it is written, "*Then was Nebuchadnezzar filled with fury*" (Gen. 3:19).

"*and darkness*" refers to Media, which darkened the eyes of Israel by making it necessary for the Israelites to fast and conduct public mourning.

" ... *great* ..." refers to Greece... .

" ... *fell upon him*" refers to Edom [Rome], as it is written, "*The earth quakes at the noise of their fall*" (Jer. 49:21).

I find this a particularly moving tableau, with darkness descending and dread falling on Jacob. That accounts, also, for the power of the ideas at hand. For this passage successfully links the cited biblical passage once more to the history of Israel. Israel's history falls under God's dominion. Whatever will happen carries out God's plan. The fourth kingdom is part of that plan, which we can discover by carefully studying Abraham's life and God's word to him. In the following selection, we see an explicit effort to calculate the time at which the end will come and Israel will be saved:

Genesis Rabbah XLIV:XVIII

1. "*Then the Lord said to Abram, 'Know of a surety [that your descendants will be sojourners in a land that is not theirs, and they will be slaves there, and they will be oppressed for four hundred years; but I will bring judgment on the nation which they serve, and afterward they shall come out with great possessions']*" (Gen. 15:13–14):

"*Know*" that I shall scatter them.

"*Of a certainty*" that I shall bring them back together again.

"*Know*" that I shall put them out as a pledge [in expiation of their sins].

"*Of a certainty*" that I shall redeem them.

"*Know*" that I shall make them slaves.

"*Of a certainty*" that I shall free them.

2. "*... that your descendants will be sojourners in a land that is not theirs and they will be slaves there, and they will be oppressed for four hundred years:*"

It is four hundred years from the point at which you will produce a descendant. [The Israelites will not serve as slaves for four hundred years, but that figure refers to the passage of time from Isaac's birth.]

Said R. Yudan, "The condition of being outsiders, the servitude, the oppression in a land that was not theirs all together would last for four hundred years, that was the requisite term."

Passage 1 parses the cited verse and joins within its simple formula the entire history of Israel, punishment and forgiveness alike. Passage 2 parses the verse to follow, trying to bring it in line with the chronology of Israel's later history.

The single most important paradigm for history emerged from the deed at Moriah, the binding of Isaac on the altar as a sacrifice to God. We shall see, in Chapter 14, how this act also forms a critical motif in synagogue art, for the philosopher-artists of synagogue decoration created their own Midrash as well. Here is how sages derive enduring rules of history and salvation from the story of the willingness of Abraham to sacrifice even his son to God:

Genesis Rabbah LVI:I

1. *"On the third day Abraham lifted up his eyes and saw the place afar off"* (Gen. 22:4):

"After two days he will revive us, on the third day he will raise us up, that we may live in his presence" (Hos.16:2).

On the third day of the tribes: *"And Joseph said to them on the third day, 'This do and live'"* (Gen. 42:18).

On the third day of the giving of the Torah: *"And it came to pass on the third day when it was morning" (Ex. 19:16).*

On the third day of the spies: "And hide yourselves there for three days" (Josh 2:16).

On the third day of Jonah: *"And Jonah was in the belly of the fish three days and three nights"* (Jonah 2:1).

On the third day of the return from the Exile: *"And we abode there three days"* (Ezra 8:32).

On the third day of the resurrection of the dead: *"After two days he will revive us, on the third day he will raise us up, that we may live in his presence"* (Hos. 16:2).

On the third day of Esther: *"Now it came to pass on the third day that Esther put on her royal apparel"* (Est. 5:1).

She put on the monarchy of the house of her fathers.

On account of what sort of merit?

Rabbis say, "On account of the third day of the giving of the Torah."

R. Levi said, "It is on account of the merit of the third day of Abraham: 'On the third day Abraham lifted up his eyes and saw the place afar off' (Gen. 22:4)."

The third day marks the fulfillment of the promise, at the end of time of the resurrection of the dead, and, at appropriate moments, of Israel's redemption. The reference to the third day at Gen. 22:2 then invokes the entire panoply of Israel's history. The relevance of the composition emerges at the end. Prior to the concluding segment, the passage forms a kind of litany and falls into the category of a liturgy. Still, the recurrent hermeneutic that teaches that the stories of the patriarchs prefigure the history of Israel certainly makes its appearance. Our final example makes the point still more explicitly, and here we close:

Genesis Rabbah LVI:II

4. "*... and we will worship [through an act of prostration] and come again to you*" (Gen. 22:5):

He thereby told him that he would come back from Mount Moriah whole and in peace [for he said that we shall come back].

5. Said R. Isaac, "And all was on account of the merit attained by the act of prostration.

"Abraham returned in peace from Mount Moriah only on account of the merit owing to the act of prostration: '*... and we will worship [through an act of prostration] and come [then, on that account] again to you*' (Gen. 22:5).

"The Israelites were redeemed only on account of the merit owing to the act of prostration: *And the people believed ... then they bowed their heads and prostrated themselves' (Ex. 4:31).*

"The Torah was given only on account of the merit owing to the act of prostration: '*And worship [prostrate themselves] you afar off*' (Ex. 24:1).

"Hannah was remembered only on account of the merit owing to the act of prostration: '*And they worshipped before the Lord*' (1 Sam. 1:19).

"The exiles will be brought back only on account of the merit owing to the act of prostration: '*And it shall come to pass in that day that a great horn shall be blown and they shall come that were lost ... and that were dispersed ... and they shall worship the Lord in the holy mountain at Jerusalem*' (Is. 27:13).

"The Temple was built only on account of the merit owing to the act of prostration: '*Exalt you the Lord our God and worship at his holy hill*' (Ps. 99:9).

"The dead will live only on account of the merit owing to the act of prostration: '*Come let us worship and bend the knee, let us kneel before the Lord our maker*' (Ps. 95:6)."

Passage 3 draws a lesson from the use of "thus" in the cited verses. The sizable construction at Passage 4 makes a simple point, to which our base verse provides its modest contribution. But its polemic is hardly simple. The entire history of Israel flows from its acts of worship ("prostration") and is unified by a single law. Every sort of advantage Israel has ever gained came about through worship. Hence what is besought, in the elegant survey, is the law of history.

The scripture then supplies those facts from which the governing law is derived. The lesson that Israel commands its own destiny through obedience to God emerges in every line of Genesis as the sages' Midrash interprets the book. In the hands of the sages of Genesis Rabbah, the book of the beginnings tells the tale of the end time. And this mode of reading Genesis typifies how the Rabbinic sages received and valued the Written Torah. Rabbinic Judaism then reads scripture as the Torah, the written part through the prism of the oral part.

PART III

Classical Judaism:
Three Important Doctrines:
Ethics, Ethos, and Ethnos

8

Way of Life: Women

FROM DOCUMENT TO DOCTRINE

The documents we have considered set forth ideas as well as interpretations of scripture, but the ideas do not reach us in a systematic way. If, nonetheless, we are to grasp Judaism, we must examine some of its main ideas or doctrines—the principles of the faith that comprise its worldview. We have, then, to move from the documents to the doctrines of Judaism. What steps do we take to generalize on the basis of episodic statements, to seek to view the whole that the parts comprise? That is an important task in studying any religion, for, in general, religions deliver their most eloquent messages through the details, leaving it up to us to identify the generalization implicit in those details.

Here we take three important questions and ask how they are answered in the Torah, Oral and Written. The first concerns women, the second, the Messiah, and, the third, the conception of Israel. For the present purpose these correspond to the categories that we have already considered in general terms: way of life, concerning women; theory of the social order, concerning Israel; and worldview, concerning the meaning and end of history, embodied in the Messiah theme. In these matters we propose to see how Judaism's system of the social order of its holy Israel actually deals with fundamental issues, what doctrines embody the system in a concrete way.[1] The doctrines before us intersect with the master narrative, woman in Israel corresponding to Eve, Israel corresponding to Adam, and Messiah standing for the restoration of Israel to Eden in the Land. So wherever we go exploring, we find ourselves not far from the foundation narrative.

How to proceed? In examining any topic of Rabbinic Judaism, our starting point is the Mishnah, and we proceed from there to examine how the Mishnah is interpreted and augmented in subsequent documents that continue its tradition. The unfolding of the documents over time conveys, also, the history of the ideas of Rabbinic Judaism that those doctrines convey. So, in this account of doctrines, first comes the Mishnah, then the later documents, in the narrative of how important ideas unfolded. We recall, also, our stress that a system says the same thing about everything, and what the system does is answer an urgent question with a response that, to the faithful, is self-evidently valid. Knowing the urgent question and the self-evidently valid answer of the system, we can predict what the system has to say about any topic it chooses to treat.

---

[1]Rabbinic Judaism possesses many other doctrines, and some of these—the principal theological ones—are expressed in the liturgy that will occupy our attention in the next part of the book.

WOMEN AS THE INDICATOR
OF THE WAY OF LIFE OR ETHOS
OF A RELIGIOUS SYSTEM

This brings us to the first and most interesting question—the way of life of Rabbinic Judaism, as its thinking about women conveys its larger conception of the social order: the classes of society and how they relate, the crises of the social life and how these are to be resolved. The social vision of the Mishnah's Judaism encompasses issues of gender, social structure, wealth and transactions in property, and the organization of the castes of society. In all these matters the system seeks the principles of order and proper classification, identifying as problems the occasions for disorder and improper disposition of persons or resources. The fact that we can find the documents saying one thing about many things tells us that they stand for a well-considered view of the whole, and, when we come to the theological and philosophical program of the same writings, that consistent viewpoint will guide us to what matters and what is to be said about what matters.

The principal focus of a social vision framed by men, such as that of the Mishnah, not only encompasses, but focuses upon, woman, who is perceived as abnormal in a world to which men are normal. But to place into perspective the Mishnah's vision of woman, we have to locate woman within the larger structure defined by the household. That is for two reasons. First of all, as a matter of definition, woman forms the other half of the whole that is the householder. Second, since, as we have already seen, the household forms the building block of the social construction envisioned by the Mishnah's framers, it is in that setting that every other component of the social world of the system must situate itself.

In the conception at hand, which sees Israel as made up, on earth, of households and villages, the economic unit also framed the social one, and the two together composed, in conglomerates, the political one, hence a political economy, initiated within an economic definition formed out of the elements of production. That explains why women cannot be addressed outside the framework of the economic unit of production defined by the household. For the Mishnah, throughout, makes a single cogent statement that the organizing unit of society and politics finds its definition in the irreducible unit of economic production. The Mishnah conceives no other economic unit of production than the household, though it recognizes that such existed; its authorship perceived no other social unit of organization than the household and the conglomeration of households in courtyards, and courtyards in villages, though that limited vision omitted all reference to substantial parts of the population perceived to be present, such as craftsmen, the unemployed, the landless, and the like. But what about woman in particular?

The framers of the Mishnah do not imagine a household headed by a woman; a divorced woman is assumed to return to her father's household. The framers make no provision for the economic activity of isolated individuals, out of synchronic relationship with a household or a village made up of house-holders. Accordingly, craftsmen and day laborers or other workers, skilled and otherwise, enter the world of social and economic transactions only in rela-tionship to the householder. The upshot, therefore, is that the social world is made up of households, and, since households may be made up of many fam-ilies—such as husbands, wives, children, all of them dependents upon the householder—households in no way are to be confused with the family. The indicator of the family is kinship, that of the household, measured by propin-quity or residence. Yet even residence is not always a criterion for membership in the household unit, since the craftsmen and day laborers are not assumed to live in the household compound at all. Accordingly, the household forms an economic unit, with secondary criteria deriving from that primary fact.

The Mishnaic law of women defines the position of women in the social economy of Israel's supernatural and natural reality—God's perspective in heaven, man's perspective on earth. That position acquires definition in rela-tionship to men, who give form to the Israelite social economy. It is effected through both supernatural and natural, this-worldly, action. What man and woman do on earth provokes a response in Heaven, and the correspondences are perfect. So the position of women is defined and secured in Heaven and here on earth, and that position, always and invariably relative to men, is what comes into consideration. The principal point of interest on Mishnah's part is the time at which a woman changes hands. That is, she becomes, and ceases to be, holy to a particular man, enters and leaves the marital union. These are the dangerous and disorderly points in the relationship of woman to man, and therefore, as I said, to society.

Five of the seven tractates of the Mishnah that pertain to women and fam-ily are devoted to the transfer of women from father to husband and back to fa-ther in the case of divorce or widowhood, thus in all to the formation and dissolution of the marital bond. Of them, three treat what by man is done here on earth—that is, formation of a marital bond through betrothal and marriage contract and dissolution through divorce and its consequences: Qiddushin (be-trothals), Ketubot (marriage contracts), and Gittin (writs of divorce). One of them is devoted to what by woman is done here on earth: Sotah (the wife ac-cused of adultery, in line with Numbers 5). Yebamot (levirate marriages, in line with Deuteronomy 25:1–5), greatest of the seven in size and informal and sub-stantive brilliance, deals with the corresponding Heavenly intervention into the formation and dissolution of marriage: the effect of death upon the marital bond, and the dissolution, through death, of that bond. The other two tractates, Nedarim (vows) and Nazir (the special vow of the Nazirite, in line with Num-bers 6), draw into one the two realms of reality, Heaven and earth, as they work out the effects of vows—generally taken by married women and subject to the confirmation or abrogation of the husband—to Heaven. These vows make a deep impact upon the marital relationship of the woman who has taken such a vow. So, in all, we consider the natural and supernatural character of the woman's relationship to the social economy framed by man: the beginning, end, and middle of that relationship.

PROPER CONDUCT WITH WOMEN

One of the many important issues worked out with special reference to women concerns proper conduct with women. Here we see how the Mishnah sets forth its ideas on avoiding improper sexual relations.

Mishnah Tractate Qiddushin 4:12–14

(4.12) A man should not remain alone with two women, but a woman may remain alone with two men.

R. Simeon says, "Also: One may stay alone with two women, when his wife is with him.

"And he sleeps with them in the same inn,

"Because his wife keeps watch over him."

A man may stay alone with his mother or with his daughter.

And he sleeps with them with flesh touching.

But if they [the son who is with the mother, the daughter with the father] grew up, this one sleeps in her garment, and that one sleeps in his garment.

(4.13) An unmarried man may not teach scribes.

Nor may a woman teach scribes.

R. Eliezer says, "Also: He who has no wife may not teach scribes."

(4.14) R. Judah says, "An unmarried man may not herd cattle.

"And two unmarried men may not sleep in the same cloak."

And sages permit it.

Whoever has business with women should not be alone with women.

And a man should not teach his son a trade which he has to practice among women.

Passage 4:13 refers to teachers of young children. They should not be brought into close association with the mothers or fathers of the children. The formal and substantive traits of what follows require no comment. We see that the Mishnah wants men and women to preserve relationships that are chaste and dignified. The authors of the document know full well that each sex desires the other—that is the foundation of the social order: family, home, household. But a well-ordered society is a predictable one, which keeps in check the natural desires of women and men. So much for the Mishnah's laws defining proper relationships between men and women. What about the theology that corresponds to those laws as set forth in Midrash exegesis of scripture?

FEMININE ISRAEL, MASCULINE ISRAEL, ANDROGYNOUS ISRAEL

The Midrash documents maintain that Israel itself serves God best through adopting the virtues that the Torah deems feminine. Indeed, when Israel adopts the feminine virtues, assigning to God the masculine ones, God appreciates Israel and responds by bringing the Messiah, at which point Israel completes its sexual identity with masculine virtues as well. So Israel must become androgynous, feminine now, masculine at the end of days. More to the point, feminine Israel is represented as God's great love, and God is represented as feminine Israel's masculine lover. This complex picture of the sexuality of Israel's and God's passionate love affair comes to full expression in the sages' interpretation of the Song of Songs (a.k.a. the Song of Solomon).

The dual Torah, beginning to end, taught that the Israelite was to exhibit the moral virtues of subservience, patience, endurance, and hope. These would translate into the emotional traits of humility and forbearance. And they would yield to social virtues of passivity and conciliation. This is expressed in terms of giving up one's wishes in favor of the wishes of the other, beginning with God:

Tractate Abot 2:4

Rabban Gamaliel, son of R. Judah the Patriarch, would say, "Make his wishes into your own wishes, so that he will make your wishes into his wishes. Put aside your wishes on account of his wishes, so that he will put aside the wishes of other people in favor of your wishes."

Not only so, but the hero was one who overcame impulses and the truly virtuous person, the one who reconciled others by giving way before the opinions of others. All of these acts of self-abnegation and self-denial, accommodation rather than rebellion, required to begin with the right attitudes, sentiments, emotions, and impulses, and the single most dominant motif of the Rabbinic writings, start to finish, is its stress on the right attitude's leading to the right action, the correct intentionality's producing the besought decision, and above all, accommodating in one's heart to what could not be changed by one's action. And that meant, the world as it was. Sages prepared Israel for the long centuries of subordination and alienation by inculcating attitudes that best suited people who could govern little more than how they felt about things.

In the definitive writings of Judaism, "our sages of blessed memory," who defined the Judaism of the dual Torah of scripture and the Mishnah and explained and expanded both into the enduring religious worldview and way of life for Israel, the Jewish people, taught what Israel is supposed to feel. And these emotions are feminine, not masculine. The feminine traits, according to Song of Songs Rabbah, are patience, submission, deep trusting; conciliation and accommodation. Israel is represented as feminine, therefore accepting and enduring. What, in concrete terms, does it mean for androgynous Israel to feel the feelings of a woman—and how do we know which emotion is feminine, which masculine? Israel is to cultivate the virtues of submission, accommodation, reconciliation, and self-sacrifice—the virtues we have now seen are classified as feminine ones. But later on, in time to come, having realized the reward for these virtues, Israel will resume the masculine virtues—again, in accord with the classification just now set forth—of aggression and domination.

A brief selection suffices to show the feminization of Israel. In the following, the relationship of Israel to God is the same as the relationship of a wife to the husband, and this is explicit in the following:

Song of Songs Rabbah to Song 7:10

Song 7:10 I am my beloved's, and his desire is for me.

XCIX.I "I am my beloved's, and his desire is for me":

There are three yearnings:

The yearning of Israel is only for their Father who is in heaven, as it is said, "I am my beloved's, and his desire is for me."

The yearning of a woman is only for her husband: "And your desire shall be for your husband" (Gen. 3:16).

The yearning of the Evil Impulse is only for Cain and his ilk: "To you is its desire" (Gen. 4:7).

R. Joshua in the name of R. Aha: "The yearning of rain is only for the earth: 'You have remembered the earth and made her desired, greatly enriching her' (Ps. 65:10).

"If you have merit, the rains will enrich it, but if not, they will tithe it [the words for enrich and tithe differ by a single letter], for it will produce for you one part for ten of seed."

Here, therefore, we find that gender relationships are explicitly characterized, and, with them, the traits associated with the genders as well. The same analogy is stated even more explicitly in the following, which reviews the principal points of the marriage liturgy in describing Israel's and God's marriage:

Song of Songs Rabbah to Song 4:10

Song 4:10 How sweet is your love, my sister, my bride! how much better is your love than wine, and the fragrance of your oils than any spice!

LIV:I.1 "How sweet is your love, my sister, my bride! how much better is your love than wine:"

R. Berekhiah and R. Helbo in the name of R. Samuel b. R. Nahman said, "There are ten passages in which Israel is called bride, six here [in the Song of Songs] and four in the prophets.

"Six here: 'Come with me from Lebanon, my bride; come with me from Lebanon. Depart from the peak of Amana, from the peak of Senir and Hermon, from the dens of lions, from the mountains of leopards' (Song 4:8); 'You have ravished my heart, my sister, my bride, you have ravished my heart with a glance of your eyes, with one jewel of your necklace' (Song 4:9); 'How sweet is your love, my sister, my bride! how much better is your love than wine, and the fragrance of your oils than any spice!' (Song 4:10); 'Your lips distil nectar, my bride; honey and milk are under your tongue; the scent of your garments is like the scent of Lebanon' (Song 4:11); 'A garden locked is my sister, my bride, a garden locked, a fountain sealed' (Song 4:12); 'I come to my garden, my sister, my bride, I gather my myrrh with my spice, I eat my honeycomb with my honey, I drink my wine with my milk. Eat, O friends, and drink; drink deeply, O lovers!' (Song 5:1).

"And four in the prophets: 'The voice of mirth and the voice of gladness, the voice of the bridegroom and the voice of the bride' (Jer. 7:34); 'And as a bride adorns herself with jewels' (Is. 61:10); 'And gird yourself with them like a bride' (Is. 59:18); 'And as the bridegroom rejoices over the bride' (Is. 62:5).

"And, correspondingly, the Holy One, blessed be he, puts on ten [nuptial] robes: 'The Lord reigns, he is clothed in majesty' (Ps. 93:1); 'The Lord is clothed' (Ps. 93:1); 'He has girded himself' (Ps. 93:1); 'And he put on righteousness as a coat of mail' (Is. 59:17); 'And he put on garments of vengeance' (Is. 59:17); ' 'For clothing' (Is. 59:17); 'This one who is glorious in his apparel' (Is. 63:1); 'Wherefore is your apparel red' (Is. 63:2); 'You are clothed with glory and majesty' (Ps. 104:1).

"This is so as to exact punishment from the nations of the world, who kept from the Ten Commandments the Israelites, who are [Simon] bound closely around them like the ornaments of a bride."

The concluding lines alert us to a rather subtle shift: Israel's relationship to God undergoes change and so, too, its relationship to the world; and, as we shall see, Israel proves androgynous, female now, male in the age to come, female to God, male to the nations of the world. Since the entire composition, we cannot overemphasize, derives from men, the metaphor proves remarkably daring and much more nuanced than we should realize were we to conclude that Israel here is only feminine, God only masculine.

The Midrash exegesis turns to everyday experience—the love of husband and wife—for a metaphor for God's love for Israel and Israel's love for God. Then, when Solomon's song says, "O that you would kiss me with the kisses of your mouth! For your love is better than wine," (Song 1:2), sages of blessed memory think of how God kissed Israel. Reading the Song of Songs as a metaphor, the Judaic sages as a matter of fact state in a systematic and orderly way their entire structure and system and, along the way, permit us to identify the traits they associate with feminine Israel and masculine God, respectively.

What sages accomplished in formulating an androgynous system was to con-ciliate two distinct constituencies to a single policy concerning gender relation-ships. On one side, women had not only to accept but to affirm and embody for the coming generations the legal position of subordination that the law prescribed for them. On the other, men had to find virtue in the political status of inferiority that history accorded to them as their lot. The solution to these distinct problems lay in the explicit androgyneity we have considered. Men must feel like women, women must act like (true, authentic, Israelite) men. But they can act like men because the authentic Israelite man exhibits virtues that, for women, come quite naturally. What was asked of the women was no more than the men themselves accepted at the hand of the nations. What was demanded of the men was no more than the relationship that their wives endured with them, which was identical to what Israel affirmed with God. The circle then is closed: God is to Israel as the nations are to Israel as man is to woman—for now. But, of course, as we have seen, that is only now; then matters will right themselves. By its femininity now, Israel will regain its masculinity.

Why did the system succeed so remarkably as it did? It was because the patriarchal gender doctrine of androgyneity, the dual Torah's unique formulation of *Halakhah* and *Aggadah*—the laws we examined in the prior section, the exegesis of the Song of Songs that is before us now—succeeded in persuading each Jew to accept what all Jews had to do to endure. Necessity defined virtue. Persuade the heart, not only the mind. Then each one privately would feel what everyone publicly had in any case to think. That accounts for not the mere persistence of sages' wise teachings but for their mythopoeic power. Sages' views on temper, their sagacious counsel on conciliating others and seeking the approval of the group—these not only made life tolerable, they in fact defined what life would mean for Israel. Society, in the canonical writings, set the style for the self's deepest sentiments. So the approved feelings retained approval for so long because emotions, in the thought of the sages of the canon at hand, followed rules. Feelings laid down judgments. Affections therefore constituted not mindless effusions but deliberate constructions. Whether or not the facts then conformed to sages' view we do not know.

When, in the Mishnah, women marry, they replicate Israel's condition and go into exile, leaving their father's house and going to their husband's, leaving their own family and joining some other. That is why the *Halakhah* has to guarantee the woman's right to return home at specified intervals and to maintain her relationships with her own home(land). And that is what happened to Israel, too. Life in "exile," viewed as living in other people's countries and not in their own land, meant life as a woman, not as a man. And that meant for Israel, as Judaism conceived Israel, a long span of endurance, a test of patience to end only with the end of time. That required Israel to live in accord with the will of others. Under such circumstances the virtues of the independent citizen, sharing command of affairs of state, the gifts of innovation, initiative, independence of mind, proved beside the point. From the end of the Second Revolt against Rome in 135 to the creation of the State of Israel in 1948, Israel, the Jewish people, faced a different task. The human condition of Israel therefore defined a different heroism, one filled with patience, humiliation, self-abnegation. Israel's heroes would exhibit the feminine virtues.

To turn survival into endurance, pariah status into an exercise in Godly living, the sages' affective program served full well. Israel's hero saw power in submission, wealth in the gift to be grateful, wisdom in the confession of ignorance. Like the cross, ultimate degradation was made to stand for ultimate power. Like Jesus on the cross, so Israel in exile served God through suffering. True, the cross would represent a scandal to the nations and foolishness to some Jews. But Israel's own version of the doctrine at hand endured and defined the nation's singular and astonishing resilience.

If I had to set forth in a single passage what I believe is at stake in androgyne Judaism, it is the system's account of God's most profound preference, which is for those traits that the system knows as feminine but wishes to nurture in men's hearts and minds as well. This comes to expression in the simple statement: God favors the pursued over the pursuer.

Leviticus Rabbah XXVII:V.1–2

"God seeks what has been driven away" (Qoh. 3:15).

R. Huna in the name of R. Joseph said, "It is always the case that 'God seeks what has been driven away' [favoring the victim].

"You find when a righteous man pursues a righteous man, 'God seeks what has been driven away.'

"When a wicked man pursues a wicked man, 'God seeks what has been driven away.'

"All the more so when a wicked man pursues a righteous man, 'God seeks what has been driven away.'

"[The same principle applies] even when you come around to a case in which a righteous man pursues a wicked man, 'God seeks what has been driven away.' "

R. Yosé b. R. Yudan in the name of R. Yosé b. R. Nehorai says, "It is always the case that the Holy One, blessed be he, demands an accounting for the blood of those who have been pursued from the hand of the pursuer.

"Abel was pursued by Cain, and God sought [an accounting for] the pursued: 'And the Lord looked [favorably] upon Abel and his meal offering' (Gen. 4:4).

"Noah was pursued by his generation, and God sought [an accounting for] the pursued: 'You and all your household shall come into the ark' (Gen. 7:1). And it says, 'For this is like the days of Noah to me, as I swore [that the waters of Noah should no more go over the earth]' (Is. 54:9).

"Abraham was pursued by Nimrod, 'and God seeks what has been driven away': 'You are the Lord, the God who chose Abram and brought him out of Ur' (Neh. 9:7).

"Isaac was pursued by Ishmael, 'and God seeks what has been driven away': 'For through Isaac will seed be called for you' (Gen. 21:12).

"Jacob was pursued by Esau, 'and God seeks what has been driven away': 'For the Lord has chosen Jacob, Israel for his prized possession' (Ps. 135:4).

"Moses was pursued by Pharaoh, 'and God seeks what has been driven away': 'Had not Moses His chosen stood in the breach before Him' (Ps. 106:23).

"David was pursued by Saul, "and God seeks what has been driven away': 'And he chose David, his servant' (Ps. 78:70).

"Israel was pursued by the nations, 'and God seeks what has been driven away': 'And you has the Lord chosen to be a people to him' (Deut. 14:2).

"And the rule applies also to the matter of offerings. A bull is pursued by a lion, a sheep is pursued by a wolf, a goat is pursued by a leopard.

"Therefore the Holy One, blessed be he, has said, 'Do not make offerings before me from those animals that pursue, but from those that are pursued: 'When a bull, a sheep, or a goat is born' " (Lev. 22:27).

The pursuer imposes, demands, insists; the pursued negotiates, yields, pleads. Since, both parts of the Torah state explicitly, in gender relationships, man is the pursuer (seeking his rib back) and woman the pursued, the pertinence of this powerful passage to the pages of this book is self-evident. That right relationship is the one that is not coerced, not manipulated, not one defined by a dominant party upon a subordinated one. It is a relationship of mutuality, negotiation, response to what is freely given through what cannot be demanded but only volunteered. Israel should relate to God in accord with these virtues, which sages explicitly classify as feminine—and, in all their patriarchal masculinity, urge upon Israel.

9

Worldview: The Messiah Theme

THE ADVENT OF THE MESSIAH
TO THE RABBINIC SYSTEM

The Written Torah contains prophecies of the coming of the Messiah at the end of days, and the Messiah theme served exceedingly well the construction of some of the Judaic systems of Second Temple times, as we saw in Chapter 3. How the Messiah theme attained prominence in the Rabbinic system that became normative in post-Temple times presents a critical problem in understanding that Judaism and the shape it would ultimately reach. We ask first about the Messiah in the Mishnah, then proceed to the successor documents' utilization of that theme and account for its prominence in the ultimate system that emerged from the formative age.

THE MESSIAH THEME IN THE
SYSTEM OF THE MISHNAH

The Messiah ("one who has been anointed for the office that he holds") is a figure in historical context, coming at the end of history to save Israel. But a Judaic system that does not define its goals through historical patterns and events will find little of consequence in the Messiah, who will be accorded a trivial role in the systemic construction. In constructing a systematic account of Judaism—that is, the worldview and way of life for Israel presented in the Mishnah—the philosophers of the Mishnah did not make extensive use of the Messiah theme in the construction of a teleology for their system.[1] *Messiah* referred to status; for example, a high priest who was anointed was differentiated from one who was confirmed in office by other means, and a priest anointed for war was a "Messianic priest." In the Mishnah there is a "Messianic priest" or a "Messianic general," therefore, but no single Messiah awaited at the end of days. The Mishnah's authorities found it possible to present a statement of goals

---

[1]This chapter reviews the results of Jacob Neusner, *The Foundations of Judaism: Method, Teleology, Doctrine*, vols. 1–3. (Philadelphia: Fortress Press, 1983–85); also *Messiah in Context: Israel's History and Destiny in Formative Judaism* (Lanham: University Press of America, 1988), Studies in Judaism series, and *Judaism and Christianity in the Age of Constantine: Issues of the Initial Confrontation* (Chicago: University of Chicago Press, 1987). Full bibliography and references are supplied in those monographs. See also Jacob Neusner and William Scott Green, eds., *Judaisms and Their Messiahs in the Beginning of Christianity* (New York: Cambridge University Press, 1987).

for their projected life of Israel that was entirely separate from appeals to history and eschatology. Since they certainly knew, and even alluded to, longstanding and widely held convictions on eschatological subjects, beginning with those in scripture, the framers thereby testified that knowing the larger repertoire, they made choices different from others before and after them. Their document accurately and ubiquitously expresses these choices, both affirmative and negative.

HOW ISRAEL COULD HASTEN
THE COMING OF THE MESSIAH

The Messiah theme, trivial in the Mishnah, moves to the forefront in the Yerushalmi, ca. 400, after world-historical events in the form of Rome's adoption of Christianity as state religion led both Christian thinkers and Judaic ones to think deeply about the meaning and end of history. The former included Eusebius, a Church Father who wrote a history of humanity from the beginning to the advent of the Christian empire, and the latter encompassed the Talmudic authorities whom we meet in this chapter. The Yerushalmi and certain associated Midrash compilations, such as Genesis Rabbah, exhibited keen interest in history and its patterns.

If the Mishnah provided a teleology without eschatology, the framers of the Yerushalmi and related Midrash compilations could not conceive of any but an utterly eschatological goal for themselves. Historical events entered into the construction of a teleology for the Yerushalmi's system of Judaism as a whole. What the law demanded reflected the consequences of wrongful action on the part of Israel. So, again, Israel's own deeds defined the events of history.

But this notion of determining one's own destiny should not be misunderstood. The framers of the Talmud of the Land of Israel were not telling the Jews to please God by doing commandments in order that they should thereby gain control of their own destiny. To the contrary, the paradox of the Yerushalmi's system lies in the fact that Israel can free itself of control by other nations only by humbly agreeing to accept God's rule. The nations—Rome, in the present instance—rest on one side of the balance, while God rests on the other. Israel must then choose between them. There is no such thing for Israel as freedom from both God and the nations, total autonomy and independence. There is only a choice of masters, a ruler on earth or a ruler in heaven.

Keeping the commandments as a mark of submission, loyalty, humility before God, is the Rabbinic system of salvation. So Israel does not "save itself." Israel never controls its own destiny, either on earth or in heaven. The only choice is whether to cast one's fate into the hands of cruel, deceitful men or to trust in the living God of mercy and love. The emphasis that Israel's arrogance alienates God, Israel's humility and submission win God's favor, cannot surprise us; this is the very point of the doctrine of emotions that defines Rabbinic Judaism's ethics. Now the same view is expressed in a still more critical area. We shall see how this position is spelled out in the setting of discourse about the Messiah in the Talmud of the Land of Israel.

THE FALSE MESSIAH: BAR KOKHBA

The Yerushalmi's compilers called attention to the failed Messiah of the second century, Bar Kokhba, who above all exemplifies arrogance against God. He lost the war because of that arrogance. His emotions, attitudes, sentiments, and feelings form the model of how the virtuous Israelite is not to conceive of matters. In particular, Bar Kokhba ignored the authority of sages:

Yerushalmi Taanit 4:5

Said R. Yohanan, "Upon orders of Caesar Hadrian, they killed eight hundred thousand in Betar."

Said R. Yohanan, "There were eighty thousand pairs of trumpeters surrounding Betar. Each one was in charge of a number of troops. Ben Kozeba was there and he had two hundred thousand troops who, as a sign of loyalty, had cut off their little fingers.

"Sages sent word to him, 'How long are you going to turn Israel into a maimed people?'

"He said to them, 'How otherwise is it possible to test them?'

"They replied to him, 'Whoever cannot uproot a cedar of Lebanon while riding on his horse will not be inscribed on your military rolls.'

"So there were two hundred thousand who qualified in one way, and another two hundred thousand who qualified in another way."

When he would go forth to battle, he would say, "Lord of the world! Do not help and do not hinder us! 'Hast thou not rejected us, O God? Thou dost not go forth, O God, with our armies'" (Ps. 60:10).

Three-and-a-half years did Hadrian besiege Betar.

R. Eleazar of Modiin would sit in sackcloth and ashes and pray every day, saying "Lord of the ages! Do not judge in accord with strict judgment this day! Do not judge in accord with strict judgment this day!"

Hadrian wanted to go to him. A Samaritan said to him, "Do not go to him until I see what he is doing, and so hand over the city [of Betar] to you. [Make peace ... for you.]"

[The Samaritan] got into the city through a drainpipe. He went and found R. Eleazar of Modiin standing and praying. He pretended to whisper something in his ear.

The townspeople saw [the Samaritan] do this and brought him to Ben Kozeba. They told him, "We saw this man having dealings with your friend."

[Bar Kokhba] said to him, "What did you say to him, and what did he say to you?"

He [R. Eleazar of Modiin] said to [the Samaritan], "If I tell you, then the king will kill me, and if I do not tell you, then you will kill me. It is better that the king kill me, and not you.

"[Eleazar] said to me, 'I should hand over my city.' ['I shall make peace... .']"

He turned to R. Eleazar of Modiin. He said to him, "What did this Samaritan say to you?"

He replied, "Nothing."

He said to him, "What did you say to him?"

He said to him, "Nothing."

[Ben Kozeba] gave [Eleazar] one good kick and killed him.

Forthwith an echo came forth and proclaimed the following verse:

"Woe to my worthless shepherd, who deserts the flock! May the sword smite his arm and his right eye! Let his arm be wholly withered, his right eye utterly blinded! (Zech. 11:17).

"You have murdered R. Eleazar of Modiin, the right arm of all Israel, and their right eye. Therefore may the right arm of that man wither, may his right eye be utterly blinded!"

Forthwith Betar was taken, and Ben Kozeba was killed.

That kick—an act of temper, a demonstration of untamed emotions and of arrogance—tells the whole story. We notice two complementary themes. First, Bar Kokhba treats heaven with arrogance, asking God merely to keep out of the way. Second, he treats an especially revered sage with a parallel arrogance. The humble, weak sage had the power to preserve Israel. Bar Kokhba destroyed Israel's one protection. The result was inevitable.

The Messiah, the centerpiece of salvation history and hero of the tale, emerged as a critical figure. The historical theory of this Yerushalmi passage is stated very simply. In their view Israel had to choose between wars, either the war fought by Bar Kokhba or the "war for Torah." "Why had they been punished? It was because of the weight of the war, for they had not wanted to engage in the struggles over the meaning of the Torah" (Yerushalmi Taanite 3:9 XVI I). Those struggles, which were ritual arguments about ritual matters, promised the only victory worth winning. Then Israel's history would be written in terms of wars over the meaning of the Torah and the decision of the law.

In the Talmud's theory of salvation the framers provided Israel with an account of how to overcome the unsatisfactory circumstances of an unredeemed present, so as to accomplish the movement from here to the much-desired future. When the Talmud's authorities present statements on the promise of the law for those who keep it, therefore, they provide glimpses of the goal of the system as a whole. These invoked the primacy of the rabbi and the legitimating power of the Torah, and in those two components of the system we find the principles of the Messianic doctrine. And these bring us back to the argument with Christ triumphant, as the Christians perceived him.

MESSIAH IN CONTEXT:
THE CHRISTIAN CHALLENGE

The context in which the Talmud of the Land of Israel and related Midrash compilations restated the received Messiah theme, representing the Messiah as a humble sage, finds its definition in the triumph of Christianity. The government's adoption of Christianity as the state religion was taken to validate the Christian claim that Jesus was, and is, Christ. Indeed, every page of Eusebius' writing bears the message that the conversion of Constantine proves the Christ-hood of Jesus, his messianic standing. History—the affairs of nations and monarchs—yields laws of society, proves God's will, and matters now speak for themselves.

For Judaism the dramatic shift in the fortunes of the competing biblical faith raised a simple and unpleasant possibility: Perhaps Israel had been wrong after all. Since the Jews as a whole, and sages among them, anticipated the coming of the Messiah promised by the prophets, the issue could be fairly joined. If history proves propositions, as the prophets and apocalyptic visionaries had maintained, then how could Jews deny the Christians' claim that the conversion of the emperor, and then of the Empire, demonstrated the true state of affairs in heaven as much as on earth?

John Chrysostom, who speaks for Christianity on the messianic issue, typifies the Christian theologians' concern that converts not proceed to the synagogue or retain connections with it. For the burden of his case was that since Christ had now been proved Messiah, Christians no longer could associate themselves with the synagogue. Judaism had lost, Christianity had won, and people had to choose the one and give up the other. At stake for Chrysostom, whose sermons on Judaism, preached in 386–87, provide for our purpose the statement of Christianity on the Messianic issue, was Christians' participation in synagogue rites and Judaic practices. He invoked the Jews' failure in the fiasco of the proposed rebuilding of the Temple in Jerusalem only a quarter of a century earlier. He drew upon the collapse of that project to demonstrate that Judaic rites no longer held any power. He further cited that incident to prove that Israel's salvation lay wholly in the past, in the time of the return to Zion, and never in the future. So the happenings of the day demonstrated proofs of the faith. The struggle between sages and theologians concerned the meaning of important contemporary happenings, and the same happenings, read in light of the same scripture, provoked discussion of the same issues. It was a confrontation.

The messianic crisis confronting the Christian theologians hardly matches that facing the Judaic sages. The one dealt with problems of triumph, the other, despair; the one had to interpret a new day, the other to explain disaster. Scripture explicitly promised that Israel would receive salvation from God's anointed Messiah at the end of time. The teleology of Israelite faith, in the biblical account, focused upon eschatology and, within eschatology, on the salvific, therefore the messianic, dimension. On the other hand, the Mishnah had for its part taken up a view of its own on the issue of teleology, presenting an ahistorical and essentially nonmessianic teleology. Sages' response to the messianic crisis had to mediate two distinct and contradictory positions. Sages explained what the messianic hope now entailed and how to identify the Messiah, who would be a sage. They further included the messianic issue in their larger historical theory. So we cannot address the question at hand as if the Christians defined the agendum. True, to Israel all they had to say was, "Why not?" But sages responded with a far-reaching doctrine of their own, deeming the question, in its Christian formulation, trivial.

But the issue confronting both Judaic sages and Christian theologians was one and the same: precisely what difference the Messiah makes. To state matters as they would be worked out by both parties, in the light of the events of the day: What do I have to do because the Messiah has come (Christian) or because I want the Messiah to come (Judaic)? That question encompasses two sides of a single issue. On the issue of the Messiahship of Jesus, all other matters depended. It follows that one party believed precisely the opposite of the other on an issue shared in identical definition by both. For Christians, the sole issue—belief or unbelief—carried a clear implication for the audience subject to address. When debate would go forward, it would center upon the wavering of Christians and the unbelief of Jews. Our exemplary figure, Chrysostom, framed matters in those terms, drawing upon the events of his own day for ample instantiation of the matter. The Christian formulation thus focused all argument on the vindication of Jesus as Christ. When Christians found attractive aspects of Judaic rite and belief, the Christian theologians invoked the fundamental issue: Is Jesus Christ? If so, then Judaism fails. If not, then Christianity fails. No question, therefore, drew the two sets of intellectuals into more direct conflict; none bore so immediate and fundamental consequences. Christians did not have to keep the Torah—that was a principal message of John Chrysostom in context.

IDENTIFYING THE MESSIAH, HASTENING HIS ADVENT

In the Talmud of the Land of Israel, we find a fully exposed doctrine not only of *a* Messiah (e.g., a kind of priest or general), but of *the* Messiah, the one man who will save Israel: who he is, how we will know him, what we must do to bring him. It follows that the Talmud of the Land of Israel presents clear evidence that the Messiah myth had found its place within that larger Torah myth that characterized Judaism in its later formative literature. A clear effort to identify the person of the Messiah and to confront the claim that a specific, named individual had been, or would be, the Messiah—these come to the fore. This means that the issue had reached the center of lively discourse, at least in some Rabbinic circles. The disposition of the issue proves distinctive to the sages: The Messiah will be a sage, the Messiah will come when Israel has attained that condition of sanctification, marked also by profound humility and complete acceptance of God's will, that signify sanctification.

These two conditions say the same thing twice: Sages' Judaism will identify the Messiah and teach how to bring him nearer. In these allegations we find no point of intersection with issues important to Chrysostom, even though the Talmud of the Land of Israel reached closure at the same time as Chrysostom's preaching. For Chrysostom dealt with the Messiah theme in terms pertinent to his larger system, and sages did the same. But the issue was fairly joined. In Chrysostom's terms, it was: Jesus is Christ, proved by the events of the recent past. In sages' terms, it was: The Messiah will be a sage, coming when Israel fully accepts, in all humility, God's sole rule. The first stage in the position of each hardly matches that in the outline of the other. But the second does: Jesus is Christ, therefore Israel will have no other Messiah. The Messiah will come, in the form of a sage, and therefore no one who now claims to be the Messiah is in fact the savior.

Once the figure of the Messiah has come on stage, there arises discussion on who, among the living, the Messiah might be. The identification of the Messiah begins with the person of David himself: "If the Messiah-King comes from among the living, his name will be David. If he comes from among the dead, it will be King David himself" (Yerushalmi Berakhot 2:3). A variety of evidence announced the advent of the Messiah as a figure in the larger system of formative Judaism. The rabbinization of David constitutes one kind of evidence. Serious discussion, within the framework of the accepted documents of Mishnaic exegesis and the law, concerning the identification and claim of diverse figures asserted to be Messiahs presents still more telling proof.

Yerushalmi Berakhot 2:4 (Translated by T. Zahavy)

Once a Jew was plowing and his ox snorted once before him. An Arab who was passing and heard the sound said to him, "Jew, loosen your ox and loosen the plow and stop plowing. For today your Temple was destroyed."

The ox snorted again. He [the Arab] said to him, "Jew, bind your ox and bind your plow, for today the Messiah-King was born."

He said to him, "What is his name?"

"Menahem."

He said to him, "And what is his father's name?"

The Arab said to him, "Hezekiah."

He said to him, "Where is he from?"

He said to him, "From the royal capital of Bethlehem in Judea."

The Jew went and sold his ox and sold his plow. And he became a peddler of infant's felt-cloths [diapers]. And he went from place to place until he came to that very city. All of the women bought from him. But Menahem's mother did not buy from him.

He heard the women saying, "Menahem's mother, Menahem's mother, come buy for your child."

She said, "I want to bring him up to hate Israel. For on the day he was born, the Temple was destroyed."

They said to her, "We are sure that on this day it was destroyed, and on this day of the year it will be rebuilt."

She said to the peddler, "I have no money."

He said to her, "It is of no matter to me. Come and buy for him and pay me when I return."

A while later he returned to that city. He said to her, "How is the infant doing?"

She said to him, "Since the time you saw him a spirit came and carried him away from me."

Said R. Bun, "Why do we learn this from [a story about] an Arab? Do we not have explicit scriptural evidence for it? 'Lebanon with its majestic trees will fall' (Isa. 10:34). And what follows this? 'There shall come forth a shoot from the stump of Jesse' (Isa. 11:1). [Right after an allusion to the destruction of the Temple the prophet speaks of the messianic age.]"

This is a set-piece story, adduced to prove that the Messiah was born on the day the Temple was destroyed. The Messiah was born when the Temple was destroyed; hence, God prepared for Israel a better fate than had appeared.

A more concrete matter—the identification of the Messiah with a known historical personality—was associated with the name of Aqiba. He is said to have claimed that Bar Kokhba, leader of the second-century revolt, was the Messiah. The important aspect of the story, however, is the rejection of Aqiba's view. The discredited Messiah figure (if Bar Kokhba actually was such in his own day) finds no apologists in the later rabbinical canon.

Yerushalmi Taanit 4:5

R. Simeon b. Yohai taught, "Aqiba, my master, would interpret the following verse: 'A star [kokhab] shall come forth out of Jacob' (Num. 24:17). "A disappointment [Kozeba] shall come forth out of Jacob.'"

R. Aqiba, when he saw Bar Kozeba, said, "This is the King Messiah."

R. Yohanan ben Toreta said to him, "Aqiba! Grass will grow on your cheeks before the Messiah will come!"

The important point is not only that Aqiba had been proved wrong. It is that the very verse of scripture adduced in behalf of his viewpoint could be treated more generally and made to refer to righteous people in general, not to the Messiah in particular. And that leads us to the issue of the age, as sages had to face it: What makes a Messiah a false Messiah? The answer, we recall, is arrogance.

The climax of the matter comes in an explicit statement that the practice of conduct required by the Torah will bring about the coming of the Messiah. That explanation of the purpose of the holy way of life, focused now upon the end of time and the advent of the Messiah, must strike us as surprising. For the framers of the Mishnah had found it possible to construct a complete and encompassing teleology for their system with scarcely a single word about the Messiah's coming when the system would be perfectly achieved. So with their interest in explaining events and accounting for history, third- and fourth-century sages invoked what their predecessors had at best found of peripheral consequence to their system. The following contains the most striking expression of the viewpoint at hand.

Yerushalmi Taanit 1:1

"The oracle concerning Dumah. One is calling to me from Seir, 'Watchman, what of the night? Watchman, what of the night?' (Is. 21:11)."

The Israelites said to Isaiah, "O our Rabbi, Isaiah, what will come for us out of this night?"

He said to them, "Wait for me, until I can present the question."

Once he had asked the question, he came back to them.

They said to him, "Watchman, what of the night? What did the Guardian of the ages tell you?"

He said to them, "The watchman says, 'Morning comes; and also the night. If you will inquire, inquire; come back again' (Is. 21:12)."

They said to him, "Also the night?"

He said to them, "It is not what you are thinking. But there will be morning for the righteous, and night for the wicked, morning for Israel, and night for idolaters."

They said to him, "When?"

He said to them, "Whenever you want, He too wants [it to be]—if you want it, he wants it."

They said to him, "What is standing in the way?"

He said to them, "Repentance: 'Come back again' (Is. 21:12)."

R. Aha in the name of R. Tanhum b. R. Hiyya, "If Israel repents for one day, forthwith the son of David will come.

"What is the Scriptural basis? 'O that today you would hearken to his voice!' (Ps. 95:7)."

Said R. Levi, "If Israel would keep a single Sabbath in the proper way, forthwith the son of David will come.

"What is the scriptural basis for this view? 'Moses said, Eat it today, for today is a Sabbath to the Lord; today you will not find it in the field' (Ex. 16:25)."

"And it says, 'For thus said the Lord God, the Holy One of Israel, "In returning and rest you shall be saved; in quietness and in trust shall be your strength." And you would not' (Is. 30:15)."

The discussion of the power of repentance would hardly have surprised a Mishnah sage. What is new is the explicit linkage of keeping the law with achieving the end of time and the coming of the Messiah. That motif stands separate from the notions of righteousness and repentance, which surely do not require it. So the condition of "all Israel," a social category in historical time, comes under consideration, and not only the status of individual Israelites in life and in death. Now history as an operative category, drawing in its wake Israel as a social entity, comes once more on the scene. But except for the Mishnah's sages, it had never left the stage.

We must not lose sight of the importance of this passage, with its emphasis on repentance on one side and the power of Israel to reform itself on the other. The Messiah will come any day that Israel makes it possible. If all Israel will keep a single Sabbath in the proper (Rabbinic) way, the Messiah will come. If all Israel will repent for one day, the Messiah will come. "Whenever you want … ," the Messiah will come. Now, two things are happening here. First, the system of religious observance, including study of Torah, is explicitly invoked as having salvific power. Second, the persistent hope of the people for the coming of the Messiah is linked to the system of Rabbinic observance and belief. In this way, the austere program of the Mishnah, with no trace of a promise that the Messiah will come if and when the system is fully realized, finds a new development.

That Mishnaic teleology—its theory of the end and goal of matters—lacking all eschatological ("end of history") dimension here in the Yerushalmi gives way to an explicitly messianic statement that the purpose of the law is to attain Israel's salvation: "If you want it, God wants it, too." The one thing Israel commands is its own heart; the power it yet exercises is the power to repent. These suffice. The entire history of humanity will respond to Israel's will, to what happens in Israel's heart and soul. And with the Temple in ruins, repentance can take place only within the heart and mind.

We have traveled no appreciable distance from the stories of Adam and Israel, each losing Paradise, at which we began in Chapter 1. The theme of exile and return now encompasses the motif that humility and an attitude of repentance will show the way of return to Paradise, such as, to begin with, was realized in Eden on the Sabbath.

10

The Doctrine of "Israel"

A RELIGIOUS STRUCTURE AND
ITS COMPREHENSIVE METAPHOR

Rabbinic Judaism defines its Israel in supernatural terms, deeming the social entity to form a transcendental community, by faith. That is shown by the simple fact that a gentile of any origin or status, slave or free, Greek or barbarian, may enter that Judaism's "Israel" on equal terms with those born into the community. They become children of Abraham and Sarah. The children of converts are Israelite without qualification. That fact bears concrete and material consequences, such as in the right to marry any other Israelite without distinction by reason of familial origin. It follows that the "Israel" of Rabbinic Judaism must be understood in a wholly theological framework. It is not an ethnic classification, based on cultural or territorial assimilation, and marrying into Israel without conversion to the God of Abraham and Sarah accomplishes no change in the status of the gentile. For that same reason this Judaism knows no distinction between children of the flesh and children of the promise and therefore cannot address a merely ethnic "Israel." That is because for Rabbinic Judaism "Israel" is always and only defined by the Torah received and represented by "our sages of blessed memory" as the word of God, never by the happenstance of secular history.

Rabbinic Judaism thus set forth a theory of the social entity formed by those who observed its way of life and who adhered to its worldview that identified that social entity with the "Israel" of which Scripture spoke. It told about itself the stories of scripture beginning with Abraham and Sarah. Scripture's narratives then were invoked as metaphor in order to explain the group and identify it. That entailed the comparison of persons—Jews—of the here and now to the "Israel" of which the Hebrew scripture—the Torah—speaks, and the identification of those Jews with that "Israel." Treating the social group—two or more persons—as other than they actually are in the present, as more than a (mere) given, means that the group is something else than what it appears to be.

"ISRAEL" IN THE MISHNAH'S
JUDAISM WITHOUT CHRISTIANITY

If we trace the unfolding of the doctrine of "Israel" within the documents of the Oral Torah from the Mishnah forward, we find that the definition shifts over time. The Mishnah, ca. 200, took shape at a time at which Christianity formed a minor irritant, perhaps in some places a competing Judaism, but not a formative component of the social order. Since Christianity was certainly not the political power that it was to become, it did not define the context in which the Rabbinic sages thought about themselves, as it would from the fourth century onward. Hence the Mishnah's framers' thinking about "Israel" in no way took account of the competing claim to form the true Israel put forth by Christianity; "Israel" remained abstract, thus intransitive, bearing no relationships to any other distinct social entity.

Defining by opposites, one would answer, "Who are we?" by saying, "Who are we not?" Here the abstraction enters in. The Mishnah's mode of thought—comparison and contrast—yielded that analogical-contrastive analysis. The opposite of "Israel" in the Mishnah is "the nations" on one side or "Levite, priest," on the other: always taxonomical, never defined out of relationship to others within the same theoretical structure. Here is how the matter is set forth in the Mishnah:

Mishnah Tractate Qiddushin 4:1

Ten castes came up from Babylonia: (1) priests, (2) Levites, (3) Israelites, (4) impaired priests, (5) converts, and (6) freed slaves, (7) Mamzers, (8) Netins, (9) "silenced ones" [*shetuqi*], and (10) foundlings.

Priests, Levites, and Israelites are permitted to marry among one another.

Levites, Israelites, impaired priests, converts, and freed slaves are permitted to marry among one another.

Converts, freed slaves, Mamzers, Netins, "silenced ones," and foundlings are permitted to marry among one another.

"Israel" here stands for a classification of Israelites, among other classifications, for the purposes of marriage: Who may marry whom? *Israel* is "not-priest" "not Levite" or "not mamzer." That is one meaning; the other is "Israel" is "not-gentile." As the Mishnah defines "Israel," the category bears two identical meanings: the "Israel" of (all) the Jews now and here, but also the "Israel" of which scripture—the Torah—spoke. And that encompassed both the individual and the group, without linguistic differentiation of any kind. Thus in the Mishnah "Israel" may refer to an individual Jew (always male) or to "all Jews," that is, the collectivity of Jews. The individual woman is nearly always called *bat yisrael,* daughter of (an) Israel(ite).

The sages in the Mishnah did not merely assemble facts and define the social entity as a matter of mere description of the given. Rather, they portrayed it as they wished to. They imputed to the social group, Jews, the status of a systemic entity, "Israel." To others within Jewry, it was not at all self-evident that "all Jews" constituted one "Israel" and that that one "Israel" formed the direct and immediate continuation, in the here and now, of the "Israel" of holy writ and revelation. The authorship of the Mishnah therefore does not differentiate among gentiles. To the system of the Mishnah, whether or not a gentile is a Roman or an Aramean or a Syrian or a Briton does not matter. That is to say, differentiation among gentiles rarely, if ever, makes a difference in the Mishnah's decision making. But later on, to the Judaic system represented by the Yerushalmi and its associated writings, "gentile" (in the collective) may be Rome or other-than-Rome, for instance, Babylonia, Medea, or Greece. That act of further differentiation—we may call it "speciation"—makes a considerable difference in the identification of gentile. In the Israel of the Mishnah's authorship, therefore, we confront an abstraction in a system of philosophy.

"ISRAEL" IN THE TWO TALMUDS' JUDAISM DESPITE CHRISTIANITY

Two metaphors, rarely present and scarcely explored in the writings of the Mishnah's stage (ca. 70–300 C.E.) in the formation of the Judaism of the dual Torah, came to prominence in the two Talmuds' stage (ca. 300–600 C.E.). These were, first, the view of "Israel" as a family, the children and heirs of the man, Israel; second, the conception of Israel as *sui generis,* a category unto itself, without counterparts. While "Israel" in the first phase of the formation of Judaism perpetually finds definition in relationship to its opposite, "Israel" in the second phase was defined in its own terms and not solely or mainly in relationship to other comparable entities. The enormous investment in the conception of "Israel" as *sui generis*—categorically unique—makes that point blatantly. But "Israel" as family bears that same trait of autonomy and self-evident definition.

Now "Israel" forms a family. An encompassing theory of society, built upon that conception of "Israel," permits us to describe the proportions and balances of the social entity at hand, showing how each component both is an "Israel" and contributes to the larger composite as well. "Israel" as *sui generis* carried in its wake a substantial doctrine of definition, a weighty collection of general laws of social history governing the particular traits and events of the social group. In comparing transitive to intransitive "Israel," we move from Israel as not-gentile and "Israel" as not-priest to powerful statements of what "Israel" is. Now to specify in concrete terms the reasons adduced to explain the rather striking shift before us.

Christianity set the external challenge. By claiming that "Israel" constituted "Israel after the flesh," the actual, living, present family of Abraham and Sarah, Isaac and Rebecca, Jacob and Leah and Rachel, the sages met head-on the Christian claim that there was—or could ever be—some other "Israel," of a lineage not defined by the family connection at all, and that the existing Jews no longer constituted "Israel." By representing "Israel" as *sui generis,* the sages moreover focused upon the systemic teleology, with its definition of salvation, in response to the Christian claim that salvation is not of Israel but of the Church, now enthroned in this world as in heaven. The sage, model for Israel, in the model of Moses, our rabbi, represented on earth the Torah that had come from heaven. Like Christ, in earth as in heaven, like the Church, the body of Christ, ruler of earth (through the emperor) as of heaven, the sage embodied what Israel was and was to be. So Israel as family in the model of the sage, like Moses our rabbi, corresponded in its social definition to the Church of Jesus Christ, the New Israel, of salvation of humanity. The metaphors given prominence in the late fourth and fifth century writings of "our sages of blessed memory" then formed a remarkable counterpoint to the social metaphors important in the mind of significant Christian theologians as both parties reflected on the political revolution that had taken place.

In response to the challenge of Christianity, the sages' thinking about "Israel" centered on the issues of history and salvation, issues made not merely chronic but acute by the political triumph. That accounts for the unprecedented reading of the outsider as differentiated, a reading contained in the two propositions concerning Rome: first, as Esau or Edom or Ishmael, that is, as part of the family, second, of Rome as the pig. Differentiating Rome from other gentiles represented a striking concession indeed, without counterpart in the Mishnah. Rome is represented as only Christian Rome can have been represented: It looks kosher but it is unkosher. Pagan Rome cannot ever have looked kosher, but Christian Rome, with its appeal to ancient Israel, could and did and moreover claimed to. It bore some traits that validate, but lacked others that validate.

The metaphor of the family proved equally pointed. The sages framed their political ideas within the metaphor of genealogy because to begin with they appealed to the fleshly connection, the family, as the rationale for Israel's social existence. A family beginning with Abraham, Isaac, and Jacob, Israel could best sort out its relationships by drawing into the family other social entities with which it found it had to relate. So Rome became the brother. That affinity came to light only when Rome had turned Christian, and that point marked the need for the extension of the genealogical net. But the conversion to Christianity also justified the sages' extending membership in the family to Rome, for Christian Rome shared with Israel the common patrimony of scripture—and said so. The character of the sages' thinking on Israel therefore proved remarkably congruent to the conditions of public discourse that confronted them.

THE METAPHOR OF THE FAMILY,
"ISRAEL'S CHILDREN"

When the fourth-century sages wished to know what (an) "Israel" was, they reread the scriptural story of "Israel's" origins for the answer. To begin with, as scripture told them the story, "Israel" was a man, Jacob, and his children were "the children of Jacob." That man's name was also "Israel," and, it followed, "the children of Israel" comprised the extended family of that man. By extension, "Israel" formed the family of Abraham and Sarah, Isaac and Rebecca, Jacob and Leah and Rachel. "Israel" therefore invoked the metaphor of genealogy to explain the bonds that linked persons unseen into a single social entity; the shared traits were imputed, not empirical. That social metaphor of "Israel"—a simple one and easily grasped—bore consequences in two ways.

First, children in general are admonished to follow the good example of their parents. The deeds of the patriarchs and matriarchs therefore taught lessons on how the children were to act. Of greater interest in an account of "Israel" as a social metaphor, "Israel" lived twice, once in the patriarchs and matriarchs, a second time in the life of the heirs as the descendants relived those earlier lives. The stories of the family were carefully reread to provide a picture of the meaning of the latter-day events of the descendants of that same family. Accordingly, the lives of the patriarchs signaled the history of Israel.

The polemical purpose of the claim that the abstraction, "Israel," was to be compared to the family of the mythic ancestor lies right at the surface. With another "Israel," the Christian Church, now claiming to constitute the true one, the sages found it possible to confront that claim and to turn it against the other side. "You claim to form 'Israel after the spirit.' Fine, and we are Israel after the flesh—and genealogy forms the link, that alone." (Converts did not present an anomaly since they were held to be children of Abraham and Sarah, who had "made souls," that is, converts, in Haran, a point repeated in the documents of the period.) That fleshly continuity formed of all of "us" a single family, rendering spurious the notion that "Israel" could be other than genealogically defined. But that polemic seems to me adventitious and not primary, for the metaphor provided a quite separate component to the sages' larger system.

The metaphor of Israel as family supplied an encompassing theory of society. It not only explained who "Israel" as a whole was but also set forth the responsibilities of Israel's social entity, its society. The metaphor defined the character of that entity; it explained who owes what to whom and why, and it accounted for the inner structure and interplay of relationship within the community, here and now, constituted by Jews in their villages and neighborhoods of towns. Accordingly, "Israel" as family bridged the gap between an account of the entirety of the social group, "Israel," and a picture of the components of that social group as they lived out their lives in their households and villages. An encompassing theory of society, covering all components from least to greatest, holding the whole together in correct order and proportion, derived from "Israel" viewed as extended family.

That theory of "Israel" as a society made up of persons who, because they constituted a family, stood in a clear relationship of obligation and responsibility to one another corresponded to what people much later would call the *social contract,* a kind of compact that in palpable ways told families and households how in the aggregate they formed something larger and tangible. The web of interaction spun out of concrete interchange now was formed not of the gossamer thread of abstraction and theory but by the tough hemp of family ties. "Israel" formed a society because "Israel" was compared to an extended family. That, sum and substance, supplied to the Jews in their households (themselves a made-up category which, in the end, transformed the relationship of the nuclear family into an abstraction capable of holding together quite unrelated persons) an account of the tie from household to household, from village to village, encompassing ultimately "all Israel."

The power of the metaphor of "Israel" as family hardly requires specification. If "we" form a family, then we know full well what links us, the common ancestry, the obligations imposed by common ancestry upon the cousins who make up the family today. The link between the commonplace interactions and relationships that make "us" into a community on one side and that encompassing entity, "Israel," "all Israel," on the other is now drawn. The large comprehends the little, the abstraction of "us" overall gains concrete reality in the "us" of the here and now of home and village, all together, all forming a "family." In that fundamental way, the metaphor of "Israel" as family therefore provided the field theory of "Israel" linking the most abstract component, the entirety of the social group, to the most mundane, the specificity of the household. One theory, framed in that metaphor of such surpassing simplicity, now held the whole together. That is how the metaphor of family provided an encompassing theory of society, an account of the social contract encompassing all social entities, Jews' and gentiles' as well, that no other metaphor accomplished.

"Israel" as family comes to expression in, among other writings of the fifth century, the document that makes the most sustained and systematic statement of the matter, Genesis Rabbah. In this theory we should not miss the extraordinary polemic utility, of which, in passing, we have already taken note. "Israel" as family also understood itself to form a nation or people. That nation-people held a land, a rather peculiar, enchanted or holy, Land, one that, in its imputed traits, was as *sui generis* as (presently we shall see) Israel also was in the metaphorical thought of the system. Competing for the same territory, Israel's claim to what it called the Land of Israel—thus, of Israel in particular—now rested on right of inheritance such as a family enjoyed, and this claim was made explicit. The following passage shows how high the stakes were in the claim to constitute the genealogical descendant of the ancestors.

Genesis Rabbah LXI:VII

"But to the sons of his concubines, Abraham gave gifts, and while he was still living, he sent them away from his son Isaac, eastward to the east country" (Gen. 25:6):

In the time of Alexander of Macedonia the sons of Ishmael came to dispute with Israel about the birthright, and with them came two wicked families, the Canaanites and the Egyptians.

They said, "Who will go and engage in a disputation with them."

Gebiah b. Qosem [the enchanter] said, "I shall go and engage in a disputation with them."

They said to him, "Be careful not to let the Land of Israel fall into their possession."

He said to them, "I shall go and engage in a disputation with them. If I win over them, well and good. And if not, you may say, 'Who is this hunchback to represent us?' "

He went and engaged in a disputation with them. Said to them Alexander of Macedonia, "Who lays claim against whom?"

The Ishmaelites said, "We lay claim, and we bring our evidence from their own Torah: 'But he shall acknowledge the first-born, the son of the hated' (Deut. 21;17). Now Ishmael was the first-born. [We therefore claim the land as heirs of the first-born of Abraham.]"

Said to him Gebiah b. Qosem, "My royal lord, does a man not do whatever he likes with his sons?"

He said to him, "Indeed so."

"And lo, it is written, 'Abraham gave all that he had to Isaac' (Gen. 25:2)."

[Alexander asked,] "Then where is the deed of gift to the other sons?"

He said to him, " 'But to the sons of his concubines, Abraham gave gifts, [and while he was still living, he sent them away from his son Isaac, eastward to the east country]' (Gen. 25:6)."

[The Ishmaelites had no claim on the land.] They abandoned the field in shame.

The metaphor as refined, with the notion of Israel today as the family of Abraham contrasted with the Ishmaelites, also of the same family, gives way. But the theme of family records persists. The power of the metaphor of family is that it can explain not only the social entity formed by Jews, but the social entities confronted by them. All fell into the same genus, making up diverse species. The theory of society before us thus accounts for all societies, and, as we shall see when we deal with Rome, it does so with extraordinary force. The passage continues:

The Canaanites said, "We lay claim, and we bring our evidence from their own Torah. Throughout their Torah it is written, 'the land of Canaan.' So let them give us back our land."

Said to him Gebiah b. Qosem, "My royal lord, does a man not do whatever he likes with his slave?"

He said to him, "Indeed so."

He said to him, "And lo, it is written, 'A slave of slaves shall Canaan be to his brothers' (Gen. 9:25). So they are really our slaves."

[The Canaanites had no claim to the land and in fact should be serving Israel.] They abandoned the field in shame.

The Egyptians said, "We lay claim, and we bring our evidence from their own Torah. Six hundred thousand of them left us, taking away our silver and gold utensils: 'They despoiled the Egyptians' (Ex. 12:36). Let them give them back to us."

Gebiah b. Qosem said, "My royal lord, six hundred thousand men worked for them for two hundred and ten years, some as silversmiths and some as goldsmiths. Let them pay us our salary at the rate of a denar a day."

The mathematicians went and added up what was owing, and they had not reached the sum covering a century before the Egyptians had to forfeit what they had claimed. They abandoned the field in shame.

[Alexander] wanted to go up to Jerusalem. The Samaritans said to him, "Be careful. They will not permit you to enter their most holy sanctuary."

When Gebiah b. Qosem found out about this, he went and made for himself two felt shoes, with two precious stones worth twenty-thousand pieces of silver set in them. When he got to the mountain of the house [of the Temple], he said to him, "My royal lord, take off your shoes and put on these two felt slippers, for the floor is slippery, and you should not slip and fall."

When they came to the most holy sanctuary, he said to him, "Up to this point, we have the right to enter. From this point onward, we do not have the right to enter."

He said to him, "When we get out of here, I'm going to even out your hump."

He said to him, "You will be called a great surgeon and get a big fee."

The same metaphor serves both "Israel" and "Canaan." Each formed the latter-day heir of the earliest family, and both lived out the original paradigm. The mode of thought imputes the same genus to both social entities, and then makes it possible to distinguish among the two species. We shall see the same mode of thought—the family, but which wing of the family—when we consider the confrontation with Christianity and with Rome, in each case conceived in the same personal way. The metaphor applies to both and yields its own meanings for each. The final claim in the passage before us moves away from the metaphor of family. But the notion of a continuous, physical descent is implicit here as well. "Israel" has inherited the wealth of Egypt.

ISRAEL AS GOD'S PEOPLE:
THE GENTILES' REJECTION OF GOD

The social entity, Israel, has therefore to be defined in its context: not-Israel/gentile. Our initial meeting with Judaism's master narrative of the human condition in Chapter 1 leads us to ask: How, in a single set of congruent stories, do the Rabbinic sages state their theory of Israel as God's people? The answer is in tales that show how the gentiles deprived themselves of the Torah because they rejected it. Showing the precision of justice, they rejected the Torah because the Torah deprived them of the very practices or traits that they deemed characteristic, essential to their being. That circularity marks the tale of how things were to begin with and in fact describes how things always are; it is not historical but philosophical. The gentiles' own character, the shape of their conscience, then, now, and always, accounts for their condition—which, by an act of will, as we have noted, they can change. What they did not want, that of which they were by their own word unworthy, is denied them. And what they do want condemns them. So when each nation comes under judgment for rejecting the Torah, the indictment of each is spoken out of its own mouth and its own self-indictment then forms the core of the matter. Given what we know about the definition of Israel as those destined to live and the gentile as those not, we cannot find surprising that the entire account is set in that age to come to which the gentiles are denied entry.

When they protest the injustice of the decision that takes effect just then, they are shown the workings of the moral order, as the following quite systematic account of the governing pattern explains:

Bavli Tractate Abodah Zarah 1:1 I.2/2–B

R. Hanina bar Pappa, and some say, R. Simlai, gave the following exposition [of the verse, "They that fashion a graven image are all of them vanity, and their delectable things shall not profit, and their own witnesses see not nor know" (Isa. 44:9)]: "In the age to come the Holy One, blessed be He, will bring a scroll of the Torah and hold it in his bosom and say, 'Let him who has kept himself busy with it come and take his reward.' Then all the gentiles will crowd together: 'All of the nations are gathered together' (Isa. 43:9). The Holy One, blessed be He, will say to them, 'Do not crowd together before me in a mob. But let each nation enter together with [2B] its scribes, 'and let the peoples be gathered together' (Isa. 43:9), and the word 'people' means 'kingdom': 'and one kingdom shall be stronger than the other' (Gen. 25:23)."

We note that the players are the principal participants in world history: the Romans first and foremost, then the Persians, the other world rulers of the age:

"The kingdom of Rome comes in first."

"The Holy One, blessed be He, will say to them, 'How have you defined your chief occupation?'

"They will say before him, 'Lord of the world, a vast number of marketplaces have we set up, a vast number of bathhouses we have made, a vast amount of silver and gold have we accumulated. And all of these things we have done only in behalf of Israel, so that they may define as their chief occupation the study of the Torah.'

"The Holy One, blessed be He, will say to them, 'You complete idiots! Whatever you have done has been for your own convenience. You have set up a vast number of marketplaces to be sure, but that was so as to set up whorehouses in them. The bathhouses were for your own pleasure. Silver and gold belong to me anyhow: "Mine is the silver and mine is the gold, says the Lord of hosts" (Hag. 2:8). Are there any among you who have been telling of "this," and "this" is only the Torah: "And this is the Torah that Moses set before the children of Israel' (Dt. 4:44)." So they will make their exit, humiliated.

The claim of Rome—to support Israel in Torah study—is rejected on grounds that the Romans did not exhibit the right attitude, always a dynamic force in the theology. Then the other world rule enters in with its claim:

> "When the kingdom of Rome has made its exit, the kingdom of Persia enters afterward."
>
> "The Holy One, blessed be He, will say to them, 'How have you defined your chief occupation?'
>
> "They will say before him, 'Lord of the world, we have thrown up a vast number of bridges, we have conquered a vast number of towns, we have made a vast number of wars, and all of them we did only for Israel, so that they may define as their chief occupation the study of the Torah.'
>
> "The Holy One, blessed be He, will say to them, 'Whatever you have done has been for your own convenience. You have thrown up a vast number of bridges, to collect tolls, you have conquered a vast number of towns, to collect the corvée, and, as to making a vast number of wars, I am the one who makes wars: "The Lord is a man of war" (Ex. 19:17). Are there any among you who have been telling of "this," and "this" is only the Torah: "And this is the Torah that Moses set before the children of Israel" (Dt. 4:44).' So they will make their exit, humiliated.
>
> "And so it will go with each and every nation."

As native categories, Rome and Persia are singled out, "all the other nations" play no role, for reasons with which we are already familiar. Once more the theology reaches into its deepest thought on the power of intentionality, showing that what people want is what they get.

But matters cannot be limited to the two world empires of the present age, Rome and Iran, standing in judgment at the end of time. The theology values balance, proportion, seeks complementary relationships, and therefore treats beginnings along with endings, the one going over the ground of the other. Accordingly, a recapitulation of the same event—the gentiles' rejection of the Torah—chooses as its setting not the last judgment but the first encounter, that is, the giving of the Torah itself. In the timeless world constructed by the Oral Torah, what happens at the outset exemplifies how things always happen, and what happens at the end embodies what has always taken place. The basic thesis is identical—the gentiles cannot accept the Torah because to do so they would have to deny their very character. But the exposition retains its interest because it takes its own course.

Now the gentiles are not just Rome and Persia but others; and of special interest, the Torah is embodied in some of the ten commandments—not to murder, not to commit adultery, not to steal. Then the gentiles are rejected for not keeping the seven commandments assigned to the children of Noah. The upshot is that the reason that the gentiles rejected the Torah is that the Torah prohibits deeds that the gentiles do by their very nature. The subtext here is already familiar from Chapter 3: Israel ultimately is changed by the Torah, so that Israel exhibits traits imparted by their encounter with the Torah. So, too, with the gentiles: By their nature they are what they are; the Torah has not changed their nature.

Once more a single standard applies to both components of humanity, but with opposite effect:

Sifré to Deuteronomy CCCXLIII:IV.1ff

Another teaching concerning the phrase, "He said, 'The Lord came from Sinai' ":

When the Omnipresent appeared to give the Torah to Israel, it was not to Israel alone that he revealed himself but to every nation.

First of all he came to the children of Esau. He said to them, "Will you accept the Torah?"

They said to him, "What is written in it?"

He said to them, " 'You shall not murder' (Ex. 20:13)."

They said to him, "The very being of 'those men' [namely, us] and of their father is to murder, for it is said, 'But the hands are the hands of Esau' (Gen. 27:22). 'By your sword you shall live' (Gen. 27:40)."

At this point we cover new ground: other classes of gentiles that reject the Torah. Now the Torah's own narrative takes over, replacing the known facts of world politics, such as the earlier account sets forth, and instead supplying evidence out of scripture about the character of the gentile group under discussion:

So he went to the children of Ammon and Moab and said to them, "Will you accept the Torah?"

They said to him, "What is written in it?"

He said to them, " 'You shall not commit adultery' (Ex. 20:13)."

They said to him, "The very essence of fornication belongs to them [us], for it is said, 'Thus were both the daughters of Lot with child by their fathers' (Gen. 19:36)."

So he went to the children of Ishmael and said to them, "Will you accept the Torah?"

They said to him, "What is written in it?"

He said to them, " 'You shall not steal' (Ex. 20:13)."

They said to him, "The very essence of their [our] father is thievery, as it is said, 'And he shall be a wild ass of a man' (Gen. 16:12)."

And so it went. He went to every nation, asking them, "Will you accept the Torah?"

For so it is said, "All the kings of the earth shall give you thanks, O Lord, for they have heard the words of your mouth" (Ps. 138:4).

Might one suppose that they listened and accepted the Torah?

Scripture says, "And I will execute vengeance in anger and fury upon the nations, because they did not listen" (Mic. 5:14).

At this point we turn back to the obligations that God has imposed upon the gentiles; these obligations have no bearing upon the acceptance of the Torah;

they form part of the ground of being, the condition of existence, of the gentiles. Yet even here, the gentiles do not accept God's authority in matters of natural law:

> And it is not enough for them that they did not listen, but even the seven religious duties that the children of Noah indeed accepted upon themselves they could not uphold before breaking them.
>
> When the Holy One, blessed be He, saw that that is how things were, he gave them to Israel.

The various gentile nations rejected the Torah for specific and reasonable considerations, concretely, because the Torah prohibited deeds essential to their being. This point is made in so many words, then amplified through a parable. Israel, by contrast, is prepared to give up life itself for the Torah.

The question becomes urgent: How has this catastrophic differentiation imposed itself between Israel and the gentiles, such that the gentiles, for all their glory in the here and now, won for themselves the grave, while Israel, for all its humiliation in the present age, inherits the world to come? And the answer is self-evident from all that has been said: The gentiles reject God, whom they could and should have known in the Torah. They rejected the Torah, and all else followed. The proposition then moves in these simple steps:

1. Israel differs from the gentiles because Israel possesses the Torah and the gentiles do not.
2. Because they do not possess the Torah, the gentiles also worship idols instead of God.
3. Therefore, God rejects the gentiles and identifies with Israel.

And where do considerations of justice and fairness enter in? Here, at a critical turning, the system reaches back into its fundamental and generative conception, that the world is ordered by justice. So the same justice that governs Israel and endows Israel with the Torah dictates the fate of the gentiles and denies them the Torah. And, predictably, that demonstration further underscores the justice of the condition of the gentiles: Measure for measure must play itself out especially here, as in Mishnah Tractate Sotah:

Mishnah-Tractate Sotah 1:7–9, poss.

By that same measure by which a man metes out [to others], they mete out to him:

> Absalom was proud of his hair, therefore, he was hung by his hair [2 Sam. 14:25–26].

And so is it on the good side:

> Miriam waited a while for Moses, since it is said, And his sister stood afar off (Ex. 2:4), therefore, Israel waited on her seven days in the wilderness, since it is said, "And the people did not travel on until Miriam was brought in again" (Num. 12:15).

PART IV

࿓

Classical Judaism:
The Torah's Theology

11

Hear, O Israel: The Unity of God

DISCERNING THE THEOLOGY OF JUDAISM
THROUGH THE PRAYERS PEOPLE SAY

A religious tradition that finds its primary mode of discourse in narrative can be expected to refer back to the master narrative at every critical juncture. The story will permeate the system. That is shown, for Judaism, in the character of its life of prayer, meaning, occasions for the community to engage in direct address to God as a "you"; in words of praise, supplication, and, in the case of Judaism above all, recapitulation: reminding the "you" of God in direct address of who is speaking and on what foundations. People at prayer make real in their conversation with God the theology that animates their system, that transforms convictions of the worldview into a system, imparts coherence to the details of religious activity that constitute the way of life, and sustains the corporate existence of their community.

Working backward from the language of the liturgy of public worship in Judaism, we seek to find the theology that transforms into principles and propositions the implicit meanings of the stories that define Judaism, stories of creation and Adam and Eve, Israel redeemed from Egyptian slavery, Sinai and the giving of the Torah, the Land, loss and restoration—that master narrative of the human condition in its Israelite version. So we move from liturgy to theology, all the time rehearsing the main themes of the narrative.

To appreciate the power of Judaic liturgy, we have to envisage a gathering of people praying silently, yet in community. Judaic worship generally involves all participants repeating all the prayers, ordinarily individually, in low voices, and part of the time together, in loud voices. The upshot is that everybody says nearly everything and since much of the liturgy rehearses theology in the language of dialogue with God, what that means is that a group of people gather together to speak each one alone yet all together to God: a community formed by prayer.

There are three main parts to Judaic worship: (1) the proclamation of the Unity of God, "Hear O Israel, the Lord our God, the Lord is One," which, fully articulated, declares the principal theological convictions of Judaism concerning creation, revelation, and redemption; (2) the Prayer, recited standing (therefore called "the Amidah," or Standing Prayer, that is, the supplications, in the form of blessings, on weekdays eighteen of them (therefore called the *Shemoneh esré*, or eighteen); and (3) a declaration of conclusion, identifying the hope of the community for the future conversion of all humanity to the worship of the one, unique God who made himself known to Israel in the Torah, called, after its opening sentence, *Alenu* ("It is incumbent on us to praise the Lord of all, to magnify to the Creator…"). In this chapter we meet the *Shema,* in Chapter 16 the Prayer/*Amidah,* and in Chapter 13 the *Alenu* prayer.

THE BLESSINGS BEFORE THE DECLARATION OF THE FAITH IN THE UNITY OF GOD: CREATION

Evening and morning, the pious Jew proclaims the unity and uniqueness of God. The proclamation is preceded and followed by blessings. The whole constitutes the theological credo of the Judaic tradition, expounding the themes of Creation, Revelation, and Redemption.

The recital of the *Shema* is introduced by a celebration of God as Creator of the world. In the morning one says,

> Praised are You, O Lord our God, King of the universe.
>
> You fix the cycles of light and darkness;
>
> You ordain the order of all creation
>
> You cause light to shine over the earth;
>
> Your radiant mercy is upon its inhabitants.
>
> In Your goodness the work of creation
>
> Is continually renewed day by day. …
>
> O cause a new light to shine on Zion;
>
> May we all soon be worthy to behold its radiance.
>
> Praised are You, O Lord, Creator of the heavenly bodies.[1]

The corresponding prayer in the evening refers to the setting of the sun:

> Praised are You. …
>
> Your command brings on the dusk of evening.
>
> Your wisdom opens the gates of heaven to a new day.
>
> With understanding You order the cycles of time;
>
> Your will determines the succession of seasons;
>
> You order the stars in their heavenly courses.
>
> You create day, and You create night,
>
> Rolling away light before darkness. …
>
> Praised are You, O Lord, for the evening dusk.[2]

---

[1]Reprinted by permission of the *Weekday Prayer Book,* edited by Gerson Hadas, © the Rabbinical Assembly, 1962, p. 42.
[2]Ibid., p. 141.

Morning and evening, the faithful Israelite responds to the natural order of the world with thanks and praise of God who created the world and who actively guides the daily events of nature. Whatever happens in nature gives testimony to the sovereignty of the Creator. And that testimony is not in unnatural disasters, but in the most ordinary events: sunrise and sunset. These, especially, evoke the religious response to set the stage for what follows.

THE BLESSINGS BEFORE THE DECLARATION OF THE FAITH IN THE UNITY OF GOD: REVELATION

For the faithful Israelite God is not merely Creator, but purposeful Creator. The works of creation serve to justify and to testify to the Torah, the revelation of Sinai. The Torah is the mark not merely of divine sovereignty, but of divine grace and love, source of life here and now and in eternity. So goes the second blessing:

> Deep is Your love for us, O Lord our God;
>
> Bounteous is Your compassion and tenderness.
>
> You taught our fathers the laws of life,
>
> And they trusted in You, Father and king,
>
> For their sake be gracious to us, and teach us,
>
> That we may learn Your laws and trust in You.
>
> Father, merciful Father, have compassion upon us:
>
> Endow us with discernment and understanding.
>
> Grant us the will to study Your Torah,
>
> To heed its words and to teach its precepts. ...
>
> Enlighten our eyes in Your Torah,
>
> Open our hearts to Your commandments. ...
>
> Unite our thoughts with singleness of purpose
>
> To hold You in reverence and in love. ...
>
> You have drawn us close to You;
>
> We praise You and thank You in truth.
>
> With love do we thankfully proclaim Your unity.
>
> And praise You who chose Your people Israel in love.[3]

Here is the way in which revelation takes concrete and specific form in the Judaic tradition: God, the Creator, revealed his will for creation through the Torah, given to Israel his people. That the Torah contains the "laws of life."

---

[3]Ibid., pp. 45–56.

The faithful Israelite, moved to worship by the daily miracle of sunrise and sunset, responds with the prayer that he or she, like nature, may enjoy divine compassion. But of what does that compassion consist? The ability to understand and the will to study the *Torah!* This is the mark of the relationship between God and the human being—the faithful Israelite in particular: that a person's eyes are open to the Torah and his or her heart is open to the commandments. These are the means of divine service and of reverence and love for God. Israel sees itself as "chosen"—close to God—because of the Torah, and it finds in its devotion to the Torah the marks of its chosenness. The covenant made at Sinai—a contract on Israel's side to do and hear the Torah; on God's side, to be the God of Israel—is evoked by natural events and then confirmed by the deeds and devotion of men.

"HEAR O ISRAEL, THE LORD OUR GOD, THE LORD IS ONE"

In the *Shema,* the Torah—revelation—leads Jews to enunciate the chief teaching of revelation:

> *Hear, O Israel, the Lord Our God, the Lord is One.*

This declaration represents accepting the yoke of the Kingdom of God upon oneself. A benediction follows:

> *Blessed be the Name of his glorious Kingdom forever and ever.*

This declaration represents accepting the yoke of the commandments, the resolve to carry out religious obligations of commission and omission. So in reciting the *Shema,* the Israelite enters the kingdom of God and accepts God's rule on earth, in everyday life.

This proclamation, by which the pious person enters the dominion of God and in attitude and action accepts God's rule, is followed by three Scriptural passages. The first is Deuteronomy 6:5–9:

> *You shall love the Lord your God with all your heart, with all your soul, with all your might.*

And further, one must diligently teach one's children these words and talk of them everywhere and always, and place them on one's forehead, doorposts, and gates.

The second set of verses of scripture is Deuteronomy 11:13–21, which emphasizes that if Jews keep the commandments, they will enjoy worldly blessings; but that if they do not, they will be punished and disappear from the good land God gives them.

The third is Numbers 15:37–41, the commandment to wear fringes on the corners of one's garments. The fringes are today attached to the prayer shawl worn at morning services by Conservative and Reform Jews, and worn on a separate undergarment for that purpose by Orthodox Jews, and they remind the faithful Israelite of *all* the commandments of the Lord.

THE BLESSING AFTER THE DECLARATION OF THE FAITH IN THE UNITY OF GOD: REDEMPTION

The proclamation is completed and yet remains open, for having created humanity and revealed his will, God is not unaware of events since Sinai. Humanity is frail, and in the contest between the word of God and the will of humanity, the Torah is not always the victor. We inevitably fall short of what is asked of us and Jews know that their own history consists of divine punishment for human failure time and again. The theme of redemption, therefore, is introduced.

Redemption—in addition to creation and revelation, the third element in the tripartite worldview—resolves the tension between what we are told to do and what we are able actually to accomplish. In the end it is the theme of God, not as Creator or Revealer, but God as Redeemer that concludes the twice-daily drama:

> You are our King and our father's King,
>
> Our redeemer and our father's redeemer.
>
> You are our creator. . . .
>
> You have ever been our redeemer and deliverer
>
> There can be no God but You. . . .
>
> You, O Lord our God, rescued us from Egypt;
>
> You redeemed us from the house of bondage. . . .
>
> You split apart the waters of the Red Sea,
>
> The faithful you rescued, the wicked drowned. . . .
>
> Then Your beloved sang hymns of thanksgiving. . . .
>
> They acclaimed the King, God on high,
>
> Great and awesome source of all blessings,
>
> The ever-living God, exalted in his majesty.
>
> He humbles the proud and raises the lowly;
>
> He helps the needy and answers His people's call. . . .
>
> Then Moses and all the children of Israel
>
> Sang with great joy this song to the Lord:
>
> Who is like You O Lord among the mighty?
>
> Who is like You, so glorious in holiness?

> So wondrous your deeds, so worthy of praise!
>
> The redeemed sang a new song to You;
>
> They sang in chorus at the shore of the sea,
>
> Acclaiming Your sovereignty with thanksgiving:
>
> The Lord shall reign for ever and ever.
>
> Rock of Israel, arise to Israel's defense!
>
> Fulfill Your promise to deliver Judah and Israel.
>
> Our redeemer is the Holy One of Israel,
>
> The Lord of hosts is His name.
>
> Praised are You, O Lord, redeemer of Israel.[4]

Redemption is both in the past and in the future. That God not only creates but also redeems is attested by the redemption from Egyptian bondage. The congregation repeats the exultant song of Moses and the people at the Red Sea, not as scholars making a learned allusion, but as participants in a narrative drama, one that concerns the story of the salvation of old and of time to come. Then the people turn to the future and ask that Israel once more be redeemed.

But redemption is not only past and future. When the needy are helped, when the proud are humbled and the lowly are raised—in such commonplace, daily events redemption is already present: God's will is realized. Just as creation is not only in the beginning but happens every day, morning and night, so redemption is not only at the Red Sea, but every day, in humble events. Just as revelation was not at Sinai alone but takes place whenever people study the Torah, whenever God opens their hearts to the commandments, so redemption and creation are daily events.

STORY, THEOLOGY, AND LITURGY

The story is told and retold, the same events recapitulated and imposing their pattern on this-worldly actions and experiences and events. Sunset, sunrise—these reenact the moment of creation. The great cosmic events of creation in the beginning, redemption at the Red Sea, and revelation at Sinai—these are everywhere, every day near at hand. The faithful Israelite views secular reality under the aspect of eternal, ever-recurrent events. What happens to the faithful Israelite and to the world, whether good or evil, falls into the pattern revealed of old and made manifest each day. The master narrative reveals the pattern, each day recapitulates its story when the Israelite accepts God's will with love. Creation, revelation, redemption—these already-realized events of the scriptural account of humanity produce a framework in which future events will find a place and by which they will be understood. Nothing that happens falls outside the paradigm.

---

[4]Ibid., pp. 50*ff.*

Before us is no random selection of scriptural narratives; those left out are many more than those selected but constantly rehearsed. The stories of creation, of the Exodus from Egypt, and of the revelation of the Torah at Sinai are repeated, not merely to tell the story of what once was and is no more. They are renewed to re-create out of the raw materials of everyday life the "true being"—life as it was, always is, and will be forever. At prayer the faithful Israelite repeatedly refers to the crucial elements of his or her narrative being, thus uncovering the sacred both in nature and in history. What happens in the proclamation of the *Shema* is story and nature are made to correspond. The particular and routine events of creation—sunset, sunrise—evoke in response the celebration of the power and the love of God, of his justice and mercy, and of revelation and redemption.

12

Coming Together: The Sanctity
of the Family

THE MASTER NARRATIVE AND THE
INDIVIDUAL'S PERSONAL STORY

How does the individual Israelite fit into the storytelling paradigm that defines Judaism? The community at prayer tells itself the story of Creation, Revelation, and Redemption. But if, as Father Greeley says, "Religion is story," then we must wonder, where in the setting of individual life the everyday affairs of the private person, does the master narrative of Israel define matters? How does the story of Adam and Israel transform the individual and his or her private life?

We turn to the most personal of all transactions, the union of husband and wife to form a family, for the answer to that question. Here, as we shall see, the narrative of Adam and Eve figures—but also the story of destruction and exile, the restoration and return to Paradise. It is difficult to imagine a more incongruous, but more logical, transformation of the everyday and the private into the theological and the public: bride and groom stand for Adam and Eve, but also their rejoicing in one another prefigures the joy of the coming redemption when Israel and the Land embrace as well. That is what takes place under the Huppah, or marriage canopy, that stands for the vault of Heaven at the creation and forms the wedding bower of Adam and Eve.

DISCERNING THE NARRATIVE
OF JUDAISM THROUGH THE
MARRIAGE LITURGY UNDER THE
HUPPAH OR WEDDING CANOPY

For the faithful Israelite the most intimate occasion—the marriage ceremony—is also intrinsically public. Here a new family in Israel begins, a household that forms the building block of the Israelite society. So when individual lover and beloved celebrate the uniqueness, the privacy of their love, they turn out to embody, to act out the very creation of the world and, as we shall see, also the restoration of Paradise in Zion. One should, therefore, expect the nuptial prayer to speak of him and her, natural man and natural woman. Yet the blessings that are said over the cup of wine of sanctification redefine the transaction in a fundamental way, by invoking two chapters of the master narrative we met in Chapter 1:

> Praised are You, O Lord our God, King of the universe, Creator of the fruit of the vine.
>
> Praised are You, O Lord our God, King of the universe, who created all things for Your glory.
>
> Praised are You, O Lord our God, King of the universe, Creator of Adam.
>
> Praised are You, O Lord our God, King of the universe, who created man and woman in his image, fashioning woman from man as his mate, that together they might perpetuate life. Praised are You, O Lord, Creator of man.
>
> May Zion rejoice as her children are restored to her in joy. Praised are You, O Lord, who causes Zion to rejoice at her children's return.
>
> Grant perfect joy to these loving companions, as You did to the first man and woman in the Garden of Eden. Praised are You, O Lord, who grants the joy of bride and groom.
>
> Praised are You, O Lord our God, King of the universe, who created joy and gladness, bride and groom, mirth, song, delight and rejoicing, love and harmony, peace and companionship. O Lord our God, may there ever be heard in the cities of Judah and in the streets of Jerusalem voices of joy and gladness, voices of bride and groom, the jubilant voices of those joined in marriage under the bridal canopy, the voices of young people feasting and signing. Praised are You, O Lord, who causes the groom to rejoice with his bride.[1]

These seven blessings say nothing of private people and of their anonymously falling in love. Nor do they speak of the community of Israel, as one might expect on a public occasion. The blessings speak of archetypal Israel, represented here and now by the bride and groom.

Israel's history begins with creation—first, the creation of the vine, symbol of the natural world. Creation is for God's glory. All things speak to nature, to the physical as much as the spiritual, for all things were made by God. In Hebrew, the blessings end, "who formed the *Adam*." All things glorify God; above all creation is Adam. The theme of ancient paradise is introduced by the simple choice of the word *Adam,* so heavy with meaning. The story of man's creation is rehearsed: Man and woman are in God's image, together complete and whole, creators of life, "life God." Woman was fashioned from man together with him to perpetuate life. And again, "blessed is the creator of Adam." We have moved, therefore, from the natural world to the realm of paradise. Before us we see not

[1]Reprinted by permission of *A Rabbi's Manual*, ed. by Jules Harlow, © The Rabbinical Assembly, 1965, p. 45.

merely a man and a woman, but Adam and Eve, once more from personal to communal, from private to paradigmatic.

But this Adam and this Eve also are Israel, children of Zion the mother, as expressed in the fifth blessing. Zion lies in ruins, her children scattered, as Psalm 137 states:

If I forget you, O Jerusalem, may my right hand forget its skill. . . . if I do not place Jerusalem above my greatest joy.

Adam and Eve cannot celebrate together without thought to the condition of the mother, Jerusalem. The children will one day come home. The mood is hopeful yet sad, as it was meant to be, for archaic Israel mourns as it rejoices and rejoices as it mourns. Quickly, then, back to the happy occasion, for we do not let mourning lead to melancholy: "Grant perfect joy to the loving companions," for they are creators of a new line in mankind—the new Adam, the new Eve— and their home: May it be the garden of Eden. And if joy is there, then "praised are you for the joy of bride and groom."

BRIDE AND GROOM, ISRAEL AND THE LAND

The concluding blessing returns to the theme of Jerusalem. This time it evokes the tragic hour of Jerusalem's first destruction. When everyone had given up hope, supposing with the end of Jerusalem had come the end of time, only Jeremiah counseled renewed hope. With the enemy at the gate, he sang of coming gladness:

Thus says the Lord:

In this place of which you say, "It is a waste, without man or beast," in the cities of Judah and the streets of Jerusalem that are desolate, without man or inhabitant or beast,

There shall be heard again the voice of mirth and the voice of gladness, the voice of the bridegroom and the voice of the bride, the voice of those who sing as they bring thank-offerings to the house of the Lord. . . .

For I shall restore the fortunes of the land as at first, says the Lord.
JEREMIAH 33:10–11

The closing blessing is not merely a literary artifice or a learned allusion to the ancient prophet. It is rather the exultant, jubilant climax of this acted-out story: Just as here and now there stand before us Adam and Eve, so here and now in this wedding, the olden sorrow having been rehearsed, we listen to the voice of gladness that is coming. The joy of this new creation prefigures the joy of the Messiah's coming, hope for which is very present in this hour. And when he comes, the joy then will echo the joy of bride and groom before us. Zion the bride, Israel the groom, united now as they will be reunited by the compassionate God—these stand under the marriage canopy.

What is striking is how the theme of Eden and loss, Land of Israel and exile, is reworked into a new pattern: from the loneliness and exile of the single life to the Eden and Jerusalem of the wedding canopy. The theme of exile and return is recapitulated, but now with the message that the joy of the bride and groom—standing, after all, for Israel and God—a foretaste of what is coming. Here the narrative life surfaces, rising above doctrines about Israel and Redemption. The personal and the public join, the individuals before us embody and reenact the entirety of Israel's holy life, past to future.

THE ACTED-OUT THEOLOGY OF HISTORY

In classical Judaism, who are Jewish men and women? They are ordinary people who live within a narrative structure that transcends and transforms their private being, and who thereby hold a view of history centered upon Israel from the creation of the world to its final redemption. Political defeats of this world are transformed by paradigmatic narrative into eternal sorrow. The natural events of human life—here, the marriage of ordinary folk—are by narrative heightened into a reenactment of Israel's life as a people. In marriage, individuals stand in the place of narrative figures yet remain, after all, scarcely a few years ago mere boys and girls. What gives their love its true meaning is the story of creation, revelation, and redemption, here and now embodied in that love. But in the end, the sacred and secular are in most profane, physical love united.[2]

The wedding of symbol and reality—the fusion and confusion of the two—these mark the classical Judaic experience shaped by stories of creation, of Adam and Eve, of the Garden of Eden, and by the historical memory of the this-worldly destruction of an old, unexceptional temple. Ordinary events, such as a political and military defeat or success, are changed into theological categories such as divine punishment and heavenly compassion. If religion is a means of ultimate transformation, rendering the commonplace into the paradigmatic, changing the here and now into a moment of eternity and of eternal return, then the marriage liturgy serves to exemplify what is *religious* in Judaic existence.

---

[2]I must stress that the marriage ceremony includes provision for bride and groom to consummate their marriage with sexual intercourse while left in private for an appropriate period. Nowadays the privacy is brief and symbolic, to be sure.

13

Going Forth:

Israel, the Holy People and God's First Love

THE POWER OF THE STORY
TO TRANSFORM

When we ask liturgy to define theology, in the case of Judaism we turn to two separate occasions of public worship and celebration to tell us who and what is the "Israel" of liturgical theology? The first is the Passover Narrative, the second the prayer recited at the end of public worship. The one defines Israel on its own; the other, Israel in relationship to the nations. Here, then, we go back over what we know about Israel in its own terms and Israel versus the nations, only in the language of prayer.

At the festival of Passover, in the spring, Jewish families gather around their tables for a holy meal. The secular eye sees a family gathering, a formal banquet. But the rite of the occasion, the Passover Seder or Order of Rite and Ritual, transforms the moment, and the family passes into history and declares itself the here-and-now embodiment of the story of the Exodus from Egypt. No more dramatic, explicit moment of transformation and renewal through narrative presents itself in the holy life of Judaism than the Passover Seder, which changes the secular into the sacred and turns the family into Israel.

THE STORY OF PASSOVER, KEY CHAPTER
IN JUDAISM'S MASTER NARRATIVE

The Israelite family retells the story of the Exodus from Egypt in times long past. With unleavened bread and sanctified wine, they celebrate the liberation of slaves from Pharaoh's bondage. How do they see themselves? These words, from the *Haggadah,* or Narrative, of Passover answer the question:

> We were the slaves of Pharaoh in Egypt; and the Lord our God brought us forth from there with a mightily hand and an outstretched arm. And if the Holy One, blessed be He, had not brought our fathers forth from Egypt, then surely we, and our children, and our children's children, would be enslaved to Pharaoh in Egypt. And so, even if all of us were full of wisdom and understanding, well along in years and deeply versed in the tradition,

we should still be bidden to repeat once more the story of the exodus from Egypt; and he who delights to dwell on the liberation is a man to be praised.[1]

Through the natural eye one sees ordinary folk, not much different from their neighbors in dress, language, or aspirations. The words they speak do not describe reality and are not meant to. When Israelites say of themselves, "We were the slaves of Pharaoh in Egypt," they know they never felt the lash; but through the eye of faith that is just what they have done. It is *their* liberation, not merely that of long-dead forebears, an event of this morning, not of three millennia ago, that they now celebrate.

To be an Israelite means to be a slave who has been liberated by God. To be Israel means to give eternal thanks for God's deliverance. And that deliverance is not at a single moment in historical time. It comes in every generation and is always celebrated. Here again, events of natural, ordinary life are transformed through story into paradigmatic, eternal, and ever-recurrent sacred moments. Israelites think of themselves as having gone forth from Egypt, and scripture so instructs them. God did not redeem the dead generation of the Exodus alone, but the living too—especially the living. Thus the family states:

> Again and again, in double and redoubled measure, are we beholden to God the All-Present: that He freed us from the Egyptians and wrought His judgment on them; that He sentenced all their idols and slaughtered all their first-born; that He gave their treasure to us and split the Red Sea for us; that He led us through it dry-shod and drowned the tyrants in it; that He helped us through the desert and fed us with the manna; that He gave the Sabbath to us and brought us to Mount Sinai; that He gave the Torah to us and brought us to our homeland—there to build the Temple for us, for atonement of our sins.[2]
>
> This is the promise which has stood by our forefathers and stands by us. For neither once, nor twice, nor three times was our destruction planned; in every generation they rise against us, and in every generation God delivers us from their hands into freedom, out of anguish into joy, out of mourning into festivity, out of darkness into light, out of bondage into redemption.[3]
>
> For ever after, in every generation, *every Israelite must think of himself or herself as having gone forth from Egypt* [italics added]. For we read in the Torah: "In that day thou shalt teach thy son, saying: All this is because of what God did for me when I went forth from Egypt." It was not only our forefathers that the Holy One, blessed be He, redeemed; us too, the living, He redeemed together with them, as we learn from the verse in

---

[1]Maurice Samuel, trans., *Haggadah of Passover* (New York: Hebrew Publishing Co., 1942), p. 9. Reprinted with permission.

[2]Ibid., p. 26.

[3]Ibid., p. 13.

the Torah: "And He brought us out from thence, so that He might bring us home, and give us the land which he pledged to our forefathers."[4]

The this-worldly people, Israel, was born in historical times. Historians, biblical scholars, and archaeologists have much to say about that event; some archaeologists and biblical historians even call into question whether these events ever "really" happened. To the Judaic faithful, they happened, really and literally, and they happen ever year in rites of transformation and renewal, literally and really: in history, in eternity.

To what is alleged in scripture and in liturgy, to the theology of Judaism, the historical question as framed by some contemporary archaeology is monumentally irrelevant, the kinds of evidence that would validate or disprove the allegations of the faith, is utterly and totally beside the point. What kind of stone serve, in attesting to the Creator's intervention into time and redemption of Israel from Egyptian slavery? What material evidence would God have had to leave behind? The redemptive promise that stood by the forefathers and "stands by us" is not a mundane historical event, though the faithful insist upon at least its historicity, but a theological interpretation of historical, natural events. Oppression, homelessness, extermination—like salvation, homecoming, renaissance—are this-worldly and profane, supplying headlines for newspapers. The story that an Israelite must think of himself or herself as having gone forth from Egypt and as being redeemed by God renders ordinary experience into a moment of celebration. If "us, too, the living, He [has] redeemed," then the observer no longer witnesses only historical men in historical time, but an eternal return to sacred time.

THE THRICE-DAILY EXODUS:
ISRAEL INTO THE EVERYDAY WORLD

The "going forth" at Passover is one sort of Exodus. Another comes morning and night when Israelites complete their service of worship and turn from holy assembly to secular pursuits. Every synagogue service concludes with a prayer prior to going forth, called *Alenu,* from its first word in Hebrew. Like the Exodus, the moment of the congregation's departure becomes a celebration of Israel's God, a self-conscious, explicitly articulated rehearsal of Israel's election into peoplehood. But now it is the end rather than the beginning of time that is important. When Israel celebrates its beginnings, it looks backward, to the redemption from Egypt; when Israelites prepare to reengage with the world at large, when the Israelites go forth, they look forward, to the end of days:

Let us praise Him, Lord over all the world;

Let us acclaim Him, Author of all creation.

---

[4]Ibid., p. 27.

He made our lot unlike that of other peoples;

He assigned to us a unique destiny.

We bend the knee, worship, and acknowledge

The King of kings, the Holy One, praised is He.

He unrolled the heavens and established the earth;

His throne of glory is in the heavens above;

His majestic Presence is in the loftiest heights.

He and no other is God and faithful King,

Even as we are told in His Torah:

Remember now and always, that the Lord is God;

Remember, no other is Lord of heaven and earth.

We, therefore, hope in You, O Lord our God,

That we shall soon see the triumph of Your might,

That idolatry shall be removed from the earth,

And false gods shall be utterly destroyed.

Then will the world be a true kingdom of God,

When all mankind will invoke Your name,

And all the earth's wicked will return to You.

Then all the inhabitants of the world will surely know

That to You every knee must bend,

Every tongue must pledge loyalty.

Before You, O Lord, let them bow in worship,

Let them give honor to Your glory.

May they all accept the rule of Your kingdom.

May You reign over them soon through all time.

Sovereignty is Yours in glory, now and forever.

So it is written in Your Torah:

The Lord shall reign for ever and ever.[5]

In secular terms Israelites know that in some ways they form a separate, distinct group. In narrative reality they thank God they enjoy a unique destiny. They do not conclude with thanks for their particular "being" but sing a hymn of hope merely that He who made their lot unlike that of all others will soon rule as sovereign over all. The secular difference, the unique destiny, is for the time being only. When the destiny is fulfilled, there will be no further difference. The natural eye beholds a social group with some particular cultural characteristics

---

[5]*Weekday Prayer Book,* ed. the Rabbinical Assembly of America Prayerbook Committee, Rabbi Jules Harlow, Secretary (New York: The Rabbinical Assembly, 1962), pp. 97–98.

defining that group. But in the perspective of the Torah, that is not how things are to be seen. Rather, "we, ourselves, personally, were slaves, whom God—and no intermediary—has redeemed, personally." The story told by the Torah transforms *difference* into *destiny*.

ISRAEL IN THE WORLD: "WE, THEREFORE, HOPE IN YOU, O LORD OUR GOD, THAT IDOLATRY SHALL BE REMOVED FROM THE EARTH, AND FALSE GODS SHALL BE UTTERLY DESTROYED"

The existence of the natural group means little, except as testimony to the sovereignty of the God who shaped the group and rules its life. The unique, the particular, the private now are no longer profane matters of culture, but facts that embody and illustrate the sacred order. They become testimonies of divine sovereignty, pertinent to all people, all groups. The particularism of the groups—Israel, the nations—is for the moment alone; the will of God is for eternity. When that will be done, then all people will recognize that the unique destiny of Israel was intended for everyone. The ordinary facts of sociology no longer predominate. The narrative of Israel has changed the secular and commonplace into a paradigm of true being.

14

The Holy Land and Jerusalem in the Age to Come

FROM HUNGER TO SATIETY AND THE THEOLOGY OF RESTORATION

No chapter in the story that Judaism tells so dominates as the one that compares Adam to Israel, Eden to the Land, the loss of the one to the loss of the other. Had Israel not sinned after entering the Promised Land, for Israel history would have ended—that is the Rabbinic sages' view. But, sages explain, because of sins of various kinds, such as are narrated in the books of Joshua, Judges, Samuel, Kings, and the prophetic writings Isaiah, Jeremiah, Ezekiel, and the Twelve Minor Prophets, Israel lost the Land and went into exile. So the Sabbath Prayerbook states, "On account of our sins we have gone into exile from our Land."

We now realize that the power of the Torah lies in its ability to transform this-worldly experiences into realizations in the here and now, reenactments, of theological convictions. In that way the way of life matches the worldview, the theology explains the religious activity, the sacred takes over and transforms the secular. No more concrete example of the capacity of the Torah's narrative to encompass the personal and the private is required than the rite under the *huppah,* or wedding canopy, that we met in Chapter 12. That leads us to ask what corresponding activity embodies in the here and now the theology of the restoration to the Land in the end of days? What human experience is available to render concrete the narrative of renewal, of salvation?

THE LAND OF ISRAEL, JERUSALEM— AND DAY-TO-DAY NOURISHMENT

The answer is, the experience of hunger followed by the eating of a meal. At the end of any meal at which bread is eaten, the Grace After Meals takes what has happened—people were hungry, so they ate bread—and in that context treats God's provision of nourishment as a foretaste of the recovery of the Land and the restoration of Zion. A meal is a this-worldly experience of salvation, redemption in the end of days.

In fact, as we have observed time and again, the great theological constructions, Creation, Revelation, Redemption, are woven together in the response
to eating a meal. How do the several salvific symbols fit together in the larger
narrative structure of creation, revelation, and redemption? In the Grace After
Meals, recited whenever pious Jews eat bread, we see their interplay. To understand the setting, we must recall that in classical Judaism the table at which meals
were eaten was regarded as the equivalent of the sacred altar in the Temple. Judaism taught that each Jew before eating had to attain the same state of ritual
purity as the priest in the sacred act of making a sacrifice. So in the classic tradition the Grace After Meals is recited in a sacerdotal circumstance.

On Sabbaths and festivals—moments of eternity in time—Jews first sing
Psalm 126: *When the Lord brought back those that returned to Zion, we were like
dreamers. Our mouth was filled with laughter, our tongue with singing. Restore our
fortunes, O Lord, as the streams in the dry Land. They that sow in tears shall reap in
joy* . . . It would be hard to miss the point: The meal is now treated as the realization in the here and now of the restoration to the Land. Then comes the
recitation of the Grace after Meals. It follows the outline: Thanks for the food
itself, thanks for the land that produces the food, supplication for restoration
of Israel to the Land, the rebuilding of Jerusalem and the renewal of the Temple offerings of atonement.

> Blessed art Thou, Lord our God, King of the Universe, who nourishes all
> the world by His goodness, in grace, in mercy, and in compassion: He
> gives bread to all flesh, for His mercy is everlasting. And because of His
> great goodness we have never lacked, and so may we never lack, suste-
> nance—for the sake of His great Name. For He nourishes and feeds
> everyone, is good to all, and provides food for each one of the creatures
> He created.
>
> Blessed art Thou, O Lord, who feeds everyone.
>
> We thank Thee, Lord our God, for having given our fathers as a
> heritage a pleasant, a good and spacious Land; for having taken us out of
> the Land of Egypt, for having redeemed us from the house of bondage;
> for Thy covenant, which Thou hast set as a seal in our flesh, for Thy Torah
> which Thou has taught us, for Thy statutes which Thou hast made known
> to us, for the life of grace and mercy Thou hast graciously bestowed upon
> us, and for the nourishment with which Thou dost nourish us and feed us
> always, every day, in every season, and every hour.
>
> For all these things, Lord our God, we thank and praise Thee; may Thy
> praises continually be in the mouth of every living thing, as it is written.
> And thou shalt eat and be satisfied, and bless the Lord thy God for the
> good Land which He hath given thee.
>
> Blessed art Thou, O Lord, for the Land and its food.
>
> O Lord our God, have pity on Thy people Israel, on Thy city
> Jerusalem, on Zion the place of Thy glory, on the royal house of David
> Thy Messiah, and on the great and holy house which is called by Thy
> Name. Our God, our Father, feed us and speed us, nourish us and make

us flourish, unstintingly, O Lord our God, speedily free us from all distress.

And let us not, O Lord our God, find ourselves in need of gifts from flesh and blood, or of a loan from anyone save from Thy full, generous, abundant, wide-open hand; so we may never be humiliated, or put to shame.

O rebuild Jerusalem, the holy city, speedily in our day. Blessed art Thou, Lord, who in mercy will rebuild Jerusalem. Amen.

Blessed art Thou, Lord our God, King of the Universe, Thou God, who art our Father, our powerful king, our creator and redeemer, who made us, our holy one, the holy one of Jacob, our shepherd, shepherd of Israel, the good king, who visits His goodness upon all; for every single day He has brought good, He does bring good, He will bring good upon us; He has rewarded us, does regard, and will always reward us, with grace, mercy and compassion, amplitude, deliverance and prosperity, blessing and salvation, comfort, and a living, sustenance, pity and peace, and all good—let us not want any manner of good whatever.[1]

The context of grace is enjoyment of creation, through which God nourishes the world in his goodness. That we have had this meal—however humble—is not to be taken for granted, but rather as a gift. Whenever one eats, he or she must reflect on the beneficence of the Creator. The arena for creation is the Land, which to the ordinary eye is commonplace, small, dry, rocky; but which to the eye of faith is pleasant good, spacious. The Land lay at the end of redemption from Egyptian bondage. Holding it, enjoying it—as we saw in the *Shema*—is a sign that the covenant is intact and in force and that Israel is loyal to its part of the contract and God to his. The Land, the Exodus, the covenant—these all depend upon the Torah, statutes, and a life of grace and mercy, here embodied in and evoked by the nourishment of the meal. Thanksgiving wells up, and the paragraph ends with praises for the Land and its food.

Then the chief theme recurs—that is, redemption and hope for return, and then future prosperity in the Land: "May God pity the people, the city, Zion, the royal house of the Messiah, the Holy Temple." The nourishment of this meal is but a foretaste of the nourishment of the messianic time, just as the joy of the wedding is a foretaste of the messianic rejoicing.

Still, it is not the messianic time, so Israel finally asks not to depend upon the gifts of mortal men but only upon those of the generous, wide-open hand of God. And then "rebuild Jerusalem." The concluding paragraph summarizes the whole, giving thanks for creation, redemption, divine goodness, every blessing. So the physical experience of hunger assuaged by eating a meal is transformed into an acting out of the narrative, which takes over and enchants everyday life. Indeed, religion is story—what else can it ever have been?

---

[1]Judah Goldin, trans., *The Grace After Meals* (New York: Jewish Theological Seminary of America, 1955), pp. 9, 15*ff.* Reprinted with permission.

PART V

Classical Judaism:
The Torah's Way of Life

15

Life under the Law of the Torah

THE SIX HUNDRED THIRTEEN COMMANDMENTS AND THEIR SINGLE PURPOSE

The written Torah not only commands Israel "to be holy, for I the Lord your God am holy" (Lev. 19:2), it defines holiness in the performance of religious duties, commandments (*mitzvot*), which are many. At the same time the Torah offers general rules of sanctification of the community of Israel, for example, "You shall love your neighbor as yourself" (Lev. 19:18).

Accordingly the master narrative of Judaism describes in vast detail the rules for living in God's kingdom under the yoke of the Torah. The commandments, enumerated at 613, 365 matching the days of the solar year, and 248 corresponding to the number of bones of the body, govern everyday life and transactions, both social and personal. Through myriads of details, it is, then, easy to lose sight of the purpose of the whole. Hence, as Moses did in Leviticus 19:2 and 19:18, so too the Rabbinic sages made every effort at teaching the purpose of the laws of the Torah, finding the main point realized in the details. In a series of stories and sayings, they declared what they deemed to form the heart and soul, the center of the system as a whole.

"THE RIGHTEOUS SHALL LIVE BY HIS FAITH"

Among many efforts at summarizing life under the law of the Torah, the most comprehensive is attributed to R. Simelai, in the following composition:

Talmud of Babylonia Makkot 23B–24A / 3:16 II.1

R. Simelai expounded, "Six hundred and thirteen commandments were given to Moses, three hundred and sixty-five negative ones, corresponding to the number of the days of the solar year, and two hundred forty-eight positive commandments, corresponding to the parts of man's body."

"David came and reduced them to eleven: 'A Psalm of David: Lord, who shall sojourn in thy tabernacle, and who shall dwell in thy holy mountain? (i) He who walks uprightly and (ii) works righteousness and (iii) speaks truth in his heart and (iv) has no slander on his tongue and (v) does no evil to his fellow and (vi) does not take up a reproach against his neighbor, (vii) in whose eyes a vile person is despised but (viii) honors those who fear the Lord. (ix) He swears to his own hurt and changes not. (x) He does not lend on interest. (xi) He does not take a bribe against the innocent' (Psalm 15)."

"Isaiah came and reduced them to six: '(i) He who walks righteously and (ii) speaks uprightly, (iii) he who despises the gain of oppressions, (iv) shakes his hand from holding bribes, (v) stops his ear from hearing of blood (vi) and shuts his eyes from looking upon evil, he shall dwell on high' (Isaiah 33:25–26)."

"Micah came and reduced them to three: 'It has been told you, man, what is good, and what the Lord demands from you, (i) only to do justly and (ii) to love mercy, and (iii) to walk humbly before God' (Micah 6:8)."

"only to do justly": this refers to justice.

"to love mercy": this refers to doing acts of loving kindness.

"to walk humbly before God": this refers to accompanying a corpse to the grave and welcoming the bread.

"And does this not yield a conclusion a fortiori: if matters that are not ordinarily done in private are referred to by the Torah as "walking humbly before God," all the more so matters that ordinarily are done in private.

"Isaiah again came and reduced them to two: 'Thus says the Lord, (i) Keep justice and (ii) do righteousness' (Isaiah 56:1).

"Amos came and reduced them to a single one, as it is said, 'For thus says the Lord to the house of Israel. Seek Me and live.' "

"Habakkuk further came and based them on one, as it is said, 'But the righteous shall live by his faith' (Habakkuk 2:4)."

If we can reduce the "whole Torah" to a handful of teachings, then clearly, the meaning of the word *Torah* has shifted. The word no longer refers to a particular body of writings. Nor does it speak mainly of God's revelation to Moses at Mount Sinai. A variety of meanings now gather around a single word, and it is time systematically to review them.

"WHAT IS HATEFUL TO YOU, TO YOUR FELLOW DON'T DO.' THAT'S THE ENTIRETY OF THE TORAH; EVERYTHING ELSE IS ELABORATION. SO GO, STUDY!"

Simlai's is only one such effort at summarizing the whole Torah in a few encompassing rules. The single most famous such statement of the "whole Torah" drives from Hillel, the first-century C.E. Pharisaic authority, whom we have met before:

Talmud of Babylonia Tractate Shabbat 30B–31A/2:5 I.12

There was another case of a gentile who came before Shammai. He said to him, "Convert me on the stipulation that you teach me the entire Torah while I am standing on one foot." He drove him off with the building cubit that he had in his hand.

He came before Hillel: "Convert me."

He said to him, " 'What is hateful to you, to your fellow don't do.' That's the entirety of the Torah; everything else is elaboration. So go, study."

This famous saying is frequently cited only in part; the part about elaboration and Torah study is left out. But, we see, Torah study is integral to life under the law of the Torah, and ignorance is the enemy of piety. So we have to ask whether the Rabbinic sages address the question of which takes priority, study or action.

"STUDY IS GREATER, FOR STUDY BRINGS ABOUT ACTION"

Everything else is elaboration, the work is to go, study. Then which is more important, doing the deed or studying about it in the Torah? That question is answered in so many words:

Talmud of Babylonia Qiddusin 1:10E–G I.2/22A

Once R. Tarfon and the elders were reclining at a banquet in the upper room of the house of Nitseh in Lud. This question was raised for them: "Is study greater or is action greater?"

R. Tarfon responded: "Action is greater."

R. Aqiba responded: "Study is greater."

All responded, saying, "Study is greater, for study brings about action."

So the point of the way of life set forth by the law of the Torah is studying the Torah so as to keep the commandments. The value of study depends on the doing of the deed. The matter is resolved by Eleazar b. Azariah in this language:

Tractate Abot 3:17

R. Eleazar b. Azariah says, "If there is no learning of Torah, there is no proper conduct.

"If there is no proper conduct, there is no learning in Torah."

He would say, "Anyone whose wisdom is greater than his deeds—to what is he to be likened? To a tree with abundant foliage, but few roots.

"When the winds come, they will uproot it and blow it down,

"as it is said, 'He shall be like a tamarisk in the desert and shall not see when good comes but shall inhabit the parched places in the wilderness' (Jer. 17:6).

"But anyone whose deeds are greater than his wisdom—to what is he to be likened? To a tree with little foliage but abundant roots.

"For even if all the winds in the world were to come and blast at it, they will not move it from its place,

"as it is said, 'He shall be as a tree planted by the waters, and that spreads out its roots by the river, and shall not fear when heat comes, and his leaf shall be green, and shall not be careful in the year of drought, neither shall cease from yielding fruit' (Jer. 17 :8)."

The picture we gain of life under the law of the Torah is a life focused on God's concerns, a life meant to respond to the expression of God's love for Israel that is embodied in the Torah. Above all, we see an insistent effort on classifying religious requirements as less or as more important, depending on the sense of proportion and purpose that animates the law as a whole.

But that is not the view of Judaism that its critics have formed, whether Jesus in his arguments with the Pharisees, or the contemporary Jewish critics of classical Judaism in their rejection of the law. A cultural bias comes into play as a result of millennia of criticism of people who care more for what goes into their mouths—kosher food—than for what comes out—gossip and slander. As we have seen, the Rabbinic sages understood full well that some commandments are more important than others, for example, that the religious duty of saving a life takes priority even over the observance of the Sabbath.

Still, when people think of law, they ordinarily imagine a religion for bookkeepers, who tote up the good deeds and debit the bad and call the result salvation or damnation, depending on the outcome. But life under the Torah brings the joy of expressing love of God through a cycle of celebration. From the generalizations embodied in efforts at expressing the whole, let us turn to the details of life under the law of the Torah.

THE CYCLE OF THE JUDAIC WAY OF LIFE:
THE RHYTHM OF THE YEAR

In fact, the Judaic way of life joins three separate cycles, one in the rhythm of the year, the second in the rhythm of the week, the third in the rhythm of a person's life.

The Judaic year follows the lunar calendar, so the appearance of the new moon marks the beginning of a month, and that is celebrated. There are two critical moments in the unfolding of the year, the first full moon after the autumnal equinox, and the first full moon after the vernal equinox. These mark the time of heightened celebration. To understand how the rhythm of the year unfolds, however, we begin with the new moon of the month of Tishré, corresponding to September. That marks the New Year, *Rosh Hashanah.* Ten days later comes the Day of Atonement, commemorating the rite described in Leviticus 16, and marking God's judgment and forgiveness of humanity. Five days afterward is the full moon, which is the beginning of the festival of Tabernacles, in Hebrew *Sukkot;* that festival lasts for eight days and ends with a day of solemn assembly, *Shemini Atzeret,* and of rejoicing of the Torah, *Simhat Torah.* So nearly the whole month of Tishré is spent in celebration: eating, drinking, praying, studying, enjoying and celebrating God's sovereignty, creation, revelation, redemption as the themes of the festivals and solemn celebrations of the season work themselves out.

The next major sequence of celebration, as we realize, follows the first new moon after the vernal equinox, which begins the month of Nisan and culminates, at its full moon, with Passover, in Hebrew *Pessah,* which commemorates the Exodus of Israel from Egypt and celebrates Israel's freedom, bestowed by God. Fifty days thereafter comes the festival of Pentecost, in Hebrew *Shavuot,* which commemorates the giving of the Torah at Mount Sinai. Other occasions for celebration exist, but, apart from the Sabbath, the New Year, the Day of Atonement, Tabernacles, Passover, and Pentecost are the main holy days.

THE CYCLE OF THE JUDAIC WAY OF LIFE:
THE RHYTHM OF THE WEEK

Second comes the rhythm of the week, the time kept by the Sabbath that commemorates creation. Just as the Days of Awe, the New Year and the Day of Atonement, and the festivals of Tabernacles, Passover, and Pentecost mark the passage of the lunar year, so the Sabbath marks the movement of time through the week. The sanctification of the Sabbath, observed on the seventh day, Saturday, is one of the Ten Commandments. It is the single happiest moment in Judaism and, coming as it does every week, the Sabbath sheds its light on the every day. On it people do no servile labor, and they devote themselves to sacred activities, including both synagogue worship and study of the Torah, as well as to eating, drinking, relaxing, and enjoying themselves. The song for the Sabbath day, Psalm 92, expresses the spirit of this observance: it is good to give thanks to the Lord. Faithful Jews find in the Sabbath the meaning of their everyday lives.

THE CYCLE OF THE JUDAIC WAY OF LIFE:
THE RHYTHM OF THE PRIVATE LIFE

The passage of the individual's life, from birth to death, marks out the third of the three cycles in the way of Torah, the cycles that convey the spirit of the

Torah, or *law,* as the word is translated. The principal points are birth, puberty, marriage, and death. In later chapters we shall review pertinent materials. What we shall see is how the master narrative supplies a chapter to tell the story of Israel on each of the turnings in the individual life cycle, whether Elijah at the circumcision, or Adam and Eve at the marriage rite, as we have already seen. Birth in the case of males is marked by circumcision on the eighth day. Nowadays in the synagogue the birth of both sons and daughters is celebrated by a rite of naming of the child. The celebration of a child's becoming responsible to carry out the religious duties that are called *mitzvot,* or commandments, entering the status known as *bar mitzvah* for the boy and *bat mitzvah* for the girl, takes place in the synagogue in a simple way. The young woman or man is called to the Torah, which she or he reads, and the prophetic passage of the day also is read by the newly responsible young adult. We have already noted the marriage ceremony; rites of death involve a clear recognition that God rules and is the true and just authority over all humanity. The memorial prayer, or *Kaddish* for mourners, expresses the worshipper's recognition of God's holiness and dominion and states the hope for the coming of the Messiah.

In a few words these events of celebration, which one might call "lifestyle events," define life under the law and explain how Judaists seek to live in accord with God's will, which is that Israel live the holy life in the here and now and await salvation at the end of time.

THE HALAKHAH

It is time to generalize on the medium by which the religious duties are translated into the details of practical living. This is through the body of Judaic law called the *Halakhah.*

The word for concrete instruction of one's duty, of the proper way of doing things, is *Halakhah,* and when we speak of life under the law we mean life in accord with the *Halakhah,* the rules and regulations of the holy life. The mythic structure built upon the themes of creation, revelation, and redemption finds expression not only in synagogue liturgy, but especially in concrete, everyday actions or action symbols—that is, deeds that embody and express the fundamental mythic life of the classical Judaic tradition.

These action symbols are set forth in *Halakhah.* This word, as is clear, is normally translated as "law," for the *Halakhah* is full of normative, prescriptive rules about what one must do and refrain from doing in every situation of life and at every moment of the day. But *Halakhah* derives from the root *halakh,* which means "go," and a better translation would be "way." The *Halakhah* is "the way": *the way* men and women live their lives; *the way* they shape their daily routines into a pattern of sanctity; *the way* they follow the revelation of the Torah and attain redemption.

For the Judaic tradition, this *way* is absolutely central. Belief without the expression of belief in the workaday world is of limited consequence. The purpose of revelation is to create a kingdom of priests and a holy people. The foundation of that kingdom, or sovereignty, is the rule of God over the lives of humanity. For the Judaic tradition, God rules much as people do, by guiding others on the path of life, not by removing them from the land of living. Creation lies behind, redemption in the future; Torah is for here and now. To the classical Jew, Torah means revealed law or commandment, accepted by Israel and obeyed from Sinai to the end of days.

The spirit of the Jewish way (*Halakhah*) is conveyed in many modes, for law is not divorced from values, but rather concretizes human beliefs and ideals. The purpose of the commandments is to show the road to sanctity, the way to God. In a more mundane sense, the following provides a valuable insight:

Babylonian Talmud Tractate Shabbat 31A

Raba [a fourth-century rabbi] said, "When a man is brought in for judgment in the world to come, he is asked, 'Did you deal in good faith? Did you set aside time for study of Torah? Did you engage in procreation? Did you look forward to salvation? Did you engage in the dialectics of wisdom? Did you look deeply into matters?' "

Raba's interpretation of the Scripture *and there shall be faith in thy times, strength, salvation, wisdom and knowledge* (Isaiah 33:6) provides one glimpse into the life of the classical Jew who followed the way of Torah.

The first consideration was ethical: Did the man conduct himself faithfully? The second was study of Torah, not at random but every day, systematically, as a discipline of life. Third came the raising of a family, for celibacy and abstinence from sexual life were regarded as sinful; the full use of man's creative powers for the procreation of life was a commandment. Nothing God made was evil. Wholesome conjugal life was a blessing. But, fourth, merely living day by day according to an upright ethic was not sufficient. It is true that people must live by a holy discipline, but the discipline itself was only a means. The end was salvation. Hence the pious people were asked to look forward to salvation, aiming their deed and directing their hearts toward a higher goal. Wisdom and insight—these complete the list, for without them, the way of Torah was a life of mere routine, rather than a constant search for deeper understanding. But life under the law of the Torah is an elaborate commentary on the text, "You shall love your neighbor as yourself...what is hateful to you, do not do to your fellow."

16

Hear Our Prayer, Grant Us Peace

PRAYER AND GOD'S PRESENCE

The life defined by the Torah's law is lived in perpetual prayer, before God's presence always. Life under the law of the Torah means praying—morning, noon, night, and at meals—both routinely and when something unusual happens. It means to remain constantly aware of the presence of God and always ready to praise and bless God for surprising events, beginning with sunset. The way of Torah is the way of perpetual devotion to God. What is the substance of that devotion? For what do those who practice Judaism ask when they pray?

Prayer expresses the most solemn aspirations of the praying community; it is what gives that community a sense of oneness and of shared hopes; it embodies the values of the community. But if it is the community in its single most idiomatic hour, it also presents the community at its least particular and self-aware, for when they pray people stand before God without the mediation of culture and ethnic consciousness. But as we shall see, that does not mean that in Judaic prayer we do not find the master narrative that embodies Judaism. We do.

THE EIGHTEEN BENEDICTIONS

In the morning, noon, and evening prayers are found the Eighteen Benedictions. Some of these, in particular those at the beginning and the end, recur in Sabbath and festival prayers. They are said silently. Each individual prays by and for himself or herself, but together with other silent, praying individuals. The Eighteen Benedictions are then repeated aloud by the prayer leader, for prayer is both private and public, individual and collective. To contemplate the meaning of these prayers one should imagine a room full of people, all standing by themselves yet in close proximity, some swaying this way and that, all addressing themselves directly and intimately to God in a whisper or in a low tone. They do not move their feet, for they are now standing before the King of Kings, and it is not meet to shift and shuffle. If spoken to, they will not answer. Their attention is fixed upon the words of supplication, praise, and gratitude. When they begin, they bend their knees—so, too, toward the end—and at the conclusion they step back and withdraw from the presence.

These, on ordinary days, are the words they say, with the topics given in italics:

Wisdom, Repentance

You graciously endow man with intelligence;

You teach him knowledge and understanding.

Grant us knowledge, discernment, and wisdom.

Praised are You, O Lord, for the gift of knowledge.

Our Father, bring us back to Your Torah;

Our King, draw us near to Your service;

Lead us back to you truly repentant.

Praised are You, O Lord who welcomes repentance.

Forgiveness, Redemption

Our Father, forgive us, for we have sinned;

Our King, pardon us, for we have transgressed;

You forgive sin and pardon transgression.

Praised are You, gracious and forgiving Lord.

Behold our affliction and deliver us.

Redeem us soon for the sake of Your name,

For You are the mighty Redeemer.

Praised are You, O Lord, Redeemer of Israel.

Heal Us, Bless Our Years

Heal us, O Lord, and we shall be healed;

Help us and save us, for You are our glory.

Grant perfect healing for all our afflictions,

O faithful and merciful God of healing.

Praised are You, O Lord, Healer of His people.

O Lord our God! Make this a blessed year;

May its varied produce bring us happiness.

Bring blessing upon the whole earth.

Bless the year with Your abounding goodness.

Praised are You, O Lord, who blesses our years.

Gather Our Exiles, Reign Over Us

South the great shofar to herald [our] freedom;

Raise high the banner to gather all exiles;

Gather the dispersed from the corners of the earth.

Praised are You, O Lord, who gathers our exiles.

Restore our judges as in days of old;

Restore our counselors as in former times;

Remove from us sorrow and anguish.

Reign over us alone with loving kindness;

With justice and mercy sustain our cause.

Praised are You, O Lord, King who loves justice.

Humble the Arrogant-Sustain the Righteous

Frustrate the hopes of those who malign us;

Let all evil very soon disappear;

Let all Your enemies be speedily destroyed.

May You quickly uproot and crush the arrogant;

May You subdue and humble them in our time.

Praised are You, O Lord, who humbles the arrogant.

Let Your tender mercies, O Lord God, be stirred

For the righteous, the pious, the leaders of Israel,

Toward devoted scholars and faithful proselytes.

Be merciful to us of the house of Israel;

Reward all who trust in You;

Cast our lot with those who are faithful to You.

May we never come to despair, for our trust is in You.

Praised are You, O Lord, who sustains the righteous.

Favor Your City and Your People

Have mercy, O Lord, and return to Jerusalem, Your city;

May Your Presence dwell there as You promised.

Rebuild it now, in our days and for all time;

Reestablish there the majesty of David, Your servant.

Praised are You, O Lord, who rebuilds Jerusalem.

Bring to flower the shoot of Your servant David.

Hasten the advent of the Messianic redemption;

Each and every day we hope for Your deliverance.

Praised are You, O Lord, who assures our deliverance.

O Lord, our God, hear our cry!

Have compassion upon us and pity us;

Accept our prayer with loving favor.

You, O God, listen to entreaty and prayer.

O King, do not turn us away unanswered,

For You mercifully heed Your people's supplication.

Praised are You, O Lord, who is attentive to prayer.

O Lord, Our God, favor Your people Israel;

Accept with love Israel's offering of prayer;

May our worship be ever acceptable to You.

May our eyes witness Your return in mercy to Zion.

Praised are You, O Lord, whose Presence returns to Zion.

Our Thankfulness

We thank You, O Lord our God and God of our fathers,

Defender of our lives, Shield of our safety;

Through all generations we thank You and praise You.

Our lives are in Your hands, our souls in Your charge.

We thank You for the miracles which daily attend us,

For Your wonders and favor morning, noon, and night.

You are beneficent with boundless mercy and love.

From of old we have always placed our hope in You.

For all these blessings, O our King,

We shall ever praise and exalt You.

Every living creature thanks You, and praises You in truth.

O God, You are our deliverance and our help. Selah!

Praised are You, O Lord, for Your Goodness and Your glory.

Peace and Well-Being

Grant peace and well-being to the whole house of Israel;

Give us of Your grace, Your love, and Your mercy.

Bless us all, O our Father, with the light of Your Presence.

It is Your light that revealed to us Your life-giving Torah,

And taught us love and tenderness, justice, mercy, and peace.

May it please You to bless Your people in every season,

To bless them at all times with Your light of peace.

Praised are You, O Lord, who blesses Israel with peace.[1]

The first two petitions pertain to intelligence. The Jew thanks God for mind: knowledge, wisdom, discernment. But knowledge is for a purpose, and the purpose is knowledge of Torah. Such discernment leads to the service of God and produces a spirit of repentance. Israelites cannot pray without setting themselves right with God, and that means repenting for what has separated them from God. Torah is the way to repentance and to return. So knowledge leads to Torah, Torah to repentance, and repentance to God. The logical next stop is the prayer for forgiveness. That is the sign of return. God forgives sin;

---

[1]Reprinted by permission of the *Weekday Prayer Book*, edited by Gerson Hadas, © Rabbinical Assembly, 1962.

God is gracious and forgiving. Once they discern what they have done wrong through the guidance of Torah, they therefore seek to be forgiven. It is sin that leads to affliction. Affliction stands at the beginning of the way to God; once they have taken that way, they ask for their suffering to end; they beg redemption. This is then specified. They ask for healing, salvation, a blessed year. Healing without prosperity means they may suffer in good health or starve in a robust body. So along with the prayer for healing goes the supplication for worldly comfort.

The individual's task is done. But what of the community? Health and comfort are not enough. The world is unredeemed. Jews are enslaved, in exile, and alien. At the end of days a great *shofar,* or ram's horn, will sound to herald the Messiah's coming. This is now besought. The Jewish people at prayer ask first for the proclamation of freedom, then for the in-gathering of the exiles to the Promised Land. Establishing the messianic kingdom, God needs also to restore a wise and benevolent government, good judges, good counselors, and loving justice.

Meanwhile—and now the master narrative takes over—Israel, the holy people, finds itself maligned. As the prayer sees things, arrogant men hating Israel hate God as well. They should be humbled. And the pious and righteous— the scholars, the faithful proselytes, the whole House of Israel that trusts in God—should be rewarded and sustained. Above all, remember Jerusalem. Rebuild the city and dwell there. Set up Jerusalem's messianic king, David, and make him to prosper. These are the themes of the daily prayer: personal atonement good health, and good fortunes; collective redemption, freedom, the end of alienation, good government, and true justice; the final and complete salvation of the land and of Jerusalem by the Messiah. At the end comes a prayer that prayer may be heard and found acceptable; then an expression of thanksgiving, not for what may come, but for the miracles and mercies already enjoyed morning, noon, and night. And at the end is the prayer for peace—a peace that consists of wholeness for the sacred community.

THE MASTER NARRATIVE FRAMES
THE ENCOUNTER WITH GOD

Here is the master narrative translated into prayer, when we speak to God. The power of the narrative presents itself: Israel and God share memories, a story in common. People who say such prayers clearly tell themselves the story of Creation and loss, restoration and return to God, that constitutes the paramount theme of the master narrative we met in Chapter 1. They arise in the morning and speak of Jerusalem. At noon they make mention of the Messiah. In the evening they end the day with talk of the *shofar* to herald freedom and the in-gathering of the exiles. Living here in the profane, alien world, they constantly talk of going there—to the Holy Land and its perfect society. They address themselves to the end of days and the Messiah's time. The praying community above all seeks the fulfillment and end of its—and humanity's—travail.

That memory calls to mind that story told in common, by each person concerning himself or herself as Israelite, by all Israelites as a common moral entity—it is that story that shapes the encounter with God as well. Here is how, in the language with which this tale of Judaism began, to practice Judaism means to act out in behavior and belief the key stories that are told in the Torah. Above all, that drama takes place when the Israelite faces God and remembers the chapters of the story: not only the theology, but also the history and the hope.

17

Sabbaths for Rest, Festivals for Rejoicing

THE STORY OF CREATION AND OF REDEMPTION REALIZED IN THE SEVENTH DAY, WHEN THE TORAH IS DECLAIMED FOR ISRAEL

Abraham J. Heschel, whom we shall meet in Chapter 20, wrote that Judaism is a religion that builds its cathedrals in temporal observance rather than spatial constructions. Not surprisingly, therefore, its great celebrations of time, the Sabbath and the festivals, all work on its principal themes of Creation, Revelation, and Redemption.

First comes the Sabbath, that single critical occasion that comes weekly, and Israel's unanimous observance of which will bring the Messiah, we recall from Chapter 9. The Sabbath day, for its part, forms the climax of creation. Israel keeps the Sabbath both as a memorial of creation and as a remembrance of the redemption from Egypt. Scripture provides two narratives of the Sabbath, invoking in the Ten Commandments both the cosmic and the social dimensions of the principal religious observance of Judaism. The cosmic narrative is familiar from Genesis 2:1–3:

> Thus the heavens and the earth were finished and all the host of them. And on the seventh day God finished his work that he had done, and he rested on the seventh day from all his work that he had done. So God blessed the seventh day and sanctified it, because on it God rested from all his work that he had done in creation.

The Ten Commandments as set forth at Exodus 20:8–11 repeat this story about the Sabbath:

> Remember the Sabbath day to keep it holy, for in six days the Lord made heaven and earth, the sea and all that is in them, and rested on the seventh day; therefore the Lord blessed the Sabbath day and sanctified it.

So Israel is to act out the climactic moment of creation, repose in the model of God's repose.

In the version of the Ten Commandments as Moses repeats them, at Deuteronomy 5:12–18, the reason for the rule invokes the Exodus from Egypt:

Observe the Sabbath day to keep it holy . . . in it you shall not do any work, you . . . or your manservant or your maidservant . . . or the sojourner who is within your gates, that your manservant and your maidservant may rest as well as you. You shall remember that you were a servant in the Land of Egypt, and the Lord your God brought you out thence with a mighty hand and an outstretched arm; therefore the Lord your God commanded you to keep the Sabbath day.

Now what is at issue is the narrative of Egyptian slavery and divine intervention, the redemption of the Israelite slaves from Egypt. Now Israel acts out the redemption from Egypt.

Judaism's generative story encompasses creation, revelation, and redemption. Here creation and redemption come into play. On the seventh day, Israel follows the model of God, celebrating creation and reposing in commemoration of God's sanctifying the day of rest from the work of creation. On that same day, Israel invokes the model of God in affording freedom from heavy labor to all who work. What of revelation? The celebration of the Sabbath focuses on the declamation of the Torah in synagogue worship on the Sabbath. So the three chief themes—creation, revelation, and redemption—are combined in the weekly observance of the seventh day—that is, from sunset Friday to sunset Saturday.

The Sabbath is protected by negative rules: One must not work; one must not pursue mundane concerns. But the Sabbath is also adorned with less concrete but affirmative laws: One must rejoice; one must rest. Nonetheless, it is a religious duty to save life, even overriding the restrictions that the Sabbath places on secular conduct. But one may not violate the Sabbath to protect one's property; for that purpose, one must wait for the sundown when Sabbath ends.

REJOICING IN THE SABBATH

The Sabbath is a foretaste of the Eden, and observing the Sabbath restores Israel to Paradise. How do faithful Israelites keep the Sabbath? All week long they look forward to it, and the anticipation enhances the ordinary days. By Friday afternoon they have bathed, put on their Sabbath garments, and set aside the affairs of the week. At home, the family—husband, wife, children—will have cleaned, cooked, and arranged their finest table. It is common to invite guests for the Sabbath meals. The Sabbath comes at sunset and leaves when three stars appear Saturday night. After a brief service the family comes together to enjoy its best meal of the week—a meal at which particular Sabbath foods are served. In the morning comes the Sabbath service—including a public reading from the Torah, the Five Books of Moses, and prophetic writings—and an additional service in memory of the Temple sacrifices on Sabbaths of old. Then home for lunch and very commonly a Sabbath nap, the sweetest part of the day. As the day wanes, the synagogue calls for a late afternoon service, followed by Torah study and a third meal.

Then comes a ceremony, *Habdalah* (separation)—effected with spices, wine, and candlelight—between the holy time of the Sabbath and the ordinary time of weekday. Its principal blessing states:

> Praised are You, Lord our God, King of the universe, who has endowed all creation with distinctive qualities and differentiated between light and darkness, between sacred and profane, between Israel and the nations, and between the seventh day and the other days of the week. Praised are you, O Lord, who differentiates between the sacred and the profane.[1]

Here, too, we see how the Sabbath captures the whole of Judaism, now corresponding among days to Israel among the nations.

This simple, regular observance has elicited endless praise. To the Sabbath-observing Jew, the Sabbath is the chief sign of God's grace:

> For thou hast chosen us and sanctified us above all nations, in love and favor has given us thy holy Sabbath as an inheritance.[2]

So states the Sanctification of the Sabbath Wine. Likewise in the Sabbath morning liturgy:

> You did not give it [Sabbath] to the nations of the earth, nor did you make it the heritage of idolaters, nor in its rest will unrighteous men find a place.
>
> But to Israel your people you have given it in love, to the seed of Jacob whom you have chosen, to that people who sanctify the Sabbath day. All of them find fulfillment and joy from your bounty.
>
> For the seventh day did you choose and sanctify as the most pleasant of days and you called it a memorial to the works of creation.

Here again we find a profusion of themes, this time centered upon the Sabbath. The Sabbath is a sign of the covenant. It is a gift of grace, which neither idolaters nor evil people may enjoy. It is the testimony of the chosenness of Israel. And it is the most pleasant of days. Keeping the Sabbath *is* living in God's kingdom:

> Those who keep the Sabbath and call it a delight will rejoice in your kingdom.

So states the additional Sabbath prayer. Keeping the Sabbath now is a foretaste of the redemption: "This day is for Israel light and rejoicing."

The rest of the Sabbath is, as the afternoon prayer affirms, "a rest granted in generous love, a true and faithful rest."

> …Let your children realize that their rest is from you, and by their rest may they sanctify your name.

---

[1] Reprinted by permission of the *Weekday Prayer Book*, edited by Gerson Hadas, © the Rabbinical Assembly, 1962.

[2] Traditional prayer; author's translation from the Hebrew.

That people need respite from the routine of work is no discovery of the Judaic tradition. That the way in which they accomplish such a routine change of pace may be made the very heart and soul of their spiritual existence is the single absolutely unique element in Judaic tradition. The word *Sabbath* simply renders the Hebrew *Shabbat;* it does not translate it, for there is no translation. In no other tradition or culture can an equivalent word be found. Certainly those who compare the Sabbath of Judaism to the somber, supposedly joyless Sunday of the Calvinists know nothing of what the Sabbath has meant and continues to mean to Jews.

In his account of the Sabbath, Abraham J. Heschel builds his theology around the meaning of the Sabbath day. He reflects:

> Judaism is a religion of time aiming at the sanctification of time. . . .
> Judaism teaches us to be attached to holiness in time, to be attached to
> sacred events, to learn how to consecrate sanctuaries that emerge from the
> magnificent stream of a year. The Sabbaths are our great cathedrals, and
> our Holy of Holies is a shrine that neither the Romans for the Germans
> were able to burn. . . . Jewish ritual may be characterized as the art of
> significant forms in time as architecture of time.[3]

Heschel finds in the Sabbath "the day on which we are called upon to share in what is eternal in time, to turn from the world of creation to the creations of the world."[4]

From this brief description of what the faithful Israelite actually does on the seventh day, we can hardly derive understanding of how the Sabbath can have meant so much as to elicit words such as those of the Judaic prayerbook and of Rabbi Heschel. Those words, like the laws of the Sabbath—not to mourn, not to confess sins, not to repent, not to do anything that might lead to unhappiness—describe something only the participant can truly comprehend and feel. Only a family whose life focuses upon the Sabbath week by week, year by year, from birth to death, can know the sanctity of which the theologian speaks, the sacred rest to which the prayers refer. The heart and soul of the Judaic tradition as set forth in the Rabbinic model, the Sabbath cannot be described—only experienced. For the student of religions, it stands as that element of Judaism that is absolutely unique and therefore a mystery.

THE PILGRIM FESTIVALS:
TABERNACLES/HUTS (*SUKKOT*)

The festivals mark the passage of time: not of the week but of the seasons. Earlier we took note of the festivals as expressions of life under the law. Let us now consider precisely how people live out those seasons of sanctification and celebration.

---

[3]Abraham J. Heschel, *The Sabbath: Its Meaning for Modern Man* (New York: Farrar, Strauss & Young, 1951), p. 8.

[4]Ibid., p. 10.

Sukkot, the feast of tabernacles, is the autumnal festival. It begins on the first full moon after the autumnal equinox, September 21. It marks the end of the dry season and of much agricultural toil. The fall crops by then were gathered in from the fields, orchards, and vineyards. The rainy season was about to begin. Special prayers for rain for the Land of Israel were recited. It was time both to give thanks for what had been granted and to pray for abundant rains in the coming months. Called "festival of the in-gathering," it was the celebration of creation par excellence. Today the principal observance is still the construction of a frail hut, or booth, for temporary use during the festival. In it Jews eat their meals out of doors. The huts are covered over with branches, leaves, fruit, and flowers, but light shows through, and at night the stars. We do not know the origin of the practice. Some have held that during the harvest it was common to build an ordinary shack in the fields for shelter from the heat of the day. In any event, the ancient practice naturally was given a historical context: When the faithful Israelites wandered in the wilderness they lived, not in permanent homes, but in frail booths. At a time of bounty it is good to be reminded of man's travail and dependence upon heavenly succor.

THE PILGRIM FESTIVALS:
PASSOVER (*PESSAH*)

Celebrating Israel's redemption, Passover, which we met in another connection in Chapter 13, is the Judaic spring festival, beginning on the first full moon after the vernal equinox of March 21, and the symbols of the Passover *seder*—hard-boiled eggs and vegetable greens—are not unfamiliar in other spring rites. But here the spring rite has been transformed into a historical commemoration. The natural course of the year, while important, is subordinated to the historical events remembered and relived on the festival. Called the feast of unleavened bread and the season of our freedom, the Passover festival preserves very ancient rites in a new framework.

It is, for example, absolutely prohibited to make use of leaven, fermented dough, and the like. The agricultural calendar of ancient Canaan was marked by the grain harvest, beginning in the spring with the cutting of barley and ending with the reaping of the wheat approximately seven weeks later.[5] The farmers would get rid of all their sour dough, which they used as yeast, and old bread as well as any leaven from last year's crop. The origins of the practice are not clear, but that the Passover taboo against leaven was connected with the agricultural calendar is beyond doubt. Just as the agricultural festivals were historicized, likewise much of the detailed observance connected with them was supplied with historical "reasons" or explanations. In the case of the taboo against leaven, widely observed today even among otherwise unobservant Jews,

---

[5]Hayyim Schauss, *The Jewish Festivals from Their Beginnings to Our Own Day* (New York: Union of American Hebrew Congregations, 1938), pp. 40*ff.*

the "reason" was that the Israelites had to leave Egypt in haste and therefore had to take with them unleavened bread, for they had not time to permit the bread to rise properly and be baked. Therefore we eat the *matzah,* unleavened bread.

THE PILGRIM FESTIVALS:
PENTECOST/WEEKS (*SHABUOT*)

Today devoted to the celebration of the revelation of the Torah at Mount Sinai, the Feast of Weeks, *Shabuot* or Pentecost, completes the pilgrim festivals trilogy, counterpart to creation, revelation, and redemption. The festival comes seven weeks after Passover. In the ancient Palestinian agricultural calendar, it marked the end of the grain harvest and was called the feast of harvest. In Temple times, two loaves of bread were baked from the wheat of the new crop and offered as a sacrifice, the first fruits of wheat harvest. So Shabuot came to be called the day of the first fruits. The Rabbinic sages further have held that the Torah was revealed on Mount Sinai on that day and celebrated it as "the time of the giving of our Torah."[6] Nowadays, confirmation and graduation ceremonies of religious schools take place on *Shabuot.*

The three historical-agricultural festivals pertain, in varying ways and combinations, to the themes we have already considered. Passover is the festival of redemption and points toward the Torah revelation of the Feast of Weeks; the harvest festival in the autumn celebrates not only creation, but especially redemption.

THE DAYS OF AWE: NEW YEAR (*ROSH HASHANAH*) AND THE DAY OF ATONEMENT (*YOM KIPPUR*)

The cycle of holy days and seasons reaches its climax in a penitential season, called the "Days of Awe," when individuals come under judgment. Now the narrative turns away from creation, revelation, and redemption to God's judgment and mercy in response to genuine repentance.

The New Year, *Rosh Hoshanah,* and the Day of Atonement, *Yom Kippur,* together mark the Days of Awe, of solemn penitence, at the start of the autumn festival season; they are followed by *Sukkot.* These are solemn times. In the narrative of classical Judaism, at the New Year humanity is inscribed for life or death in the heavenly books for the coming year, and on the Day of Atonement the books are sealed. The synagogues on that day are filled with penitents. The New Year is called the birthday of the world: "This day the world

---

[6]Ibid., pp. 86ff.

was born." It is likewise a day of remembrance on which the deeds of all creatures are reviewed. On it God asserts his sovereignty, as in the New Year Prayer:

> Our God and God of our Fathers, Rule over the whole world in Your honor...and appear in Your glorious might to all those who dwell in the civilization of Your world, so that everything made will know that You made it, and every creature discern that You have created him, so that all in whose nostrils is breath may say, "The Lord, the God of Israel is king, and His kingdom extends over all."[7]

The themes of the liturgy are divine sovereignty, divine memory, and divine disclosure. These correspond to creation, revelation, and redemption. Sovereignty is established by creation of the world. Judgment depends upon law: "From the beginning You made this, Your purpose known. ..." And therefore, since people have been told what God requires of them, they are judged:

> On this day sentence is passed upon countries, which to the sword and which to peace, which to famine and which to plenty, and each creature is judged today for life or death. Who is not judged on this day? For the remembrance of every creature comes before You, each man's deeds and destiny, words and way...

The theme of revelation is further combined with redemption; the ram's horn, or *shofar,* which is sounded in the synagogue during daily worship for a month before the *Rosh Hashanah* festival, serves to unite the two:

> You did reveal yourself in a cloud of glory. ...Out of heaven you made them [Israel] hear Your voice. ...Amid thunder and lightning You revealed yourself to them, and while the shofar sounded You shined forth upon them. ...Our God and God of our fathers, sound the great Shofar for our freedom. Lift up the ensign to gather our exiles. ...Lead us happily to Zion Your city, Jerusalem the place of Your sanctuary.

The complex themes of the New Year, the most "theological" of Judaic holy occasions, thus weave together the central narrative categories we have already discovered elsewhere.

The most personal, solemn, and moving of the Days of Awe is the Day of Atonement, *Yom Kippur,* the Sabbath of Sabbaths. It is marked by fasting and continuous prayer. On it, the faithful Israelite makes confession:

> Our God and God of our fathers, may our prayer come before You. Do not hide yourself from our supplication, for we are not so arrogant or stiff-necked as to say before You. ...We are righteous and have not sinned. But we have sinned.
>
> We are guilt laden, we have been faithless, we have robbed...

---

[7]Traditional prayer; author's translation from the Hebrew.

We have committed iniquity, caused unrighteousness, have been presumptuous.

We have counseled evil, scoffed, revolted, blasphemed....[8]

The Hebrew confession is built upon an alphabetical acrostic following the letters of the Hebrew alphabet, as if by making certain every letter is represented, God, who knows human secrets, will combine them into appropriate words. The very alphabet bears witness against us before God. Then:

> What shall we say before You who dwell on high? What shall we tell You who live in heaven? Do You not know all things, both the hidden and the revealed? You know the secrets of eternity, the most hidden mysteries of life. You search the innermost recesses, testing men's feelings and heart. Nothing is concealed from You or hidden from Your eyes. May it therefore be Your will to forgive us our sins, to pardon us for our iniquities, to grant remission for our transgressions.[9]

A further list of sins follows, built on alphabetical lines. Prayers to be spoken by the congregation are all in the plural: "For the sin which we have sinned against You with the utterance of the lips. ...For the sin which we have sinned before You openly and secretly. ..." The community takes upon itself responsibility for what is done in it. All Israel is part of one community, one body, and all are responsible for the acts of each. The sins confessed are mostly against society, against one's fellow men; few pertain to ritual laws. At the end comes a final word:

> O my God, before I was formed, I was nothing. Not that I have been formed, it is as though I had not been formed, for I am dust in my life, more so after death. Behold I am before You like a vessel filled with shame and confusion. May it be Your will...that I may no more sin, and forgive the sins I have already committed in Your abundant compassion.[10]

So the faithful Israelite in the classical Judaic tradition sees himself or herself before God: possessing no merits, yet hopeful of God's love and compassion. To be a classical Jew is to be intoxicated by faith in God, to live every moment in God's presence, and to shape every hour by the paradigm of Torah. The day with its worship in the morning and evening, the week with its climax at the Sabbath, the season marked by nature's commemoration of Israel's sacred history all shape life into rhythms of sanctification, and thus make all of life an act of worship. How does an individual enter into and leave that life— and what stories accompany Israelites on their journey to and fro? That is the question we answer in the next chapter.

---

[8]Jules Harlow, trans., *Mahzor* (New York: Rabbinical Assembly, rep. 1995).

[9]Ibid.

[10]Ibid.

18

Rites of Passage:

Birth, Maturity, Death

Rites for the private person, as distinct from those for the celebration of the holy people as a community, tend to be simple; they ordinarily take place at home and not in the synagogue. These are rites for birth, puberty, marriage, and death. Two of the four, the ones for birth and marriage, are transformed by the master narrative into events in the story of holy Israel; we have already noted, in the case of the *huppah* (Chapter 12), how the private lives of bride and groom embody the public events of the union of Adam and Eve on one side and the loss and restoration of Jerusalem on the other. The story that turns the birth of the male child into a reenactment of a moment in Israel's history proves dramatic and underscores the anomaly that puberty and death, equally critical turnings in the life of Israelite individuals, are left out of the narrative repertoire of Judaism. Puberty and death make no impact upon the holy community that is subject to the sacred story; nothing changes once the Israelite is born, and as to death, that, too, is just an episode in life eternal.

BIRTH: THE COVENANT RENEWED, THE STORY REENACTED

The Torah marks the first of these rites of passage—circumcision of the male penis as an act of the covenant between God and Israel beginning with Abraham—and treats it as critical to the formation of the holy people. The individual, not only holy Israel, stands in a covenanted relationship with God. For males, that is concrete and physical. The covenant between God and Israel is not a mere theological abstraction, nor is it effected only through laws of community and family life. It is quite literally engraved on the flesh of every male Jewish child through the rite of circumcision, *Berit milah* (the covenant of circumcision, not to be confused with a surgical operation performed in a hospital for hygienic reasons).

Performed on the eighth day after birth (the infant's health permitting), normally in the presence of a quorum of ten adult males, the rite of *Berit milah* works like the rite of the *huppah*. It transforms the birth of the child to the parents from a private and personal happening in the natural family to a public and momentous event. Now the individual embodies a chapter in the narrative of the supernatural family of Israel on earth and of God in heaven. An operation of possible medical value becomes the mark of the renewal of the agreement between God and Israel, the covenant carved into the flesh of the penis of every Jewish male.

There are four aspects in which the operation is turned into a rite.

When the rite begins, first, the assembly and the mohel together recite the following:

> The Lord spoke to Moses saying, "Phineas, son of Eleazar, son of Aaron, the priest, has turned my wrath from the Israelites by displaying among them his passion for me, so that I did not wipe out the Israelite people in my passion. Say therefore I grant him my covenant of peace."

Commenting on this passage, Lifsa Schachter states, "Phineas is identified with zealously opposing the…sins of sexual licentiousness and idolatry. He is best known for an event which occurred when the Israelites, whoring with Moabite women in the desert, were drawn to the worship of Baal-Peor …Phineas leaped into the fray and through an act of double murder…quieted God's terrible wrath."[1]

Second, a chair is set called the "chair of Elijah," so that the rite takes place in the presence of a chair for Elijah, the prophet. The newborn son is set on that chair, and the congregation says, "This is the chair of Elijah, of blessed memory." Elijah had complained to God that Israel neglected the covenant (I Kings 19:10–14). So he comes to bear witness that Israel observes the covenant of circumcision. Then, we see, before the surgical operation a blessing is said.

To understand the invocation of Elijah we first recall the pertinent biblical passage:

1 Kings 19:10–14

Suddenly the word of the Lord came to him: "Why are you here, Elijah?"

"Because of my great zeal for the Lord the God of hosts," he said. "The people of Israel have forsaken your covenant, torn down your altars, and put your prophets to death with the sword. I alone am left, and they seek to take my life."

The answer came: "Go and stand on the mount before the Lord."

For the Lord was passing by: a great and strong wind came rending mountains and shattering rocks before him, but the Lord was not in the wind; and after the wind there was an earthquake, but the Lord was not in the earthquake; and after the earthquake fire; but the Lord was not in the fire; and after the fire a still small voice.

When Elijah heard it, he muffled his face in his cloak and went out and stood at the entrance of the cave. Then there came a voice: "Why are you here, Elijah?"

---

[1] Lifsa Schachter, "Reflections on the Berit Mila Ceremony," *Conservative Judaism* 1986 38 (1986): 38–41.

"Because of my great zeal for the Lord God of hosts," he said. "The people of Israel have forsaken your covenant, torn down your altars, and put your prophets to death with the sword. I alone am left, and they seek to take my life."

So, too, the "messenger of the covenant" (Malachi 1:23) is the prophet Elijah, and he is present whenever a Jewish son enters the covenant of Abraham, which is circumcision. God therefore ordered him to come to every circumcision so as to witness the loyalty of the Israelites to the covenant. Elijah then serves as the guardian for the newborn, just as he raised the child of the widow from the dead (1 Kgs. 17:17–24).

Along these same lines, on the Seder table of Passover, a cup of wine is poured for Elijah, and the door is opened for Elijah to join in the rite. Setting a seat for Elijah serves to invoke the presence of the guardian of the newborn and the zealous advocate of the rite of the circumcision of the covenant. Celebrating with the family of the newborn are not "all Israel" in general, but a very specific personage indeed. The gesture of setting the chair silently sets the stage for an event in the life of the family not of the child alone, but of all Israel. The chair of Elijah, filled by the one who holds the child, sets the newborn baby into Elijah's lap.

Third, the blessing is said before the rite itself, that is, as the *mohel,* the person who performs this rite, takes the knife to cut the foreskin:

> Praised are You…who sanctified us with Your commandments and commanded us to bring the son into the covenant of Abraham our father.

The explicit invocation of Abraham's covenant turns the concrete action in the here and now into a simile of the paradigm and archetype: I circumcise my son just as Abraham circumcised Isaac at eight days, and Ishmael. What I do is like what he did. Things are more than what they seem. Then I am a father, like Abraham, and—more to the point—my fatherhood is like Abraham's.

Fourth, after the operation a blessing is said over a cup of wine. Once more invoking the story of Abraham:

> Praised are You, Lord our God, who sanctified the beloved from the womb and set a statute into his very flesh, and his parts sealed with the sign of the holy covenant. On this account, Living God, our portion and rock, save the beloved of our flesh from destruction, for the sake of his covenant placed in our flesh. Blessed are You…who makes the covenant.
>
> Praised are You…who sanctified us with Your commandments and commanded us to bring the son into the covenant of Abraham our father.

By virtue of the rite, the child enters the covenant, meaning that he joins that unseen "Israel" that through blood enters an agreement with God. Then the blessing of the covenant is owing to the child. For covenants or contracts cut both ways.

After the father has recited the blessing, "…who has sanctified us by his commandments and has commanded us to induct him into the covenant of our father, Abraham," the community responds:"just as he has entered the covenant, so may he be introduced to Torah, the *Huppah* [marriage canopy] and good deeds."

It is not possible to interpret the rite of *Berit milah* without invoking the Torah's narrative. Three separate chapters of the story are invoked in the names of Elijah, Phineas, and Abraham. In this connection Schachter interprets those who are present: "In the presence of Elijah...to Torah—as against idolatry; in the presence of Phineas...to the *huppah,* as against sexual licentiousness; in the presence of Abraham...to good deeds: 'For I have singled him out that he may instruct his children and his posterity to keep the way of the Lord by doing what is just and right' (Gen. 18:18)."[2]

PUBERTY: BAR OR BAT MITZVAH

The advent of puberty is marked by the *bar mitzvah* rite for a young man, and in Reform, Reconstructionist, and Conservative Judaism a *bat mitzvah* rite for a young woman, at which a young person becomes obligated to keep the commandments; *bar* means son and *bat* means daughter, with the sense that "one is subject to...," and *mitzvah* means commandment. The young person is called to pronounce the benediction over a portion of the Torah lection in the synagogue and is given the honor of reading the prophetic passage as well. In olden times it was not so important an occasion as it now is in modern America where it has become an occasion of extravagance. Recently Agudath Israel, the organization of classical Orthodox Judaism, issued instructions limiting the expenditure of funds on the celebration.

Only when an Israelite achieves mature intelligence and self-consciousness, normally at puberty, is he or she expected to accept the full privilege of *mitzvah* (commandment) and to regard himself or herself as part of Israel at Sinai, personally *commanded* by God. In the language we have used time and again, at that point the young Israelite tells about himself or herself personally the tale that the Torah tells about Israel: personally redeemed from Egypt, personally present at Sinai.

Judaism perceives the commandments as expressions of one's acceptance of the yoke of the kingdom of heaven and submission to God's will. That acceptance cannot be coerced but requires thoughtful and complete affirmation. The *bar* or *bat mitzvah* thus represents the moment that the young Israelite first assumes full responsibility before God to keep the commandments. But the Israelite changes the face of Israel upon birth, and neither reaching maturity nor death affects the holy community. For the Israelite, once born, never dies for eternity; death is a moment between life and resurrection: "All Israel has a portion in the world to come" (Mishnah Tractate Sanhedrin 11:1) says it all. Marriage does make a difference, for the reasons the liturgy makes explicit, in the narrative of holy Israel.

---

[2]Schachter. "Reflections," p. 41.

BURIAL RITES

Death, a moment in the life of the individual but marking only an interval in the journey to life eternal in the Garden of Eden, is not subject to a narrative in the way in which, as we have seen, birth and marriage are. Rites of death are simple and brief. The natural process of death is treated as a normal chapter of life but not as a tragedy, and not the end of the tale.

At issue in the rites of death and burial is the condition of the soul of the individual Israelite: Death atones for sin, the way in which the Day of Atonement atones for sin, and prepares the Israelite to "stand in judgment" and to enter into the Garden of Eden, there to await the resurrection of the dead and the restoration of Israel to the Land. So the focus is on atonement and reconciliation with God. At the onset of death, the dying Israelite says a confession.

My God and God of my fathers, accept my prayer....

Forgive me for all the sins that I have committed in my lifetime....

Accept my pain and suffering as atonement and forgive my wrongdoing for against You alone have I sinned....

I acknowledge that my life and recovery depend on You.

May it be Your will to heal me.

Yet if You have decreed that I shall die of this affliction,

May my death atone for all sins and transgressions which I have committed before You.

Shelter me in the shadow of Your wings.

Grant me a share in the world to come.

Father of orphans and Guardian of widows, protect my beloved family....

Into Your hand I commit my soul. You redeem me, O Lord God of truth.

Hear O Israel, the Lord is our God, the Lord alone.

The Lord He is God.

The Lord He is God.[3]

The corpse is carefully washed and always protected. The body is covered in a white shroud, then laid in a coffin and buried. Normally burial takes place on the day of death or on the following day. Once the body has been placed in the grave, three pieces of broken pottery are laid on eyes and mouth as signs of their vanity. A handful of dirt from the Land of Israel is laid under the head.[4]

The family recites the *Kaddish,* an eschatological prayer of sanctification of God's name that looks forward to the messianic age and the resurrection of the dead.

---

[3]Reprinted by permission of *A Rabbi's Manual*, edited by Jules Harlow, © the Rabbinical Assembly, 1965, p. 96.

[4]A. Z. Idelsohn, *The Ceremonies of Judaism* (New York: National Federation of Temple Brotherhoods, 1930) p. 133.

Magnified and sanctified be the glory of God in the world created according to his will.

May his sovereignty soon be acknowledged during your lives and the life of all Israel.

May the glory of God be eternally praised, hallowed and extolled, lauded and exalted, honored and revered, adored and worshipped,

Beyond all songs and hymns of exaltation, beyond all praise that man can utter is the glory of the Holy One, blessed be he.

May there be abundant peace from heaven and life's goodness for us and for all Israel.

He who ordains the order of the universe will bring peace to us and to all Israel.[5]

Death is not mentioned. The prayer expresses the hope that the Messiah ("his sovereignty") will soon come, "speedily, in our days," and that "he who brings harmony to the heavens will make peace on earth." The mourners remain at home for a period of seven days and continue to recite the memorial *Kaddish* for eleven months. The life cycle for the private individual is simple, but for the individual as part of Israel, God's holy people, it is rich, absorbing, and encompassing. Life is lived with people, God's people, in God's service.

---

[5]Reprinted by permission of the *Weekday Prayer Book*, edited by Gerson Hadas, © Rabbinical Assembly, 1962, p. 315.

PART VI

Four Types of Judaic Piety

19

The Philosopher

TYPES OF RELIGIOUS EXPRESSION

The mark of a successful religion is its power to accommodate diverse types of personality, to make a place for everybody, man and woman, rich and poor, practical and spiritual, simple and brilliant. In the nature of things, any community contains different kinds of people. Catholic Christianity, for instance, finds a place for people who wish to spend their lives at prayer, for others who want to serve, and for still others who find their vocation in everyday community life. In this section we take up four types of human being. We review how Rabbinic Judaism accommodates each of them: the intellectual (Chapter 19), the mystic (Chapter 20), the ordinary man (Chapter 21), and extraordinary women (Chapter 22). In this way we see how one and the same system makes its impact upon quite exceptional sorts of people.

Life under the Law of the Torah is in this way made real in the context of everyday life of various types of Israelites. A common denominator emerges: the highest common denominator, the Torah. Specifically, what we see is how the Torah infuses each type of personality, giving the philosopher problems for thought, the mystic an encounter with the living God, the everyday man the ethics to guide him in ordinary life, and the exceptional woman the promise—fulfilled only in our own day—that she too may find a place in the life of learning God's will and a life of leadership in Holy Israel. The philosopher, the mystic, the ordinary man, the exceptional woman—all four pursue that singular logic that pervades the way of the Torah and that imparts coherence to diversity.

THE PHILOSOPHICAL FORMULATION
OF THE DUAL TORAH

Up to now we have dealt with those enduring formations of the Judaism of the dual Torah that had come into being in Late Antiquity, the first seven centuries of the Common Era, from the destruction of the Temple in 70 to the Muslim conquest of the Near and Middle East from 640 onward. But as Chapter 2 has shown, the Judaism of the dual Torah survived the world-historical changes represented by the shift from Christian to Muslim rule of territories in which Jews lived, such as the Land of Israel and Babylonia. The rise of Islam brought important intellectual changes because of the character of Islamic culture: intellectually rigorous, sophisticated, enlightened, and philosophical in the classical sense.

Specifically, Muslim theologians, who could read Greek or who read Greek philosophy translated (often by Judaism's intellectuals) into Arabic, developed a mode of thought along philosophical lines that was rigorous, abstract, and scientific, with special emphasis on a close reading of Aristotle. That mode of thought and its consequent expression posed a challenge to the Rabbinic system. While in ancient times a school of Judaic philosophy in the Greek-speaking Jewish world, represented by Philo of Alexandria, read scripture in the light of a Greek philosophical framework, the sages of the Talmud did not follow that generalizing and speculative mode of thought. True, they thought philosophically, pursuing the modes of inquiry of natural history to clarify the Torah. But they presented the results in the form of exegesis of cases, not exposition of general principles resulting from a process of classification and hierarchization.

Now, as the Judaic intellectuals of Islam faced the challenge of Muslim rationalism and philosophical rigor, they read scripture and the Oral Torah as well in the familiar framework of natural history, but they had to express the results in a new way: in the philosophical idiom. The task at hand was to reconcile and accommodate the one with the other, Torah and philosophy. For just as today most Judaists—faithful believers all—cannot imagine denying the established truths of science while affirming the revelation of the Torah—no one thinks the world is flat, for instance, and a one-dimensional, literal reading of the story of a seven-day creation is set aside as well—so in medieval Islam no Judaic intellectuals could rest easy in the admission that scripture and science, in its philosophical form, came into conflict.

That is why alongside study of Torah—meaning spending one's life in learning the Babylonian Talmud and later codes, commentaries, and rabbinical court decisions—a different sort of intellectual-religious life flourished in Judaism. It was the study of the Torah tradition through the instruments of reason and the discipline of philosophy: the quest for generalization, a critical sifting of evidence, and above all, harmony between the generalizations of the Torah and the scientific principles of Aristotle. They had to harmonize, for example, the scriptural notion that God changes his mind with the Aristotelian principle that change indicates imperfection or that miracles interrupt the course of nature with the philosophical principle that the laws of nature are immutable. If God is arbitrary, then God is no philosopher. But for Judaic, Christian, and Islamic theology, God is the source of all truth.

For whom did these questions of the harmony of religion and philosophy or science prove urgent? For the whole history of the Judaism in the age of cogency, from early medieval to modern times and beyond, "study of Torah" in its exegetical formulation predominated. The philosophical enterprise of testing truths and skepticism attracted small numbers of elitists and mainly served their specialized spiritual and intellectual needs. That does not mean the philosophical way was unimportant. Those who followed it included the thoughtful and the perplexed—those who took the statements of the tradition most seriously and, through questioning and reflection, intended to examine and then validate them by the medium of rationality. The philosophers, moreover, were not persons who limited their activities to study and teaching; they frequently both occupied high posts within the Jewish community and served in the high society of politics, culture, and science outside the community as well. Though not numerous, the philosophers exercised considerable influence, particularly over the mind of an age that believed reason and learning, not wealth and worldly power, were what really mattered.

The way of Torah study formed the path everywhere and always. By contrast, the philosophical way proved attractive only at specific times and under unique circumstances, while the way of Torah was always and everywhere characteristic in premodern times. Philosophy proved uniquely important to Jews living in close contact with other cultures and traditions, like those of Hellenistic Alexandria in the first century C.E., of ninth-century Muslim Baghdad, of Spain in the eleventh and twelfth centuries, of Christian Germany in the nineteenth century, and of twentieth-century America. In such settings, Jews coexisted in an open society with gentiles—encompassing pagans, Muslims, Christians, Zoroastrians.

The received theology of the undifferentiated gentiles conflicted with the obvious fact that Muslims and Christians believed in one God, were ethical monotheists just as much as were Israelites. They did not live isolated from, or in ignorance of, the dominant spiritual currents of the day. On the contrary, each particular group felt called upon to explain its chief ideas and doctrines in terms accessible to all others. Reason was conceived as the medium for such discourse, and in the world of Islam, shared by Judaism, Arabic was the language of intellectual sophistication and universal discourse. In most circumstances, where it ruled, Islam was a religion of peace, enlightenment, and tolerance. The Judaic sages had no difficulty in acknowledging Islam as a monotheist religion, even while unable to concede that Muhammad was the "seal of prophecy." As Maimonides put it in his thirteen principles of faith (regularly sung in synagogue worship to this very day): "There has not arisen a prophet of the character of Moses ever again," thus excluding from the Torah that was Judaism both Christ and Muhammad and their revelations.

All groups in the day-to-day encounter of differing cultures and traditions, therefore, attained a high degree of self-consciousness; so that something called Judaism or Christianity or Islam could be defined by contrast to—against the background of—other sorts of "isms" and "ities." The total, all-encompassing world view of Torah, on the other hand, quite unself-consciously spoke of "person," in the assumption that people were pretty much alike because they were Jews. The "good way" for a human being could be defined in a homogeneous setting. But the heterogeneity of the world of intersecting Islam, Christianity, and Judaism, in medieval Spain and in early modern Turkey and the Muslim Balkans, for example, was only one of detail. Philosophy flourished in a world of deep religious conviction—a conviction common to the several disparate communities. The issues of philosophy were set, not by lack of belief, but by deep faith. Few, if any, denied providence, a personal God, and a holy book revealed by God through his chosen messenger.[1] Everyone believed in reward and punishment, in a last judgment, and in a settling of accounts.

The Judaic philosopher had to cope with problems imposed not only by the Torah's conflict with philosophy, but also by the anomalous situation of the Jews themselves. Here again, the enduring ecology left no choice: the issues that faced Jews in times past, present, and future, would dictate a set of issues that philosophy, too, had to take up. For instance, what was the meaning of the strange, unfortunate history of the Jews? How was philosophy to account reasonably for a homelessness of God's people, who were well aware that they lived as a minority among powerful, prosperous majorities—Christian or Muslim? If Torah were true, why did different revelations claiming to be based upon it—but to complete it—flourish, while the people of Torah suffered? Why, indeed, ought one to remain a Jew, when every day one was confronted by the success of the daughter religions? Conversion was always a possibility—an inviting one even under the best of circumstances—for a member of a despised minority.[2]

These problems pressed upon the philosopher in particular—a marginal figure both in Jewry and in the urban civilization of the day. For him, the easy answers—"we are still being punished for our sins," or "we suffer now but our reward will be all the greater later on"—were transparently self-serving, and unsatisfactory because they were too easy. He was, further, concerned with the eternal questions facing all religious people: Is God just: What is the nature of humanity? What is the meaning of revelation? Where were answers to be found?

The search was complicated by the formidable appeal of Greek philosophy to medieval Christian and Islamic civilization. Its rationalism, its openness, its search for pure knowledge challenged all revelations. Philosophy called into question all assertions of truth verifiable not through reason, but only through appeals to a source of truth not universally recognized. Reason thus stood, it seemed, against revelation. Mysterious divine plans came into conflict with allegations of the limitless capacity of human reason. Free inquiry might lead anywhere and so would not reliably lead to the synagogue, church, or mosque. And not merely traditional knowledge, but the specific propositions of faith and the assertions of a holy book had to be measured against the results of reason. Faith or reason—this seemed to be the choice.

For the Jews, moreover, the very substance of faith—in a personal, highly anthropomorphic God who exhibited traits of character not always in conformity with humanity's highest ideals and who in Rabbinic hands looked much like the rabbi himself—posed a formidable obstacle. Classical conundrums of philosophy were further enriched by the obvious contradictions between belief in free will and belief in divine providence. Is God all knowing? Then how can people be held responsible for what they do? Is God perfect? Then how can he change his mind or set aside his laws to forgive people?

---

[1]Abraham S. Halkin, "The Judeo-Islamic Age," in *Great Ages and Ideas of the Jewish People,* ed. Leo W. Schwarz (New York: Random House, 1956), p. 235.

[2]Ibid., pp. 238–239.

No theologian in such a cosmopolitan, rational age could begin with an assertion of a double truth or a private, relative one. The notion that something could be true for one party and not for another, or that faith and reason were equally valid and yet contradictory, were ideas that had little appeal. And the holy book had to retain the upper hand: "Scripture as the word of God contained, of course, absolute truth, while philosophy as a human activity could find its truth only in reasoning."[3] The two philosophers we shall now consider represent the best efforts of medieval Judaic civilization to confront these perplexities.

MOSES MAIMONIDES

The first is Moses Maimonides (1141–1205), who was at the same time a distinguished student of the Talmud and of Judaic law in the classical mode, a community authority, a great physician, and a leading thinker of his day. He mastered the Halakhah and imposed on it a complete reorganization and recategorization. First, he produced a commentary to the Mishnah, the first one in a thousand years that treated the Mishnah as an autonomous document, not merely as subsumed within the Talmud. Then, second, he rewrote the Mishnah into the Mishneh Torah, a law code organized around more rational, topical category formations than the Talmuds or the Mishnah. A comparison of the Mishnah's topics and their organization with those of the Mishneh Torah will show the impact of the philosophical mind upon the Halakhic system. So he recast the entire Halakhic system of Judaism, along lines of philosophical rationalism with its stress on the purposive character of creation.

When it comes to the received corpus of scriptural exegesis and *Aggadah,* his achievement was to synthesize a NeoPlatonic Aristotelianism with biblical revelation. His *Guide to the Perplexed,* published in 1190, was intended to reconcile the believer to the philosopher and the philosopher to faith. For him philosophy was not alien to religion but identical with it, for truth was, in the end, the sole issue. Faith is a form of knowledge; philosophy is the road to faith.

How, specifically, did Moses Maimonides enlist Greek philosophy in the service of the Torah? Let us address the most fundamental question of all: God. His proof for the existence of God was Aristotelian. He argued from creation to Creator but accepted the eternity of the world. Julius Guttmann describes his view as follows:

> Since, in addition to bodies which are both moving and moved, there are other bodies which are moved and yet are not causes of movement, there must also exist a being which moves without being moved. The second proof is based not on the movement of bodies but on their transition from potency to act: the transition presupposed the existence of an actualizing

---

principle which is external to the being thus changed. The impossibility of an infinite regression of causes, just as it led in the first proof to prime mover, now serves to establish the existence of a first actualizing principle, free of all potentiality and hence also immaterial in nature. ...
Maimonides can prove the origin of the world as a whole, from God, only by deduction from the contingent existence of things.[4]

God becomes, therefore an "absolutely simple essence from which all positive definition is excluded."[5] One can say nothing about the attributes of God. He is purged of all sensuous elements. One can say only that God is God—nothing more—for God can only be known as the highest cause of being.

What then of God's self-revelation? Did God not say anything about himself? And if he did, what need for reasonings such as these? For Maimonides, prophecy, like philosophy, depends upon the Active Intellect. But in the case of the prophets, "the Active Intellect impresses itself especially upon their imaginative faculty, which is why they express their teachings in a poetic or literary form, rather than in the ratiocinative form of the philosophers."[6] Prophecy is a gift bestowed by God upon man. The Torah and commandments are clearly important but are not ultimately beyond question or reasonable inquiry. They, however, survive the inquiry unimpaired. The Torah fosters a sound mind and body:

> All its precepts and teachings conspire to guide a man to the greatest
> benefits, moral and intellectual. Everything in the Torah, whether it be a
> law or a narrative or genealogy, is significant...intended to inculcate a
> moral or intellectual truth, to wean men away from wrong beliefs,
> harmful excesses, or dangerous indulgences. In its entirety, the Law is the
> supreme means whereby man realizes himself most fully.[7]

The greatest good, however, is not to study Torah in the sense described earlier, but rather to know God—that is, to worship and love him. Piety and knowledge of Torah serve merely to prepare people for this highest achievement. Study of Torah loses its character as an end in itself and is rendered into a means to a philosophical goal. This constituted the most striking transformation of the old values. Philosophical knowledge of physical and metaphysical truths "culminates in a purified conception of the nature of God. It is this kind of understanding that engenders the longing for God and the love of him."[8]

Maimonides provided a definition of Judaism—a list of articles of faith he thought obligatory on every faithful Jew. These are as follows: (1) existence of God, (2) his unity, (3) his incorporeality, (4) his eternity; (5) the obligation to

---

[4]Julius Guttmann, *Philosophies of Judaism: The History of Jewish Philosophy from Biblical Times to Franz Rosenzweig,* trans. David Silverman (New York: Holt, Rinehart and Winston, 1964), p. 158.

[5]Ibid., p. 158.

[6]Halkin, "The Judeo-Islamic Age," from Schwartz, *Great Ages,* 1956, p. 253. Reprinted with permission.

[7]Ibid., p. 251.

[8]Ibid., pp. 251–252.

worship him alone, (6) prophecy, (7) Moses as the greatest of the prophets, (8) the divine origin of Torah, (9) the eternal validity of Torah, (10) God's knowledge of man's deeds, (11) God punishes wicked actions and rewards righteous ones, (12) his promise to send a Messiah, and (13) his promise to resurrect the dead. These philosophical principles were hotly debated and much criticized, but ironically, achieved a place in the life of Judaic piety. Although subjected to debate and criticism, in the end they were sung as a prayer in a hymn, *Yigdal,* which is always sung at the conclusion of synagogue prayer. (The same principles of faith are set forth in yet another, equally popular synagogue hymn, Adon Olam, the Lord of the world.)

1. The living God we praise, exalt, adore
   He was, he is, he will be evermore.

2. No unity like unto his can be
   Eternal, inconceivable is he.

3. No form or shape has the incorporeal one
   Most holy he, past all comparison.

4. He was ere aught was made in heaven or earth
   But his existence has no date or birth.

5. Lord of the Universe is he proclaimed
   Teaching his power to all his hand has framed.

6. He gave his gift of prophecy to those
   In whom he gloried, whom he loved and chose.

7. No prophet ever yet has filled the place
   Of Moses, who beheld God face-to-face.

8. Through him (the faithful in his house) the Lord
   The law of truth to Israel did accord.

9. This Law of God will not alter, will not change
   For any other through time's utmost range.

10. He knows and heeds the secret thoughts of man:
    He saw the end of all ere aught began.

11. With love and grace doth he the righteous bless,
    He metes out evil unto wickedness.

12. He at the last will his anointed send
    Those to redeem who hope and wait the end.

13. God will the dead to life again restore.
    Praised by his glorious name for evermore.[9]

The esoteric words of the philosopher were thus transformed into a message of faith, at once sufficiently complex to sustain critical inquiry according to the canons of the day and simple enough to bear the weight of the faith of ordinary

[9]Alice Lucas, trans., quoted in Bernard Martin, *Prayer in Judaism* (New York & London: Basic Books, 1968), pp. 84–85.

folk and to be sung. The "God without attributes" is still guide, refuge, stronghold. It is a strange and paradoxical fate for the philosopher's teachings. Who would have supposed at the outset that the way of the philosopher would lead to the piety of the people?

JUDAH HALEVI

Many, indeed, came to no such supposition. They found the philosophers presumptuous, inadequate, and incapable of investigating the truths of faith. But the critics of "philosophy" were themselves philosophers. The greatest was Judah Halevi (1080–1141), who produced *not* a work of sustained philosophical; argument and analysis, but a set of dialogues between a king—the King of the Khazars, a kingdom which did, in fact, adopt Judaism several centuries earlier—in search of true religion and the advocates of the several religious and philosophical positions of the day, including Judaism. Judah Halevi, poet and mystic, objected to the indifference of philosophy to the comparative merits of the competing traditions. In philosophy's approach, "the ultimate objective is the knowledge of God. Religion is recommended because it inculcates the proper moral qualities in men, but no attention is paid to the question of *which* system of religious morality one ought to follow."[10] For the majority religions in the West—Islam and Christianity—such an indifference may have been tolerable, but *not* for a minority destined any day to have to die for the profession of faith.

The philosophers had to address generations of Jews facing martyrdom. The Crusades in Christian Europe, beginning in 1096, when Halevi was sixteen years old, confronted the Jews with armies of Christians out to do battle with infidels, and the Jewish "unbelievers" near at hand provided an easier target, and a more irritating provocation in their unbelief, than the distant Muslims they marched off to fight for possession of the Holy Land. Down the Rhineland marched Crusader armies, massacring Jewish communities that refused to accept Jesus Christ and his gospel of love. Jews began to escape toward the frontier lands of Eastern Europe, down the Rhine and the Danube into new territories, laying the foundations for the vast communities of Judaism that would develop in medieval and early modern times in Poland, Lithuania, White Russia, Ukraine, Rumania, Hungary, Bohemia, Moravia, and elsewhere in the east. And in Spain and North Africa, Islamic counterparts to Crusaders took over; over time, Islam would show a fanatical face to Judaic faithful. Maimonides, too, had to escape from Muslim Spain to Muslim Egypt, where he found safety.

This brings us to the challenge that philosophy faced in the practical crisis confronting Judaism: how to prepare the people of God for the martyrdom that awaited. Here the critics of the rationalists had their say. Martyrdom will not be evoked by the unmoved mover, the God anyone may reach either through revelation or through reason. Only for the God of Israel will a Jew give up his or

---

[106]Halkin, "The Judeo-Islamic Age," from Schwartz, *Great Ages*, 1956, p. 253. Reprinted with permission.

her life. By its nature, philosophy is insufficient for the religious quest: "It starts with assumptions and ends with mere theories."[11] It can hardly compete with— let alone challenge—the *history* of the Israelite people—a history recording extraordinary events starting with revelation. What has philosophy to do with Sinai, with the land, with prophecy? On the contrary, the Jew, expounding religion to the king of the Khazars, begins not like the philosopher with a disquisition on divine attributes, nor like the Christian who starts with the works of creation and expounds the Trinity, nor like the Moslem who acknowledges the unity and eternity of God, but as follows:

> I believe in the God of Abraham, Isaac, and Israel, who led the Israelites out of Egypt with signs and miracles; who fed them in the desert and gave them the Land, after having made traverse the sea and the Jordan in a miraculous way; who sent Moses with His Torah and subsequently thousands of prophets, who confirmed His law by promises to those who observed and threats to the disobedient. We believe in what is contained in the Torah—a very large domain.[12]

The king then asks: Why did the Jew not say he believes in the creator of the world and in similar attributes common to all creeds? The Jew responds that the evidence for Israel's faith is *Israel,* the people, this history and endurance, and not the kinds of reasonable truths offered by other traditions. The *proof* of revelation is the testimony of those who were *there* and wrote down what they heard, saw, and did.

If so, the king wonders, what accounts for the despised condition of Israel today? The Jew compares Israel to the dry bones of Ezekiel:

> …these bones, which have retained a trace of vital power and have once been the seat of a heart, head, spirit, soul, and intellect, are better than bones formed of marble and plaster, endowed with heads, eyes, ears, and all limbs, in which there never dwelt the spirit of life.[13]

God's people is Israel; he rules them and keeps them in their present status:

> Israel amid the nations is like the heart amid the organs: it is the most sick and the most healthy of them all. …The relationship of the Divine power to us is the same as that of the soul to the heart. For this reason it is said, *You only have I known among all the families of the earth, therefore I will punish you for all your iniquities* [Amos 3:2]. …Now we are oppressed, while the whole world enjoys rest and prosperity. But the trials which meet us serve to purify our piety, cleanse us, and to remove all taint from us.[14]

The pitiful condition of Israel is, therefore, turned into the primary testimony and vindication of Israel's faith. That Israel suffers is the best assurance of divine

---

[11] Ibid., p. 253.

[12] Cited in Isaak Heinemann, "Judah Halevi, Kuzari," in *Three Jewish Philosophers,* ed. Isaak Heinemann, Alexander Altmann, and Hans Lewy (Philadelphia: Jewish Publication Society, 1960), p. 33. Reprinted with permission.

[13] Ibid., p. 72.

[14] Ibid., p. 75.

concern. The suffering constitutes the certainty of coming redemption. In the end, the Jew parts from the king in order to undertake a journey to the Land of Israel. There he seeks perfection with God:

> The invisible and spiritual *Shekhinah* [presence of God] is with every born Israelite of pure life, pure heart, and sincere devotion to the Lord of Israel. And the Land of Israel has a special relation to the Lord of Israel. Pure life can be perfectly lived only there.[15]

To this the king objects. He thought the Jew loved freedom, but the Jew finds himself in bondage by imposing duties obligatory in residing in the Land of Israel. The Jew replies that the freedom he seeks is from the service of men and the courting of their favor. He seeks the service of one whose favor is obtained with the smallest effort: "His service is freedom, and humility before him is true honor." He, therefore, turns to Jerusalem to seek the holy life. He closes his remarks:

> "Thou shalt arise and have mercy upon Zion; for it is time to favor her, the moment is come. For thy servants love her stones and pity her dust" (Psalm 102:14–15). This means, Jerusalem can only be rebuilt when Israel yearns for it to such an extent that we sympathize even with its stones and its dust.[16]

Here we find no effort to identify Judaism with rational truth, but rather the claim that the life of the pious Jew stands above—indeed constitutes the best testimony to—truth.

The source of truth is biblical revelation; it was public, complete, fully in the light of history. History, not philosophy, testifies to the truth and in the end constitutes its sole criterion. Philosophy claims reason can find the way to God. Halevi says only God can show the way to God, and he does so through revelation, and therefore in history. For the philosopher, God is the object of knowledge.[17] For Halevi, God is the subject—the source—of knowledge: "The yearning heart seeks the God of Abraham; the labor of the intellect is directed toward the God of Aristotle."[18] And Israel has a specifically religious faculty that mediates the relationship to God; so we have seen in the references to the role of Israel among the nations as similar to the role of the heart among the limbs.

Halevi seeks to explain the supernatural status of Israel. The religious faculty is its peculiar inheritance and makes it the core of humanity. He thus "predicates...the supernatural religious faculty."[19] But while the rest of humanity is subject to the laws of nature, Israel is subject to supernatural, divine providence, manifested in reward and punishment. The very condition of the Jews,

---

[15]Ibid., p. 75.

[16]Ibid., pp. 126–129.

[17]Guttmann, *Philosophies of Judaism,* p. 125.

[18]Ibid., p. 125.

[19]Ibid., p. 126.

in that God punishes them, verifies the particular and specific place of Israel in the divine plan. The teaching of prophecy thus returns in Halevi's philosophy.

PHILOSOPHICAL JUDAISM

These two philosophers were part of a number of important thinkers who attempted to meet the challenge of philosophy and of reason by constructing a comprehensive theological system. But the uses or reason were not exhausted by the philosophical enterprise. Reason played a central role in the study of Torah. The settings, however, were vastly different. Still, so far as reasoning power "is one of the modes of human awareness through which man constructs human experience,"[20] the classic Judaic tradition fully explored this mode.

If, in Judaic tradition, salvation was never reduced to a "confession of a creed or theological agreement," still important efforts were made, such as the one of Maimonides, to produce just such a creed. It is not, as is often asserted, that Judaism had (or has) no theology. Such a statement is manifestly absurd. It is simply that the theological idiom of the Judaic tradition often diverged from that of the Christian West. In Maimonides, we meet a theological mind quite capable of addressing itself to the issues confronting any religious tradition perplexed by philosophical reason.

While like the Muslim and Christian intellectuals in mentality, the Judaic philosophers had more in common with the Talmudic rabbis then with gentile philosophers. The rabbis accepted the Bible and the Talmud as the "whole Torah," and so did the Judaic philosophers. Both groups devoted themselves to the articulation of the role of Torah in the life of Israel, to the meaning of the fate of Israel and to the effort to form piety and shape faith. And for both, *reason* was the means of reaching into Torah—of recovering and achieving truth. Both agreed that words could contain and convey the sacred, and, therefore, reason—the examination of the meaning and referents of words—was the golden measure. They differed only in the object of reason; the one studied law, the other, philosophy. Yet Maimonides, the complete and whole Jew, studied both and made a lasting impact upon the formation not only of both sorts of Judaic tradition, but also of the pious imagination of the ordinary Jew. That is because he translated his philosophical and theological principles and convictions into his presentation of the concrete, practical law. And it is in the study and practice of the Torah and its law that Judaism finds its being.

---

[20]Frederick J. Streng, *Understanding Religious Man* (Belmont, CA: Dickenson, 1968), p. 92.

20

The Mystic

MYSTICAL KNOWLEDGE AND
EXPERIENCE IN RABBINIC JUDAISM

The Judaism of the dual Torah, both in ancient times and also in the medieval and modern ages, welcomed and placed a high value on mystical experience attained through prayer, asceticism, and devotion to godly service. It furthermore made a place within Torah for holy books of mystical doctrine. In ancient times, it is clear, a mystical experience involving visions of God in the levels of the firmament was available to some sages. A continuing tradition of speculation about matters of mystical knowledge and experience flourished from Late Antiquity forward. That tradition came to its zenith in the most important work of mystical speculation and experience, the *Zohar,* a thirteenth-century work of immense proportions and commensurate influence. It suffices to say that the dual Torah of Judaism encompassed not only scripture and the Mishnah and other writings of the oral tradition of the ancient rabbis, but also yet a third powerful and important "torah" as well, the Torah of religious experience of an intense and mystical confrontation with the living God. The *Zohar* is that third component of the Judaism of the dual Torah.

THE ZOHAR AND MOSES DE LEÓN

The principal document for conveying Judaism's story in mystical form was the *Zohar,* "the book of Splendor, Radiance, Enlightenment."[1] The word *Zohar* sustains various interpretations, each pertaining to an important aspect of the book. It was written in the thirteenth century as a multilayered commentary to the Five Books of Moses and to the Five Scrolls (Esther, Ruth, Song of Songs, Qohelet/Ecclesiastes, and Lamentations). It is an anthology of texts composed and redacted over a long period of time, from the latter part of the thirteenth century into the fourteenth century. The main, but not the sole, author was Moses de León, who worked in Spain between 1281 and 1286. We can speak of a completed book of the *Zohar* only from the sixteenth century, when Kabbalists began to prepare the manuscripts for printing; we are best of speaking of "Zoharic literature" until that time.

---

[1] Daniel Chanan Matt, *Zohar: The Book of Enlightenment. Translation and Introduction* (New York, Ramsey, and Toronto: Paulist Press, 1983), xv. I found this the best introduction to the *Zohar* in the English language.

We cannot be surprised that the *Zohar* speaks in the name of important second-century rabbis. For the mystics before and after the *Zohar* took for granted that their doctrines were tradition, part of the Torah, and derived from the same authorities who gave them the Mishnah and other parts of the Oral Torah.

The *Zohar* is made up of diverse writings, most of them interpretations or biblical passages or short sayings or longer disquisitions, many of them attributed to second-century Rabbinical authority, Simeon bar Yohai and his disciples. Hidden meanings of scripture are spelled out. These hidden meanings include the story of the Creation and the cosmos that unfolds in the structure of the ten Emanations (*Sefirot*) of God. They provide the paradigmatic plan of all that unfolds from the supreme deity, called the *En Sof*, or infinity. So the *Zohar* provides another way of telling the story, registering its theological points through narrative. A single passage suffices to show how this is carried on:

> " 'And God said, Let there be light, and there was light' (Gen. 1:3):
>
> "This is the primal light that God made. It is the light of the eye. This
> light God showed to Adam, and by means of it he was enabled to see
> from end to end of the world. This light God showed to David, and he,
> beholding it, sang forth his praise, saying, 'Oh, how abundant is thy
> goodness, which you have laid up for them that fear thee' (Ps. 31:20). This
> is the light through which God revealed to Moses the land of Israel from
> Gilead to Dan. Foreseeing the rise of three sinful generations, the genera-
> tion of Enoch, the generation of the Flood, and the generation of the
> Tower of Babel, God put away the light from their enjoyment. Then he
> gave it to Moses in the time that his other was hiding him, for the first
> three months after his birth. When Moses was taken before Pharaoh, God
> took it from him, and did not give it again until he stood upon the mount
> of Sinai to receive the Torah. Thenceforth Moses had it for his until the
> end of his life, and therefore he could not be approached by the Israelites
> until he had put a veil upon his face (Ex. 23:33)."[2]

On the surface, we are given an account of the primordial light and how it was preserved. The doctrine of the disposition of that light and its cosmic meaning is hinted at but hardly articulated. The upshot is that the Torah is "cosmic law, a blueprint of creation. The *Zohar* illuminates the cosmic aspect of Torah...the literal sense is sanctified, but readers are urged to 'look under the garment of Torah.' "[3] The meaning of this counsel is that, for the unenlightened, there is a rift between the plain sense and the mystical sense, exoteric and esoteric, but the enlightened can see through the veil of scripture and understand that the deep meaning is the mystical meaning. But if all the garments are removed, there is nothing to see, since the ultimate reality of the Torah is the infinite light of God, which in and of itself has no form.

---

[2]Gershom Scholem, ed., *Zohar: The Book of Splendor, Basic Readings from the Kabbalah* (New York: Schocken Books, 1963), p. 29–30.

[3]Matt, *Zohar*, p. 24.

Indeed, the main purpose of mysticism for Judaism is that God is very real, He is accessible in the scriptural texts that the Kabbalists read in its interpretation in the *Zohar,* and the desire of the mystic is "to feel and to enjoy Him; not only to obey but to approach Him"; so says Abraham J. Heschel, the great theologian of Judaism in the twentieth century, who goes on: "They want to taste the whole wheat of spirit before it is ground by the millstones of reason. They would rather be overwhelmed by the symbols of the inconceivable than wield the definitions of the superficial."[4]

Obviously, in so fresh and original a system, all the antecedent symbols and conceptions of Judaism are going to be revised and given new meanings. The single most striking revision is in the very definition of Torah. We know that for classical Judaism Torah means revelation, and revelation is contained in various documents—some of them written down and handed on from Sinai, others transmitted orally, also from Sinai. It is clear that the mystic finds in the Torah meanings and dimensions not perceived elsewhere. In many ways the mysterious power of the mystic is to see what lesser eyes cannot perceive. Thus, Torah came to include both the literal meaning of the words and the deeper or symbolic meaning—the level of meaning far more profound than meets the eye.

THE BOOK OF THE PIOUS

So much for the theoretical exercise, counterpart to philosophy, in the Judaic mystical writings. What about the this-worldly effects of the mystical doctrines? This is how the practical expression of ascetic mysticism is described in a thirteenth-century book of mysticism, the *Book of the Pious:*

> At all times you should love your Creator with all your heart and all your soul and take council with your heart and a lesson from man who is but worms; if a person give you ten gold pieces or more, how deeply engraved would his love be in your heart. And if he provides your support and the support of your children and of your household you would certainly think, "This man which I have never seen and who has extended to me such kindness I would not be able to repay for all the goodness he has shown me should I live a thousand years. I would love him with all my heart and with all my soul; he could not command me to do anything that I would not do for him, because both my wealth and my being are his." As with the love of man so with the love of the Holy One, blessed be He, raised and exalted be His fame. It is He who gives sustenance to all, how much better that we should cleave to the love of the Creator, fear

[4]Abraham J. Heschel, "The Mystical Elements of Judaism," in *The Jews: Their History, Culture, and Religion,* ed. Louis Finkelstein (New York: Harper & Row, 1971), p. 284. Reprinted with permission.

Him, nor transgress His commands whether great or small. For we do not know the reward of each commandment, and the punishment for transgressions though they appear light in our eyes, as it is written, *When the iniquity of my supplanters compasseth me about* (Psalm 49:6). The transgressions to which a man becomes habituated in this world will encompass him on the Day of Judgement. If he is deserving his good deeds will bear witness for him. True and firm it is that we are not to transgress the commandments of our Creator even one of the small ones for a house full of gold and silver. If an individual says, "I will transgress a commandment and with the gold and silver they give me I will fulfill the difficult commandments. With this I will support the poor, invite wayfarers, I will do very many favors." These are the futile thoughts, for perhaps soon after the transgression he will die and not succeed to the gift. Moreover, if he should not die the money would soon be dissipated so that he dies in his sin. Come and see how much you should love your Creator and who does wonderful kindnesses with you, He creates you from a decayed drop, He gives you a soul, draws you forth from the belly, then gives you a mouth with which to speak, a heart to understand, ears to hear the pure words of His mouth, which are refined as silver and pure gold. It is He who leads you on the face of earth, who gives sustenance to all, who causes death and gives life to all. In His hand are the souls of all the living. It is He who distributes your share of bread. What is there to say? For the mouth is unable to speak, the ear unable to hear, for to Him all praise is as silence, there is no end to the length of His days, His years will have no end, He is the King of kings, the Holy One, blessed be His name and His fame. It is He who has created the heavens and earth, sea, and all that is therein. He is the provider of all, for His eyes are open upon all men's paths recompensing each according to his ways and the fruit of his deeds, whether good or bad. Behold it is He who sets forth before men two paths, the path of life and the path of death and says to you, *Choose life* (Deuteronomy 30:19). In spite of all this, we who are filled with worms do not think and do not set our hearts but to fill our appetites freely. We do not think that man's days are numbered, today he is here, tomorrow in the grace, that suddenly he dies. For no man rules over his spirit retaining it (forever). Therefore it is good for man to remove himself from all appetites and direct his heart to love and fear the Lord with all his heart at all times and revile the life of vanity. For we will not be able to humble ourselves and subdue our passion which thrusts us from the land of the living, except through subduing our heart and returning to our Maker in complete repentance, to serve Him and to do His will with a whole heart. Our sages have said, "Bread and salt shalt thou eat and water in measurement shall you drink and beware of gazing at women which drives a person from the world. Love humans and judge all people in the scale of merit." And this is what the Torah has said, *But in righteousness shalt thou judge they neighbor* (Leviticus 19:15). Be humble before all, busy yourself with Torah, which is whole, pure and upright and do not praise yourself for it, because for this were you created.[5]

Some may ask how this intense religious experience is particularly mystical, since the generality of religious people seek to attain that same unity of life and thought with God. But when, in Chapter 21, we meet the piety of an ordinary Israelite, not labeled a Kabbalist or a mystic, we shall find an equivalently intense encounter with the living God of the Torah.

ABRAHAM JOSHUA HESCHEL'S ACCOUNT
OF MYSTICISM IN JUDAISM

That is not surprising, for Kabbalah took shape within the very heart and center of the Judaic intellectual community, and many of the greatest masters of the Talmud also devoted themselves to Kabbalah. To no one in holy Israel was the goal of Kabbalah, encounter with God, alien. The doctrines were particular, the experience was commonly sought, if not commonplace in accomplishment.

Indeed, the main purpose of mysticism for Judaism is that God is very real, and the desire of the mystic is "to feel and to enjoy Him; not only to obey but to approach Him"; so says Abraham J. Heschel, the greatest theologian of Judaism in the twentieth century, who goes on: "They want to taste the whole wheat of spirit before it is ground by the millstones of reason. They would rather be overwhelmed by the symbols of the inconceivable than wield the definitions of the superficial."[6] What, then, is the mystic doctrine of God in Judaism? This is how Heschel answers that question:

> Mystic intuition occurs at an outpost of the mind, dangerously detached from the main substance of the intellect. Operating as it were in no-mind's land, its place is hard to name, its communications with critical thinking often difficult and uncertain and the accounts of its discoveries not easy to decode. In its main representatives, the Kabbalah teaches that man's life can be a rallying point of the forces that tend toward God, that this world is charged with His presence and every object is a cue to His qualities. To the Kabbalist, God is not a concept, a generalization, but a most specific reality; his thinking about Him full of forceful directness. But He who is "the Soul of all souls" is "the mystery of all mysteries." While the Kabbalists speak of God as if they commanded a view of the Beyond, and were in possession of knowledge about the inner life of God, they also assure us that all notions fail when applied to Him, that He is beyond the grasp of the human mind and inaccessible to meditation. He is the *En Sof,* the Infinite, "the most Hidden of all Hidden." While there is

---

[5]Scholom Alchanan Singer, trans., *Medieval Jewish Mysticism: The Book of the Pious* (Northbrook, IL: Whitehall, 1971), pp. 37–38. Reprinted with permission.

[6]Heschel, "Mystical Elements of Judaism," p. 284–285. Reprinted with permission.

an abysmal distance between Him and the world, He is also called All. "For all things are in Him and He is in all things. ...He is both manifest and concealed. Manifest in order to uphold the all and concealed, for He is found nowhere. When He becomes manifest He projects nine brilliant lights that throw light in all directions. So, too, does a lamp throw brilliance in all directions, but when we approach the brilliance we find there is nothing outside the lamp. So is the Holy ancient One, the Light of all Lights, the most Hidden of all Hidden. We can only find the light which He spreads and which appears and disappears. This light is called the Holy Name, and therefore All is One."

Thus, the "Most Recondite One Who is beyond cognition does reveal of Himself a tenuous and veiled brightness shining only along a narrow path which extends from Him. This is the brightness that irradiates all." The *En Sof* has granted us manifestations of His hidden life: He had descended to become the universe; He has revealed Himself to become the Lord of Israel. The ways in which the Infinite assumes the form of finite existence are called *Sefirot*. These are various aspects or forms of Divine action, spheres of Divine emanation. They are, as it were, the garments in which the Hidden God reveals *Himself* and acts in the universe, the channels through which His light is issued forth.[7]

Obviously, in so fresh and original a system, all the antecedent symbols and conceptions of Judaism are going to be revised and given new meanings. The single most striking revision is in the very definition of Torah. We know that for classical Judaism Torah means revelation, and revelation is contained in various documents—some of them written down and handed on from Sinai, others transmitted orally, also from Sinai. But for the mystic, Torah also becomes a "mystic reality," as Heschel explains:

The Torah is an inexhaustible esoteric reality. To enter into its deep, hidden strata is in itself a mystic goal. The Universe is an image of the Torah and the Torah is an image of God. For the Torah is "the Holy of Holies"; it consists entirely of the name of the Holy One, blessed be He. Every letter in it is bound up with that Name."

The Torah is the main source from which man can draw the secret wisdom and power of insight into the essence of things. "It is called Torah (lit.: showing) because it shows and reveals that which is hidden and unknown; and all life from above is comprised in it and issues from it." "The Torah contains all the deepest and most recondite mysteries; all sublime doctrines both disclosed and undisclosed; all essences both of the higher and the lower grades, of this world and of the world to come are to be found there." The source of wisdom is accessible to all, yet only few resort to it. "How stupid are men that they take no pains to know the ways of the Almighty by which the world is maintained. What prevents

---

[7]Ibid., pp. 284–285.

them? Their stupidity, because they do not study the Torah; for if they were to study the Torah they would know the ways of the Holy One, blessed be He."

The Torah has a double significance: literal and symbolic. Besides their plain, literal meaning, which is important, valid and never to be overlooked, the verses of the Torah possess an esoteric significance, "comprehensible only to the wise who are familiar with the ways of the Torah." "Happy is Israel to whom was given the sublime Torah, the Torah of truth. Perdition take anyone who maintains that any narrative in the Torah comes merely to tell us a piece of history and nothing more! If that were so, the Torah would not be what it assuredly is, to wit, the supernal Law, the Law of truth. Now if it is not dignified for a king of flesh and blood to engage in common talk, much less to write it down, is it conceivable that the most high King, the Holy One, blessed be He, was short of sacred subjects with which to fill the Torah, so that He had to collect such commonplace topics as the anecdotes of Esau, and Hagar, Laban's talks to Jacob, the words of Balaam and his ass, those of Balak, and of Zimri, and such-like, and make of them a Torah? If so, why is it called the 'Law of Truth?' Why do we read *The Law of the Lord is perfect. ... The testimony of the Lord is sure. ... The Ordinances of the Lord are true. ...More to be desired are they than gold, yea, than much fine gold" (Psalm 19:8–11).* But assuredly each word of the Torah signifies sublime things, so that this or that narrative, besides its meaning in and for itself, throws light on the all-encompassing Rule of the Torah."[8]

In this statement of Heschel's, we see how it was that the long and influential tradition of mysticism in Judaism was able to reinforce and vivify Rabbinic Judaism in its Talmudic mode. It is clear that the mystic finds in Torah meanings and dimensions not perceived in the earlier phases of Talmudic Judaism. In many ways the mysterious power of the mystic is to see what lesser eyes cannot perceive. But the perception is there, and to the mystic and his audience it was very real. So Torah took on a richer meaning that it had had, even for the rabbi. Thus, Torah came to include both the literal meaning of the words and the deeper or symbolic meaning—the level of meaning far more profound than meets the eye. Torah was made to yield the meanings not solely of its sentences, but now of each and every individual letter.

GERSHOM SCHOLEM'S ACCOUNT
OF MYSTICISM IN JUDAISM

The essence of the mystic way is not contained within the notion of the deeper layers of meaning to be found within Torah. Rather, the essence of mysticism

---

[8]Ibid., pp. 292–293.

is the inquiry into the very essence of God. What made mysticism a powerful force in Judaism is the vivid encounter with God made possible in mysticism as it was not in any other mode of Judaism or Judaic religiosity. This is how Gershom Scholem, another great twentieth-century master of Kabbalistic learning, explains the mystic encounter with God:

> The mystic strives to assure himself of the living presence of God, the God of the Bible, the God who is good, wise, just and merciful and the embodiment of all other positive attributes. But at the same time he is unwilling to renounce the idea of the hidden God who remains eternally unknowable in the depths of His own Self, or, to use the bold expression of the Kabbalists "in the depths of his nothingness." This hidden God may be without special attributes—the living God of whom the Revelation speaks, with whom all religion is concerned, must have attributes, which on another plane represent also the mystic's own scale of moral values: God is good, God is severe, God is merciful and just. ... The mystic does not even recoil before the inference that in a higher sense there is a root of evil even in God. The benevolence of God is to the mystic not simply the negation of evil, but a whole sphere of divine light, in which God manifests Himself under this particular aspect of benevolence to the contemplation of the Kabbalist.[9]

In many ways, then, mysticism must be seen as the ultimate, logical conclusion of that mode of Judaism which took shape in the aftermath of the messianic disasters of the first and second century. For the encounter with God outside history and time—the direct realization of the knowledge of God, who in some measure is hidden and unknowable in the depths of His nothingness—removes the mystic from the one thing that Rabbinic Judaism to begin with proposed to neutralize; namely, the vagaries of history. The essentially ahistorical quality of mystical thinking accounts for the ready home provided to mysticism by that form of Judaism which began with the Mishnah and the Talmud and, we now see, came to fruition and fulfillment—in the minds of many great Talmudists—in the mystical realization of the encounter with God's hidden self. In Chapter 29 we shall meet Kabbalah again, this time in its formulation in Hasidism, a movement within the Judaic systems of modern times.

To what degree did the values of the rabbis of the Talmud and of the great philosophers and mystics actually influence the lives of ordinary folk? Were Jews truly the "people of Torah" that the rabbis, philosophers, and mystics wanted them to be? Next we turn to an ordinary man, and then we shall look at the spiritual traits of an ordinary woman—both of whom lived in the long centuries during which Judaism in its classical form predominated. When, at the end, we discover in the writing of a pious and traditional woman an essentially fresh aspiration, we shall know that it is time to ask what has changed in the modern period in the history of Judaism, and why that change has taken place.

---

[9]Gershom Scholem, "Major Trends in Jewish Mysticism," in *Understanding Rabbinic Judaism,* ed. Jacob Neusner (New York: Ktav, 1974), pp. 253–254.

21

An Ordinary Jew

HOSTILE STEREOTYPES OF ORDINARY JEWS AND OF JUDAISM

In normative Judaism, to be "Israel"—part of the community, an individual Israelite—means to model life in the image, after the likeness, of God as made known in the Torah. Every human being is in God's image, after God's likeness, and the Torah—so Judaism maintains—defines what that means.

But in the everyday world Jews are subjected to negative stereotypes; Judaism has been denigrated as well. Any negative experience someone may ever have had with an individual of Jewish origin, whether or not a practitioner of Judaism, is taken to represent all the Jews and Judaism, too. In a university classroom in Christchurch, New Zealand, for instance, I found Judaism unashamedly represented by students as "not a religion so much as a certain attitude toward money,"[1] and the same sort of denigration of the faith and people of Israel is common everywhere. Christian anti-Semites have described life under the law, that is, under the Torah, in derogatory terms, denying that any true piety can emerge under the burden of so many petty rules and regulations. Lutheran theologians in pre-Nazi Germany characterized Judaism as a "religion for book-keepers," and "life under the law," a religion for robots. Not to be outdone, secular anti-Semites attribute to the fault of the Jews everything they find wrong with the world.

LIFE UNDER THE LAW OF THE TORAH: COVENANTAL NOMISM

The kind of human being the Torah (that is, "Judaism") means to nurture therefore requires attention. When we examine the statements of ordinary people, we find rich evidence of a profound ethical life with God: women and men devoted to the holy way of life because they love God and want to live their lives and form their communities in accord with the covenant that God made with

---

[1] The same university, Canterbury University, bestowed an MA degree on a dissertation of Holocaust revisionism, one that claimed to "disprove the Holocaust," and out of shame the university had to rescind the degree. The quite routine anti-Semitism of the educated classes of New Zealand has its counterparts elsewhere—in Sweden, France, and Britain, for example. To the credit of three generations since the Holocaust World War II, Germany has repudiated the racist and cultural and theological anti-Semitism and anti-Judaism that produced the Holocaust.

Israel at Mount Sinai. Life under the law has rightly been characterized by the New Testament scholar E. P. Sanders as a life of *covenantal nomism,* meaning that Israel keeps the Torah in obedience to the covenant made by God with the holy people through the Torah.

So, we come to ask, what of the common folk who lived out their days in a community shaped by the values of the Torah? What were their ideals? One insight is to be derived from the "ethical wills" written by fathers for their children. In an ethical will, the one who made the will would divide not his earthly property but his highest ideals, and he would ask his heirs to carry out those ideals. Such wills obviously present the father at his best, facing the prospect of death and judgment and hoping to show his best side and urge upon his children the highest and noblest ideals. But that is what makes the ethical wills interesting, for they mirror ordinary folk ideals at an extraordinary moment.

ELEAZAR OF MAINZ

The ideals of an average Jew are represented by the testament of Eleazar of Mainz, who died in 1357:

> These are the things which my sons and daughters shall do at my request. They shall go to the house of prayer morning and evening, and shall pay special regard to the Prayer and the *Shema.* So soon as the service is over, they shall occupy themselves a little with the Torah, the Psalms, or with works of charity.
>
> Their business must be conducted honestly, in their dealing both with Jew and gentile.
>
> They must be gentle in their manners, and prompt to accede to every honorable request. They must not talk more than is necessary: by this will they be saved from slander, falsehood and frivolity.
>
> They shall give an exact tithe of all their possessions; they shall never turn away a poor man empty-handed, but must give him what they can, be it much or little. If he beg a lodging overnight, and they know him not, let them provide him with the wherewithal to pay an innkeeper. Thus shall they satisfy the needs of the poor in every possible way.
>
> My daughters must obey scrupulously the rules applying to women; modesty sanctity, reverence, should mark their married lives. Marital intercourse must be modest and holy, with a spirit of restraint and delicacy, in reverence and silence. They shall be very punctilious and careful with their ritual bathing. They must respect their husbands, and must be invariably amiable to them. Husbands, on their part, must honor their wives more than themselves, and treat them with tender consideration. If they can by any means contrive it, my sons and daughters should live in communities, and not isolated from other Jews, so that their sons and daughters may learn the ways of Judaism. Even if compelled to solicit

from others the money to pay a teacher, they must not let the young, of both sexes, go without instruction in the Torah. Marry your children, O my sons and daughters, as soon as their age is ripe, to members of respectable families.

Every Friday morning, they shall put themselves in careful trim for honoring the Sabbath, kindling the lamps while the day is still great, and in winter lighting the furnace before dark, to avoid desecrating the Sabbath (by kindling fire thereon). For due welcome to the Sabbath, the women must prepare beautiful candles.

In their relation to women, my sons must behave continently, avoiding mixed bathing and mixed dancing and all frivolous conversation, while my daughters ought not to speak much with strangers, nor jest nor dance with them. They ought to be always at home, and not be gadding about. They should not stand at the door, watching whatever passes. I ask, I command, that the daughters of my house be never without work to do, for idleness leads first to boredom, then to sin. But let them spin, or cook, or sew.

I earnestly beg my children to be tolerant and humble to all, as I was throughout my life. Should cause for dissension present itself, be slow to accept the quarrel; seek peace and pursue it with all the vigor at your command. Even if you suffer loss thereby, forbear and forgive, for God has many ways of feeding and sustaining His creatures. To the slanderer do not retaliate with counter-attack; and though it be proper to rebut false accusations, yet is it most desirable to set an example of reticence. You yourselves must avoid uttering any slander, for so will you win affection. In trade be true, never grasping at what belongs to another. For by avoiding these wrongs—scandal, falsehood, money-grubbing—men will surely find tranquility and affection. And against all evils, silence is the best safeguard.

Whatever happiness befalls you, be it in monetary fortune or in the birth of children, be it some signal deliverances of any other of the many blessings which may come to you, be not stolidly unappreciative, like dumb cattle that utter no word of gratitude. But offer praises to the Rock who has befriended you, saying: "O give thanks unto the Lord, for He is good, for His mercy endureth for ever. Blessed art Thou, O Lord, who are good and dispenses good." Besides thanking God for His bounties at the moment they occur, also in your regular prayers let the memory of these personal favors prompt your hearts to special fervor during the utterance of the communal thanks. When words of gratitude are used in the liturgy, pause to reflect in silence on the goodness of God to you that day. And when you make the response: "May Thy great Name be blessed," call to mind your own personal experiences of the divine favor.

Be very particular to keep your houses clean and tidy. I was always scrupulous on this point, for every injurious condition, and sickness and poverty, are to be found in foul dwellings. Be careful over the benedictions; accept no divine gift without paying back the Giver's part; and His part is man's grateful acknowledgment.

Every one of these good qualities becomes habitual with him who studies the Torah; for that study indeed leads to the formation of a noble character. Therefore, happy is he who toils in the Law! For this gracious toil fix daily times, of long or short duration, for it is the best of all works that a man can do. . . .

Be of the first ten in Synagogue, rising betimes for the purpose. Pray steadily with the congregation, giving due value to every letter and word, seeing that there are in the *Shema* 248 words, corresponding to the 248 limbs in the human body.

I beg of you, my sons and daughters, my wife and all the congregation, that no funeral oration be spoken in my honor. Do not carry my body on a bier but in a coach. Wash me clean, comb my hair, trim my nails, as I was wont to do in my life-time, so that I may go clean to my eternal rest, as I went clean to Synagogue every Sabbath day. If the ordinary officials dislike the duty, let adequate payment be made to some poor man who shall render this service carefully and not perfunctorily. At a distance of thirty cubits from the grave, they shall set my coffin on the ground, and drag me to the grave by a rope attached to the coffin. Every four cubits they shall stand and wait awhile, doing this in all seven times, so that I may find atonement for my sins. Put me in the ground at the right hand of my father, and if the space be a little narrow, I am sure that he loves me well enough to make room for me by his side. If this be altogether impossible, put me on his left, or near my grandmother, Yuta. Should this also be impractical, let me be buried by the side of my daughter.[2]

Where does the "way of Torah" lead? The human being before us clearly shapes his life and values by what Torah was supposed to mean. He stresses a life of prayer, study, and good deeds. A disciple of the sages should not bring Torah into disrepute by false dealing, and no distinction is made between Jew and gentile. The disciple must be gentle and modest, must not talk too much, and must be careful to avoid slander. He must tithe and generously receive the poor man. Daughters must be modest and sons solicitous. Jews must live with other Jews, so as to sustain one another during the long exile. Living as a nation within other nations, governed by their own laws and under their own administrations, Jews had best seek one another out. Above all, one should borrow—even impoverish oneself—to make certain one's children study Torah. The Sabbath comes next in order of interest and then again, an appeal for modesty, sobriety, and tolerance. Life is to be lived as a gift from God. Whatever happens, one must thank God, in public and private worship, on every possible occasion. The difference between man and beast is *gratitude*. And once more, all these virtues are the habits of the student of Torah. Study leads not to learning but to nobility.

---

[2]Israel Abrahams, *Hebrew Ethical Wills,* vol. 2 (Philadelphia: Jewish Publication Society of America, 1948), pp. 207–218. Reprinted with permission.

As to the rituals of death, they should be humble—even degrading—so that penance on earth may produce felicity in heaven.

One may well doubt that any ordinary person could live up to these high ideals. Indeed, the homely touch at the end of Eleazar's testament reminds us of his humanity: "Put me in the ground at the right hand of my father...he loves me well enough to make room...or near my grandmother...[or] by the side of my daughter." Life under Torah law was meant to produce a saint. Being men of flesh and blood, Jews cannot be assumed everywhere and always to have replicated the values of the Torah; but what is important is that these values set the standard.[3] Until modern times, no others were widely adopted by Jews living within the Jewish community. Studying Torah, living in the traditional community, following the stable and serene way of life from Sabbath to Sabbath and from season to season—these were what it meant to be a Jew: always Israel, only Israel. It was a sweet life—sweeter than honey—full of piety, reverence, and beauty. So the pious Jew prayed—and continues to pray—day by day: "How good our lot! How pleasant our portion!"

---

[3]For an excellent account of medieval Jewish life, see Cecil Roth, "The European Age," in *Great Ages and Ideas of the Jewish People,* ed. Leo W. Schwarz (New York: Random House, 1956), pp. 267–314.

22

Two Extraordinary Women

THE FEMININE HALF OF HOLY ISRAEL

At the end of our description of the way of Torah explored by Jews from antiquity to the present, we return to the position of women. This is for two reasons. First, the matter is intrinsically important. We cannot understand a religion unless we make some sense of the role and position that religion accords to half its adherents—women—just as we must attend to the values and ideals shaped for that religion's male adherents. Second—and still more important—one of the principal traits of the advent of the new era in the history of Judaism will be a shift in the status and role of women on one side and in women's aspirations for such a shift to take place on the other. So, as usual, women supply the key to the system for the social order set forth by a religion.

We may point to important roles taken by women in Israelite politics, culture, and religion in biblical times. The Hebrew scripture speaks of women who were important political figures, such as generals, heads of state, and prophets. Women form the center of important biblical narratives from the time of Miriam, the sister of Moses, through Deborah to Ruth, Esther, Bathsheba, and others. So there is no doubt that within the complexities of a mosaic of biblical documents, one continuing trait is that women may come to the center of the stage and play a leading role. That this was so in exceptional circumstances—that men generally were the heads of state, prophets, generals, and other important political figures—is beside the point. Women could and did attain prominence.

There was one institution in ancient times in which women were afforded no role whatsoever and from which, in point of fact, women were essentially excluded. That was the Temple, and with it, the priesthood, which was no mean exclusion. The priestly law codes contained within Leviticus and Numbers take women very seriously and devote much attention to the status of women within the priesthood. But women's status was solely dependent on the priests, all of whom were males, and it was principally a vehicle for the sanctification of the priesthood. While some rites (e.g., those performed after childbirth) were defined for women, no rites could be performed by women, who were not permitted into the holier part of the Temple buildings and were kept out in a women's courtyard. We cannot now speculate on why the imagination of the priesthood should have excluded all roles for women while, by contrast, the royal house could put forward queens as well as kings, the prophetic movement could put forward a Hulda along with a Jeremiah, and the great writers could pay attention to a Ruth and an Esther as much as to a David and a Solomon. We have to recognize that exclusion from Temple and priesthood as a fact.

When, in the first and second centuries, movements took shape out of the priesthood and around the priestly ideals, the consequence of that fact became clear. Just as the priesthood excluded women, so its successor, the rabbinate, found little place for women. After the second century, we hear of a few, if any women in the all-male society of the rabbinical schools (*Yeshivot*). And for the next eighteen hundred years there is not a *single* woman associated with the writing of a commentary to the Talmud, the conduct of a rabbinical court, or the administration of the Jewish community as a rabbinical authority. The exclusion of women from the centers of learning and leadership does not, of course, mean that women were abused or disgraced. The contrary is the case. Every effort was made to preserve the rights, property, and dignity of women. But women could not preserve their own rights, property, or dignity. They formed a subordinated caste within the community of Judaism.

GLÜCKEL OF HAMELN

Now we must ask ourselves: Does the fact of their subordination mean women were alienated by the system? In the writings of Glückel of Hameln (1646–1724) we find that was not so. Indeed, if we now compare Glückel's letter to her children with the ethical will of Eleazar of Mainz—written three hundred years earlier!—we find pretty much the same beliefs and ethical values. Glückel's message is the same and expresses precisely the same religious world view as Eleazar's, which we met in Chapter 21.

> In my great grief and for my heart's ease I begin this book in the year of Creation 5451—God soon rejoice us and send us His redeemer soon. Amen.
>
> With the help of God, I began writing this, my dear children, upon the death of your good father in the hope of distracting my soul from the burdens laid upon it, and the bitter thought that we have lost our faithful shepherd. In this way I have managed to live through many wakeful nights, and springing from my bed have shortened the sleepless hours.
>
> I do not intend, my dear children, to compose and write for you a book of morals. Such I could not write, and our wise men have already written many. Moreover, we have our holy Torah in which we may find and learn all that we need for our journey through this world to the world to come. Of our beloved Torah we may seize hold. ...We sinful men are in the world as if swimming in the sea and in danger of being drowned. But our great, merciful and kind God, in His great mercy, has thrown ropes into the sea that we may take hold of them and be saved. These are our holy Torah where is written what are the rewards and punishments for good and evil deeds. ...

I pray you this, my children: be patient, when the Lord, may He be praised, sends you a punishment, accept it with patience and do not cease to pray to Him; perhaps He will have mercy upon you. ...Therefore, my dear children, whatever you lose, have patience, for nothing is our own, everything is only a loan. ...We men have been created for nothing else but to serve God and to keep His commandments and to obey the Torah, "for that is thy life, and the length of the days."

The kernel of the Torah is: "Thou shalt love thy neighbor as thyself." But in our days we seldom find it so, and few are they who love their fellowmen with all their heart. On the contrary, if a man can contrive to ruin his neighbor nothing pleases him more. ...

The best thing for you, my children, is to serve God from your heart without falsehood or deception, not giving out to people that you are one thing while, God forbid, in your heart you are another. Say your prayers with awe and devotion. During the time for prayers do not stand about and talk of other things. While prayers are being offered to the Creator of the world, hold it a great sin to engage another man in talk about an entirely different matter—shall God Almighty be kept waiting until you have finished your business?

Moreover, set aside a fixed time for the study of the Torah, as best you know how. Then diligently go about your business, for providing your wife and children with a decent livelihood is likewise a mitzvah—the command of God and the duty of man. We should, I say, put ourselves to great pains for our children, for on this the world is built, yet we must bear in mind that if children did as much for their parents, the children would quickly tire of it.

A bird once set out to cross a windy sea with its three fledglings. The sea was so wide and the wind so strong that the father bird was forced to carry his young, one by one, in his claws. When he was half-way across with the first fledgling the wind turned to a gale, and he said: "My child, look how I am struggling and risking my life in your behalf. When you are grown up, will you do as much for me and provide for my old age?" The fledgling replied: "Only bring me to safety, and when you are old I shall do everything you ask of me." Whereat the father bird dropped his child into the sea, and it drowned, and he said: "So shall it be done to such a liar as you." Then the father bird returned to the shore, set forth with his second fledgling, asked the same question, and receiving the same answer, drowned the second child with the cry "You, too, are a liar!" Finally he set out with the third fledgling, and when he asked the same question, the third and last fledgling replied: "My dear father, it is true you are struggling mightily and risking your life in my behalf, and I shall be wrong not to repay you when you are old, but I cannot bind myself. This though I can promise: when I am grown up and have children of my own, I shall do as much for them as you have done for me." Whereupon the father bird said: "Well spoken, my child, and wisely; your life I will spare and I will carry you to shore in safety."

Above all, my children, be honest in money matters, with both Jews and Gentiles, lest the name of Heaven be profaned. If you have in hand money or goods belonging to other people, give more care to them than if they were your own, so that, please God, you do no one a wrong. The first question put to a man in the next world is, whether he was faithful in his business dealings. Let a man work ever so hard amassing great wealth dishonestly, let him during his lifetime provide his children fat dowries and upon his death a rich heritage—yet woe, I say, and woe again to the wicked man who for the sake of enriching his children has lost his share in the world to come! For the fleeting moment he has sold Eternity.[1]

If we look in vain for evidence that Glückel is discontented with her status as a woman, it is because, within the system, her work is as important as her husband's. She is one who shapes and transmits Judaism, as much as her husband, but she does it in a different context; she has a different job to do. And she carried out her work unself-consciously and in a thoroughly accepting spirit.

HENRIETTA SZOLD

A dramatic shift took place in the consciousness and culture of the Jewish people of Europe and America in the nineteenth and twentieth centuries. That change profoundly affected the Judaic religious system that had prevailed for nearly two millennia. We shall devote the rest of this account to what happened to Judaism in modern times. But, treating women as the key to the system, we ask in this very context for an example of that shift captured in a single document of explicit feminism—a letter written by one woman in 1906. The contrast between Glückel and Henrietta Szold captures the transition from classical to contemporary times in the history of Judaism.

Henrietta Szold, in the very heart of Judaic religious expression, exemplifies the fact that in modern times women would become conscious of their subordinated and secondary role in Judaism and would undertake to change that role. Szold was one of the earliest and certainly the single most effective of the leaders in this movement. She founded the Women's Zionist Movement (Hadassah) and formed it into the single most important organization in American and world Zionism. But that is not the reason Szold provides a contrast with Glückel. Rather, it is because she represents an event in Judaism, not only in the national or ethnic history of the Jewish people. For what makes her es-

---

[1] Franz Kobler, *A Treasury of Jewish Letters*, vol. 2 (Philadelphia: Jewish Publication Society of America, 1954), pp. 565–567. Reprinted with permission.

pecially interesting in an account of the history of Judaism is a poignant moment, the advent of Judaic feminism in a single prophetic gesture.

The event had to do with the mourning rites of Judaism: Do women participate? Specifically, until recent times, men recited the *Kaddish;* women were
not expected to. When her mother died, Szold insisted on saying the memorial
Kaddish in her mother's memory and refused the offer of a well-meaning male
to say it in her behalf. This is what she replied in her letter.

> It is impossible for me to find words in which to tell you how deeply I
> was touched by your offer to act as "*Kaddish*" for my dear mother. I
> cannot even thank you—it is something that goes beyond thanks. It is
> beautiful, what you have offered to do—I shall never forget it.
>
> You will wonder, then, that I cannot accept your offer. Perhaps it
> would be best form not to try to explain to you in writing, but to wait
> until I see you to tell you why it is so. I know well, and appreciate what
> you say about, the Jewish custom; and Jewish custom is very dear and
> sacred to me. And yet I cannot ask you to say *Kaddish* after my mother.
> The *Kaddish* means to me that the survivor publicly and markedly
> manifests his wish and intention to assume the relation to the Jewish
> community which his parent had, and that so the chain of tradition
> remains unbroken from generation to generation, each adding its own
> link. You can do that for the generations of your family, I must do that for
> the generations of my family.
>
> I believe that the elimination of women from such duties was never
> intended by our law and custom—women were freed from positive duties
> when they could not perform them, but not when they could. It was
> never intended that, if they could perform them, their performance of
> them should not be considered as valuable and valid as when one of the
> male sex performed them. And of the *Kaddish* I feel sure this is particu-
> larly true.
>
> My mother had eight daughters and no son; and yet never did I hear a
> word of regret pass the lips of either my mother or my father that one of
> us was not a son. When my father died, my mother would not permit
> others to take her daughters' place in saying the *Kaddish,* and so I am sure
> I am acting in her spirit when I am moved to decline your offer. But
> beautiful your offer remains nevertheless, and, I repeat, I know full well
> that it is much more in consonance with the generally accepted Jewish
> tradition than is my or my family's tradition. You understand me, don't
> you?[2]

It would not be possible to adduce a more eloquent statement of the shift
toward modernity—represented for us by the change in the consciousness and

---

[2]"The Jewish Woman: An Anthology," in *Response* 18(1973): 76.

aspirations of Jewish women in the practice of Judaism—than this simple, deeply traditional statement. In the modern age some women would no longer accept the role, assigned to them in classical Judaism, of silent partner and member of a protected but subordinated caste. It is time to ask: What other changes took place? And how shall we account for them?[3]

---

[3]For scholarly views of women in classical and contemporary Judaism, see these works of Judith R. Baskin, *Midrashic Women: Formations of the Feminine in Rabbinic Literature* (Hanover, NH: Brandeis University Press/University Press of New England, 2002); "Jewish Women in the Middle Ages," in *Jewish Women in Historical Perspective*, 2nd ed. Detroit: Wayne State University Press, 1998) pp. 101–127 "Women in Contemporary Judaism," in *The Blackwell Companion to Judaism*, ed. Jacob Neusner and Alan J. Avery-Peck (Oxford: Blackwell, 2001) pp. 393–414. In addition, see these works by Mayer I. Gruber: *The Motherhood of God and Other Studies*, University of South Florida Studies in the History of Judaism, no. 57 (Atlanta: Scholars Press, 1992); "The Status of Women in Ancient Judaism," in *Judaism in Late Antiquity*, vol. 3, *Where We Stand: Issues and Debates in Ancient Judaism, Part Two*, ed. Jacob Neusner and Alan J. Avery-Peck (Leiden: E. J. Brill, 1999), pp. 151–176; and "Women in the Religious System of the Dead Sea Scrolls," in *Judaism in Late Antiquity*, vol. 5, *The Judaism of Qumran: A Systematic Reading of the Dead Sea Scrolls*, ed. Alan J. Avery-Peck, Bruce D. Chilton, and Jacob Neusner (Leiden: E. J. Brill, 2000), pp. 173–196.

PART VII

Classical Judaism in Modern Times: Reform, Orthodox, Conservative Judaisms and Zionism

23

Modern Times

CHRISTIANITY AND JUDAISM TOGETHER MEET COMPETITION IN SECULARISM

From the time of Constantine in the fourth century down to the nineteenth century, Jewry in Christendom had sustained itself as a recognized and ordinarily tolerated minority. The contradictory doctrines of Christianity—the Jews as Christ killers to be punished, the Jews as witnesses to be kept alive and ultimately converted at the second coming of Christ—held together in an uneasy balance. Official policy—preserve the Jews alive, but do not reward their perfidy—accounts for the Jews' survival in some of the Christian realms, particularly those on the frontiers of Christian Europe, south and east. The pluralistic character of some multiethnic societies, such as that in Spain, explains the welcome accorded entrepreneurs in opening territories. These were, for instance, Norman England, Lithuania, Poland and Russia, White Russia and Ukraine, in the early centuries of their development.

What of the Judaism that flourished from antiquity to modern times? The Rabbinic system to begin with had addressed the agenda of Christianity and for long centuries had given answers that, for holy Israel, proved self-evidently valid. Judaism had framed its normative system by answering the question made urgent by Christianity's triumph: What is Israel in the divine plan? This it did by appeal to the sanctification of Israel and its future salvation. So normative Judaism had taken shape in response to the challenge of Christianity. So long as Christianity defined the issues in Christian lands, Judaism would flourish without effective competition within Jewry, absorbing and accommodating new issues and ideas. The same was true of Islam and the character of Judaism in the Muslim world. That was so for Islam right down to 1948, when the creation of the state of Israel led to the expulsion of Jews from some of the Muslim lands, where they had lived from antiquity: Iraq (1949), Egypt (1956), Algeria (1965), Iran (1979), and the like. And in the Christian West from the Enlightenment onward, just as Christianity faced competition from militant secularism, communism, Nazism, nationalism, and hedonism (among others), so those same competing views of the world provoked the formation of Judaisms in response.

THE NEW "URGENT QUESTION"
FACING JEWS

In the received system of normative Judaism, which reached definition from the fourth century C.E. onward, "Israel"—that is, the supernatural community of the Torah, not to be confused with the "Jews" as an ethnic group or nation—seeks sanctification now to attain salvation at the end of time: "The Messiah will come when all Israel sanctifies a single Sabbath." That conviction explained why a Jew should adhere to the holy way of life of the holy Israel formed by the Jewish community. Thus the normative system could explain how and why Jews should be solely "Israel." But that system could not explain how they could be both "Israel" and something—anything—else. None required such an explanation. No one until the nineteenth century had ever imagined that a Jew belonged to any community other than the community of Judaism, "Israel." A secular definition of "Israel" lay beyond the community's imagining. Nor could "Israel" accommodate Jews who adopted Islam or Christianity status as "Israel" was permanent, however, so upon reversion to Judaism ex-apostates were received home without much ado.

In modern times, faced with the political changes brought about by the American Constitution of 1787 and the French Revolution of 1789, Jews in Western Europe and the United States aspired to a position equivalent to that of the majority population: citizenship and equality before the law. Then the urgent question emerged: How and why be *both* Jewish *and* German or Jewish and French or Jewish and British?[1] From the earliest decades of the nineteenth century new Judaisms took shape, dealing with other agendas of urgent questions and answering those questions in ways self-evidently right for those who believed. They offered explanations of how a Jew could be not solely "Israel" but something—anything—in addition to Israelite. For that purpose people had to uncover a neutral realm in the life of individuals and consequently of the community as well, a realm left untouched by the processes of sanctification leading to salvation that had for so long made Jews into "Israel," the community of Judaism. Each of these Judaisms claimed to continue in linear succession the Judaism that had flourished for so long, to develop in an incremental succession and so to connect, through the long past, to Sinai. But in fact each one responded to contemporary issues deemed urgent among one or another group of Jews.

---

[1]The issue was drawn in categories of religion and nationality: thus, Jewish by religion and German, say, by nationality. It would be drawn in the late twentieth-century United States in terms of religion and ethnicity: thus Christian by religion and Jewish by ethnic identification.

THE PRINCIPAL JUDAISMS
OF MODERNITY: THE REFORM,
ORTHODOX, AND CONSERVATIVE
JUDAIC RELIGIOUS SYSTEMS

The three main Judaisms born in the aftermath of the advent of modern politics have now to be specified. All of them continued the Torah as set forth in
Rabbinic Judaism and adopted the Torah as their generative symbol and myth,
its law as their norms, its theology as their touchstone. Between 1800 and 1850
the main systems had taken shape.

First in time is Reform Judaism, coming to expression in the early part of
the nineteenth century and making changes in liturgy, then in doctrine and in
way of life, of the received Judaism of the dual Torah. Reform Judaism recognized the legitimacy of making changes and regarded change as reform, yielding Reform.

Second was the reaction to Reform Judaism, called Orthodox Judaism,
which in many ways was continuous with the Judaism of the dual Torah but in
some ways as selective of elements of that Judaism as was Reform Judaism. Orthodox Judaism reached its first systematic expression in the middle of the nineteenth century. Orthodox Judaism addressed the same issue, that of change, and
held that Judaism lies beyond history; it is the work of God and constitutes a set
of facts of the same order as the facts of nature. Hence change is not reform,
and Reform Judaism is not Judaism—so Orthodoxy. But, at the same time, in
principle no different from Reform Judaism, Orthodox Judaism affirmed that
one could devote time to science, not only Torah study; that affirmation stood
for an accommodation with contemporary politics and culture, different only
in degree from the Reform compromise.

Third in line and somewhat after Orthodox Judaism came positive Historical Judaism, known in America as Conservative Judaism, which occupied the
center between the two other Judaisms of continuation of the dual Torah. This
Judaism maintained that change *could* become reform, but only in accord with
the principles by which legitimate change may be separated from illegitimate
change. Conservative Judaism would discover those principles through historical study. In an age in which historical facts were taken to represent theological truths, the historicism of Conservative Judaism bore compelling weight.
The positivism and dependence on history to validate theological conviction
would serve Conservative Judaism poorly when archaeologists would call into
doubt the principal parts of the scriptural narrative, as they have in the current
generation.

POLITICAL CHANGE AND RELIGIOUS
TRANSFORMATION: "EMANCIPATION"

The changes in the status and aspiration of the Jews took shape in politics not only in the life of intellect, and they affected the community of Jewry at large, not only a handful of philosophers. To explain the circumstance in which Jews asked new questions, we have to examine the political changes that followed from the American Constitution, the French Revolution, and their counterparts in other nations in Western Europe in particular. In both Christendom and Islam, Jews had long found themselves subjected to legal restrictions on where they might live and how they might earn a living. They enjoyed political and social rights of a most limited character. In the multiethnic empires of Central and Eastern Europe—Germany, Austria-Hungary, and Russia—where most Jews lived, they governed their own communities through their own administration and law. Few aspired to a place in an open society, which, in those empires, lay beyond imagining.

Like other ethnic groups, the Jews lived as "holy Israel." They formed an island in an archipelago. They spoke their own language, Yiddish, just as other ethnic groups spoke their respective languages; they wore distinctive clothing; they ate only their own food; they controlled their own sector of the larger economy and ventured outside it only seldom; and, in all, they formed a distinct and distinctive group. Commonly, the villages in which they lived found Jews and Christians living side by side, but in many of those villages Jews formed the majority of the population. They were always Israel and only Israel. They did not aspire to be anything else but what God had made them. They had no difficulty identifying themselves in the stories they read in scripture, their way of life in the laws set forth in the Mishnah, their view of matters in the exegeses of scripture laid out in the Midrash. So the Jews for a long time formed a caste, a distinct and clearly defined group—but within the hierarchy ordered by the castes of the society at hand.

For reasons having little to do with the Jews, political change aimed at breaking down the differences that distinguished one caste (as just now defined) from another and to form of them all a single nation, a body of citizens equal before the law. A process called *Emancipation,* part of a larger movement of emancipation of serfs, women, slaves, and Catholics (in Protestant countries such as Great Britain), over time would encompass the Jews as well. They, too, would find a place in the nation-state and in its undifferentiated workforce—at least, in theory. The historian Benzion Dinur defines this process of emancipation as follows:

> Jewish emancipation denotes the abolition of disabilities and inequities applied specially to Jews, the recognition of Jews as equal to other citizens, and the formal granting of the rights and duties of citizenship. Essentially the legal act of emancipation should have been simply the expression of the diminution of social hostility and psychological aversion toward Jews in the host nation…but the antipathy was not obliterated and constantly

hampered the realization of equality even after it had been proclaimed by the state and included in the law.[2]

The political changes that fall into the process of the Jews' emancipation began in the eighteenth century, and in a half-century affected the long-term stability that had characterized the Jews' social and political life from the time of Constantine onward. These political changes raised questions not previously found urgent and, it follows, also precipitated reflection on problems formerly neglected. The answers to the questions flowed logically and necessarily from the character of the questions themselves.

Dinur traces three periods in the history of the Jews' Emancipation: from 1740 to 1789, ending with the French Revolution, then from 1789 to 1878, from the French Revolution to the Congress of Berlin, and from 1878 to 1933, from the Congress of Berlin to the rise of the Nazis to power in Germany. The adoption of the American Constitution in 1787 confirmed the U.S. position on the matter: Jewish males enjoyed the rights of citizens along with all other white males. The first period marked the point at which the emancipation of the Jews first came under discussion, the second marked the period in which Western and Central European states accorded to the Jews the rights of citizens, and the third brought to the fore a period of new racism that in the end simply wiped out Jewish communities in vast parts of Europe where Jews had lived for more than a thousand years and came very close to annihilating all the Jews of Europe.[3]

1740–1789   Advocates of the Jews' emancipation maintained that religious intolerance accounted for the low caste status assigned to the Jews. Liberating the Jews would mark another stage in overcoming religious intolerance. During this first period the original ideas of Reform Judaism came to expression, although the important changes in religious doctrine and practice were realized only in the earlier part of the nineteenth century.

1789–1878   The French Revolution brought Jews political rights in France, Belgium, Netherlands, Italy, Germany, and Austria-Hungary. The French Army tore down the walls within which Italian Jews were required to live in the Papal States of Italy. As Germany and Italy attained unification and Hungary independence, the Jews were accorded the rights and duties of citizenship. Dinur explains: "It was stressed that keeping the Jews in a politically

---

[2]Benzion Dinur, "Emancipation," *Encyclopaedia Judaica,* vol. 6 (Jerusalem: Keter, 1971), cols. 696–718.

[3]This matter can be followed up in a simple way. *The Encyclopaedia Judaica,* published in 1971, scarcely twenty-five years after the gas chambers at Auschwitz were blown up by the retreating Germans to hide what they had done, has an entry on nearly every location in Europe where Jews ever lived. For all the towns and cities in the territories occupied by the Germans, the entries run in the same pattern: Jews first came in such and such a time, they lived in such and such a way, and then what happened in the Holocaust is described to the day and to the hour: the German army came and upon arrival did thus and so; then the Jews were forced into a tiny area ("ghetto") and kept there to starve and die of disease; then, on such and such a day, there was a roundup and the Jews were forced to dig a mass grave and were then machine gunned; or the Jews were rounded up and shipped off to . . . , with the death factory to which the Jews of that place were shipped then named. That encyclopedia forms the detailed monument to nearly every event in the Holocaust; in scholarship it represents an amazing achievement in so short a time.

limited and socially inferior status was incompatible with the principle of civic equality…'it is the objective of every political organization to protect the natural rights of man,' hence, 'all citizens have the right to all the liberties and advantages of citizens, without exception.' "[4] Jews at that time entered the political and cultural life of the Western nations, including their overseas empires (hence Algerian Jews received French citizenship).

During this second period, Reform Judaism reached its first stage of development, beginning in Germany. The Reform movement made it possible for Jews to hold together the two things they deemed inseparable: their desire to remain Jewish and their wish also to be one with their "fellow citizens." By the middle of the nineteenth century, Reform had reached full expression and had won the support of a sizable part of German Jewry. In reaction against Reform ("the excesses of…"), Orthodoxy came into existence. As we shall see, Orthodoxy no less than Reform asked how "Judaism" could coexist with "German-ness," meaning citizenship in an undifferentiated republic of citizens. A centrist position, mediating between Reform and Orthodoxy, was worked out by theologians in what was then called the Historical School and what in twentieth-century America took the name of Conservative Judaism. The period from the French Revolution (1789) to the Congress of Berlin (1878) therefore saw the full efflorescence of all of the Judaisms of political modernization. All of these Judaisms characterized the Jews of Western Europe and, later on, of America.[5]

1878–1933   A political and social movement, anti-Semitism—a secular, racist political doctrine, nurtured by but distinct from Christian anti-Judaism—attained power. Jews began to realize that, in Dinur's words, "the state's legal recognition of Jewish civic and political equality does not automatically bring social recognition of this equality." The Jews continued to form a separate group; they were "racially inferior." The impact of the new racism would be felt in the twentieth century.

Clearly, in the nineteenth century, particularly in Western countries, a new order revised the political settlement covering the Jews in place for nearly the entire history of the West. From the time of Constantine forward, the Jews' essentially autonomous life as a protected minority had raised political questions that found answers of an essentially supernatural and theological character. But now the Emancipation redefined those questions, asking about Jews not as a distinct group but Jews as part of some other polity altogether than the Jewish one. Those Jews who simply passed over retain no interest for the study of Judaism. Few retained an ethnic connection to the Jewish group for more than a second generation.

---

[4]Dinur, "Emancipation," col. 696.

[5]But in America Reform, Orthodoxy, and the Historical School or Conservative Judaism radically changed in character, responding to the urgent issues of a different circumstance, producing self-evidently valid answers of a character not compatible with the nineteenth-century statements of those same systems. We see the Americanization of Judaism in the "American Judaism of Holocaust and Redemption," addressed in Chapter 29.

But vast numbers of Jews in the West determined to remain Jewish and also to become something else, something they deemed compatible with what they defined as "Judaism." Their urgent question addressed the issue of defining Israel in terms compatible with the politics that defined all else. But—we cannot overstress—the normative Judaism that defined Israel as solely holy, only and always Israel and nothing else, continued to govern the vast majority of those that practiced Judaism. These enormous populations found themselves unaffected by the political changes of Western Europe and the United States, and the received Judaic religious system continued to answer precisely the question they found urgent: Why should Israel the holy people endure through history? And the answer remained the same for them as it had been for millennia: because it is God's will for Israel to remain a people dwelling apart, loyal to the one true God, who has made his will known in the Torah. That Judaic system would survive the Holocaust intact and would define the normative system of Judaism for much of that part of the Jewish community that practiced any Judaic system at all.[6]

WHAT IS ZIONISM AND HOW DOES IT PARTICIPATE IN THE HISTORY OF JUDAISM IN MODERN TIMES?

Reform, Orthodox, and Conservative Judaisms were joined, at the end of the nineteenth century, by a secular Jewish system, one that viewed the Jews as a political community, not a religious one at all. That system, Zionism, replicated the classical paradigm of exile and return that had animated the normative system, beginning with scripture's own narrative from Genesis through Kings, as we saw in Chapter 1. But it took the secular view, within the established paradigm, that the Jews outside the land of Israel were politically in exile from their Land. Zionism advocated a return to Zion in the here and now, before the Messiah's intervention. It regarded "Israel" as the Jewish people, one people, and its intellectuals wrote a single, unitary, continuous, harmonious history of the Jewish people, the story of a people that had functioned in history through its state, that in 70 had lost its state and left history, and that in the twentieth century should (and did) regain its state and return to history. Its "Israel" then should realize its political calling to form a nation of its own and to resume the history of Israel, the Jewish people.

---

[6]That formulation excludes the secular portion of Jewry, which defined "being Jewish" in ethnic terms in the United States and much of the Diaspora, and in nationalist terms in the state of Israel; and the apostate portion of Jewry, which adopted a Christianity instead of a Judaism. Subsequent generations of ethnic Jews retained some connection with Jewry, but the children and grandchildren of "Messianic Jews," as the apostates to Christianity called themselves, would be absorbed within Christian circles and rarely identified themselves as Jews in any material manner. Jewish origins, such as a Jewish grandparent, figure not at all except as a curiosity. From the viewpoint of the history of Judaism, the ethnic and the apostate Jews supply no data for the study of Judaism, its systems, and their structures.

Zionism was founded in 1897 and fifty years later reached fulfillment of its program in 1947 with the United Nations approval of a Jewish state and an Arab state in Palestine. In 1948, the Jewish state advocated by Zionism came into existence, calling itself, predictably, the "State of Israel," a name capturing the radical claim that Zionism laid upon the Jews: return from the exile in the here and now of a secular age and activity. When the Holocaust came, Zionism could explain what had happened and set forth a program of what to do in response to keep such a thing from ever again happening, and with its success in creating and maintaining the state of Israel, Zionism would form one of the most successful systems of modern and contemporary Jewry: a Jewish system, if not a Judaic system.

Even though it was not a religious system,[7] Zionism belongs in an account of modern Judaisms because it responded to the Judaic systems of the nineteenth century and to the problem they took as urgent and proposed to solve in a self-evidently correct manner. Specifically, Zionism rejected the religious systems' certainty that the Jews could attain emancipation from their legal, cultural, and social disabilities and become French, German, or British citizens of the Judaic persuasion. At the end of the century, Zionism offered an essentially secular and negative answer to that same question of being Jewish and something else: The Jews cannot become party to the nation-states where they now live because anti-Semitism is endemic. Zionism, with its own definition of "Israel," met fierce opposition from Reform Judaism, with its account of how Jews could be good Germans "of the Mosaic persuasion," that is, German by nationality and Jewish by religion, as well as from the Judaism of the dual Torah that dominated in Eastern Europe.[8] Now let us examine the Judaic systems of the nineteenth and twentieth centuries and their secular competition, Reform, Orthodox, Conservative Judaisms and Zionism.

[7]But in the complex organization of Zionism were important and influential communities of Judaism that affirmed the political program of Zionism within their reading of the laws of the Torah.

[8]But Zionism maintained constant dialogue with the Judaic religious systems of the age, and by the second third of the twentieth century would convert the systems that had originally opposed it, Reform and Orthodox Judaisms, to its goals. American Reform Judaism affirmed Zionism by the 1930s, and some of the Torah camp of Orthodox Judaism encompassed Zionism long before. Indeed, the settlement of Jewish towns beyond the frontiers of the state of Israel in 1967, in Samaria and Judea (a.k.a. the "West Bank"), was undertaken principally by a movement called "The Greater Land of Israel," centered in Orthodox religious parties and theologies.

24

Reform Judaism

From the perspective of the political changes taking place from the American and French Revolutions onward the received system of Judaism simply answered the wrong questions in responding to the challenge of not citizenship but triumphant Christianity. For the issue no longer found definition in the claims of regnant Christianity. A new question, emerging from forces not contained within Christianity, demanded attention from Jews affected by those forces. For those Jews, the fact of change derived its self-evidence from shifts in political circumstances. When the historians began to look for evidence of precedents for changing things, it was because their own circumstance had already persuaded them that change matters—change itself effects change. What they sought, then, was a picture of a world in which they might find a place, and, it went without saying, that picture would include a portrait of a Judaic system—a way of life, a worldview, a definition of the Israel to live the one and believe the other.

Reform Judaism in the nineteenth century saw its most accessible authoritative statement come to expression in America. In 1885, an assembly in Pittsburgh of Reform rabbis, the Central Conference of American Rabbis, defined Israel, its way of life and its worldview. Since a Judaic religious system will commence its work by defining the "Israel" of which it speaks, we may not find surprising the Pittsburgh Platform's heavy emphasis on who is Israel. That doctrine exposes the foundations of the way of life and worldview that these rabbis had formed for the Israel they conceived:

> We recognize in the Mosaic legislation a system of training the Jewish people for its mission during its national life in Palestine, and today we accept as binding only its moral laws and maintain only such ceremonies as elevate and sanctify our lives, but reject all such as are not adapted to the views and habits of modern civilization. ...We hold that all such Mosaic and rabbinical laws as regular diet, priestly purity, and dress originated in ages and under the influence of ideas entirely foreign to our present mental and spiritual state. ...Their observance in our days is apt rather to obstruct than to further modern spiritual elevation. ...We recognize in the modern era of universal culture of heart and intellect the approaching of the realization of Israel's great messianic hope for the establishment of the kingdom of truth, justice, and peace among all men.

> We consider ourselves no longer a nation but a religious community and
> therefore expect neither a return to Palestine nor a sacrificial worship
> under the sons of Aaron nor the restoration of any of the laws concerning
> the Jewish state. . . .

Difference is acceptable at the level of religion, not nationality, a position that
accords fully with the definition of citizenship of the Western democracies. Israel once was a nation ("during its national life") but today is not a nation. It
once had a set of laws that regulate diet, clothing, and the like. These no longer
apply because Israel now is not what it was then. Israel forms an integral part
of Western civilization. The reason to persist as a distinctive group was that the
group has its work to do, namely, to realize the Messianic hope for the establishment of a kingdom of truth, justice, and peace. For that purpose Israel no
longer constitutes a nation. It now forms a religious community.

   So issues of sanctification fall away, but issues of salvation endure. The
worldview then lays heavy emphasis on an as-yet unrealized but coming perfect age. The way of life admits to no important traits that distinguish Jews from
others, since morality, in the nature of things, forms a universal category, applicable in the same way to everyone. The theory of Israel then forms the heart
of matters, and what we learn is that Israel constitutes a "we," that is, that the
Jews continue to form a group that, by its own indicators, holds together and
constitutes a cogent social entity.

WHAT IS REFORM JUDAISM?

The original Judaic system of Reform appeals to the eighteenth-century
scholar of Judaism and Enlightenment philosophy, Moses Mendelssohn, for its
intellectual foundations. Mendelssohn presented, in the words of Michael A.
Meyer, an appeal "for a pluralistic society that offered full freedom of conscience
to all those who accepted the postulates of natural religion: God, Providence,
and a future life."[1] Issues dominant from Mendelssohn's time forward concerned what was called the "Emancipation," discussed in the preceding chapter,
meaning the provision, for Jews among others, of the rights of citizens. Reform
theologians took the lead in the struggle for such rights. To them it was self-
evident that Jews not only should have civil rights and civic equality. It also was
obvious that they should want them. A Judaism that did not explain why the
Jews should want and have full equality as part of a common humanity ignored
the issues that preoccupied those who found, in Reform Judaism, a corpus of
self-evident truths. To those truths, the method—the appeal to historical facts—
formed a contingent and secondary consideration.

   The original changes, in the first decades of the nineteenth century, produced a new generation of rabbis. Some forty years into the century, these rab-

---

[1]Michael A. Meyer, *The Origins of the Modern Jew: Jewish Identity and European Culture in Germany, 1749–1824*
(Detroit: Wayne State University Press, 1967), p. 48.

bis gave to the process of change the name of Reform and created those institutions of Reform Judaism that would endow the inchoate movement with a
politics of its own. In the mid-1840s a number of rabbinical conferences
brought together the new generation of rabbis. Trained in universities, rabbis
who came to these gatherings turned backward, justifying the changes in prayer
rites long in place, effecting some further mostly cosmetic changes in the observance of the Sabbath and in the laws covering personal status through marriage and divorce. In 1845 a decision to adopt for some purposes German in
place of Hebrew led to the departure of conservative Reformers, who founded
what they called the "Historical School" in Germany and Conservative Judaism
in the United States. But the Reformers appealed for their apologia to the received writings, persisting in their insistence that they formed a natural continuation of the processes of the "tradition."

LEGITIMATING CHANGE BY
CALLING IT "REFORM"

To begin with, the issue involved not politics, Emancipation and civil rights,
but merely justification for changing anything at all. The Reformers maintained
that change was all right because historical precedent proved that change was
all right. But change long had defined the constant in the ongoing life of the
received system of Judaism. Generative causes and modes of effecting change
marked the vitality of the system. Rabbinic Judaism, normative from its fourth-
century formation forward, endured, never intact but always unimpaired, because of its power to absorb and make its own the diverse happenings of culture
and society. So long as the structure of politics remained the same, with Israel
an autonomous entity, subordinated but recognized as a cogent and legitimate
social group in charge of some of its own affairs, the system answered the paramount question. The trivial ones could work their way through and become
part of the consensus, to be perceived in the end as "tradition," too. A catalogue
of changes that had taken place over fifteen hundred years, therefore, will list
many more dramatic and decisive sorts of change than those matters of minor
revision of liturgy, such as sermons in the vernacular, that attracted attention at
the dawn of the age of change become Reform.

   When people could take a stance external to the received system and effect
change as a matter of decision and policy, we know that, for those people, Judaism in its received form had already died. And that marks the move from self-
evidence to self-consciousness. What had brought about the demise of the
received system as definitive and normative beyond all argument is something
we do not know. Nothing in the earliest record of liturgical reform tells us. The
constructive efforts of the first generation, only later on recognized not as people who made changes or even as reformers but as founders of Reform Judaism,
focused upon synagogue worship. The services were too long; the speeches
were in a language foreign to participants; the singing was not aesthetic; the

prayers were in a language no one understood. But that means some people recited the prayers as a matter of duty, not supplication; did not speak the language of the faith; formed other than received opinions on how to sing in synagogue; saw as alien what earlier had marked the home and hearth. Those people no longer lived in that same social world that had for so long found right and proper precisely the customs now seen as alien.

When the heritage forms an unclaimed, unwanted legacy, out of duty people nonetheless accept it. So the changes, called "reform," that produced Reform Judaism introduced a shortened service, a sermon in the language people spoke, a choir and an organ, prayers in the vernacular. Clearly, a great deal of change had taken place before it was recognized that something had changed. People no longer knew Hebrew; they no longer found pleasing received modes of saying the prayers. We look in vain to the consequent reforms for answers to the question of why people made these changes, and the reasons adduced by historians settle no interesting questions for us.

The more interesting question is: Why the persistence of engagement and concern? For people always had the option, which many exercised, of abandoning the received Judaism of the two Torahs and all other Judaisms, too. Among those for whom these cosmetic changes made a difference, much in the liturgy, and far more beyond, retained powerful appeal. The premise of change dictated that Jews would say the old prayers in essentially the old formulation. And that premise carried much else: the entire burden of the faith, the total commitment to the group, in some form, defined by some indicators—if not the familiar ones, then some others. So we know that Reform Judaism, in its earliest manifestation in Germany in the early nineteenth century, constituted an essentially conservative, profoundly constructive effort to save for Jews the received Judaism by reforming it in some (to begin with) rather trivial ways.

REFORM'S HISTORICIST THEOLOGY: REFORM AS THE NATURAL NEXT STEP IN THE HISTORY OF JUDAISM

What formed the justification for these changes was the theory of the incremental history of a single, linear Judaism. That argument from history played a powerful role in the creative age of Reform Judaism. The ones who made changes to begin with rested their case on an appeal to the authoritative texts. Reform even at the outset claimed to restore, to continue, to persist in the received pattern. The justification of change always invoked precedent. People who made changes had to show that the principle that guided what they did was not new, even though the specific things they did were.

But there was a more radical claim than the one from precedent. It was this: Change restores, reverts to an unchanging ideal. So the Reformer claims not to change at all, but only to regain the correct state of affairs, one that others, in the interval, themselves have changed. That forms the fundamental attitude of the people who make changes and call the changes Reform. The appeal to history, a common mode of justification in the politics and theology of the nineteenth century, therefore defined the principal justification for the new Judaism: It was new because it renewed the old and enduring, the golden Judaism of a mythic age of perfection. Arguments on precedent drew the Reformers to the work of critical scholarship, as we shall see, as they settled all questions by appeal to the facts of history.

We cannot find surprising, therefore, the theory that Reform Judaism stood in a direct line with the prior history of Judaism. Judaism, the theory stated, is one. Judaism has a history, that history is single and unitary, and it was always leading to its present outcome: Reform Judaism. Others later on would challenge these convictions. Orthodox Judaism would deny that Judaism has a history at all. Conservative, or positive Historical Judaism, would discover a different goal for history from that embodied by Reform Judaism. But the mode of argument, appealing to issues of a historical and factual character, and the premises of argument, insisting that history proved, or disproved, matters of theological conviction, characterized all the Judaisms of the nineteenth century. And that presents no surprises, since the Judaisms of the age took shape in the intellectual world of Germany, with its profoundly philosophical and historical mode of thought and argument.

The Protestant Reformation had provided the model. Reform began in Germany, and the earliest theologians had before them the precedent of Martin Luther, the leader of the Protestant Reformation in Germany. Luther supplied the model, demanding reversion to the pure and primitive faith of the Gospels. The Reform theologians took the same route when they rejected long-established customs as historically inauthentic. Then history stood in judgment on tradition, the pure faith of old upon the accretions of time, just as in the Protestant Reformation. Reform renews; recovers the true condition of the faith; selects, out of a diverse past, that age and that moment at which the faith attained its perfect definition and embodiment. Not change but restoration and renewal of the true modes, the recovery of the way things were in that perfect, paradigmatic time, that age that formed the model for all time—these deeply mythic modes of appeal formed the justification for change, transforming mere modification of this and that into Reform.

REFORM MOVEMENTS IN JUDAISM: THE APPEAL TO HISTORICAL PRECEDENT

Let us consider a concrete example of historicist theology as Reform Judaism practiced it. In his preface to Abraham Cronbach's classic work *Reform Movements in Judaism,* Jacob Rader Marcus, a principal voice in Reform Judaism in the twentieth century, provides a powerful statement of the Reform view of its place in history. Marcus recognizes that diverse Judaisms have flourished in the history of the Jews. What characterizes them all is that each began as a reform movement but then underwent a process we might characterize as "traditional-ization." That is to say, change becomes not merely reform but tradition, and the only constant in the histories of Judaisms is that process of transformation of the new to the conventional, or, in theological language, the traditional. This process Marcus describes as follows:

> All [Judaisms] began as rebellions, as great reformations, but after receiving widespread acceptance, developed vested 'priestly' interests, failed their people, and were forced to retreat before the onslaught of new rebellions, new philosophies, new challenges.[2]

So the fundamental theological method of Reform Judaism in its initial phase, the appeal to facts of history for the validation of theological propositions, en-dures. But the claim that everything always changes yields a challenge, which Marcus forthrightly raises:

> Is there then nothing but change? Is change the end of all our history and all our striving? No, there is something else, the desire to be free.... In the end [the Jew] has always understood that changelessness is spiritual death. The Jew who would *live* must never completely surrender himself to one truth, but...must reach out for the farther and faint horizons of an ever Greater God. ...This is the meaning of Reform.[3]

Marcus thus treats as self-evident—obvious because it is a fact of history—the persistence of change. And denying that that is all there is to Reform, at the end he affirms the simple point that change sets the norm. It comes down to the same thing. The something else of Marcus's argument presents its own problems. Appeal to the facts of history fails at that point at which a construc-tive position demands articulation. "The desire to be free" bears a predicate: free of what? Free to do, to be what? If Marcus fails to accomplish the whole of the theological task, however, he surely conveys the profoundly construc-tive vision that Reform Judaism afforded to its Israel.

For his part, Cronbach in his theology sets forth as the five precedents for the present movement the Deuteronomic Reformation, the Pentateuchal Re-formation, the Pharisaic Reformation, the Karaite Reformation, and the Ha-sidic Reformation. His coming reformation appeals to social psychology and aims at tolerance: "Felicitous human relationships can be the goal of social wel-fare and of economic improvement. ...Our Judaism of maturity would be ded-icated to the ideal of freedom. Corollary of that ideal is what we have just observed about courtesy toward the people whose beliefs and practices we do not share."[4]

---

[2]Jacob Rader Marcus, Preface, in Abraham Cronbach, *Reform Movements in Judaism* (New York: Bookman Associ-ates, 1963), p. 7.

[3]Ibid., p. 9.

[4]Cronbach, *Reform Movements,* p. 11.

More than half of U.S. Jews who practice a Judaism call themselves Reform Jews, and the Reform approach characterizes other American Judaisms as well. So far as Orthodox Judaism takes up an integrationist position, it affirms the principle of Reform, not its details. So Reform Judaism must be judged to have defined accurately the question Jews in modern times in the Western democracies would deem urgent. With acuity, perspicacity, and enormous courage, the Reformers, nineteenth and twentieth century alike, took the measure of the world and made ample use of the materials they had in hand in manufacturing something to fit it. And Reform did fit those Jews, and they were, and are, very many, to whom the issue of Israel as a supernatural entity remained vivid. For, after all, the centerpiece of Reform Judaism remained its powerful notion that Israel does have a task and a mission, on which account Israel should endure as Israel. Reform Judaism persuaded generations from the beginning to the present of the worth of human life lived in its Judaic system. More than that we cannot ask of any Judaism.

25

Orthodox Judaism

ORTHODOXY AND THE "TRADITION"

All Orthodox systems of Judaism affirm that, in a literal sense, God revealed the Torah to Moses at Sinai in dual form, oral and written, and that the Torah of Sinai sets forth God's will for Israel for eternity. But Orthodox Judaisms break down into two camps, the segregationist, rejecting accommodation with the politics and culture of the secular world, and the integrationist, maintaining that total adherence to the Torah allowed for participation in everyday politics, culture, and economic life as well. In the nineteenth and early twentieth centuries, before communism shut down Judaic religious life in the former Soviet Union, segregationist Orthodoxy persisted where political change did not lend urgency to the issue of integration. Integrationist Orthodoxy flourished in countries where Jews had reason to hope for political emancipation. The state of Israel today shelters both kinds of Orthodoxy and differentiates between them. In the United States segregationist Orthodoxy flourishes in two distinct venues. The first is the world of Yeshiva communities, centers for Torah study surrounded by the pious faithful. The second is in highly sectarian Hasidic communities, centered on the holy man, the Rebbe, not Torah study. These are Judaists who, in addition to the dual Torah, value a heritage of mysticism centered around holy men, or rebbes, as the nexus between God and the world. We shall meet the single most important American example of these groups in Chapter 28.

Reform Judaism precipitated the formation of an integrationist-Orthodox Judaism, one that accepted its premises but not its policies. Integrationist Orthodoxy distinguished itself from self-segregationist Orthodoxy in matters of learning when Jews who kept the law of the Torah—for example, as it dictated food choices and use of leisure time (to speak of the Sabbath and festivals in secular terms)—sent their children to secular schools, in addition to, or instead of, solely Jewish ones. When Jewish schools included in the curriculum subjects outside the sciences of the Torah, they crossed the boundary between the received and the new Judaism. For the notion that science or German or Latin or philosophy deserved serious study in the nineteenth century struck as wrong those for whom the received system remained self-evidently right. Those Jews did not send their children to gentile schools, and their Jewish schools did not include in the curriculum any subject other than Torah study.

DEFINING INTEGRATIONIST
ORTHODOX JUDAISM IN ITS
WESTERN POLITICAL CONTEXT

Integrationist Orthodox Judaism is that Judaic system that does two things. First, it maintains the worldview of the received dual Torah, constantly citing its sayings and adhering with only trivial variations to the bulk of its norms for the everyday life. At the same time, Orthodoxy holds second that Jews adhering to the dual Torah may wear clothing that non-Jews wear and do not have to wear distinctively Jewish (even Judaic) clothing; live within a common economy and not practice distinctively Jewish professions (however, in a given setting, these professions may be defined), and, in diverse ways, take up a life not readily distinguished in important characteristics from the life lived by people in general.

So for Orthodoxy a portion of holy Israel's life may prove secular, in that the Torah does not dictate and so sanctify all details under all circumstances. Since the received Judaic system presupposed not only the supernatural entity, Israel, but also a way of life that in important ways distinguished that supernatural entity from the social world at large, the power of Orthodoxy to find an accommodation for Jews who valued the received way of life and worldview and also planned to make their lives in an essentially integrated social world proves formidable. The difference between Orthodoxy and the system of the dual Torah therefore comes to expression in social policy: integration, however circumscribed, versus the total separation of the holy people.

The word *Orthodoxy* takes on meaning only in the contrast to Reform, so in a simple sense, integrationist, or Western, or modern, Orthodoxy owes its life to Reform Judaism. The term first surfaced in 1795[1] and over all covers all Jews who believe that God revealed the dual Torah at Sinai and that Jews must carry out the requirements of Jewish law contained in the Torah as interpreted by the sages through time. Obviously, so long as that position struck as self-evident the generality of Jewry at large, Orthodoxy as a distinct and organized Judaism did not exist. It did not have to. What is interesting is the point at which two events took place: first, the recognition of the received system, the "tradition" as Orthodoxy, second, the specification of the received system as religion. The two, of course, go together. So long as the received Judaic system enjoys recognition as a set of self-evident truths, those truths add up not to something so distinct and special as "religion," but to a general statement of how things are: all of life explained and harmonized in one whole account, culture, politics, religion, the social order all integrated in a single coherent system.

---

[1]Nathaniel Katzburg and Walter S. Wurzburger, "Orthodoxy," *Encyclopaedia Judaica,* vol. 12 (Jerusalem: Keter, 1971), cols. 1486–1493.

The former of the two events—the view that the received system was "traditional"—came first. The matter of the self-aware recognition of "Judaism" as "religion" comes later. That identification of truth as tradition came about when the received system met the challenge of competing Judaisms. Then, in behalf of the received way of life and worldview addressed to supernatural Israel, people said that the received Judaic system was established of old, the right, the only way of seeing and doing things, how things have been and should be naturally and normally: "tradition." But that is a category that contains within itself an alternative, namely, change, as in "tradition and change."

It is when the system lost its power of self-evidence that it entered, among other apologetic categories, the classification "*the* tradition." And that came about when Orthodoxy met head on the challenge of change become Reform. We understand why the category of tradition, the received way of doing things, became critical to the framers of Orthodoxy when we examine the counter-claim. That is, just as the Reformers justified change, the Orthodox theologians denied that change was ever possible, so Walter Wurzburger: "Orthodoxy looks upon attempts to adjust Judaism to the 'spirit of the time' as utterly incompatible with the entire thrust of normative Judaism which holds that the revealed will of God rather than the values of any given age are the ultimate standard."[2]

To begin with the issue important to the Reformers, the value of what was called "Emancipation," meaning, the provision to Jews of civil rights, defined the debate. When the Reform Judaic theologians took a wholly one-sided position affirming Emancipation, numerous Orthodox ones adopted the contrary view. The position outlined by those theologians followed the agenda laid forth by the Reformers. If the Reform made minor changes in liturgy and its conduct, the Orthodox rejected even those that under other circumstances might have found acceptance. Saying prayers in the vernacular, for example, provoked strong opposition. But everyone knew that some of the prayers, said in Aramaic, in fact were in the vernacular of the earlier age. The Orthodox thought that these changes, not reforms at all, represented only the first step of a process leading Jews out of the Judaic world altogether, so, as Wurzburger says, "The slightest tampering with tradition was condemned."

If we ask where the received system of the dual Torah prevailed, and where, by contrast, Orthodoxy came to full expression, we may follow the spreading out of railway lines, the growth of new industry, the shifts in political status accorded to, among other citizens, Jews; changes in the educational system; in all, the entire process of political change, economic and social, demographic and cultural shifts of a radical and fundamental nature. Where the changes came first, there Reform Judaism met them in its way—and Orthodoxy in its way. Where change came later in the century, as in the case of Russian Poland, the eastern provinces of the Austro-Hungarian empire, and Russia itself, there, in villages contentedly following the old ways, the received system endured.

---

[2]Ibid., col. 1487.

Again, in an age of mass migration from Eastern Europe to America and other Western democracies, those who experienced the upheaval of leaving home and country met the challenge of change either by accepting new ways of seeing things or articulately and in full self-awareness reaffirming the familiar ones once more, Reform or Orthodoxy. We may, therefore, characterize the received system as a way of life and worldview wedded to an ancient people's homelands, the villages and small towns of Central and Eastern Europe, and Orthodoxy as the heir of that received system as it came to expression in the towns and cities of Central and Western Europe and America. That rule of thumb, with the usual exceptions, allows us to distinguish between the piety of a milieu and the theological conviction of a self-conscious community. Or we may accept the familiar distinction between tradition and articulate Orthodoxy, a distinction with its own freight of apologetics, to be sure.

When, therefore, we explain by reference to political and economic change the beginnings of Reform Judaism, we also understand the point of origin of Orthodoxy as distinct and organized and articulated. Clearly, the beginnings of Orthodoxy took place in the areas where, in response to fundamental political change, Reform made its way, hence in Germany and in Hungary. In Germany, where Reform attracted the majority of numerous Jewish communities, the Orthodox faced a challenge indeed. Critical to their conviction was the notion that "Israel," all of the Jews, bore responsibility to carry out the law of the Torah. But the community's institutions in the hands of the Reform did not obey the law of the Torah as the Orthodox understood it. So, in the end, Orthodoxy took that step that marked it as a self-conscious Judaism. Orthodoxy separated from the established community altogether. The Orthodox set up their own organization and seceded from the community at large. The next step prohibited the Orthodox from participating in non-Orthodox organizations altogether. Isaac Breuer, a leading theologian of Orthodoxy, would ultimately take the position that "refusal to espouse the cause of separation was interpreted as being equivalent to the rejection of the absolute sovereignty of God."[3]

The matter of accommodating to the world at large, of course, did not allow for so easy an answer as mere separation. The specific issue—integration or segregation—concerned preparation for life in the larger politics and economic life of the country, and that meant secular education, involving not only language and science, but history and literature, matters of values. Orthodoxy proved diverse, with two wings to be distinguished, one rejecting secular learning as well as all dealing with non-Orthodox Jews, the other cooperating with non-Orthodox and secular Jews and accepting the value of secular education. That position in no way affected loyalty to the law of Judaism, such as, belief in God's revelation of the one whole Torah at Sinai. The point at which the received system and the Orthodox split requires specification. In concrete terms, we know the one from the other by the evaluation

---

[3]Ibid., col. 1488.

of secular education. Proponents of the received system never accommodated themselves to secular education, while the Orthodox in Germany and Hungary persistently affirmed it. That represents a remarkable shift, since central to the received system of the dual Torah is study of Torah—Torah, not philosophy.

Explaining where we find the one and the other, Katzburg works with the distinction we have already made, between an unbroken system and one that has undergone a serious caesura with the familiar condition of the past. He states:

> In Eastern Europe until World War I, Orthodoxy preserved without a break its traditional ways of life and the time-honored educational framework. In general, the mainstream of Jewish life was identified with Orthodoxy, while Haskalah [the Jewish Enlightenment, which applied to the Judaic setting the skeptical attitudes of the French Enlightenment] and secularization were regarded as deviations. Hence there was no ground wherein a Western type of Orthodoxy could take root. . . . European Orthodoxy in the 19th and the beginning of the 20th centuries was significantly influenced by the move from small settlements to urban centers . . . as well as by emigration. Within the small German communities there was a kind of popular Orthodoxy, deeply attached to tradition and to local customs, and when it moved to the large cities this element brought with it a vitality and rootedness to Jewish tradition.[4]

Katzburg's observations provide important guidance. He authoritatively defines the difference between Orthodoxy and "tradition." So he tells us how to distinguish between the received system accepted as self-evident and an essentially selective, therefore by definition new system, called Orthodoxy. In particular he guides us in telling the one from the other and where to expect to find, in particular, the articulated, therefore, self-conscious affirmation of "tradition" that characterizes Orthodoxy but does not occur in the world of the dual Torah as it glided in its eternal orbit of the seasons and of unchanging time.

SAMSON RAPHAEL HIRSCH

The principal voice of integrationist Orthodoxy in Germany, Samson Raphael Hirsch (1808–1888), set forth a theology of joining Torah with secular education, producing a synthesis of Torah and modern culture. He represents the strikingly new Judaism at hand, exhibiting both its strong tie to the received system but also its innovative and essentially new character. Hirsch's stress on the possibility of living in the secular world and sustaining a fully Orthodox life rallied the Jews of the counter-reformation. But Hirsch and his followers took over one principal position of Reform, the possibility of integrating Jews in modern society. What made Hirsch significant was that he took that view not

---

[4]Ibid., col. 1490.

only on utilitarian grounds but on the foundations of the Torah itself. Hirsch himself studied at the University of Bonn, specializing in classical languages, history, and philosophy, so he did not think one had to spend all his time studying Torah, and in going to a university he implicitly affirmed that he could not define, within Torah study, all modes of learning. Gentile professors knew things worth knowing. But continuators of the Judaism of the dual Torah thought exactly the opposite: Whatever is worth knowing is in the Torah.

In his rabbinical posts, Hirsch published a number of works to appeal to the younger generation. His ideal for them was the formation of a personality that would be both enlightened and observant, that is, educated in Western knowledge and observant of the Judaic way of life. This ideal took shape through an educational program that encompassed Hebrew language and holy literature, and also German, mathematics, sciences, and the like. In this way he proposed to respond to the Reformers' view that Judaism in its received form constituted a barrier between Jews and German society. The Reformers saw the received way of life as an obstacle to the sort of integration they thought wholesome and good. Hirsch concurred in the ideal and differed on detail. Distinctive Jewish clothing, in Hirsch's view, enjoyed a low priority. Quite to the contrary, he himself wore a ministerial gown at public worship, which did not win the approbation of the traditionalists, and when he preached, he encompassed not only the law of the Torah but other biblical matters, equally an innovation. Hirsch argued that Judaism and secular education could form a union. This would require the recognition of externals, which could be set aside, and the emphasis on principles, which would not change. So Hirsch espoused what, in the ideas of those fully within the mentality of self-evidence, constituted selective piety and, while the details differed, therefore fell within the classification of reform.

In his selections Hirsch included changes in the conduct of the liturgy, involving a choir, congregational singing, sermons in the vernacular—sure marks of Reform a generation earlier. He required prayers to be said only in Hebrew and Jewish subjects to be taught in that language. He opposed all changes in the Prayerbook. At the same time he sustained organizational relationships with the Reformers and tried to avoid schism. By mid-career, however, toward the middle of the century, Hirsch could not tolerate the Reformers' abrogation of the dietary laws and those affecting marital relationships, and he made his break, accusing the Reformers of disrupting Israel's unity. In the following decades he encouraged Orthodox Jews to leave the congregations dominated by Reform, even though, in the locale, such was the only synagogue. Separationist synagogues formed in the larger community.

We come now to Hirsch's framing of issues of doctrine, with special attention to the matter of history, so important to Reform Judaism. Hirsch for his part stressed that the teachings of the Torah constitute facts beyond all doubt, as much as the facts of nature do not allow for doubt. This view of the essential facticity—the absolute givenness—of the Torah led to the further conviction that human beings may not deny the Torah's teachings even when they do not grasp the Torah's meaning. Wisdom is contained within the Torah, God's will is to be found there. Just as the physical laws of nature are not conditioned by human search, so the rules of God's wisdom are unaffected by human search. The Torah constitutes an objective reality. What makes Israel different is that they gain access to the truth not through experience but through direct revelation. Gentile truth is truth but derives from observation and experience. What Israel knows through the Torah comes through a different medium: The Jewish people then stand outside of history and *do not* have to learn religious truth through the passage of history and changes over time. Israel then forms a supernatural entity, a view certainly in accord with the Judaism of the dual Torah.

Hirsch's theory of who Israel is stood at the opposite pole from that of the Reformers. To them, as we have seen, Israel fell into the classification of a religious community, that alone. To Hirsch, Israel constituted a people, not a religious congregation, and Hirsch spoke of "national Jewish consciousness": "The Jewish people, though it carries the Torah with it in all the lands of its dispersion, will never find its table and lamp except in the Holy Land." Israel performs a mission among the nations, to teach "that God is the source of blessing." Israel then falls between, forming its own category, because it has a state system, in the land, but also a life outside. In outlining this position, Hirsch of course reaffirmed the theory of the supernatural Israel laid forth in the dual Torah.

CONTINUITY OR NEW CREATION?

Both—but, therefore, by definition, new creation. Piety selected is by definition piety invented, and Samson Raphael Hirsch emerges as one of the intellectually powerful creators of a Judaism. "Torah and secular learning" defined a new worldview, dictated a new way of life, and addressed a different Israel from the Judaism of the dual Torah. To those who received that dual Torah as self-evident what the Torah did not accommodate was secular learning. The Torah as they received it did not approve changes in the familiar way of life and did not know an Israel other than the one at hand. So the perfect faith of Orthodoxy sustained a wonderfully selective piety. What was the human greatness of Hirsch and the large number of Jews who found self-evident the possibility of living the dual life of Jew and German or Jew and American? It lay in the power of the imagination to locate in a new circumstance a rationale for inventing tradition.

The human achievement of Orthodoxy demands more than routine notice. Living in a world that only grudgingly accommodated difference and did not like Jews' difference in particular, the Orthodox followed the rhythm of the week to the climax of the Sabbath, of the seasons to the climactic moments of the festivals. They adhered to their own pattern of daily life, with prayers morning, noon, and night. They married only within the holy people. They ate only food that had been prepared in accord with the rules of sanctification. They honored philosophy and culture, true, but these they measured by their own revealed truth as well. It was not easy for them to keep the faith when so many within Jewry, and so many more outside, wanted Jews to be pretty much the same as everyone else.

The human costs cannot have proved trivial. To affirm when the world denies, to keep the faith against all evidence—that represents that faith that in other settings people honored. It was not easy for either the integrationist Orthodox of Germany or the immigrant Jews of America, who in an ocean voyage moved from the world of self-evident faith to the one of insistent denial of the faith. But Jews throughout the Western world did respond to the agenda of political change in a manner radically different from the response of Reform Judaism, and integrationist Orthodoxy has remained predominant in post-Holocaust Europe and, while overshadowed by segregationist Orthodox Judaisms, still deeply influential in the state of Israel as well. What we learn about Judaism from Orthodoxy is what we learn about humanity from religion, which is that different people reach different conclusions about the same questions. Religion cannot be reduced to a function of politics or economics or even culture. It is an independent variable.

26

Conservative Judaism

BETWEEN REFORM AND ORTHODOXY

Between Reform and Orthodoxy, the Historical School, a group of nineteenth-century German scholars of Judaism, and Conservative Judaism, a twentieth-century Judaism in America, took the middle position, each in its own context.[1] We treat them as a single Judaism because they hold in common to moderation in making change, accommodation between "the tradition" and the requirements of modern life, above all, adaptation to circumstance. Toward the end of the nineteenth century rabbis of this same centrist persuasion organized the Jewish Theological Seminary of America in 1886–1887, and from that Rabbinical school the Conservative movement developed. The order of the formation of the several Judaisms of the nineteenth century therefore is, first, Reform, then Orthodoxy, finally, Conservatism—the two extremes, then the middle. The Historical School shaped the worldview, and Conservative Judaism later on brought that view into full realization as a way of life characteristic of a large group of Jews, for a time nearly half, and now at least a third of all American Jews who practice a Judaism identify themselves with Conservative Judaism.

EAT KOSHER AND THINK *TRAIF*

The ambivalence of Conservative Judaism, speaking in part for intellectuals deeply loyal to the received way of life but profoundly dubious of the inherited worldview, came to full expression in the odd slogan of its intellectuals and scholars: "Eat kosher and think *traif*." *Traif* refers to meat that is not acceptable under Judaic law, and the slogan announced a religion of orthopraxy: Do the right thing and it doesn't matter what you believe. That statement meant people should keep the rules of the holy way of life but ignore the convictions that made sense of them. *Orthopraxy* is the word that refers to correct action and unfettered belief, as against *orthodoxy*, right doctrine. Some would then classify Conservative Judaism in America as an orthoprax Judaism defined through works, not doctrine. Some of its leading voices even denied Judaism set forth doctrine at all in what is called "the dogma of dogma-less Judaism."

---

[1] Arthur Hertzberg, "Conservative Judaism," *Encyclopaedia Judaica*, vol. 5 (Jerusalem: Keiter, 1971), cols. 901–906.

The middle position then derived in equal measure from the two extremes. The way of life was congruent in most aspects with that of integrationist Orthodoxy, the worldview, with that of Reform. The two held together in the doctrine of "Israel" that covered everyone. Conservative Judaism laid enormous stress on what the people were doing, on the consensus of what one of its founders called "catholic Israel," meaning the ethnic-religious group whole. Conservative Judaism saw the Jews as a(nother) people, not merely a(nother) religious community, as Reform did, nor as a unique and holy people, as Orthodoxy did. That Judaism celebrated the ethnic as much as the more narrowly religious side to the Jews' common life. Orthodoxy took a separatist and segregationist position, leaving the organized Jewish community in Germany as that community fell into the hands of Reform Jews. Reform Judaism, for its part, rejected the position that the Jews constitute a people, not merely a religious community. Conservative Judaism emphasized the importance of the unity of the community as a whole and took a stand in favor of Zionism as soon as that movement got under way.

What separated Conservative Judaism from Reform was the matter of observance. Fundamental loyalty to the received way of life distinguished the Historical School in Germany and Conservative Judaism in America from Reform Judaism in both countries. When considering the continued validity of a traditional religious practice, the Reform asked why, the Conservatives why not. The Orthodox, of course, would ask no questions to begin with. The fundamental principle, that the worldview of the Judaism under construction would rest upon (mere) historical facts, came from Reform Judaism. Orthodoxy could never have concurred. The contrast to the powerful faith despite the world, exhibited by integrationist Orthodoxy's stress on the utter facticity of the Torah, presents in a clear light the positivism of the Conservatives, who, indeed, adopted the name "the *positive* Historical School."

The emphasis on research as the route to historical fact, and on historical fact as the foundation for both theological change and also the definition of what was truly authentic in the theological tradition, further tells us that the Historical School was made up of intellectuals. In America, too, a pattern developed in which essentially nonobservant congregations of Jews called upon rabbis whom they expected to be observant of the rules of the religion. As a result, many of the intellectual problems that occupied public debate concerned rabbis more than laypeople, since the rabbis bore responsibility—so the community maintained—for not only teaching the faith but, on their own, embodying it. An observer described this Judaism as "Orthodox rabbis serving Conservative synagogues made up of Reform Jews."

But in a more traditional liturgy, in an emphasis upon observance of the dietary taboos and the Sabbath and festivals—which did, and still does, characterize homes of Conservative more than of Reform Jews—Conservative Judaism in its way of life as much as in its worldview did establish an essentially mediating position between Orthodoxy and Reform Judaisms. And the conception that Conservative Judaism is a Judaism for Conservative rabbis in no way accords with the truth. That Judaism for a long time enjoyed the loyalty of fully half of the Jews in America and, while losing ground, today still retains the center and the influential position of Judaism in America. The viewpoint of the center predominates even in the more traditional circles of Reform and the more modernist sectors of Orthodoxy.

RESPONDING TO REFORM JUDAISM

The point of movement of a school's viewpoint into the status of a Judaism is not difficult to locate. The school—the Historical School in Germany, a handful of moderate rabbis in America—defined itself as a movement in Judaism (in my terms, a Judaism) in response to a particular event. It was the adoption, by the Reform rabbis, of the Pittsburgh Platform of 1885, cited earlier. At that point a number of European rabbis now settled in America determined to break from Reform and establish what they hoped would be simply "traditional" Judaism in America. In 1886 they founded the Jewish Theological Seminary of America, and that is the point at which Conservative Judaism as a religious movement began. The actual event was simple. The final break between the more traditional and the more radical rabbis among the non-Orthodox camp produced the formation of a group to sponsor a new rabbinical school for "the knowledge and practice of historical Judaism."[2]

The power of Reform Judaism to create and define the character of its own opposition—Orthodoxy in Germany, Conservative Judaism in America—tells us how accurately Reform had outlined the urgent questions of the age. Just as Reform had created Orthodoxy, it created Conservative Judaism. Reform, after all, had treated as compelling the issue of citizenship ("Emancipation") and raised the heart of the matter: How could Jews aspire to return to the Holy Land and form a nation and at the same time take up citizenship in the lands of their birth and loyalty? Jews lived a way of life different from that of their neighbors, with whom they wished to associate. A Judaism had to explain that difference.

Both in Germany in the middle of the century and in America at the end, the emphasis throughout lay on "knowledge and practice of historical Judaism as ordained in the law of Moses expounded by the prophets and sages in Israel in Biblical and Talmudic writings," as the articles of Incorporation of the Jewish Theological Seminary of America Association stated in 1887. Calling themselves "traditionalists" rather than "Orthodox," the Conservative adherents accepted for most Judaic subjects the principles of modern critical scholarship. Conservative Judaism therefore exhibited traits that linked it to Reform but also to Orthodoxy, a movement very much in the middle. Precisely how the Historical School related to the other systems of its day—the mid- and later-nineteenth century—requires attention to that scholarship that, apologists insisted, marked the Historical School off from Orthodoxy.

---

[2]Ibid., col. 902.

HISTORY AND RELIGION:
THE POWER OF HISTORICISM

The principal argument in validation of the approach of the Historical School and Conservative Judaism derived from these same facts of history. Change now would restore the way things had been at that golden age which set the norm and defined the standard. So by changing, Jews would regain that true Judaism that, in the passage of time, had been lost. The Lutheran model governed, as we noted in Chapter 24. Reform added up to more than mere change to accommodate the new age, as the Reforms claimed. This kind of reform would conserve, recover, restore. That is what accounts for the basic claim that the centrists would discover how things had always been. By finding out how things had been done, what had been found essential as faith, in that original and generative time, scholarship would dictate the character of the Judaic system. It would say what it was and therefore what it should again become, and, it followed, Conservative Judaism then would be "simply Judaism."

Reform identified its Judaism as the linear and incremental next step in the unfolding of the Torah. The Historical School and Conservative Judaism later on regarded its Judaism as the reversion to the authentic Judaism that in time had been lost. Change was legitimate, as the Reform said, but only that kind of change that restored things to the condition of the original and correct Judaism. That position formed a powerful apologetic because it addressed the Orthodox view that Orthodoxy constituted the linear and incremental outgrowth of "the Torah" or "the tradition," hence the sole legitimate Judaism. It also addressed the Reform view that change was all right. Conservative Judaism established a firm criterion for what change was all right: the kind that was, really, no change at all. For the premise of the Conservative position was that things should become the way they had always been.

Here we come to the strikingly secular character of the reformist Judaisms: their insistence that religious belief could be established upon a foundation of historical fact. The category of faith, belief in transcendent things, matters not seen or tangible but nonetheless deeply felt and vigorously affirmed—these traits of religiosity hardly played a role. Rather, fact, ascertained by secular media of learning, would define truth. And truth corresponded to here-and-now reality: how things were. Scholarship would tell how things had always been and dictate those changes that would restore the correct way of life, the true worldview, for the Israel composed of pretty much all the Jews—the center. Historical research therefore provided a powerful apologetic against both sides.

That is why history was the ultimate weapon in the nineteenth century in the struggle among the Judaisms of the age. We therefore understand how much authority was carried by the name "Historical School" in the Germany of the mid-nineteenth century. The claim to replicate how things always had been and should remain thus defined historical research, of a sort, as the ultimate weapon. That was, specifically, a critical scholarship that did not accept at face value as history the stories of holy books, but asked whether and how they were true, and in what detail they were not true. That characteristically critical approach to historical study would then serve as the instrument for the definition of Conservative Judaism, the Judaism that would conserve the true faith, but would also omit those elements, accretions of later times, that marred that true faith.

At issue in historical research into secular facts, out of which the correct way of life and worldview would be defined, was the study of the Talmudic literature—that is, the Oral Torah. The Hebrew scripture enjoyed immunity. Both the Reformers and the Historical School theologians stipulated that the Written Torah was God given. The Conservatives and Reformers concurred that God gave the Written Torah, humans made the Oral Torah. So the two parties of change, Reformers and Historical School alike, chose the field of battle, declaring the Hebrew scripture to be sacred and outside the war. They insisted that what was to be reformed was the shape of Judaism imparted by the Talmud, specifically, and preserved in their own day by the rabbis whose qualification consisted in learning in the Talmud and approval by those knowledgeable therein.

That agreement on the arena for critical scholarship is hardly an accident. The Reform and Historical School theologians revered scripture. Wanting to justify parting company from Orthodox and the received tradition of the Oral Torah, they focused on the Talmud because the Talmud formed the sole and complete statement of the one whole Torah of Moses our rabbi, to which Orthodoxy and, of course, the traditionalists of the East appealed. Hence in bringing critical and skeptical questions to the Talmud but not to the Hebrew scripture, the Conservatives and Reformers addressed scholarship where they wished, and preserved as revealed truth what they in any event affirmed as God's will. That is why the intellectual program of the Historical School in Germany and Conservative Judaism in America consisted of turning the Talmud, studied historically, into a weapon turned against two sides: against the excessive credulity of the Orthodox, but also against the specific proposals and conceptions of the Reformers.

The role of scholarship being critical, Conservative Judaism looked to history to show which changes could be made in the light of biblical and Rabbinic precedent, "for they viewed the entire history of Judaism as such a succession of changes," Arthur Hertzberg explains.[3] The continuity in history derives from the ongoing people. The basic policy from the beginning, however, dictated considerable reluctance at making changes in the received forms and teachings of the Judaism of the dual Torah. The basic commitments to the Hebrew language in worship, the dietary laws, and the keeping of the Sabbath and festivals distinguished the Historical School in Europe and Conservative Judaism in America from Reform Judaism. The willingness to accept change and to affirm the political emancipation of the Jews as a positive step marked the group as different from the Orthodox. So far as Orthodoxy claimed to oppose all changes of all kinds, Conservative Judaism did take a position in the middle of the three.

---

[3]Ibid., col. 901.

THE BIRTH OF A JUDAISM

Conservative Judaism formed a deeply original response to a difficult human circumstance. In its formative century it solved the problem of alienation: People who had grown up in one place, under one set of circumstances, now lived somewhere else, in a different world. They cherished the past, but they themselves had initiated the changes they now confronted. In the doctrine of orthopraxy they held onto the part of the past they found profoundly affecting, and they made space for the part of their present circumstance they did not, and could not, reject. A Judaism that joined strict observance to free thinking kept opposed weights in equilibrium—to be sure, in an unsteady balance.

By definition such a delicate juxtaposition could not hold. Papered over by a thick layer of words, the abyss between the way of life, resting on supernatural premises of the facticity of the Torah, and the worldview, calling into question at every point the intellectual foundations of that way of life, remained. But how did the successor generation propose to bridge the gap so to compose a structure resting on secure foundations?

We look for the answer to a representative Conservative theologian of the second generation, active from the 1920s to the 1970s, the high tide of Conservative Judaism. The claim of Reform Judaism to constitute an increment of Judaism, we recall, rested on the position that the only constant in "Judaism" is change. The counterpart for Conservative Judaism comes to expression in the writings of Robert Gordis, since, for their day, they set the standard and defined the position of the center of the religion. Specifically, we seek Gordis's picture of the Judaism that came before and how he proposes to relate Conservative Judaism to that prior system. We find a forthright account of "the basic characteristics of Jewish tradition" as follows:

> The principle of development in all areas of culture and society is a fundamental element of the modern outlook. It is all the more noteworthy that the Talmud . . . clearly recognized the vast extent to which Rabbinic Judaism had grown beyond the Bible, as well as the organic character of this process of growth. . . . For the Talmud, tradition is not static—nor does this dynamic quality contravene either its *divine origin* or its *organic continuity* [all italics his]. . . . Our concern here is with the historical fact, intuitively grasped by the Talmud, that *tradition grows*.[4]

Gordis's appeal is to historical precedent. Without the slightest concern for anachronism, the Conservative theologians found in the tradition ample proof for precisely what they proposed to do, which was, in Gordis's accurate picture, to preserve in a single system the beliefs in both the divine origin and the "organic continuity" of the Torah: that middle-ground position, between Orthodoxy and Reform, that Conservative Judaism so vastly occupied. For Gordis's generation the argument directed itself against both Orthodoxy and Reform.

---

[4]Robert Gordis, *Understanding Conservative Judaism,* ed. Max Gelb New York: Rabbinical Assembly, 1978), pp. 26–27.

In the confrontation with Orthodoxy Gordis points to new values, institutions, and laws "created as a result of new experiences and new felt needs."

But with Reform Gordis points out "instances of accretion and of reinterpretation, which . . . constitute the major modes of development in Jewish tradition." That is, change comes about historically, gradually, over time, and change does not take place by the decree of rabbinical convocations. The emphasis of the positive Historical School upon the probative value of historical events, we now recognize, serves the polemic against Reform as much as against Orthodoxy. To the latter, history proves change, to the former, history dictates modes of appropriate change.

Gordis thus argues that change deserves ratification after the fact, not deliberation before hand: "Advancing religious and ethical ideals were inner processes, often imperceptible except after the passage of centuries." Gordis, to his credit, explicitly claims, on behalf of Conservative Judaism, origin in an incremental and continuous linear history of Judaism. He does so in an appeal to analogy:

> If tradition means development and change . . . how can we speak of the continuity or the spirit of Jewish tradition? An analogy may help supply the answer. Biologists have discovered that in any living organism, cells are constantly dying and being replaced by new ones. . . . If that be true, why is a person the same individual after the passage of . . . years? The answer is twofold. In the first instance, the process of change is gradual. . . . In the second instance, the growth follows the laws of his being. At no point do the changes violate the basic personality pattern. The organic character and unit of the personality reside in this continuity of the individual and in the development of the physical and spiritual traits inherent in him, which persist in spite of the modifications introduced by time. This recognition of the organic character of growth highlights the importance of maintaining the method by which Jewish tradition . . . continued to develop.[5]

The incremental theory follows the modes of Reform thought, with their stress on the continuity of process and that alone. Here, too, just as Marcus saw the permanence of change as the sole continuity, so Gordis sees the ongoing process of change as permanent. The substance of the issues, however, accords with the stress of Orthodoxy on the persistence of a fundamental character to Judaism. The method of Reform then produces the result of Orthodoxy, at least so far as practice of the way of life would go forward. The differences between Conservative and Reform Judaisms mattered to the virtuosi, mostly rabbis, but to ordinary folk, the two Judaisms said mostly the same things to the same people, and that sufficed.

---

[5]Ibid., pp. 39–40.

THE MIDDLE OF THE ROAD IS
NEVER CROWDED

The middle did not hold. Aiming at the best of all worlds, Conservative Judaism got the worst. In the mid-1950s, Conservative Judaism was the largest Judaism in the United States and Canada, encompassing half of the entire Judaic population of North America. At the end of the twentieth century, it had fallen to second place, behind Reform Judaism, and held scarcely a third. The center had collapsed. The elite of Conservative Judaism found its way to Orthodoxy, and the masses to Reform Judaism.

The most recent scholarship on Conservative Judaism sees the movement at a turning point:

> All those who were part of its founding or were educated by the founders have passed away or retired. The new generation taking the lead . . . is a product of the postwar flowering and was influenced by the institutions created in that flowering. . . . The defection of the most traditional wing to the Union for Traditional Judaism, developments affecting the Masorti Movement in Israel . . . the decision of the University of Judaism to found its own rabbinical school . . . challenge Seminary and United Synagogue leadership to rethink the structure of the Movement.[6]

Conservative Judaism is in decline but has hope: "Even as its overall membership is declining, there seems to be emerging a generation of Conservative Jews who take Conservative Judaism seriously." Most significantly, after a century of development, at this time "no more than 40,000 to 50,000 members . . . live up to the standards of Conservative Judaism as defined by its leadership," out of an estimated million and a half Jews affiliated with that Judaism. The system is best defined, then, as a Conservative synagogue where an Orthodox rabbi serves Reform Jews.

---

[6]Daniel J. Elazar and Rela Mintz Geffen, *The Conservative Movement in Judaism. Dilemmas and Opportunities* (Albany: State University of New York Press, 2000), p. 102.

27

Zionism

EXILE AND RETURN IN A
SECULAR SYSTEM: ZIONISM

The master narrative of the human condition, set forth in Chapter 1, is retold in countless variations and chapters and media in the history of Judaism. It tells the tale of exile and return, first of Adam and Eve, cast out
of Eden to work and death, then of Israel cast out of Jerusalem but brought back
through repentance, then the second exile, which precipitated the formation of
the Rabbinic road to return: sanctification now, salvation at the end. With that
scriptural paradigm so deeply etched into the Judaic consciousness, reenacted
through repetition of the Torah in the cycle of the years and their seasons and
repeated in so many words three times a day, we need hardly wonder what became of the master narrative in the secular circumstance of modern times. For
we recall, not only did Judaic systems of the nineteenth century respond to that
circumstance, but Jews also did. Not a few of them in the Western countries
opted out of the supernatural version of the master narrative. They stopped
telling the story and took up other stories. But some undertook to rehearse the
Judaic story in a secular framework.

For these, the story of exile and return became a political myth. That narrative, told in a secular spirit with man, not God, as the principal actor, furthermore animated a political movement of return from exile. Zionism, born as a
secular political movement aiming at the creation of the Jewish state in the Land
of Israel, took up this-worldly media for the realization of the Judaic story of exile and return. Now the Jews (not holy Israel) are in exile (not from God and the
Land but from political normality) and on their own (not with the Messiah's intervention) should take up the challenge of returning to the Land—there to
build the state of Israel! It was a daring, original, unprecedented recapitulation
of the same story that for millennia was repeated in reading from the Torah.

THE URGENT QUESTION
ADDRESSED BY ZIONISM:
RACIST POLITICAL ANTI-SEMITISM

For the assimilated and secular Western Jews of Berlin, Paris, Vienna, and London, the rise of virulent scientific and political anti-Semitism during the last

third of the nineteenth century raised significant doubts. Nor did the political situation of Eastern European Jewry—in Poland, White Russia, Lithuania, Latvia, Estonia, Ukraine, Rumania, and neighboring lands, which was characterized by pogroms, repression, and outright murder, provide reassurance. Humankind did not seem to be progressing very quickly toward that golden day of which Reform Judaism dreamed.

Zionism responded to a political crisis: the failure, by the end of the nineteenth century, of promises of political improvement in the Jews' status and condition. Zionism called to the Jews to emancipate *themselves* by facing the fact that gentiles in the main hated Jews. Therefore Zionism aimed at founding a Jewish state where Jews could free themselves of anti-Semitism and determine their own destiny. The Zionist system of Judaism declared that the Jews form a people, one people, and should transform themselves into a political entity and build a Jewish state. Simply defined, therefore, Zionism is the Judaic system that defined its "Israel" as an ethnic and political entity. It spoke of "the Jews"—not holy Israel of scripture and liturgy, and it held that the Jews form a people, one people, and should create a nation-state of their own. That nation-state should be founded in the Land of Israel (a.k.a. Palestine), the historic homeland of the Jewish people. Its worldview and its way of life followed from its definition of the system's "Israel," as we shall see.

Political Zionism—as distinct from the Messianic Zionism of the Judaic narrative—represented a peculiar marriage of Western romantic nationalism and Judaic piety. The virtuosi of the movement were mostly Western, but the masses of followers were in the East. The Western Jewish intellectuals found that European culture barred them. Fustel de Coulanges's saying, "True patriotism is not love of the soil, but love of the past, reverence for the generations which have preceded us," in his book *The Ancient City* at once excluded Jews (who were newcomers to French culture and could hardly share love for a French past that included banishment of their ancestors) and invited some of them to rediscover their own patriotism—that is, Zionism. The Jews could not share the "collective being" and could not be absorbed into a nation whose national past they did not share.

The Dreyfus trial of 1893–94 involved one of the handful of Jewish officers in the French army who had been falsely accused of selling military secrets to Germany. Because of widespread anti-Semitism, Dreyfus was represented as an example of the bigoted notion that Jews were not loyal citizens. When he was publicly disgraced, the crowds did not shout "Down with the traitor!" but "Down with the Jews!" That fact forced upon the Viennese reporter Theodor Herzl a clear apprehension that the "Jewish problem" could be solved only by complete assimilation or complete evacuation. It occurred to no one in the West that extermination was an option, though the czarist Russians thought of it.

In response to the Dreyfus trial, Herzl published *Der Judenstaat* (*The Jew State*), from whose appearance in 1896, with the consequent founding of the World Zionist Organization in Basel in 1897, is conventionally dated the foundation of modern Zionism (though there were some earlier movements as well). One can hardly overemphasize the secularity of Herzl's vision. He did not appeal to religious sentiments, but to modern secular nationalism. His view of anti-Semitism ignores the religious dimension altogether and stresses only economic and social causes. He did not attend to two millennia of Christian preaching against the "perfidious Jews" and Church demonization of the Jews and its supersessionism—the doctrine that Christianity has replaced Judaism. Modern anti-Semitism grows out of the emancipation of the Jews and their entry into competition with the middle classes. The Jews cannot cease to exist as Jews, for affliction increases their cohesiveness. So Zionism—a state built by the Jews for the Jews—was the only solution. No one foresaw Germany's "Final Solution," the systematic murder of the entire Jewish population.

A JEWISH SYSTEM OF THE SOCIAL ORDER: THEORY OF ISRAEL

But why consider a secular political movement of Jews in the context of the Judaic systems that realize the paradigmatic story of the Torah? After all, not everything Jewish in an ethnic or national sense pertains to the study of Judaism, a religious system of the social order comparable to other religions. But the reason is that Zionism, though secular, recapitulated the main themes of the Judaic system.

That was not the founder's intent. Herzl's solution was wholly practical and in no way motivated by the narrative of restoration: Choose a country to which Jews could go—perhaps Argentina. In fact, Uganda was made available by the British government a few years later, but the Zionist Congress of the day—infused with Jews inspired by the Judaic narrative—rejected that possibility, opting for Palestine (the "Land of Israel") alone. What was important to Herzl was a rational plan: The poor would go first and build the infrastructure of an economy; the middle class would follow to create trade, markets, and new opportunity. The first Zionist Congress was not a gathering of messianists, but of sober women and men. Herzl's statement, "At Basel I founded the Jewish state," was not, however, a sober statement; nor was his following one: "The State is already found in essence, in the will of the people of the State." All that remained were mere practicalities.

Had Zionism led to Uganda, one could have believed it. When, however, Herzl proposed Uganda, he was defeated. The masses in the East had been heard from. They bitterly opposed any "Zion" but Jerusalem. To them, Zionism could mean only Zion; Jerusalem was in one place alone. The classical messianic language—much of which was already associated with Zion in the messianic era—was taken over by the Zionist movement, and it evoked a much more than political response in the Jewish hearts. After the mass murder of most of European Jewry, Zionism swept the field, and in the mid-twentieth century even the Reform movement affirmed it and contributed some of its major leaders. Only small groups within extreme Reform and Orthodox circles resisted. In the state of Israel today there are, in addition to Orthodox religious-political parties, such as Mizrachi, also Orthodox religious-political parties that are not Zionist and do not affirm the Jewish state.

From the creation of the state of Israel forward, "Israel" came to stand not so much for the holy people as for the nation-state. To "go to Israel" meant a locative action, to take a trip to a place, and "Israel" stood for a location rather than a social entity that flourished in a variety of places. That fact has created complications for Judaic religious discourse because for every Judaic religious system, "Israel" stands for the supernatural entity, the holy people, corresponding to Church as the mystical body of Christ—and not for the nation-state. Scripture, the Oral Torah, and the liturgy alike all concur on that point. When we reach the American Judaism of Holocaust and Redemption we shall see some of these complications.

ZIONIST THEORIES OF ZION
AND JUDAIC THEORIES OF ZION

Three main streams of theory flowed abundantly and side by side in the formative decades. The first, a theory concerning the shared culture of the Jews, represented by Ahad HaAm, laid stress on Zion as a spiritual center, to unite all parts of the Jewish people. Ahad HaAm and his associates laid emphasis on spiritual preparation, ideological and cultural activities, and the long-term intellectual issues of persuading the Jews of the Zionist premises.[1]

Another stream, the political one, maintained from the beginning that the Jews should provide for the emigration of the masses of their nation from Eastern Europe, then entering a protracted state of political disintegration and already long suffering from economic dislocation, to the land of Israel—or somewhere, anywhere. Herzl in particular placed the requirement for legal recognition of a Jewish state over the location of the state. In doing so, he set forth the policy that the practical salvation of the Jews through political means would form the definition of Zionism. Herzl stressed that the Jewish state would come into existence in the forum of international politics.[2] The instruments of state—a political forum, a bank, a mode of national allegiance, a press, a central body and leader—came into being in the aftermath of the first Zionist congress in Basel. Herzl spent the rest of his life—less than a decade—seeking an international charter and recognition of the Jews' state.

---

[1] S. Ettinger, "Hibbat Zion," under "Zionism," *Encyclopaedia Judaica,* vol. 16 (Jerusalem: Keter, 1971), cols. 1031–1178.

[2] Arthur Hertzberg, "Ideological Evolution," under "Zionism," *Encyclopaedia Judaica,* vol. 16, cols. 1044–1045.

A third stream, derived from socialism, expressed a Zionist vision of socialism or a socialist vision of Zionism. The Jewish state was to be socialist, as indeed, for its first three decades, it was. Socialist Zionism in its earlier theoretical formulation (before its near-total bureaucratization) emphasized that a proletarian Zionism would define the arena for the class struggle within the Jewish people to be realized. In the reading on socialism and Yiddishism as a Judaic system, we shall learn more about socialist Zionism.

Cultural Zionism precipitated the conflict between Zionist and religious Jews. Ahad HaAm made the explicit claim that Zionism would succeed Judaism, and Hertzberg states:

> The function that revealed religion had performed in talmudic and medieval Judaism, that of guaranteeing the survival of the Jews as a separate entity because of their belief in the divinely ordained importance of the Jewish religion and people, it was no longer performing and could not be expected to perform. The crucial task facing Jews in the modern era was to devise new structures to contain the separate individual of the Jews and to keep them loyal to their own tradition. This analysis of the situation implied . . . a view of Jewish history which Ahad HaAm produced as undoubted . . . , that the Jews in all ages were essentially a nation and that all other factors profoundly important to the life of this people, even religion, were mainly instrumental values.[3]

Hertzberg contrasts that statement with one made a thousand years earlier by Saadiah, a tenth-century theologian and philosopher of Judaism in Islamic Baghdad: "The Jewish people is a people only for the sake of its Torah." That statement of the position of the Judaism of the dual Torah contrasts with the one of Zionism and allows us to set the one against the other, both belonging to the single classification, a Judaism. For, as is clear, each proposed to answer the same type of questions, and the answers provided by each enjoyed that same status of not mere truth but fact, not merely fact but just and right and appropriate fact.

Herzl's thesis, by contrast to Ahad HaAm's, laid stress on the power of anti-Semitism to keep the Jews together, and that was the problem he proposed to solve. So Ahad HaAm's conception serves more adequately than Herzl's to express a worldview within Zionism comparable to the worldview of a Judaism. Hertzberg points out that Ahad HaAm described the Jews' "national spirit as an authoritative guide and standard to which he attributed a majesty comparable to that which the religious had once ascribed to the God of revelation." That conception competed with another, which laid stress on the re-creation of the Jews in a natural and this-worldly state. Hertzberg again: "a bold and earthy people, whose hands would not be tied by the rules of the rabbis or even the self-doubts of the prophets."[4]

---

[3]Ibid., col. 1046.

[4]Ibid., col. 1047.

THE IDEOLOGY OF "JEWISH HISTORY" AS THE CONTINUOUS, UNITARY STORY OF "A PEOPLE, ONE PEOPLE"

Given the Jews' diversity, people could more easily concede the supernatural reading of Judaic existence than the national construction given to it. For, scattered across the European countries as well as in the Moslem world, Jews did not speak a single language, follow a single way of life, or adhere in common to a single code of belief and behavior. What made them a people, one people, and further validated their claim and right to a state, a nation, of their own, constituted the central theme of the Zionist worldview. Apart from having in common the status of hated object, Jews all together could identify no facts of perceived society to validate that view. In no way, except for a common fate, did the Jews form a people, one people.

We should not miss the intellectual power of the Zionist rereading of Jews' histories as Jewish History, single, continuous, unitary, starting somewhere and ending up there. Because of the diversity of the Jews, spread over many countries and speaking many languages, Zionist theory sought roots for its principal ideas in the documents of the received Judaism of the dual Torah. Zionist theory had the task of explaining how the Jews formed a people, one people, and in the study of "Jewish History" read as a single and unitary story, Zionist theory solved that problem. The Jews all came from some one place, traveled together, and were going back to that same one place: one people. Zionist theory therefore derived strength from the study of history, much as had Reform Judaism, and in time generated a great renaissance of Judaic studies as the scholarly community of the nascent Jewish state took up the task at hand. The sort of history that emerged took the form of factual and descriptive narrative. But its selection of facts, its recognition of problems requiring explanation, its choice of what mattered and what did not—all of these definitive questions found answers in the larger program of nationalist ideology. So the form was secular and descriptive, the substance ideological.

At the same time, Zionist theory explicitly rejected the precedent formed by that Torah, selecting as its history not the history of the faith, of the Torah, but the history of the nation, Israel construed as a secular entity. Zionism defined episodes as history, linear history, Jewish History with a capital H. That History appealed to those strung-together events, all of a given classification to be sure, as vindication for its program of action. Zionism went in search of heroes unlike those of the present, warriors, political figures, and others who might provide a model for the movement's future, and for the projected state beyond. So instead of rabbis or sages, Zionism chose figures such as David or Judah Maccabee or Samson. David the warrior king, Judah Maccabee, who had led the revolt against the Syrian Hellenists, Samson the powerful fighter— these provided the appropriate heroes for a Zionism that proposed to redefine Jewish consciousness, to turn storekeepers into soldiers, lawyers into farmers, corner grocers into builders and administrators of great institutions of state and government. Zionism gave pride to beggars and purpose to perpetual victims. The Judaism of the dual Torah treated David as a rabbi. The Zionist system of Judaism saw David as a hero in a more worldly sense: a courageous nation builder.

In its eagerness to appropriate a usable past, Zionism and its successor Israeli nationalism dug for roots in the sands of history, finding in archaeology links to the past, even proofs for the biblical record to which, in claiming the Land of Israel, Zionism pointed. So in pre-state times and after the creation of the state of Israel in 1948, Zionist scholars and institutions devoted great effort to digging up the ancient monuments of the Land of Israel, finding in archaeological work the link to the past that the people, one people, so desperately sought. Archaeology uncovered the Jews' roots in the Land of Israel and became a principal instrument of national expression, much as, for contemporary believers in scripture, archaeology would prove the truths of the biblical narrative. It was not surprising, therefore, that in the Israeli War of Independence, 1948–1949, and in later times as well, Israeli generals explained to the world that by following the biblical record of the nation in times past, they had found hidden roads, appropriate strategies—in all, the key to victory.

So Zionism framed its worldview by inventing—or selecting—a past for itself. Its appeal for legitimation invoked the precedent of history, or, rather, Jewish History, much as Reform did. But Orthodoxy, in its (quite natural) appeal to the past as the record of its valid conduct in the present, produced an argument of the same sort. None of the exemplary figures Zionism chose for itself, of course, served as did their counterpart components in Reform, Orthodox, and Conservative Judaisms, to link the new movement to the received Torah. Zionism sought a new kind of hero as a model for the new kind of Jew it proposed to call into being. Zionism in its appeal to history represented a deliberate act of rejection of the received Torah and construction of a new system altogether.

THE RENAISSANCE OF THE
SCRIPTURAL NARRATIVE

Zionism's particular stress, as time went on, focused upon the biblical portrait of Israel's possession of the Land of Israel. The Torah (only in written form, hence the "Bible," omitting reference to its Christian half!) represented for Zionism, as much as for the Judaism of the two Torahs, the validation of Israel's claim to the land. But it also contributed a usable past, in place of the one now found wanting, that is, the past made up of the dual Torah's sages and their teachings on one side as well as their iron control of the politics of the traditional sector of Israel, the people, on the other.

So we should not find surprising the power of Zionism to appropriate those components of the received writings that it found pertinent and to reshape them into a powerful claim upon continuity, indeed in behalf of the self-evidence of the Zionist position: The Jews form a people, one people, and should have the land back and build a state on it. Above all, Zionism found in the writings of the biblical prophets about the return to Zion ample precedent for its program, linking today's politics to something very like God's will for Israel, the Jewish people, in ancient times. So calling the new Jewish city Tel Aviv invoked the memory of Ezekiel's reference to a Tel Aviv, and that only symbolizes much else. It was a perfectly natural identification of past and present, an appeal not for authority alone to a historical precedent, but rather a reentry into a perfect world of mythic being, an eternal present. Zionism would reconstitute the age of the Return to Zion in the time of Ezra and Nehemiah, so carrying out the prophetic promises. The mode of thought, again, is entirely reminiscent of that of Reform Judaism, which, to be sure, selected a different perfect world of mythic being, a golden age other than the one that to Zionism glistened so brightly.

Alongside the search of scripture, Zionism articulated a very clear perception of what it wished to find there. And what Zionism did not find, it deposited on its own: celebration of the nation as a secular, not a supernatural category, imposition of the nation and its heroism in place of the heroic works of the supernatural God. A classic shift took the verse of Psalms, "Who will retell the great deeds of God?" and produced "Who will retell the great deeds of Israel?" And that only typifies the profound revisioning of Israel's history accomplished by Zionism. For Israel in its dual Torah (and not only in that Judaism by any means) formed a supernatural entity, a social unit unlike any other on the face of the earth. All humanity divided into two parts, Israel and the (undifferentiated) nations. The doctrine of Israel in the Judaism given literary expression in Constantine's day, moreover, maintained that the one thing Israel should not do is arrogant deeds. That meant waiting on God to save Israel, assigning to Israel the task of patience, loyalty, humility, obedience, all in preparation for God's intervention. The earliest pronouncements of a Zionist movement, received in the Jewish heartland of Eastern Europe like the toxin of the coming Messiah, for that same reason impressed the sages of the dual Torah as blasphemy. God will do it—or it will not be done. Considerable time would elapse before the avatars of the dual Torah could make their peace with Zionism, and some of them never did.

JUDAISM AND ZIONISM:
COMPETITION AND CONCILIATION

The notion that the Jews form a secular nation, not just a holy people, dismayed most Rabbinic authorities before the end of the nineteenth century. For until modern times, the category "secular Jew" or "ethnic Jew" was unknown; no one imagined that a Jew would not also be a Judaist, one who practiced Judaism. Israel always meant the holy people, awaiting redemption in the end of days. The definition of the Jews as a political entity, without regard to supernatural considerations, developed in the late nineteenth century, a byproduct of the invention of Judaism as a religion distinct from the secular aspect of life, and therefore the formulation of the Jews as an ethnic (or in nineteenth-century terms, a racial) and (in due course) a political body.

Ludwig Philippson wrote:"Formerly the Jews had striven to create a nation . . . but now their goal was to join other nations. . . . It was the task of the new age to form a general human society which would encompass all peoples organically. In the same way, it was the task of the Jews not to create their own nation . . . but rather to obtain from the other nations full acceptance into their society." Similarly, the West London Synagogue of British Jews heard from its first rabbi in 1845:"To this land [England] we attach ourselves with a patriotism as glowing, with a devotion as fervent, and with a love as ardent and sincere as any class of our British non-Jewish fellow citizens."[5] One could duplicate that statement—and with it, its excessive protest—many times.

The reformation represented by Reform Judaism emphasized that Judaism could eliminate the residue of its nationalistic phase that survived in traditional doctrine and liturgy. The reformers saw messianism not as Zionist doctrine, but as a call to the golden age in which a union of nations into one peaceful realm to serve their one true God would take place. It has not happened yet.

If Judaic systems objected to Zionism, Zionism acknowledged the competition of Judaism. The Zionist worldview explicitly competed with the religious one. The formidable statement of Jacob Klatzkin (1882–1948) provides the solid basis for comparison:

> In the past there have been two criteria of Judaism: the criterion of religion, according to which Judaism is a system of positive and negative commandments, and the criterion of the spirit, which saw Judaism as a complex of ideas, like monotheism, Messianism, absolute justice, etc. According to both these criteria, therefore, Judaism rests on a subjective basis, on the acceptance of a creed . . . a religious denomination . . . or a community of individuals who share in a *Weltanschauung*. . . . In opposition to these two criteria, which make of Judaism a matter of creed, a third has now arisen, the criterion of a consistent nationalism. According to it, Judaism rests on an objective basis: to be a Jew means the acceptance of neither a religious nor an ethical creed. We are neither a denomination or a school of thought, but members of one family, bearers of a common history. . . . The national definition too requires an act of will. It defines our nationalism by two criteria: partnership in the past and the conscious desire to continue such partnership in the future. There are, therefore, two bases for Jewish nationalism—the compulsion of history and a will expressed in that history.[6]

---

[5]Joseph L. Blau, *Modern Varieties of Judaism* (New York: Columbia University Press, 1966), pp. 121, 124.

[6]Cited in Hertzberg, "Ideological Evolution," p. 317.

Klatzkin's stress on "a will expressed in history" carries us back to the appeals of Reform and Conservative theologians to facts of history as precedents for faith. The historicism at hand falls into the same classification of thought. But for the theologians the facts proved episodic and ad hoc, mere precedents. Zionists would find it necessary to reread the whole of the histories of Jews and compose of them Jewish History, a single and linear system leading inexorably to the point that, to the Zionist historians, seemed inexorable: the formation of the Jewish state on the other end of time. Klatzkin defined being a Jew not as something subjective but something objective: "on land and language. These are the basic categories of national being."[7]

That definition, of course, would lead directly to the signal of calling the Jewish state the "state of Israel," so making a clear statement of the doctrine formed by Zionism of who is Israel. In contributing, as Klatzkin said, "the territorial-political definition of Jewish nationalism," Zionism offered a genuinely fresh worldview:

> Either the Jewish people shall redeem the land and thereby continue to live, even if the spiritual content of Judaism changes radically, or we shall remain in exile and rot away, even if the spiritual tradition continues to exist.[8]

It goes without saying that, like Christianity at its original encounter with the task of making sense of history, so Zionism posited that a new era began with its formation: "not only for the purpose of making an end to the Diaspora but also in order to establish a new definition of Jewish identity—a secular definition."[9]

In this way Zionism clearly stated the intention of providing a worldview instead of that of the received Judaism of the dual Torah and in competition with all efforts of the continuators of that Judaism. Klatzkin states: "Zionism stands opposed to all this. Its real beginning is *The Jewish State* [italics his], and its basic intention, whether consciously or unconsciously, is to deny any conception of Jewish identity based on spiritual criteria." Obviously, Klatzkin's was not the only voice. But in his appeal to history, in his initiative in positing a linear course of events of a single kind leading to one goal, the Jewish state, Klatzkin did express that theory of history that would supply Zionism with a principal plank in its platform. What the several appeals to the facts of history would mean, of course, is that the arena of scholarship on what ("really") happened would define the boundaries for debate on matters of faith. Consequently the heightened and intensified discourse of scholars would produce judgments not on secular facts but on deeply held truths of faith, identifying not correct or erroneous versions of things that happened but truth and heresy, saints and sinners. In its radical historicism, Zionism conformed to the pattern of the nineteenth-century Judaic systems of Israel's social order.

---

[7]Cited in ibid., p. 318.

[8]Cited in ibid., p. 319.

[9]Klatzkin, cited in ibid., p. 319.

HISTORY PROVES . . . :
ZIONISM AND THE HOLOCAUST

Zionism won, and it won over the greater number of Judaic religious systems that had offered competing narratives, though not all of them. "History" did prove Zionism right—so most Jews, and most Judaists, practitioners of a Judaism, have decided.

Zionism succeeded in persuading most Judaic systems of the Israelite social order that the Jews should adopt its program. That is for reasons of theory, not only of historical fact. That is, Zionism not only answered its urgent question—Israel and anti-Semitism—but the political success of racist anti-Semitism also secured for that question the highest position on the Jewish agenda.

First, Zionism enunciated a powerful and attractive doctrine of Israel. It appealed to Jews' sense of their distinctive character as a group, which appealed to this-worldly, not other-worldly considerations. It was now not God who identified the Jews as a single social entity, but anti-Semitism. The anti-Semites made no distinctions among Jews, and therefore Jews saw themselves as unified even while lacking much in common. Thus so many concurred on this-worldly, political grounds that the Jews indeed form a people, one people.

Second, the world confirmed the worst prognostications of Zionism and made the Zionist conception of the power of anti-Semitism seem moderate and understated. Zionism faced reality, explained it, and offered a program, inclusive of a worldview and a way of life, that worked. The power of the Zionist theory of the Jews' existence came to expression not only at the end of World War II, when Zionism offered world Jewry the sole meaningful explanation of how to endure; it led at least some Zionists to realize as early as 1940 what Hitler's Germany was going to do. At a meeting in December 1940, Berl Katznelson, an architect of socialist Zionism in the Jewish community of Palestine before the creation of the state of Israel, announced that European Jewry was finished:

> The essence of Zionist awareness must be that what existed in Vienna will never return, what existed in Berlin will never return, nor in Prague, and what we had in Warsaw and Lodz is finished, and we must realize this! . . . Why don't we understand that what Hitler has done and what existed before will never exist again. . . . And I declare that the fate of European Jewry is sealed. . . .[10]

Zionism, in the person of Katznelson, even before the systematic mass murder got underway, grasped that after World War II Jews would not wish to return to Europe, certainly not to those places in which they had flourished for a thousand years, and Zionism offered the alternative: the building, outside Europe, of the Jewish state.

---

[10]Anita Shapira, *Berl* (New York: Oxford University Press, 1983), p. 290.

Third, events showed that Zionism had taken a position of prophecy and had found its prophecy fulfilled. Its fundamental dogma about the character of the Diaspora as Exile found verification in the destruction of European Jewry. And Zionism's further claim to point the way forward proved to be Israel's salvation in the formation of the state of Israel on the other side of the Holocaust. So Katznelson maintained: "If Zionism wanted to be the future force of the Jewish people, it must prepare to solve the Jewish question in all its scope." The secret of the power of Zionism lay in its power to make sense of the world and to propose a program to solve the problems of the age. In its context, brief though it turned out to be, Zionism formed the counterpart, in power and success and self-evidence, to the received Judaic system of the dual Torah of the fourth through nineteenth centuries.

And that carries us to the twentieth century, the age of ruin and reconstruction, and its urgent question. Through the nineteenth century Reform, Orthodox, Conservative Judaisms and Zionism all took for granted that the urgent question facing the Jews was Emancipation. All responded within the premise that an integrationist system is required. But prominent in the twentieth century practice of Judaism in modern and contemporary North America—the United States and Canada—in addition to those Judaisms are a variety of self-segregationist ones. None of them fits easily into the pattern formed by Reform, integrationist Orthodoxy, Conservative Judaism, and Zionism. That is because, self-segregationist in basic conviction, they dismissed as simply irrelevant the urgency of the question of Emancipation. They asked questions of sanctification in a century polluted by mass murder—and in so doing kept the faith, as we shall now see.

PART VIII

The Practice of Judaism in Contemporary North America

28

Beyond "Emancipation"

Agudath Israel and Habad Hasidism in Contemporary North America

JUDAIC SYSTEMS UNTOUCHED
BY EMANCIPATION

Conventional accounts of Judaisms in modern times encompass Reform, Orthodox, and Conservative Judaisms and deal also with Zionism, a secular system. It is common to include, for contemporary times, other integrationist Judaic systems, some (Reconstructionism, for example) with a this-worldly theology, others (such as "New Age Judaism,") offering a subjective, spiritual Judaism. All of the modern Judaisms are modest in numbers and influence. Each tells variations of a single story: the history not of holy Israel forming God's kingdom from Sinai but of the "Jews," a religious community among other religions, not God's unique domain.

True, significant, prominent communities of Judaism continue to tell themselves the classical story in the familiar way: the story of Creation and Eden, Revelation and Sinai, Redemption and the Land in the end of days. These Judaic systems rehearse the old, familiar story of Exile and Return as the master narrative of the human condition. They ask the received urgent question and respond in the established pattern. They are self-segregated systems. But accounts of Judaism in modern times tend to omit self-segregationist Orthodox Judaisms from their picture of "modern Judaisms." These they think they cover when they treat "premodern" or classical Judaic systems. So, in response to the urgent question of Emancipation, observers do not take up the story the self-segregationist Orthodox Judaisms tell, phrase the urgent question they ask; set forth the self-evidently valid answers they put forth. That is so even though they too speak to contemporary Jewry and win a huge hearing, as a matter of fact.

But whether or not we assign them the adjective *modern,* the Jews who adhere to self-segregationist Judaic systems flourish in the same century and respond to the same issues of politics and culture as do those that identify with Reform, Orthodox, or Conservative Judaisms. They simply read matters differently, in their own proportions and foci. Numerous, well-organized, with strong institutions and effective leadership, self-segregationist Judaisms are temporally just as "modern" as the integrationist groups. They know the same things, they address the same cultural and political facts. But they respond differently to the challenges that yield the now-familiar theologies of "Israel." In terms of our analytical model, they find their urgent question other than the one captured in the word "Emancipation." And their self-evidently valid answer does not explain how one may ever be—or would want to be—anything other than Israel, God's people, subject to the Torah of Sinai: the people that dwells apart, for God's sake.

These groups themselves prove diverse. We briefly consider one and, at some greater length, another of them. The first of the two that represent self-segregationist Orthodoxy, Agudath Israel, forms a response to Zionism, taking shape in the early part of the twentieth century in Europe. The second, Hasidism, with special reference to Habad Hasidism, originates in Eastern Europe in the eighteenth century and finds a place in the United States and Canada only in the time of the destruction of its home communities of Poland, Hungary, and other lands of Eastern Europe, in and after World War II. That Judaism became a great power among world Judaisms only in the last third of the twentieth century. It is today the single most vigorous community of Judaism, possessing the power to change Jews' lives and convert them to their Torah. Reform, integrationist-Orthodox, and Conservative Judaisms, not to mention Reconstructionism and New Age Judaism, compete but cannot excel in that same venture.

What of the urgent question the self-segregationist systems ask? To each group in its own way, God and the Torah defined the self-evident response to the urgent question addressed by God and by the century of Auschwitz to humanity: "Adam, Where are you?" (Gen. 3:9). Both found Israel's self-evident answer in the Torah.

AGUDATH ISRAEL

Among the segregationist Judaisms, one type, represented by Agudath Israel, continues the normative Judaism of Mishnah, Talmuds, and Midrash-centered Torah study and observance in the classical framework. The other type, the various Hasidic systems, add on their own doctrines and practices to the received ones. The former, pure in their classicism, defined by the Written and Oral Torah and its extensions, commentaries, and codes, take shape around great *Yeshivot,* sustained by neighborhoods where the Judaic way of life predominates. They find intensely relevant the urgent question of the ages—God's question to Adam—and they answer that question in the same terms as ever. They deny the possibility of a secular Jewish culture, such as Zionism wished to found from the early part of the twentieth century, and they do not equate "Torah" and "modern learning" as equally legitimate media of knowledge, as integrationist Orthodoxy does. The Judaic narrative is not "Jewish History" but rather that of the Torah. The Jewish people should be united under the rule of the Torah, classically understood: charged to form "a kingdom of priests and a holy people."

Agudath Israel was organized in Central Europe in 1912, in response to the Fourth Zionist Congress's decision to foster a secular Jewish culture. Agudath Israel then undertook to defend the received Torah as the sole valid "culture." It achieved great influence in Poland and other parts of Eastern Europe not subjugated by communism, where the practice of Judaism in any form was proscribed. Agudath Israel was organized in the United States in 1939 and today exercises considerable influence in public opinion in all traditionalist Judaisms, beyond the numbers of its affiliates and their memberships.[1] Its public voice undertakes to criticize other Judaic systems and their positions on theological as much as political issues, exemplifying utter seriousness about the truth claims of the Torah. Nothing is negotiable, just as Moses insists in Deuteronomy.

So Agudath Israel fits well into the narrative of modernization, dealing as it does with Emancipation, whether mediated by Reform Judaism or by Zionism. But it offers other answers than those of integrationist Orthodoxy, as follows: Israel remains separate from the nations because it is holy to God. It does not seek integration among the nations. The Torah governs, and the sages who have mastered the sciences of the Torah decide. When Agudath Israel speaks in public debate, it finds for contemporary issues the position authentic to the classical teachings without compromise or apology.

HASIDISM IN THE UNITED STATES

Like Agudath Israel, arriving on the North American scene in the aftermath of the Holocaust but much more prominent in the public eye, Hasidism had reached its full definition in eighteenth- and nineteenth-century Poland, Ukraine, White Russia, and elsewhere, where Emancipation meant nothing. There anti-Semitism presented no surprise and required no special explanation, being part of the theory of "Israel" that accounted for gentile hostility by appeal to the Torah, which God gave to Israel alone.

While Reform and Conservative Judaisms cohere, respectively, in national and institutional rabbinical bodies and congregational unions, Hasidism presents an institutionally more diverse appearance. That is because it organizes itself in communities around particular holy men. The freestanding communities are named after the towns where those holy men resided in Eastern Europe—thus the Satmar, Lubavitcher [Habad], Bobover, Belzer, Vishnitzer, Gerer, Klausenberger, Skverer, and Bratslaver Hasidim.[2] Gall states: "Brooklyn, New York, has North America's largest concentration of Hasidim—an estimated 150,000, located mainly in the neighborhoods of Boro Park, Williamsburg, and Crown Heights. There are also well-established Hasidic communities elsewhere in New York City, as well as in such diverse cities as Cleveland, Detroit, Los Angeles, Baltimore, Miami, St. Louis, Philadelphia, and Denver."[3]

The adherents of the diverse Hasidic communities also cohere in common customs; on holy days such as the Sabbath, for instance, all wear the exotic

---

[1] Maurice Friedberg, "Agudat Israel," *Encyclopaedia Judaica,* vol. 2 (Jerusalem Keter, 1971), cols. 421–426.

[2] Timothy L. Gall, ed., *Worldmark Encyclopedia of Culture and Daily Life,* vol. 3, *Asia & Oceania* (Cleveland, OH: Eastword Publications Development, 1998), p. 776. Particularly helpful is the information set forth at www.adherents.com, which contains the information cited here.

[3] Ibid., p. 776.

costume-clothing of an earlier era of Eastern Europe, the black caftan and broad-brimmed hat. The men preserve their sidelocks.

The segregated communities of adherents interact with outsiders only as required. Clearly, these communities of Judaism have taken a different view of Emancipation from the one of Reform, integrationist Orthodoxy, and Conservatism. Along with self-segregationist Orthodoxy, they reject it out of hand. But these are superficial traits. The differences between all Hasidic Judaic systems and the received Judaic system of the dual Torah prove fundamental and doctrinal.

HASIDISM: THE EUROPEAN ORIGINS

Hasidic Judaism originated at the same period as Reform Judaism, at the end of the eighteenth and beginning of the nineteenth centuries, and its earliest writings, stories of the Hasidic holy men, were published in the early decades of the nineteenth centuries, at the same time as the initial publications of Reform Judaism. Emerging in mid-eighteenth century Ukraine and Poland, the mystical movement began with doctrines and emphases quite at variance with those of the standard Rabbinic Judaism. What distinguished Hasidism from the Rabbinic system set forth in the Mishnah, Talmuds, and Midrash and their continuators was the Hasidic focus on holy men as media of divine grace. These holy men—some of them endowed with profound learning in the Torah, some not—were all exemplars of purity and piety. Hasidic groups, taking shape around such charismatic personalities, favored holy men having a direct encounter with God over sages meeting God in the Torah.

The mystic circles in Ukraine and Poland in the eighteenth century where Hasidism developed furthermore carried on certain practices that marked them as different from other Jews—such as special prayers, distinctive ways of observing certain religious duties, and the like. The first of the movement of ecstatics, Israel ben Eliezer Baal Shem Tov, the "Besht," worked as a popular healer. From the 1730s onward he undertook travels and attracted to himself circles of followers in Podolia (Ukraine), Poland and Lithuania, and elsewhere. When he died in 1760, he left disciples who organized the movement in southeastern Poland and Lithuania. Dov Ber inaugurated the institution of the Hasidic court and dispatched disciples beyond Podolia to establish courts on their own. Most of the major Hasidic circles originate in his disciples. Leadership of the movement then passed to a succession of holy men, about whom stories were told and preserved. In the third generation, from the third quarter of the eighteenth century into the first of the nineteenth, the movement spread and took hold. Diverse leaders, called *Zaddikim,* holy men and charismatic figures, developed their own standing and doctrine.

Given the controversies that swirled around the movement, we should expect that many of the basic ideas would have been new. But that was hardly the case. The movement drew heavily on available Kabbalistic mystical books and doctrines, which from medieval times onward had won a place within the faith as part of the Torah. Emphasis on the distinctive doctrines of Hasidic thinkers should not obscure the profound continuities between the modern movement and its medieval sources.

To take one example of how the movement imparted its own imprint on an available idea, Menahem Mendel of Lubavitch (an early principal of Habad Hasidism) notes that God's oneness—surely a given in all Judaisms—means more than that God is unique. It means that God is all that is:

> There is no reality in created things. This is to say that in truth all creatures are not in the category of something or a thing as we see them with our eyes. For this is only from our point of view, since we cannot perceive the divine vitality. But from the point of view of the divine vitality which sustains us, we have no existence and we are in the category of complete nothingness like the rays of the sun in the sun itself. . . .
> From which it follows that there is no other existence whatsoever apart from his existence, blessed be he. This is true unification."[4]

Since all things are in God, the suffering and sorrow of the world cannot be said to exist. So to despair is to sin.

Hasidism lay great stress on joy and avoiding melancholy. It further maintained that the right attitude must accompany the doing of religious deeds: The deed could only be elevated when carried out in a spirit of devotion. The doctrine of Hasidism moreover held that "in all things there are 'holy sparks' waiting to be redeemed and rescued for sanctity through man using his appetites to serve God. The very taste of food is a pale reflection of the spiritual force which brings the food into being."[5] Before carrying out a religious deed, the Hasidism would recite the formula, "For the sake of the unification of the Holy One, blessed be he, and his *Shekhinah* [presence in the world]." On that account they were criticized.

But most criticized of all was the Hasidic doctrine of Zaddikism: the *Zaddik,* or holy man, had the power to raise the prayers of the followers to Heaven and to work miracles. The *Zaddik* was the means through which grace reached the world, the one who controlled the universe through his prayers. The *Zaddik* would bring humanity nearer to God and God closer to humanity. The Hasidim were well aware that this doctrine of the *Zaddik*—the pure and elevated soul that could reach to that realm of heaven in which only mercy reigns— represented an innovation. So, too, did the massive opposition to Hasidism organized by the great sages of the Torah of that time.

By the end of the eighteenth century powerful opposition, led by the most influential figures of Eastern European Judaism, characterized Hasidism as heretical. Hasidism, true to the optimistic spirit of eighteenth century revivalism, thought that humanity was capable of transcendence. The opposition,

---

[4]Cited by Louis Jacobs, "Basic Ideas of Hasidism," *Encyclopaedia Judaica,* vol. 7 (Jerusalem: Keter, 1971), col. 1404.

[5]Ibid., col. 1405.

called Mithnagdism," took a more pessimistic view of humanity's possibilities. Hasidism held that we may meet God in this world. Mithnagdism found in death the beginning of an authentic life with God. The scholar of opposition to Hasidism, Allan Nadler, states it simply, "As far as the Mithnagdim were concerned, the attainment of Kabalistic erudition or mystical union with God was possible, if at all, only in the world to come." Hasidism held that ordinary folk could master difficult writings, Mithnagdism doubted it. Hasidism exalted prayer over Talmud Torah, Mithnagdism insisted upon the classic priority of learning over spiritualism. Mithnagdism held that "only the full and final obliteration from the created cosmos offered man complete salvation from a physical world so far removed from God and so saturated with the evil desire . . . for many of the Mithnagdim only physical death allowed man to attain that proximity to the Lord that is his final good."[6] Mithnagdism affirmed the received definition of the religious leader in the Torah world, while Hasidism framed a theory of the Zaddik out of "a general theological monism and its mystical notions of cosmic harmony and restoration."

Above all, Mithnagdism preserved a more realistic, more pessimistic view of human potentiality, which Nadler describes as follows:

> In the process of attaining . . . communion with God, the Hasid inevitably departs from the traditional, restricted modes of organized religious and social behavior. He then appears to those who are faithful to the normative limits of social, legal, and religious protocol as at best eccentric or somewhat deranged and at the very worst fraudulent. . . . The Mithnagdim . . . simply could not accept that such significant numbers from among the Jewish masses had legitimately reached the level of its attainment. Consequently, they could not tolerate the concerted attempts by the early Hasidic theoreticians to spread the knowledge and practice of Jewish mysticism as widely as possible.[7]

So, Nadler concludes:

> The Mithnagdim did not dispute the fundamental teachings of Jewish mysticism in principle. They shared . . . the religious conviction that God is immanent in the created universe and that it is possible for the ideal man . . . to commune with the divine presence inherent in the world. The Mithnagdim harbored . . . a very pessimistic view of the common man of their day; they believed that he was simply unable . . . ever to attain such a mystical state. . . . In sum, the Mithnagdim allowed man no genuine mystical experiences in this life. . . . Because of this very limited assessment of the human condition, the Mithnagdim restricted their attention almost exclusively to carefully controlled and well-defined religious disciplines. . . . The Mithnagdim . . . offered the individual Jew

---

[6]Allan Nadler, *The Faith of the Mithnagdim: Rabbinic Responses to Hasidic Rapture,* Johns Hopkins Jewish Studies, ed. Sander Gilman and Steven T. Katz (Baltimore & London: The Johns Hopkins University Press, 1997).

[7]Ibid., p. 12.

no path of redemption from his estranged, shattered existence in this world and no remedy for his divided nature and afflicted spirit.[8]

So the issues are real, the choices consequential. The Hasidic stress on ecstasy, visions, miracles of the leaders, its way of life of enthusiasm—these were seen as delusions, and the veneration of the Zaddik was interpreted as worship of a human being. The stress on prayer to the denigration of study of the Torah likewise called into question the legitimacy of the movement. In the war against Hasidism, the movement found itself anathematized, its books burned, its leaders vilified. Nadler cites the following: "They must leave our communities with their wives and children . . . and they should not be given a night's lodging . . . it is forbidden to do business with them and to intermarry with them or to assist at their burial."

Under these circumstances, the last thing anyone would anticipate would have been for Hasidism to find a place for itself within what would at some point be deemed the embodiment of Orthodoxy. But it did. By the 1830s, the original force of the movement had run its course, and the movement, beginning as a persecuted sect, now defined the way of life of the Jews in Ukraine, Galicia, and central Poland, with offshoots in White Russia and Lithuania on one side and Hungary on the other. The waves of emigration from the 1880s onward carried the movement to the West, and, in the aftermath of World War II, to the United States and the state of Israel as well. Today the movement forms a powerful component of Orthodox Judaism.

HABAD OR LUBAVITCH HASIDISM

The single most prominent Hasidic community in contemporary Judaism is Habad, the neologism formed of the first letter of the Hebrew words for wisdom, understanding, and knowledge. Centered around the Hasidic dynasty deriving from the town of Lubavitch, Habad ultimately found a central place in its piety for Torah study. The combination of ecstatic piety, Zaddikism, and Torah learning as well distinguished Habad Hasidism from the other Hasidic circles.

Louis Jacobs tells us: "The branch of the Habad tendency in Hasidism with many thousands of followers all over the Jewish world. The second Rebbe of Habad, Dov Baer, settled in the Russian town of Lubavitch, after which this group of Hasidism is called. The sixth master, Rabbi Joseph Isaac Schneerson (1880–1950), settled in Brooklyn, USA, in 1940, where he was succeeded by his son-in-law, Rabbi Menahem Mendel Schneerson (1902–1994), the seventh and to date, the last, Lubavitcher Rebbe, who established a worldwide network of educational institutions and a major publishing house."[9] Habad has grown rapidly since World War II after its transfer to the United States (with its center

---

[8]Ibid., p. 13.

[9]Louis Jacobs, *Oxford Concise Companion to the Jewish Religion,* (Oxford, UK: Oxford University Press, 1999), pp. 138–139.

at 770 Eastern Parkway, Brooklyn) and to the state of Israel (with its center at Kefar Habad, featuring a replica of the building at 770 Eastern Parkway as the heart of the Israeli office): "Since mid-century," Jacob says, "the number of Lubavitchers has doubled about every ten years, so that by the mid-1990s there were perhaps a quarter of a million of them worldwide (making them the largest of the Hasidic courts today)."[10] Other estimates place the number at 50,000 full-fledged Lubavitch Hasidim, fewer than in the Satmar community, which makes the influence of Habad all the more remarkable.

Habad undertakes vigorous missionary activity among Jews, whom they seek to convert to their particular Judaic system. They tend to neglected Jews, those living isolated from larger communities. They build Habad Houses in locations ignored by the more conventional Judaic groups. They have been very active in proselytizing among Jews in Russia, Ukraine, White Russia, and Siberia, as well as in locations where Jews gather. In Nepal, for example, they hold a Passover Seder that attracts hundreds, even thousands, of Israeli youth, engaged in a year of wandering after their army service. "Lubavitchers have remained most active in the U.S. on college campuses, Habad Houses have offered Sabbath dinners and services to young Jews living away from home. Several dozen *yeshivas* (religious schools) have been established around the country. So have summer camps, attended by tens of thousands of children each year. In the early 1990s, there were about 1,500 Lubavitcher outposts—schools, camps, synagogues, and other centers—worldwide, with most of them in the U.S."[11] Through the Aleph Society, Habad ministers to Jewish prisoners in penitentiaries, providing them with opportunities to practice Judaism, a constituency neglected by mainstream organized Jewry. Habad competes with integrationist and with self-segregationist Orthodoxy as well. It wins support from many Jews who themselves do not practice the faith either in its manner or at all.

With 2,600 institutions worldwide, the adherence of as much as 50 percent of the English rabbinate, control of most of Judaism in Italy and possession of the chief rabbinate of Russia, spending $20 million a year in Russia alone against one-twenty-second of that amount by Reform Judaism—with immense resources, in short, joined to the claim to Halakhic authenticity, Habad represents the most powerful force in contemporary world Judaism. It is the single most powerful force within the Torah camp of organized Judaism, and far exceeds any integrationist Judaism, whether Reform of Orthodox, in its commitment to proselytism among Jews for their particular Judaic system.

HABAD AND "HALAKHIC CHRISTIANITY"

But there is another side to Habad, which is also by far the most controversial Judaism on the contemporary scene. And that is for a very specific reason. The tradition of opposition to Hasidism outlined by Allan Nadler—the accusation

---

[10]Tricia Andryszewski, *Communities of the Faithful: American Religious Movements Outside the Mainstream* (Brookfield, CT: Millbrook Press, 1997, p. 95.

[11]Ibid., p. 95.

that it is inauthentic to the Torah—was renewed when Habad found for itself a story to tell out of the resources of Christianity, not of Judaism. That story involved the Messiahship of the Habad Rebbe, Menahem Mendel Schneerson, even before his death in 1994, but even more so since then. Then the received narrative of how the Messiah would appear at the end of days and restore Israel to the Land of Israel no longer served: Schneerson had died. But the Christian narrative of the Messiah risen from the dead provided the model of an explanation for Habad to offer. "Messiah now," the Habad slogan of the 1980s and early 1990s, involved the resurrection of the deceased Rebbe (which to date has not taken place).

While regarded—perhaps superficially—as "ultra-Orthodox," Habad thus deviated from the norms of the classical Judaic tradition of the dual Torah in one important way. On this matter, specifically, when Rabbi Schneerson died in 1994, powerful voices and parties in Habad, though not the entire leadership of the group, formed the doctrine that he would rise from the dead and return to save the world. Louis Jacobs states:

> Many of Rabbi Menahem Mendel's followers hailed him as the Messiah, and went about singing in public places: "We want the Messiah now," in the hope that God would reveal to the Rebbe his true identity as the hoped-for redeemer, to the consternation of most of the other Hasidim and traditional Orthodox Rabbis. The latter were now slow to point out the dangers of unbridled Messianic fervor, especially when the Messiah is identified with a particular, known leader. Even after the Rebbe's death many of his followers still retained belief in his Messianic role.[12]

On the messianic claim set forth in behalf of, and possibly by, Rabbi Schneerson, Professor Ithamar Gruenwald comments:

> Nobody in the Habad group seems to care that he appointed no successor to lead the Habad dynasty. Quite the contrary is the truth: The Messiah has no successor. He passed directly to heaven, and there he abides the time until his second coming. Holding to the Land of Israel in its entirety plays an important role in this respect even to people, like Habad, who view themselves as fulfilling Messianic missions on the international scene. In this respect, the similarities between the Habad movement and early Christianity can hardly be overlooked.[13]

Now, years after his death, Habad Hasidim in large numbers continue to work and pray for the resurrection of the deceased Rebbe, and no successor to the position of Rebbe has been chosen. Such a doctrine of a Messiah who dies and rises from the grave tracks Christian, not Judaic, messianic thinking and has no basis whatsoever in the normative Torah, scripture, Mishnah, Midrash, or Talmuds, down to the present day.

---

[12]Jacobs, *Oxford Concise Companion*, pp. 138–139.

[13]Personal communication, July 9, 2002.

Since Habad also adheres most firmly to the rules of the *Halakhah,* the law of Judaism, while adopting a manifestly Christian view of the Messiah risen from the dead, it has been called "Halakhic Christianity." That is because, in the name of the *Halakhah,* which it claims authentically to carry out, Habad proclaims its deceased rabbi to be the royal Messiah and—for many Hasidim, not for all—the embodiment of God, who will rise from the dead to do what he did not do in his initial life on earth. To this claim the "Messianic Jews" and "Jews for Jesus"—in both cases ethnic Jews who have apostatized from Judaism and adopted Christianity—and even an Episcopalian bishop responded, "Right idea, wrong man."

The leading critic of Habad's doctrine of the resurrection of the Rebbe as Messiah, himself a Rabbi of integrationist Orthodoxy, is David Berger, professor of Jewish studies at Brooklyn College. Berger has set forth this specific indictment of the Habad Messianists, who affirm, he asserts, the following propositions:

1. "A specific descendant of King David may be identified with certainty as the Messiah even though he died in an unredeemed world. The criteria always deemed necessary for a confident identification of the Messiah—the temporal redemption of the Jewish people, a rebuilt Temple, peace and prosperity, the universal recognition of the god of Israel—are null and void.

2. "The messianic faith of Judaism allows for the following scenario: God will finally send the true Messiah to embark upon his redemptive mission. The long-awaited redeemer will declare that all preparations for the redemption have been completed and announce without qualification that the fulfillment is absolutely imminent. He will begin the process of gathering the dispersed of Israel to the Holy Land. He will proclaim himself a prophet, point clearly to his messianic status, and declare that the only remaining task is to greet him as Messiah. And then he will die and be buried without having redeemed the world. To put the matter more succinctly, the true Messiah's redemptive mission, publicly proclaimed and vigorously pursued, will be interrupted by death and burial and then consummated through a Second Coming."[14]

Rabbi Berger's critique has produced heated debate both within Orthodoxy and in the larger community of Judaism. But it has not affected the growth of Habad. Berger points out that Hasidim who proclaim this belief hold significant religious positions sanctioned by major Orthodox authorities with no relationship to their movement. Berger has therefore advocated denying the *kashrut*—the suitability for Israelite consumption of food in accord with the laws of the torah—of Habad restaurants. He further calls into question the status of legitimacy of its public worship, its synagogues, and the status of authen-

---

[14]David Berger, *The Rebbe, the Messiah, and the Scandal of Orthodox Indifference* (London and Portland OR.: The Littman Library of Jewish Civilization, 2001), pp. 42.

ticity of its books, unless careful investigation has determined that the specific Habad rabbi in question rejects non-Orthodox beliefs, especially in light of the widespread conviction that Rebbe Schneerson is a manifestation of pure divinity. Even a Torah scroll written by a Habad Messianist is not to be used for Judaic declamation; even for a *minyan* (a quorum for worship) a Habad Messianist is not to be counted, any more than a "Messianic Jew" and his Torah-scroll would serve. Rabbi Berger does not stand alone in calling into question the bona fides of Habad's system.

IN CONTEXT: EXEMPLARS OF TRADITION OR ONLY A NOTEWORTHY MINORITY?

The Judaic systems that identify as critical the issues of Emancipation form a group over against those that press the urgent question of the normative system. No picture of contemporary North American Judaism can exclude one or the other set of systems. But every system is self-validating and lays claim on the Torah as mark of its authenticity. How shall we situate North American Judaisms in the context of the history of Judaism?

One perspective is this: Which Judaic system attracts Jews to Judaism? When it comes to exercising the power to win Jews to Judaism and to bring about a reversion to the Torah and a renewal of tradition, with their heavy demands for meticulous, life-changing observance of the law of the Torah, though exotic and alien to the American scene, Habad and Agudath Israel compete with the integrationist Judaisms on equal terms and with favorable results. That is because, when secular Jews go in search of the authentic tradition, the Torah set forth as normative without apologetics, they more often than not find their way to self-segregationist Orthodox Judaisms, which, on that account, flourish in North America.

The argument from sociology, as against that from theology, favors the self-segregated Orthodox systems over the integrationist ones, and the integrationist Orthodox system over the Reform, Conservative, and other reformist ones. Certainly among Orthodox Judaisms, levels of observance are markedly higher than among the Reform and Conservative ones. Thus, the sociologist of contemporary Conservative Judaism Jack Wertheimer states,

> Synagogue attendance twelve or more times annually is claimed by 55% of self-identified Orthodox Jews, 21% of Conservatives, and 12% of self-proclaimed Reform Jews. By contrast, 45% of the Orthodox claimed to attend synagogue once or more a week, compared with only 8% of Jews who identified themselves as Conservative and 2.5% who identified as Reform. . . . Synagogue attendance twelve or more times annually is claimed by 55% of self-identified Orthodox Jews, 21% of Conservatives, and 12% of self-proclaimed Reform Jews. By contrast, 45% of the Orthodox claimed to attend synagogue once or more a week, compared

with only 8% of Jews who identified themselves as Conservative and 2.5% who identified as Reform.[15]

So much for both integrationist and segregationist Orthodox Judaisms. In light of such findings of mass indifference to the way of life of the non-Orthodox integrationist systems, it therefore is easy to see Orthodox communities—integrationist or self-segregationist—as exemplary, and to call upon them for evidence of the "tradition" today.

And the argument from sociology moreover favors the more exotic over the more commonplace. The levels of observance in the Hasidic community exceed (if only marginally) the norms of Orthodoxy in general. And wearing Jewish clothes and speaking a Jewish language (Yiddish)—what could be more traditional than that! But here is where the argument from theology enters in. For among Judaic systems are some, such as Agudath Israel, that affirm the classical tradition in a form far more congruent with the received normative Judaic system set forth in the Torah, Written and Oral. It has been said that if the Written Torah and its oral continuation in Mishnah, Talmuds, and Midrash were lost, they could be reconstructed in their main lines of *Halakhah* and *Aggadah,* and their narrative could be recovered, by closely observing the way of life and public discourse of Agudath Israel. That may represent an exaggeration, but the reality is not far behind.

What makes the study of Judaism difficult is that all the Judaic systems—integrationist Orthodoxy, Agudath Israel, Habad Hasidism, Reform and Conservative Judaisms—justify themselves by appeal to the same Torah. But enjoying the status of self-evidence in vast populations of Jewry and affecting the framing of otherwise diverse Judaisms, there is a Judaic system that does not appeal to the Torah in any form. Yet it forms the most effective competition, within North American Judaisms, to the worldview and way of life and definition of "Israel" of the Torah-centered Judaisms. This Judaism's worldview shapes the popular imagination, and its way of life establishes the norm: what is required, what is expendable. Its definition of Israel prevails. And in the forming of the three components of its system, the narrative of the Torah and its consequent theology and its law, none of the established heritage enters in.

The competition in North America facing all the Judaisms of the past two centuries, and many centuries before, comes from a different version of the Judaic story, a variation on the theme of exile and return particularly suited to the twentieth century. To that system, the American Judaism of Holocaust and Redemption, we now turn.

---

[15]Jack Wertheimer, *A People Divided: Judaism in Contemporary America* (New York: Basic Books, 1993). [Orig. source: Nine City Sample, North American Jewish Data Bank], pp. 53.

29

The American Judaism
of Holocaust and Redemption

WHAT IS "THE AMERICAN JUDAISM
OF HOLOCAUST AND REDEMPTION"?

The American Judaism of Holocaust and Redemption is a Judaic religious system that, in the North American context,[1] tells as a connected narrative of salvation the story of the destruction of European Jewry from 1933–1945 and of the creation of the state of Israel in 1948. It is a religious system because it invokes the specified theological categories, not mass murder but "Holocaust," not political event but "Redemption." It furthermore sees in those events a divine purpose and a plan. This Judaism came to expression after the Six Day War of June 1967. In its North American context, it answers the question Jews ask: Why should I be Jewish? And what should I do because I am Jewish? The answers are framed in this-worldly secular terms and activities.

This Judaism's worldview stresses the unique character of (1) the murder of millions of European Jews, matched by (2) the providential meaning of the creation of the state of Israel. Its way of life requires two things. First are acts of memorialization of the Holocaust. Second comes active work in raising money and political support for the state of Israel. Different from Zionism, which held that Jews should not only favor and support but should actually *live* in the Jewish state, this system gives Jews residing in North America a reason and an explanation for being different. It tells why they should opt for continuing to form a distinct ethnic group in the open society of American and Canadian democracy.

Why did a secular event, the Six Day War, precipitate the shaping of what is now the most influential system of all contemporary Judaisms? Professor Ithamar Gruenwald perspicaciously explains:

> Two events stand out in modern Judaic history—the Holocaust and the Establishment of the State of Israel. In the eyes of many, the two events are connected. The State of Israel is the Judaic answer to the traumatic events of the Holocaust. In the context of Judaism, the State of Israel was the event in which God showed that he still cared for His People.

---

[1]The Judaism of Holocaust and Redemption in its North American formulation is what concerns us here, not its counterpart within Israeli nationalism. The Holocaust and the founding of the state of Israel shape a comparable but separate narrative in the context of Israeli culture. European Jewry has its own history and culture and is not under discussion here; its Judaic systems respond to a quite different cultural politics from the North American one.

However, since the State of Israel was a secular entity, a more religiously configured event had to come about to show that underlying modern Jewish secular history had a religious dynamic. The occasion for this event came in 1967, when people translated the victory of the Israel Defense Army over the Arab countries into the notions of a war of liberation. The victory of 1948 was a War of Independence, clearly a secular notion.

Liberation and redemption are notions crafted in religious thought and tradition. They enabled a new theology to develop, in which old Messianic hopes became a major driving force. These thoughts awakened in the Judaic world various chain reactions, some of which were channeled into the realms of Messianic realization.[2]

So Gruenwald explains the connection, deemed self-evident, that forms the premise of the question: How in light of the creation of the state of Israel are we—"the Jews"—to make secular sense of the Holocaust? It is an ethnic question; the religious Judaic systems ask and answer in other terms altogether.

Focused on the same themes, Zionism and the American Judaism of Holocaust and Redemption deserve comparison. The two systems exhibit in common a lack of interest in invoking the presence and activity of God. Both concur that the Jews form an ethnic group, not a religious community (in the category formation of Reform Judaism in its formative stage) and also not a unique, holy people, a kingdom of priests and a holy people (in the category formation of the Torah).

But they also contrast. For Zionism appealed to scripture, to the Land and to actually restoring Israel to the Land. It responded to the enduring paradigm of exile and return. It retold "Jewish History" as its sacred narrative, with stress on scripture. Above all, Zionism speaks of experiences people actually undergo or should undergo, evokes natural emotions. For its part, the American Judaism of Holocaust and Redemption makes remarkably slight use of the received Judaic heritage of theology and law, scripture and story. Its repertoire of narrative derives from the horrors of the German war against the Jews, its holy places are museums and memorials. It speaks of experiences no one would want to have, conveyed in the word *Holocaust,* and actions no one is required to take—specifically, participating in the actual realization of the Jewish state, the state of Israel. Its devotees weep at memorials of events they only imagine, and they give money so other Jews will bring the Jewish state into being. Not surprisingly, therefore, its imperatives have little density or depth. A famous one is, "The 614th commandment [beyond the six hundred thirteen we met earlier]: Stay Jewish so as not to hand Hitler any more victories." This opaque advice is fabricated as "the commanding voice of Auschwitz." And that is no exaggeration. For pilgrimages, the American Judaism of Holocaust and Redemption takes the faithful, particularly young people, to Auschwitz, followed by a trip to the Western Wall of the destroyed Temple of Jerusalem.

---

[2]Personal communication, July 9, 2002.

To proponents of Holocaust and Redemption Judaism God presents a massive problem. It is framed as the "problem of evil": How can the unique, just, all-powerful God have permitted such wickedness? That problem is worked out within Judaic systems through the nineteenth century, all of which framed theologies that could explain why bad things happen to good people. It remains insoluble for any Judaism not continuous with the classical Rabbinic system.[3]

For these reasons the American Judaism of Holocaust and Redemption defines a theory of the Jewish social order that scarcely relates to, or can be classified as, a religion at all; it is essentially a system of ethnic Jewishness, and shows us, as does Zionism, that not all Judaic religious systems need to take shape within the framework of religion at all, though to the middle of the twentieth century most have.

Here is the point at which the development of the ethnic and secular Jew impinges upon the history of Judaisms.[4] For once Jews continued as an identifiable social group that was not defined by religion, then some Jews would identify themselves as a part of a social entity that was Jewish but not religious. They could then formulate a worldview and a way of life to match their sense of ethnic identification—that is, to realize their particular version of "being Israel." This they could do even while opting for a religion other than Judaism—Buddhism, for example.

TO WHOM DOES THE AMERICAN JUDAISM OF HOLOCAUST AND REDEMPTION PRESENT SELF-EVIDENT TRUTHS?

The Judaism of Holocaust and Redemption forms an important creation of the third and fourth generation of Jewish Americans. It gives meaning to the experiences of that generation, first, of bitter anti-Semitism from the 1920s to the 1950s, then of greater toleration of ethnic (and racial) difference from the late

---

[3]See Zachary Braiterman, (*God*) *After Auschwitz: Tradition and Change in Post-Holocaust Jewish Thought* (Princeton: Princeton University Press, 1998). Compare Braiterman's data with Gershon Greenberg, "Wartime Orthodox Jewish Thought About the Holocaust: Christian Implications," www.jcrelations.net, also published in *Journal of Ecumenical Studies* 35 (Summer-Fall 1998): 3–4. There is scarcely a point of intersection between Greenberg's wartime Orthodox theology of the calamity and Braiterman's post-1967, mostly ethnic-cultural philosophizing on the part of the "After-Auschwitz" theologians.

[4]Another such point is the advent, for the first time in the history of the Jews, of apostates from Judaism who wish to belong to the Jewish community. Until the end of the twentieth century, when Jews converted to another religion, for instance, to Christianity, they cut their ties to Jewry and excluded themselves; they went to Church, raised their children as Christians, and desired no further affiliation with the Jewish group. In the final decades of this millennium, by contrast, "Jews for Jesus" practicing "Messianic Judaism" converted to Christianity but wished to remain active members of the (secular) Jewish community; converts to Christianity migrated to the state of Israel and claimed citizenship under the Law of Return that accords automatic citizenship to all (ethnic) Jews, without religious test. Converts to Christianity in San Antonio remained on the board of Hadassah, the Women's Zionist Organization, and in Utica remained officeholders of the synagogue itself. These are some of the complications for the life of Jewry brought about by the secularization and ethnicization of the category of Rabbinic Judaism, Holy Israel.

1950s onward. Those who find the system self-evidently so are the grandchildren and great-grandchildren of the wave of immigrants from central and Eastern Europe who came to the United States in the great migration of 1880–1920. They form the third or fourth generation beyond the transfer of populations. The immigrants found "being Jewish" a self-evident fact of life; they exhibited the traits of a highly distinctive and coherent ethnic group.

The First Generation   The numerous immigrants of the later nineteenth and early twentieth centuries (from 1880 to 1920, more than 3.5 million Jews came to the United States from Russia, Poland, Rumania, Hungary, and Austria) spoke Yiddish all their lives. They pursued a limited range of occupations and lived mainly in crowded Jewish neighborhoods of a few great cities. So the facts of language, occupation, and residence, not just religion, reinforced their separateness. Their several Judaic systems then explained it. In this period, moreover, other immigrant groups of the same era—Italian, German, Greek, Bohemian, Polish, Irish, for example—together with their churches likewise found themselves constituting tight enclaves of the old country in the new.

The Second Generation   The children of the immigrants, that is, the second generation in America, by contrast, adopted the American language and American ways of life. Its medium of Americanization involved Conservative Judaism, which thrived in the areas to which the second generation moved, as well as Reform Judaism, which vastly changed in character and definition because of this second generation. The two reformist Judaisms accommodated to the assimilationist aspirations of the second generation, and Zionism exercised a great attraction for a portion of that generation as well. Further, the second generation grew up and lived in a period of severe anti-Semitism at home and in Europe, especially in the 1930s and 1940s. While trying to forget the immigrant heritage, the second generation found the world a school for Jewish consciousness, with lessons of a distinctively negative sort. They did not have to go to class to learn what it meant to be a Jew.

The context defined matters. America was a country of racial and ethnic minorities at that time, many of which found themselves excluded, vilified, and placed in a pariah caste (among many pariah castes of the time). Coming to maturity in the Depression and in World War II, the second generation did not have to decide whether or not to "be Jewish," nor were many decisions about what "being Jewish" demanded of them. Gentiles wanted no part of them, so out-marriage was not an issue.

The Third Generation   That set of decisions, amounting to the framing of a situation of genuine free choice, awaited the third generation, reaching its maturity some time after World War II. In the later 1950s the civil rights movement led by African Americans, with ample support from Jews and liberals, undertook to create a hate-free environment for racial and ethnic minorities. Surveys of anti-Semitic opinion turned up progressively diminishing levels of

Jew hatred. The third generation therefore saw cracks in the walls of exclusion that surrounded the community.

More important, while the second generation had strong memories of Yiddish-speaking parents and lives of a distinctively Jewish character, it chose not to speak Yiddish with its children and not to practice Judaism in such a way that Judaism impeded social integration. But in line with Marcus Lee Hanson's law, which says that the third generation wants to remember what the second generation has tried to forget, a renewal of interest in Judaism and Jewish ethnicity characterized the third generation. Now, the third generation had to make a decision to learn what it did not know, indeed, what it had no natural reason, in its upbringing and family heritage, to know. And that was the foundations of "being Jewish." These were defined in religious terms, for America would tolerate difference in the aspect of religion, which it treated as trivial ("It doesn't matter what you believe, as long as you're a good man" captured the age.

Jewish but Not Too Jewish   The upshot may be simply stated. The American Jews[5] of the third generation were eager to be Jewish—but not too Jewish. They did not want to be so Jewish that they could not also take their place within the undifferentiated humanity of which they fantasized. They had been taught lessons of ethnicity, and religiosity did not fit. The underlying problem was understanding what the ambiguous adjective *Jewish* is supposed to mean when the noun *Judaism* in its received meanings has been abandoned. Here the system of Holocaust and Redemption found its place. In the ethnic framework that system answered the question: Who are you? What should you do? What do you make of the other? The urgent question reflected, then, on the actualities of anti-Semitism on one side and on ethnic engagement on the other. What of the way of life of sanctification en route to the worldview of salvation afforded by the received system? Chapter 30 will show us how the second generation afforded its children and grandchildren only a superficial encounter with Judaism, the religion, in any of its received systems.

THE WORLDVIEW OF "HOLOCAUST AND REDEMPTION" JUDAISM

So the narrative of Holocaust and Redemption Judaism scarcely intersects with the narrative of the Torah. Its chapters do not coincide with creation, revelation, redemption, and its story does not concern exile and return. It is a personal story of ethnic identification, not a public account of the formation and

---

[5]The Canadian Jewish pattern was quite different. See Gerald Tulchinsky, *Taking Root: The Origins of the Canadian Jewish Community* (Toronto: Lester Publishing), and Gerald Tulchinsky, *Branching Out: The Transformation of the Canadian Jewish Community* (Toronto: Lester Publishing).

purpose of a group. Then here is how the story might go, as I would attempt to tell the tale in behalf of the second and part of the third generations:

> Once upon a time, in the 1930s and 1940s, when I was a young man, I felt helpless before the world. I was a Jew, when being Jewish was a bad thing. As a child, I saw my old Jewish grandparents, speaking a foreign language and alien in countless ways, isolated from America. And I saw America, dimly perceived to be sure, exciting and promising, but hostile to me as a Jew. I could not get into a good college. I could not aspire to medical school. I could not become an architect or an engineer. I could not even work for an electric utility.
>
> When I took my vacation, I could not go just anywhere, but had to ask whether Jews would be welcome, tolerated, embarrassed, or thrown out. Being Jewish was uncomfortable. Yet I could not give it up. My mother and my father had made me what I was. I could hide, but could not wholly deny, not to myself even if to others, that I was a Jew. And I could not afford the price in diminished self-esteem of opportunity denied, aspiration deferred, and insult endured. Above all, I saw myself as weak and pitiful. I could not do anything about being a Jew, nor could I do much to improve my lot as a Jew.
>
> Then came Hitler and I saw that what was my private lot was the dismal fate of every Jew. Everywhere Jew hatred was raised from the gutter to the heights. Not from Germany alone, but from people I might meet at work or in the streets I feared that being Jewish was a metaphys- ical evil. The "Jews" were not accepted, but debated. Friends would claim we were not all bad. Enemies said we were. And we had nothing to say at all.
>
> As I approached maturity, a still more frightening fact confronted me. People guilty of no crime but Jewish birth were forced to flee their homeland, and no one would accept them. Ships filled with ordinary men, women, and children searched the oceans for a safe harbor. And I and they had nothing in common but one fact, and that fact made all else inconsequential. Had I been there, I should have been among them. I, too, should not have been saved at the sea.
>
> Then came the war and, in its aftermath, the revelation of the shame and horror of holocaust, the decay and corrosive hopelessness of the displaced person camps where survivors of the war were warehoused, the contempt of the nations who would neither accept nor help the saved remnants of hell.
>
> At the darkest hour came the dawn. The state of Israel saved the remnant and gave meaning and significance to the inferno. After the dawn, the great light: Jews no longer helpless, weak, unable to decide their own fate, but strong, confident, decisive.
>
> And then came the corrupting doubt: if I were there, I should have died in hell, but now has come redemption and I am here, not there.

How much security in knowing that if it should happen again I shall not be lost. But how great a debt paid in guilt for being where I am and who I am!

This is the narrative expression of the worldview that shapes the mind and imagination of most American Jewry. It supplies the correct interpretation and denotes the true significance of everyday events. So the generations that lived through disaster and triumph, darkness and light, understand the world in terms of a salvific story of an entirely this-worldly character. How do we know the power of the narrative? Nearly all American Jews identify with the state of Israel and regard its welfare as more than a secular good, but a metaphysical necessity: the other chapter of the Holocaust, as Professor Gruenwald lays matters out. Nearly all American Jews not only support the state of Israel, they also regard their own "being Jewish" as inextricably bound up with the meaning they impute to the Jewish state.

THE SELF-EVIDENCE OF HOLOCAUST AND REDEMPTION JUDAISM AS A JUDAISM: FROM MASS MURDER TO "HOLOCAUST," FROM MILITARY VICTORY TO "REDEMPTION"

Three factors, among the Jews, reinforced one another in turning the Judaism of Holocaust and Redemption into a set of self-evident and descriptive facts. These events placed the truths beyond all argument: (1) the Six Day War of 1967, to which we have already made reference; (2) the transformation of the mass murder of European Jews into the symbol of cosmic evil, and (3) the reethnicization of American life. We address the first two as a pair now, and the third on its own in the next unit.

Specifically, Jews underwent a transforming experience, covered by factors 1 and 2, and that experience formed a Jewish counterpart to what was happening in American society in general. Just as the return to religion of the 1950s found a Jewish counterpart in the construction of suburban synagogues—a Jewish way of being American—so the renaissance of ethnicity among Jews formed the Jewish way of responding to the renewed freedom accorded to ethnic, religious, racial, and other "minorities" to be different.

First comes the engagement of American Jews with the state of Israel at a very particular moment, matched by its discovery that the murder of millions of European Jews constituted the "Holocaust." Why, in other words, date the birth of the Judaism of Holocaust and Redemption so precisely to the 1967 war?

The question is counterintuitive. Was the state of Israel not always the focus of American Jewish affairs? People take as routine the importance of the state of Israel in American Jewish consciousness. But in the 1940s and 1950s, American Jewry had yet to translate its deep sympathy for the Jewish state into intense political activity on one side and the shaping element for local cultural activity and sentiment on the other. So, too, the memory of the destruction of European Jewry did not immediately become the "Holocaust," as a formative event in contemporary Jewish consciousness.

In fact the reethnicization of the Jews in the model of Holocaust and Redemption probably could not have taken the form that it did—a powerful identification with the state of Israel as the answer to the question of the "Holocaust"—without a single, catalytic event. That was, specifically, experiencing the fear of another Holocaust. The trauma of the weeks preceding the 1967 war, when the Arabs promised to drive the Jews into the sea and no other power intervened or promised help, renewed for the third generation the nightmare of the second. Once more the streets and newspapers became the school for being Jewish. On that account the Judaism in formation took up a program of urgent questions—and answered them.

In the trying weeks before June 5, 1967, American Jewry relived the experience of the second generation and the third in the 1930s and 1940s, the age of Hitler's Germany and the murder of the European Jews in death factories. Every day's newspaper brought and taught the lessons of Jewish history. Everybody knew that were he or she in Europe, death would be the sentence because of the crime of Jewish birth. And as before, the world was then indifferent. No avenues of escape were opened to the Jews who wanted to flee, and many roads to life were deliberately blocked by anti-Semitic foreign service officials. What, then, was the contemporary parallel? In 1967, the Arab states threatened to destroy the state of Israel and murder its citizens. The Israelis turned to the world, without response. The world again ignored Jewish suffering, and a new "Holocaust" impended.

But now the outcome was quite different. The entire history of the century at hand came under a new light. A moment of powerful and salvific weight placed into a fresh perspective everything that had happened from the beginning to the present. The third generation now had found its memory and its hope. It now could confront the murder of the Jews of Europe, in the very context of its parents' and its own experience of exclusion and bigotry. No longer was it necessary to avoid painful, intolerable memories. Now what had happened had to be remembered, because it bore within itself the entire message of the new day in Judaism.

That is, putting together the murder of nearly 6 million Jews of Europe with the creation of the State of Israel transformed both events. One became the "Holocaust," the unique, the purest statement of evil in all of human history. The other became salvation or redemption in the form of "the first appearance of our redemption" (as the language of the Jewish prayer for the state of Israel has it). Accordingly, a moment of stark epiphany captured the entire experience of the age and imparted to it that meaning and order that a religious system has the power to render self-evidently true. The self-evident system of American Judaism, then, for the third generation encompassed a salvific story deeply and personally relevant to the devotees. That story made sense at a single instant equally of both the world and the self, of what the newspapers had to say and of what the individual understood in personal life.

THE ETHNICIZATION OF JUDAISM

But why did an ethnic narrative take over, in the American context in particular, to make sense of the Jews' experience of fear and renewed confidence? Whence the ethnic model of difference? It was a development in contemporary American politics and society. From the late 1950s onward, American society began to come to grips with distinctions that made a difference and could not be trivialized, as religious differences could be treated as marginal. That was the contribution of the black community to American society. Numerous ethnic and other minorities benefited.

The African-American civil rights movement of the late 1950s and 1960s, culminating in the Civil Rights acts, legitimated ethnic and racial difference, not only difference by reason of religion. Then the question became, "Who are we in relationship to everybody else?" The black community affirmed that "black is beautiful," and thereby supplied everyone else with models and heroes of self-respect and dignity. Other distinctive groups, different by reason of ethnic heritage, followed suit. All stopped apologizing for being different from the norm. More precisely: A new norm took shape.

The utility of the "Holocaust" in this context is not difficult to see, once we realize that the TV counterpart to "Holocaust" was the series *Roots,* the highly successful dramatization of many generations of black suffering under slavery and post-Emancipation racism. Unstated in this simple equation "Roots" = "Holocaust" is the idea that being Jewish is an ethnic, not primarily a religious, category. In that context, the "Holocaust" became the Jews' special thing. It was what set them apart from others while giving them a claim upon those others. That is why Jews would insist on the uniqueness of the Holocaust. If blacks on campus have soul food, the Jews will have kosher meals—even if they do not keep the dietary laws under ordinary circumstances. To state the matter in more general terms: For nearly a century American Jews had persuaded themselves and their neighbors they fell into the religious—and therefore acceptable—category of being "different," and not into the ethnic—and therefore crippling and unwanted—category of "different." Now that they had no Jewish accent, they were willing to be ethnic.

The question then arises: What did the received systems of Reform, integrationist Orthodox, and Conservative Judaisms lack that only the American Judaism of Holocaust and Redemption supplied? That formulation misses the mark. More to the point: What did the religious Judaisms require that the American Judaism of Holocaust and Redemption did not demand? That Judaism supplied an immediate access to emotional engagement, direct involvement at the depths of personality. Clearly, third- and fourth-generation American Jews found the continuator Judaisms of the synagogue lacking in emotional appeal. But there is a reason: The classical Judaic system and its several continuator systems of the nineteenth century—including Zionism, as a matter of fact—demanded literacy in the Torah. Each, more important, required participation in its way of life. The classical and continuator systems all shaped lives through the Sabbath or through the Passover Seder. They supplied memories and shaped expectations through realized patterns of life. They shaped emotions and framed intellect—but only through participation.

The ethnic experience of the third and fourth generations, with their superficial engagement with the synagogue and none with the Torah, did not provide access to so subtle and exotic a worldview as that of the Judaism of the dual Torah. To make of those continuator Judaisms the model for a viable life—an explanation of the world, an account of how to live—Jews found they had to give what they did not have: personal response to the compelling experience that would be acquired in direct participation in the way of Torah. What was demanded, then, was education that few possessed, access to the memories and the habits of the faith denied by the second generation to their children. The third generation affirmed religion without direct knowledge of piety, sentiment without memory, nostalgia without knowledge. True, from a barren upbringing, some would make the effort to locate a road back. In Chapter 31, we shall meet those who in the 1980s and 1990s became reversioners to the faith. But they did not dominate their cohorts.

In this context we explain the success of the American Judaism of Holocaust and Redemption. It answered the question of how to engage the emotions without experience, with sentiment lacking the mediation of learning in the Torah. What Judaic system could claim self-evidence without the experience of encounter with God in the commandments and the Torah? And along these same lines, that Judaism knew how to define a way of life that imparted the condition of group distinction without making much material difference. The Judaism of Holocaust and Redemption afforded immediate access to wells of emotion: Who can keep back tears at the narrative of Auschwitz? But it provided tears first, and then cheers, upon demand. And for the rest, for the way of life and worldview, it made no demands upon its Israel.

To state matters in a homely way, what distinctively Judaic way of life would allow devotees to eat whatever they wanted and to marry whomever they wished without separation from the ethnic group? The fourth and fifth American generations, raised in the Judaism of Holocaust and Redemption, produced rates of out-marriage—Jews and non-Jews—in proportions unknown from the time of mass immigration. Upwards of half of all Jews who got married in those generations chose gentile spouses.

So here is the question that lay at the foundations of the American Judaism of Holocaust and Redemption: How, *without leaving the faithful terribly different from everybody else,* to gain access to the life of feeling and experience, to the way of life that made one distinctive? Now we see the answer that emerged in the American Judaism of Holocaust and Redemption. This system presented an immediately accessible emotional experience and an uncomplicated message. The former was cast in extreme emotions of terror and triumph, the latter in a corresponding ethnic triumphalism.

But then we come full circle: Neither the emotions nor the message directly derived from the life experience of the devotees. They were not in Auschwitz, and now they do not live in Jerusalem. So the American Judaism of Holocaust and Redemption builds on foundations removed from experience and authentic emotion. And as for its imperatives, the round of endless activity demanded only spare time, no change of life. In all, the American Judaism of Holocaust and Redemption realized in a poignant way the conflicting demands of Jewish Americans to be intensely Jewish, but only once in a while and then not for long, and surely not at much of a cost in meaningful difference from others. It was a love affair for a motel: intense but brief.

30

How Jews Practice Judaism
in North America

WHAT THE BOOKS SAY,
WHAT THE PEOPLE DO

The holy books say one thing about a religion, the people who believe in and practice that religion do quite another. Trying to understand the difference between official religion, defined by the religious virtuosi, and the believed and practiced religion of the faithful defines a central problem in making sense of religion as we see it in today's world. Apart from small circles of the truly and consistently pious, practitioners do make choices in religions about what counts and what does not or, more to the point, what can be compromised or neglected, and what is going to matter.

In describing the Judaic religious systems of past and present, we have focused on ideal types portrayed in legal, theological, and narrative writing. We have described in their pure theoretical form the communities of Judaism comprised by the respective Judaic systems: their respective theories of Israel, ways of life, and worldviews. That approach affords ready access to sets of ideas and how they hold together. But describing ideal types yielded by the holy books conveys the misleading impression that the systems exist not only in theory but in social reality. They do not.

The systems rarely exist in pure form. Closest to its ideal type is the workaday practice of self-segregated Orthodoxy. Thousands in the self-segregated Orthodox communities attend daily classes in Talmud study and ethical lectures. One Talmud lecture in Brooklyn draws nearly 1,500 people each Saturday night, and the once-in-seven-years celebration of a complete cycle of daily study of the Talmud of Babylonia brought 70,000 celebrants together when it last happened. These facts may be multiplied many times over to describe the everyday life of a vigorous religious community, one where the facts of workaday observance match the theories of the legal and theological writings.

But the picture of other Judaisms for the most part is quite different. What the books say, the people sometimes do, sometimes not, and the books raise expectations that are rarely met. For one thing, Conservative, Reform, integrationist-Orthodox Judaisms commonly tell both their own stories and also the story of the American Judaism of Holocaust and Redemption. Delegations of secular, Reform, Orthodox, Reconstructionist, Zionist, and other Jews join together in pilgrimages to Auschwitz and to the Western Wall. The complexities of Reform belief and behavior comprise a long catalogue of do's and don'ts. Not only so, but the distinct communities of Judaism sometimes meet in marriage. In Chapter 28, we considered as completely separate and at odds the Hasidic system and its opposition, represented by Agudath Israel. But families within self-segregationist Orthodox Judaisms encompass both Hasidim and members of Agudath Israel. Intermarriage between Reform and Conservative Jews is routine and not noteworthy. Synagogues affiliated with the national institutions of both Reform and Conservative Judaisms are not uncommon. A signal of Orthodoxy is the separation, at worship, of women and men; but some integrationist-Orthodox synagogues make provision for both separate seating and what they call "family seating," by which husbands and wives sit together.

People other than the religious virtuosi of those Judaisms—rabbis, for example—tend to pick and choose what they will do from among what the several systems, respectively, set up as norms. That is a striking trait of Conservative Judaism, for example, which advocates dietary laws few observe and sanctification of the Sabbath that only a tiny minority of congregants remembers. Reform Judaism advocates regular Sabbath observance, including synagogue worship. Its rabbis face rows and rows of empty seats at Sabbath morning services. Even Orthodox Judaisms contend with backsliding and compromise. So in order to describe the practice of Judaism in the United States, it is time to move from the ideal types of the several Judaic systems to the realities of conduct. In the U.S. community of Judaism viewed whole and in the aggregate, to what extent do the people do what the books say?

The question facing us is: How do we explain the difference, how do people know the difference, between what is required and what—acceptably, amiably, with all the good will in the world—is actually done? And what do we learn about Judaism from the choices people make?

WHAT THE JEWISH PEOPLE
IN NORTH AMERICA DO:
A SOCIAL SCIENCE PORTRAIT
OF THE ACTUAL PRACTICE OF JUDAISM

Current social studies of Judaism in America yield a consensus that all surveys have produced.[1] Among the many religious occasions and obligations set forth by the Torah, American Jews in the aggregate do practice some and do not

---

[1] I mainly rely upon Steven M. Cohen, *Content or Continuity? Alternative Bases for Commitment* (New York: American Jewish Committee, 1991), Jack Wertheimer, "Recent Trends in American Judaism," *American Jewish Yearbook, 1989* (New York and Philadelphia: American Jewish Committee and Jewish Publication Society, 1989); and Barry A. Kosmin, Sidney Goldstein, Joseph Waksberg, Nava Lerer, Ariella Keysar, and Jeffrey Scheckner, *Highlights of the CJF [Council of Jewish Federations] 1990 National Jewish Population Survey* (New York, 1991: Council of Jewish Federations, 1991). More recent studies have produced comparable results, so the basic picture is constant.

practice others. Take demography, for starters. The United States counts as a "Jewishly identified population" some 6,840,000. Of these, 4.2 million identify themselves as born Jews who practice the religion Judaism. They embody all the Judaisms that flourish in North America. Another 1.1 million call themselves born Jews with no religion. Adults of Jewish parentage who practice some other religion than Judaism number 415,000. Born of Jewish parents, raised as Jewish, and converted to some other religion are 210,000. Jews by choice (converts to Judaism) are 185,000. Children under age eighteen being raised in a religion other than Judaism are 700,000.[2] It follows that the "core Jewish population" is 5.5 million, of which approximately 80 percent—4.4 million—are Jews by religion.

"ISRAEL": WHAT DO THE JEWS THINK THEY ARE—RELIGION, CULTURE, ETHNIC GROUP, OTHER?

Beginning with the component "Israel," let us examine popular opinion on whether the Jews are a religious group, an ethnic group, a cultural group, or a nationality. Kosmin's report states: "Being Jewish as defined by cultural group membership is the clear preference of three of the four identity groups [Jews by birth, religion, Judaism; Jews by choice, converts; Jews by birth with no religion; born and raised Jewish, converted out; adults of Jewish parentage with another current religion]. Definition in terms of ethnic group was the second highest and was cited more frequently than the religious concept by every Jewish identity group."[3] Jews who thought of themselves as a religious group were 49 percent of those who said they were born Jews, religion Judaism; 35 percent of born Jews with no religion; 56 percent of born and raised Jews who converted out; and 40 percent of adults of Jewish parents with another current religion.

The further figure that affects our study—besides the 4.4 million, which defines its parameters—concerns intermarriage patterns. At this time, 68 percent of all currently married Jews by birth (1.7 million) are married to someone who was also born Jewish. But, in the language of Kosmin's report:

> The choice of marriage partners has changed dramatically over the past few decades. In recent years just over half of born Jews who married, at any age, whether for the first time or not, chose a spouse who was born a Gentile and has remained so, while less than 5 percent of these marriages include a non-Jewish partner who became a Jew by choice. As a result, since 1985, twice as many mixed couples, that is, born Jew with gentile

---

[2]Kosmin et al., *Highlights*, p. 4.

[3]Ibid., p. 28.

spouse, have been created as Jewish couples (Jewish with Jewish spouse). This picture . . . tends to underestimate the total frequency, because it does not include currently born-Jews divorced or separated from an inter-marriage nor Jew–Gentile unmarried couple relationships and living arrangements.[4]

Wertheimer too comments on the matter of intermarriage, in these terms: "Intermarriage has exploded on the American Jewish scene since the mid-1960s, rapidly rising in incident to the point where as many as two out of five Jews who wed marry a partner who was not born Jewish." In Reform Judaism he reports, 31 percent of the lay leaders of Reform temples reported having a child married to a non-Jewish spouse.[5] So the first thing that captures our attention is that the single most important building block of Judaism, the family, expression in the here and now of the sacred genealogy of Israel, that is, "the children of Israel," wobbles. None of the Judaic systems we have described provides for such mixtures. When Reform Judaism accommodated being more than "Israel"—being Jewish and something else—it had in mind secular citizenship, not practice of both Judaism and some other religion in the same family, even by the same person.

WORLDVIEW

Restricting our attention to the Judaists and the ethnic Jews (Kosmin's categories: born Jews, religion Judaism and born Jews with no religion), what do we learn about religious beliefs?

1. The Torah is the actual word of God: 13 percent concur (but 10 percent of born Jews with no religion do too, not a very impressive differential).

2. The Torah is the inspired word of God, but not everything should be taken literally word for word: 38 percent of Judaists, and 19 percent of the ethnicists concur.

3. The Torah is an ancient book of history and moral precepts recorded by man: 45 percent of the Judaists and 63 percent of the ethnicist Jews concur.

And 4 percent of the Judaists and 8 percent of the ethnicists had no opinion.

It follows that, by the criterion of belief in the basic proposition of the Judaism of the dual Torah, that the Torah is the word of God: To this statement, 13 percent of the Judaists concur; another 38 percent agree that the Torah is the inspired word of God but not literally so; and another 45 percent value the Torah. If we were to posit that these numbers represent Orthodox, Conservative, and Reform Judaisms, we should not be far off the mark.

---

[4]Ibid., p. 281.

[5]Wertheimer, "Recent Trends," p. 8.

In fact, the denominational figures Kosmin's report gives are as follows (current Jewish denominational preferences of adult Jews by religion = our "Judaists"):

	Percentage of Those Polled	Percentage of Households
Orthodox	6.6	16
Conservative	37.8	43
Reform	42.4	35
Reconstructionist	1.4	2
"Just Jewish"	5.4	

Of the Judaists, 80 percent are Reform or Conservative, approximately 7 percent Orthodox; and the high level of identification with Orthodoxy is strictly a phenomenon in the greater New York City area.[6] Elsewhere, the percentage of Orthodox Jews in the community of Judaists is still lower.[7] The denominational choice of the rest is scattered. A slightly earlier study by Kosmin (for 1987) divided the Jews in general as: 2 percent Reconstructionist, 9 percent Orthodox, 29 percent Reform, 34 percent Conservative, and 26 percent "other" or "just Jewish." It is not clear whether the distinction between Jews and Judaists is reflected in these figures, but the upshot is not in doubt.[8] Recent surveys have yielded a plurality of Reform over Conservative affiliations.

Kosmin further observes that there is "a general trend of movement away from traditional Judaism. While one quarter of the born Jewish religion Judaism group was raised in Orthodox households, only 7 percent report themselves as Orthodox now." Not only so, but "nearly 90 percent of those now Orthodox were raised as such, thus indicating any movement toward Orthodoxy is relatively small. In contrast to the Orthodox, the Conservative and Reform drew heavily from one or both of the major denominations; one third of the Conservatives were raised as Orthodox, and one-quarter of the Reform as Conservative, with an additional 12 percent having been raised Orthodox."[9] Wertheimer too observes that the trend is away from Orthodoxy and from Conservatism as well and toward Reform Judaism: "Nationally, the Conservative movement still commands the allegiance of a plurality of Jews, albeit a shrinking plurality. The main beneficiary of Orthodox and Conservative losses seems to be the Reform movement."[10]

As to synagogue affiliation, Kosmin comments: "Synagogue affiliation is the most widespread form of formal Jewish connection, but it characterized only 41 percent of the entirely Jewish households." He further notes that there is a discrepancy between calling oneself Reform and belonging to a Reform temple: "The distribution of the 860,000 households reporting synagogue mem-

---

[6]Kosmin et al., *Highlights,* p. 281.

[7]Westheimer, "Recent Trends," p. 80.

[8]Cf. Wertheimer, "Recent Trends." pp. 80–81.

[9]Kosmin et al., *Highlights,* p. 32.

[10]Wertheimer, "Recent Trends," p. 80.

bership across the denominations shows that the Reform plurality, which was evidence in denominational preferences, does not translate directly into affiliation. By contrast, the Orthodox are more successful in affiliating their potential constituency."[11]

WAY OF LIFE

How about religious practice of the Judaists—the center of concern for this inquiry? Here the figures cover only three matters:

Fast on the Day of Atonement	61%
Attend synagogue on high holidays	59%
Attend synagogue weekly	11%

Every study for several decades has replicated these results: lots of people go to Passover seders, a great many also observe the so-called High Holy Days (in the Torah, the Days of Awe, that is, Rosh Hashanah, the New Year, and Yom Kippur, the Day of Atonement). So we may ask: Why do people who in community do not pray weekly (or daily) come to synagogue worship for the New Year and the Day of Atonement, that is, why do approximately half of the Judaists who worship in community at all do so only three days a year? How do they know what is fit and proper: this day, not that?

As to rites at home and household practices, Kosmin shifts to entirely Jewish households as against mixed Jewish and gentile households, that is, from the Judaist to the Jewish (and a sensible shift at that):

Attend Passover seder	86%
Never have Christmas tree	82%
Light Hanukkah candles	77%
Light Sabbath candles	44%
Belong to a synagogue	41%
Eat kosher meat all the time	17%

What makes Passover different from all other holidays? Clearly, that question must come up first of all. What makes Sabbath candles (all the more so, the weekly Sabbath as a holy day of rest) only half so important as Hanukkah candles (one week out of the year)?

Since the Torah devotes considerable attention to the foods that may sustain the life of holy Israel and since the ethnic Jews too identify foods as particularly Jewish, we may ask about the matter of observance of dietary rules in Conservative Judaism, which affirms these rules and regards them as a key indicator of piety. Charles S. Liebman and Saul Shapiro report that among the Conservative

---

[11]Kosmin et al., *Highlights*, p. 37.

Jews they surveyed, 5 percent of the men and 6.4 percent of the women report that they observe the dietary laws both at home and away (by the standards of Conservative Judaism, which are somewhat more lenient then those of Ortho-doxy); 29.2 percent of the men and 28.8 percent of the women have kosher homes but do not keep the dietary taboos away from home. Approximately a third of the Conservative homes, then, appear to be conducted in accord with the laws of kosher food.[12]

Liebman and Shapiro comment that the home of the parents of those in this group also was kosher, and observance of the dietary laws correlates with Jew-ish education: "of the children receiving a day school education, 66 percent come from kosher homes; of all those who attended Camp Ramah [a Jewish education summer camp run by the Conservative movement], 53 percent came from kosher homes; this despite the fact that only 34 percent of the parents re-port their homes are kosher. The differences are even more dramatic if one bears in mind that a disproportionate number of older Conservative synagogue members have kosher homes, which means that their children were educated at a time when day school education was much less widespread in the Jewish community."

Along these same lines Steven M. Cohen introduces the metaphor of "an artichoke syndrome," where, he says, "the outer layers of the most traditional forms of Jewish expression are peeled away until only the most essential and minimal core of involvement remains, and then that also succumbs to the forces of assimilation. . . . according to assimilationist expectations, ritual observance and other indicators of Jewish involvement decline successively from parents to children." But current studies do not "support a theory predicting uniform de-cline in ritual practice from one generation to the next. Rather, it suggests in-tergenerational flux with a limited movement toward a low level of observance entailing Passover Seder attendance, Hanukkah candle lighting, and fasting on Yom Kippur."[13] In yet other studies, Cohen speaks of "moderately affiliated Jews," who nearly unanimously "celebrate High Holidays, Hanukkah and Passover, belong to synagogues when their children approach age 12 and 13, send their children to afternoon school or Sunday school, and at least occa-sionally support the Federation [United Jewish Appeal] campaigns."[14] Cohen speaks of "broad affection for Jewish family, food, and festivals."

Here, Cohen's report provides especially valuable data. He explains "why Jews feel so affectionate toward their holidays":

> One theme common to the six items [celebrated by from 70 to over 90 percent surveyed] is family. Holidays are meaningful because they connect

---

[12]Charles S. Liebman and Saul Shapiro, *A Survey of the Conservative Movement and Some of Its Religious Attitudes,* unpublished ms, September 1979, Library of the Jewish Theological Seminary of America. The figures probably overestimate contemporary practice.

[13]Cohen, *American Assimilation of Jewish Revival?* pp. 80, 81.

[14]Cohen, *Content or Continuity,* p. 4. Cohen distinguishes between "the Jewish-identity patterns of the more involved and passionate elites from those of the more numerous, marginally affiliated Jews, those with roughly average levels of Jewish involvement and emotional investment. . . . One may be called 'commitment to content' and the other 'commitment to continuity.' Alternative . . . 'commitment to ideology' versus 'commitment to identity.' "

Jews with their family-related memories, experiences, and aspirations. Respondents say that they want to be with their families on Jewish holidays, that they recall fond childhood memories at those times, and that they especially want to connect their own children with Jewish traditions at holiday time. Moreover, holidays evoke a certain transcendent significance; they have ethnic and religious import; they connect one with the history of the Jewish people, and they bear a meaningful religious message. Last, food . . . constitutes a major element in Jews' affection for the holidays.[15]

The holidays that are most widely celebrated in this report remain the same as in the others: Passover, Hanukkah, and the High Holy Days. By contrast, "relatively few respondents highly value three activities: observing the Sabbath, adult Jewish education, and keeping kosher." The question comes to the fore once again: Why those rites and not others? The answers are not difficult to locate when Hanukkah is considered. That day is important because it is the holiday of Judaism closest to Christmas. Passover is a rite of the home. The Holy Days focus the liturgy on the condition of the individual. So home and family rites define the way of life of American Jews who practice Judaism, and holidays of that speak to corporate, public "Israel," the holy people, in a way that Tabernacles or the Sabbath, do not.

THE AMERICAN JUDAISM
OF HOLOCAUST AND REDEMPTION

Where do American Judaists stand on Israeli matters? Among the Judaists, 31 percent have visited the state of Israel, 35 percent have close family or friends living there; among the ethnic Jews (not Judaists), the figures are 11 percent and 20 percent. Here is another question: what makes the state of Israel so important to the Judaists?

Along the same lines comes charity, including Israel-centered charity (the United Jewish Appeal, for instance). Once more speaking of entirely Jewish households:

Contributed to a Jewish charity in 1989	62%
Contributed to UJA/Federation campaign in 1989	45%
Celebrate Israeli independence day	18%

And, for comparison:

Contributed to a secular charity in 1989	67%
Contributed to a political campaign in 1988–1990	36%

---

[15]Ibid., pp. 14–15.

Commenting on the Kosmin report, Ari L. Goldman commented, "In a radical change from just a generation ago, American Jews today are as likely to marry non-Jews as Jews. But even as this assimilation accelerates, Jews are clinging to religious traditions. . . . These trends—one away from tradition, the other maintaining tradition—are spelled out."[16]

Covering a variety of issues, Jack Wertheimer proposes to "evaluate the state of contemporary Jewish religious life" with special attention to changing patterns of religious observance, which concern this inquiry into the contrast between book-Judaism and practiced Judaism. Orthodoxy, conceded by all parties to be closest in popular observance to the Judaism described in the holy books, retains its young people, but at the same time loses its older population, a disproportionately large component of its numbers, to death, with from two to three times as many Orthodox Jews over age 65 as between 18 and 45; so the gap between the books as lived by everyday Jews and the conduct of the generality of Jews is in fact growing wider. Synagogue attendance rates vary, but decline. In the early 1980s, Wertheimer says, approximately 44 percent of Americans claimed they attended services weekly, and 24 percent of American Jews did; but that figure is high. Wertheimer says, "In most communities between one third and one-half of all Jews attend religious services either never or only on the High Holy Days."[17]

THE VITAL CENTER: ETHNICALLY JEWISH AND RELIGIOUSLY JUDAIC

If, then, we wish to describe the large center of American Jews, those who are both ethnically Jewish and religiously Judaic—estimated by Steven M. Cohen to number about half of the American Jews—we may do so in the terms Cohen has provided. He gives these generalizations that pertain to our problem:

The moderately affiliated are proud of their identity as Jews, of Jews generally, and of Judaism.

They combine universalist and particularist impulses; they are ambivalent about giving public expression to their genuinely felt attachment to things Jewish.

They are especially fond of the widely celebrated Jewish holidays as well as the family experiences and special foods that are associated with them.

They celebrate High Holidays, Hanukkah and Passover as well as most major American civic holidays . . .

They vest importance in those Jewish activities they perform; and they regard those activities they fail to undertake as of little import. Accord-

[16]Ari L. Goldman, *New York Times,* June 7, 1991.

[17]Wertheimer, *Recent Trends,* pp. 63, 85.

ingly, they are happy with themselves as Jews; they believe they are "good Jews."

Their primary Jewish goal for their children is for them to maintain Jewish family continuity . . .

The Holocaust and anti-Semitism are among the most powerful Jewish symbols . . .

The moderately affiliated believe God exists, but they have little faith in an active and personal God.

They are voluntarists, they affirm a right to select those Jewish customs they regard as personally meaningful, and unlike many intensive Jews, most of the moderately affiliated reject the obligatory nature of halakhah [laws, norms].

They endorse broad, abstract principles of Jewish life (such as knowing the fundamentals of Judaism) but fail to support narrower, more concrete normative demands (such as regular text study or sending their children to Jewish day schools).

The moderately affiliated prefer in-marriage but fail to oppose out-marriage with a great sense of urgency.

They support [the state of] Israel, but only as a subordinate concern, one lacking any significant influence on the private sphere of Jewish practice.

To the moderately affiliated, "good Jews" are those who affiliate with other Jews and Jewish institutions.[18]

We have before us the description of a mass of Judaists who in some ways conform, and in other ways do not conform, to book Judaism. Their religion presents us with a problem of interpretation: how do these people know the difference between what matters and what doesn't, Passover as against Pentecost (*Shabuot*) fifty days later; circumcision as against intermarriage; the Holocaust and anti-Semitism as against the state of Israel; the existence of God as against God's active caring. The key lies in Cohen's description: "They affirm a right to select." On what basis do they choose?

WHY THIS, NOT THAT? THE AMERICAN PROTESTANT MODEL: RELIGION IN PRIVATE, POLITICS IN PUBLIC

In North American society, historically defined as it has been by Protestant conceptions, it is permissible to be different in religion, and *religion is a matter of what is personal and private*. That reading of religion as separate from public affairs has

---

[18]Cohen, *Content or Continuity*, pp. 41–42.

remained firm, despite the affirmation of ethnic or racial difference too. Hence Judaism as a religion encompasses what is personal and familial. But that definition of religion proves insufficient.

The Jews (among other religious and ethnic groups) also constitute a corporate community. They put forth as a political entity a separate system, one that concerns not religion, but public policy. Judaism in public policy produces political action in favor of the state of Israel or other important matters of the corporate community. That is the American norm for ethnic groups, which do enter public life and make demands upon public policy.

That pattern which keeps religion private and accommodates ethnicity in public, conforms to the Protestant model of religion. The Jews have accomplished conformity to it by the formation of two Judaisms, the one for the home, the other for the public square.

Specifically, the data of social science have shown us that American Jews practice two Judaisms, a version of the classical one at home, the secular system of Holocaust and Redemption in public. The rites of the received Judaisms, Reform, Conservative, and integrationist-Orthodox Judaisms, prevail in the home. These are Passover, bar mitzvah, marriage, and burial—all of them matters of private life and family concern. They are defined by the received systems of Judaism. But when that Judaism in its normative or derivative formulations speaks of corporate life, it loses its audience. The public and communal celebrations of that same set of Judaic systems attract modest interest. For example, large numbers of people do not come together regularly for public worship, except on occasions involving private life (the Days of Awe) or the Holocaust and the state of Israel.

Rather, when it comes to the corporate, ethnic Jewish community, the rites of the American Judaism of Holocaust and Redemption are practiced. Trips to the state of Israel provide an example. Just now, a huge public project has undertaken to supply a ten-day trip to the state of Israel free of charge to *every* young Jewish American or Canadian who has not undertaken such a secular pilgrimage. The organized Jewish community, niggardly in its support for Jewish education, leaving to the parents nearly the entire cost of day schools, has found massive resources for "Project Birthright."

Accordingly, the Judaic narratives of home and family and individual life register, the Judaic narratives of corporate Israel do not. It is not that they cannot compete with the ethnic narratives of Holocaust and Redemption. Rather, they are incongruent and cast aside as implausible, irrelevant.

1. *Personal, private, familial Judaism:* American Jews at home, in the family, identify with the religious world of the received Judaic system. Circumcision and the Passover Seder bear in common a single social referent: family, home, and experiences of essentially private life. The narrative message of the rites corresponds to the social experience of the faithful that practice those rites.

2. *Public, corporate, communal Jewishness:* Rites of Judaism such as the Sabbath or the Festival of Tabernacles that focus on community and public affairs, by contrast, fail to attract a large constituency, because they invoke in common another social referent: Judaic society beyond individual and family. The Sabbath

observed in synagogue worship and declamation of the Torah, for example, does not define the routine of large numbers of American Jews who practice Judaism. Public, corporate Jewishness involves a different narrative and different rites.

So people commonly see religion as something personal and private. There the received Judaic system and its continuators flourish. But when it comes to a corporate message, the Jews turn to the ethnic system of secular Jewishness. That is why, whatever the books say, the people do what to them is self-evidently right—and dismiss what does not fit. The Protestant model best explains the Judaic data.

31

Reversionary Judaisms: Forward to "Tradition"?

FROM SECULARITY TO RELIGIOSITY
IN CONTEMPORARY JUDAIC LIFE

The last third of the twentieth century and the early years of the twenty-first witness a movement of "return to tradition," or reversion, affecting all of the Judaic systems of the past two hundred years, from Orthodoxy to Reform, inclusive of American, European, and Israeli Jewry. Quite what people mean by "tradition" was not always clear, but in general the movement has involved formerly secular and non-observant Jews, often quite divorced from Jewish ethnic life, undertaking some type of religious observance. They adopt a religious viewpoint and move from the secular and ethnic to the religious and theological framework of (a) Judaism. Among some who were formerly disengaged from all ethnic and religious connection, it may involve joining a Reform synagogue. Sometimes the pattern of reversion brings a Reform Jew into a Conservative rabbinical seminary, or a Conservative Jew into an Orthodox Yeshiva.

Sometimes reversion has meant that a formerly indifferent ("assimilated") Jew discovered his or her Jewishness and determined to engage with the organized Jewish community, in activities involving Holocaust memorialization or political support for the state of Israel. Reversion came about for some in a personal crisis, for others in an event involving the state of Israel. In general, the pattern of reversion is marked by the movement from the life of an isolated individual to participation in a Jewish social entity (the "community" in one or another definition). In this way, personal and private religiosity or utter secularity lost their hold, and public and social religiosity took over.

The single most striking trait of the contemporary Judaic religious world in all its diversity is the return to Judaism on the part of formerly secular Jews on one side or the movement from less rigorous to more complete observance of the holy way of life on the other. All together, the diverse phenomena fall under the category of *reversion,* that is, "return to tradition," in the theological language of the matter, or renewed religiosity, in more descriptive terms. Reversion both marks a movement and also defines a particular Judaic system.

JEWS CONVERTING TO JUDAISM

When, as happens not uncommonly, Jews in America make a decision to observe the dietary laws and the Sabbath, to say prayers every day and to identify with a Torah study circle in a yeshiva, they adopt a way of life and a worldview new to them. For the generality of American Jews have defined their lives in other terms. Reversion marks the entry of Jews not born and brought up within the Judaic system of the dual Torah into the way of life defined by the dual Torah and the adoption of the viewpoint and values of that same Torah. Reversioners enter into the Israel to whom the received Judaic systems speak, entering an intense social life lived in a round of daily and Sabbath prayers, study sessions, celebrations. Not a few reversioners dismiss the Judaic systems that favor or accommodate integration. Instead they choose a Judaic system that, in effect if not in articulated policy, creates a life of segregation. The shift from world to world marks entry into a stunningly powerful Judaic system.

Yet in interpreting the Judaic mode and system of reversion, we may not take for granted that we witness a mere "return to tradition." Some maintain that the "return" is exactly that. Quite to the contrary, whatever is meant by "tradition," reversioners in their context represent new, not traditional choices. The reversioners do undertake to redefine—for themselves, but they are exemplary—that way of life and worldview that they received as traditional from their parents. But that was *not* the received system of the dual Torah, its worldview, its way of life. So to the reversioners the new is what (they say) is old, even as what was old is new to them. Accordingly, our analysis requires us to treat as fresh not the received system, but the way the reversioners receive it: A system of reversion is fresh, even though that to which people return draws them (in its own terms) upward to Sinai.

All of the Judaic systems of the last third of the twentieth century bore the marks of a renewal of observance and a return to more classical formulations of the faith. But a particular reversionary system also took shape, the one that led utterly secular, but searching young Jews into one or another of the Orthodox-Judaic systems of the age, both in America and in the state of Israel. Let us speak first of the movement, which imparted a style of its own to existing Judaisms, all of which, in the end of the twentieth century, saw themselves as "more traditional" than they had earlier been.

WHO CONVERTS? THE WORLDVIEW, THE WAY OF LIFE

Reversion to Judaism in America began among the third generation, that is, with the grandchildren of the immigrant generations of the period 1880–1920, whom we meet in Chapter 29. But it reached its height with the fourth and beyond, and, it now is obvious, reversion will mark the formation of Judaic systems well into the twenty-first century. That movement that I have called reversion uses the language of "return," which, in Hebrew, as *teshubah,* bears the further sense of repentance. The Judaic systems of return or repentance invoke profoundly moral and theological dimensions, not characteristic, as we have seen, of the four movements just now reviewed. For all of the Judaic systems of the late nineteenth and twentieth centuries explained a process of distance, that is, a movement away from the "tradition," while the Judaic style and system of the present propose to account for the opposite: a return, a closing of the gap between the Jew and the Torah.

That is the explanation for the word choice at hand, *return* to the Judaic way of life and worldview in one of its religious formulations, rather than its secular ones. Why the stress on "return"? The worldview of reversionary Judaisms sees Israel as God's people, who by *nature and by definition* should keep the Torah. All Jews who do not ought to return to their true calling and character as the people of the Torah. So the title of the movement expresses its worldview and its theory of who is Israel and what it is natural for Israel to become. The worldview of the movement perceives the Jews as alienated from the "tradition" to which they must "return." The way of life, on the surface, is simply that mode of behavior prescribed by the "tradition" for whatever chair the reversioner chooses to occupy.

We may wonder why Jews growing up in secular circumstances opt for a religious Judaism. And, more important, we want to know how that tendency on the part of individuals became a movement and generated a Judaism, the Judaic system(s) of return, indeed, the one fresh Judaism that we see as we turn toward the twenty-first century. To answer these questions, we have to take note of the highly secular character of American Judaism, a Judaism that, over all, lays stress on institutions and organizations rather than on the inner life of faith, learning, and observance. That system has provided a mode of "being Jewish" in the context of an open and free society, when one wanted to be both Jewish and also part of an undifferentiated society. It involved essentially secular activity—fundraising, political organizing—and left untouched the inner life and values of the participants. But the success of American Judaism had an unexpected effect. People took seriously the powerful emotions elicited by the appeals, characteristic of fundraising and organizational propaganda, for instance, rehearsals of the "Holocaust" and engagement with the ongoing crises of the state of Israel. They were sold, and find partial and incomplete the Judaism that they had bought.

As the 1970s unfolded, the stress of the community at large on a high level of emotion, joined to only occasional activity and then activity of an essentially neutral character, affected younger people in a curious way. People sold on the centrality of "being Jewish" in their lives required modes of expression that affected their lives more deeply, and in more ways, than the rather limited way of life offered by American Judaism. In search, once more, for values, rejecting what they deemed the superficial, merely public Jewish activities of their parents, they resolved that tension between being Jewish and not being too Jewish generated, for the third generation, by American Judaism. They were sold on "being Jewish" and looked not for activity but for community, not for an occasional emotional binge but for an enduring place and partnership: a covenant. In America reversioners have come from Reform or secular backgrounds, Conservative or Orthodox ones. It hardly matters. In all cases we find a conversion process, a taking up of a totally new way of life and a rejection of the inherited one, the parents' way of life. In the state of Israel, reversioners derive from three different sources of Jews: America, Israelis of European background, and Israelis of Asian or African origin.[1] The movement of reversion dates from the mid-1960s, coincident with the Judaism of Holocaust and Redemption, and it begins in a rejection of Western culture. So much for reversion as a generalized characteristic of diverse Judaic systems.

REVERSIONARY JUDAISM AS A JUDAIC RELIGIOUS SYSTEM IN ITS OWN RIGHT

But reversion has formed not only a mode and a style for Judaic systems of all sorts, but also a Judaic system on its own. Janet Aviad's definitive chronicle of the matter provides not only a systematic picture of the ideology and way of life but a synoptic portrait of the movement as a whole. Still, enough is in hand to generalize. The movement's American component derived, she says, from the youth rebellion of the 1960s. So Aviad:

> Protesting a war they regarded as immoral, a situation that permitted terrible injustices to ethnic minorities, what appeared as a wasteful directionless use of technology, youth struck out in various directions. One direction was toward new forms of a religious life.[2]

Involved was a rejection of the "tradition of skeptical, secular intellectuality which has served as the prime vehicle for three hundred years of scientific and technical work in the West." The reversioners described here had earlier in the 1960s experimented with diverse matters, including drugs, poetry, and religion. And, among the religions, some Jews tried out Judaism.

The quest involved travel, and Judaism "was often only the end station of a long search."[3] Coming to Judaism came about by chance meetings with rabbis or religious Jews, but staying there was because of the yeshivas that received the reversioners. Yet another group of reversioners derived from Reform and Conservative synagogues; they came to improve their knowledge and raise their level of practical observance of piety. A further group, Israelis of Western background, compared, over all, with this second group. They had seen themselves

---

[1] Janet Aviad, *Return to Judaism: Religious Renewal in Israel* (Chicago: University of Chicago Press, 1983), ix.

[2] Ibid., p. 2.

[3] Ibid., p. 4.

as secular but sought to become, in Israeli terms, religious. Their search for meaning brought them to the yeshivas ready to receive them. The final group Aviad surveys were Israelis of poorer and Asian or African origin, and to them, too, reversion represented a religious conversion, from life "experienced as empty or meaningless to one experienced as fully, whole, and holy."[4]

In all as in the ethnic Jewishness embodied by the Judaism of Holocaust and Redemption, so here too, we deal with a Jewish expression of a common, international youth culture of the 1970s and 1980s, just as much as we found in American Judaism a version, in a Judaic idiom, of a larger cultural development in American life of the 1960s and early 1970s. When the massive rise in the birthrate following World War II took place, it pointed the way to, among other things, the youth culture that would emerge twenty years later. When we find that Jews rejected the values they deemed secular and shallow and opted for a new way of life they found authentic and Godly, we do well to wonder whether, in other groups, young people were reaching the same conclusions. A generation in search, a shared quest for something to transcend the ("merely") material achievements—that generation grew up in the prosperity that followed the end of World War II.

Children of successful parents with leisure and resources to go in quest, some turned to drugs, others to social concerns, still others to a search for a faith that would demand more than the (to them shallow, compromising) religiosity of their parents. Whether Roman Catholic Pentecostalism, Protestant Biblical affirmation (called "fundamentalism"), Judaic reversion, Islamic renewal from Malaya to Morocco (also called "fundamentalism" or "extremism"), the international youth movement exhibits strikingly uniform traits: young people in rebellion against the parents' ways, in search of something more exacting and rigorous. If, as we noticed, the Judaism of the dual Torah insisted that Jews are not only Jews all the time, but never anything else, then we may characterize as a return to that theory of Israel the movement of reversion. But it is only in that sense. For as an acutely contemporary movement, part of a large-scale rejection of secular, humanistic, and liberal values of a generation concerned to live an affable life, the reversion to Judaism presented much that was fresh, unprecedented, but, above all, selective.

The system of reversion drew its categories, its values, its goals from a larger setting as well. These it then adapted to the Judaic circumstance: a totally fresh, totally new, totally autonomous Judaic system. A Judaism invented or discovered? Both, to begin with, invented. In her description of reversion in the state of Israel, Janet Aviad, whom I shall cite at length, uses such language as this: "who turned outward . . . who noticed a change in the spiritual climate." That is a mark of invention, I think. But then, assuredly it was also a Judaism discovered and recovered. So the idiom, as Aviad says, may have proved new, but the content was more than welcome: It was what they had brought with them. The worldview of reversionism in the present form constitutes part of a larger

---

[4]Ibid., p. 10.

and international style, a Judaic statement of what a great many people were saying, all of them in the language and categories of their own.

ORTHODOX JUDAISMS RESPOND
TO THE REVERSIONARY MOVEMENT

The movement of reversion flourishes throughout the Jewish world. It attains realization as a system, however, in the *Yeshivat* or yeshivas—the centers for full-time study of Torah, comparable to monasteries in providing for a holy way of life for all their participants. The ones in the state of Israel lead the movement of reversion and give full expression to its worldview and way of life. But, interestingly, the yeshivas that succeed in embodying the ideals of reversion derive not from Israeli Orthodox rabbis but from American ones living in Jerusalem. It was American Orthodox rabbis trained in yeshivas who saw the opportunity and the issue. They understood as self-evident of course that all Jews should live by the Torah and study it, but they had the wit to recognize a generation of young Jews who were prepared to revert to that way of life and worldview . And they further undertook to give form and full expression to the system of reversion. The yeshivas that received the newcomers came into being because of American rabbis settled in Jerusalem:

> They discerned a new openness to religion. . . . They felt strongly that Orthodox Judaism would appeal to the young Jews being drawn to non-Jewish religious groups . . . the problem seemed merely technical: how to make young people aware of orthodox values and beliefs as a way of life.[5]

What these rabbis found points to the freshness of the movement at hand, for in fact the established yeshivas took no interest in the possibilities at all. They did not think they could absorb the types of students coming their way. So the rabbis founded autonomous schools.

That fact alerts us to the presence of an innovative system. A system that, to begin with, finds itself rejected and ignored by another system of the same family will have difficulty in claiming to form an incremental outcome of the system the institutions of which prove—by their own word—utterly incompatible. In the movement of reversion, as well as in the systemic formulations of"return," there is a transvaluation of that critical value: Gifts of the spirit take priority and endow the gifted with status out of all relationship to his (or her) intellectual attainment. The addition of the "or her," of course, provides another signal of a system aborning, for the familiar yeshiva world makes slight provision for women's participation in its Judaism. But the Judaic system of reversion worked out within the Judaic system of the dual Torah flourishing in

---

[5]Ibid., p. 16.

the state of Israel founded yeshivas for women and understood the importance of equality, within the received system, for them, an astounding and important mark of innovation and renewal.

That is only one indicator that we deal with something fresh and novel. The initiative involved in identifying the opportunity further provides solid evidence that a new system is under way. The total negation of Western culture that forms the centerpiece of the worldview at hand finds no ample precedents in the received dual Torah, which found itself entirely at home in diverse circumstances and drew both deliberately and unself-consciously on the world in which it flourished. We need hardly point to obvious precedents for a policy of selecting what was appropriate. The policy of rejecting the entire world beyond moreover finds few precedents and, in the balance, presents an egregious exception to a long history of—not integration but—mediation. But if we look toward another wellspring for the view at hand, we readily discern it. The worldview of reversion, resting on the principle of total rejection of "Western culture," in fact corresponded point by point with the worldview of comparable movements of its time and circumstance. It was the youth revolution of the 1960s. Rejecting the parents and their values, the authority of their youth, and the conventions of society, the juvenile revolutionaries sought radical change, finding it in politics, music, clothing, food, and drugs of their choice rather than their parents'—and, for some, in religion.

The view that the reversion was a homecoming, that the values of reversionism simply replicated, for the occasion, the theology of the Judaic system of the dual Torah, contradicts the particular structure and points of value and emphasis of reversionism. The questions at hand come from the circumstance, the answers then derive from a process of selection and arrangement of proof-texts provided by the canonical writings on one side and—if truth be told—the everyday way of life of the Judaic system of the dual Torah on the other. The whole then compares to other wholes, other Judaic systems: a work of selection along lines already determined, a system dictated by its own inventive framers to answer questions urgent to themselves in particular, a Judaism. To begin with, the matter of context requires attention. The movement of reversion came about in exactly the same time marked by massive out-marriage, apostasy to other religions, a turning away from engagement with Jewry in any terms. At the end of World War II, British Jewry numbered approximately 500,000; had natural growth marked its number, the community would be substantially larger than its present number of approximately 300,000 to 350,000! And, we cannot forget, World War II left the Jews as a group decimated, about one-third of all the Jews in the world alive in 1939 having been murdered by 1945. These demographic facts raised the question, are we the end? And the question confronted individuals as well: Am I the last Jew on earth, as a novella by Arthur A. Cohen, within his *Days of Simon Stern,* put matters? So the natural ecology of the Jews once more defined a crisis, and the response of one sector of the Jews was to revert to (a) Judaism, to (a formulation of) tradition—to reaffirm Israel the holy people in the face of extinction.

JUDAIC RESPONSE TO THE
HOLOCAUST THROUGH THE POWER
OF THE JUDAIC NARRATIVE

The source of the rebirth is the world as it is, the motive and the power, the teachings of the Torah. For the reversionary Judaisms begin in a mix of resentment of a social present with a right and natural reflection on an awful, near-at-hand past. The reversion to the dual Torah marked the generations beyond the murder of the Jews of Europe, facing the demographic loss. It affected the generations that made the state of Israel, addressing the perpetual insecurity of the bastion become beleaguered fortress. It touched deeply the great-grandchildren of the immigrants who formed American Jewry, the children of the framers of American Judaism, looking backward at integration fully realized and forward toward what they feared would be no future at all.

With no family untouched by out-marriage, and with many families' lives framed out of all relationship with distinctively Judaic or even culturally Jewish activity (however defined), the future came under doubt. The reversionary Judaic systems for their part say no to two hundred years of Judaic system building. They reject the premises and the programs not only of the Judaic systems of an essentially economic and political character—Zionism, for example—but also the ones that affirm religious viewpoints and ways of life. Since these systems by definition come into being as the creation of children—great-great-grand-children, really—of the nineteenth-century reformers, they mark the conclusion off the age of modernization.

The pressing problem they address seems to me clear. The Jews en route to the Torah in its dual statement once more ask very profound, very pressing human questions. They want to know the answers to such questions as: Why do I live? What do I do to serve God? What should I do with my life? No wonder Orthodoxy cannot cope with them. The reversioners come to study Torah as God's word, not as a source of historical facts. They take up a way of life quite alien to that they knew from their parents as an act of conversion to God, not as a means of expressing or preserving their Jewishness. They repudiate, yes, but only to affirm. If I had to explain, in a single sentence, the remarkable power of reversionary Judaisms—whether to Reform or to Israeli yeshiva Orthodoxy—I would invoke a single consideration. The one question ignored by the former Judaic systems, the human question, found its answer here, and, after two hundred years of change, the final turning of the wheel brought up the original issue afresh.

For what questions had the Judaic system of the dual Torah set at the center of discourse, if not the ones of living a holy and a good life? For those long centuries in which Christianity defined the frame of reference for all Western society, the Jews understood that that question pressed, its answers demanded attention. The Judaism of the dual Torah addressed that Jew who was always a Jew and who was only a Jew, delivering the uncompromising lesson that God demanded the human heart, and that Israel was meant to be a kingdom of priests and a holy people, and that the critical issues of life concerned conduct with God, the other, and the self. That piety which explained from day to day what it meant to be a *Mensch,* a decent human being, answered the question that through the Christian centuries the West understood as critical: How shall I live so as decently to die? For all of us owe God one death, and the worthy make it a good one: one out of a good life.

The issues of modern times shifted from the human questions framed by humanity in God's image and in God's likeness to an altogether different set of urgent concerns. These had to do with matters of politics and economics. The received Torah echoed with the question: Adam, where are you? The Torahs of the nineteenth century answered the question: Jew, what *else* can you become? For millennia Jews had not wanted to be more than they were, and now the Jewish question, asked by gentiles and Jews alike, rested on the premise that to be Jewish did not suffice. Now Jews wished not totally to integrate, but also not entirely to segregate themselves. They no longer had in mind a place in a people that dwells alone.

The Judaic systems of the twentieth century, with their stress on politics for professionals and ephemeral enthusiasm for everybody else, reconstituted the people that dwells alone—for fifteen minutes at a time. No wonder, then, that at the end of two hundred years the heirs of a set of partial systems would go in search of a whole and complete one: one that provided what all the established ones did not, that same sense of center and whole that, for so long, was precisely what Jews did not want for themselves. The protracted love affair over, some Jews reengaged with the received Torah, the one in two parts, in a long-term union. Not many, not experienced, sometimes awkward, often forced and unnatural, they in time would find their path—and in ways they could not imagine or approve, lead the Jewish world.

The capacity of Judaic systems drawing upon the Judaism of the dual Torah to come to grips with the acutely contemporary issues of Jews' lives forms the source of their remarkable power to change lives, to bring about what in secular terms one would call conversion, and in Judaic terms return. The reversionary Judaisms—and they include Reform, Orthodoxy, Conservatism, each one in its many formulations—take up today's concerns and draw them into the framework of an enduring program of lively reflection. That capacity to form a relationship between the individual here and now and the social entity of holy, supernatural Israel, in the far reaches of time and unto eternity, takes the measure of Judaic systems. By that criterion, the systems of reversion, however limited their actual effect in numbers, exercise moral authority and therefore enjoy remarkable success.

32

Facing the Twenty-First Century
Ethnic and Religious
in Contemporary Judaism

ETHNIC AND RELIGIOUS

We conclude where we began: with definitions of Judaism. We started with "Judaism is the religion of the Old Testament," a definition we found necessary but insufficient. We conclude with another commonplace. Judaism is commonly identified as the religion of the Jews. But that is only partially right, therefore wholly wrong.

First, the Jews in Western democracies form an ethnic group, and in the state of Israel they constitute a nation.

Second, not all Jews practice Judaism. Some are secular. Others practice a religion other than Judaism while continuing to regard themselves as "Jews" in an ethnic, not a religious, sense. Jews who practice Judaism, the religion, supply information about that religion.

The ethnic secular Jews who do not practice Judaism and the Jews who practice a religion other than Judaism help define the Jews as an ethnic group but do not claim to attest to the character of the religion Judaism. Hence while Judaism is the religion of most Jews who practice a religion, it is not the "religion of the Jews" viewed as a group.

In the United States and Canada, Western Europe and Hispanic America, the Jews form an ethnic group, part of which also practices the religion Judaism. In the state of Israel, the Jews form the vast majority of the population of a nation, only part of which also practices the religion Judaism. Judaism is not the culture of an ethnic group, nor is it the nationalism of a nation-state, even though it is nourished by, and helps to define, both Diaspora ethnicity and Israeli national identify. Why does the distinction between ethnic and religious make a difference? The reason is that the ethnic self-understanding of North American Jewry and the view of the Jewish people as a nation affect the integrity of Judaism as a religion.

That is for two reasons. First, people identify what Jews believe with the religion Judaism, which then emerges as the sum total of Jews' opinions on various topics. Then, to take a common instance, when people want to know what Judaism teaches about life after death, they will be told, " 'The Jews' don't believe in that . . . ," even while, as we saw in Chapter 16, the prayer said three times a day explicitly blesses God for raising the dead.

Second, when portrayed as a matter of ethnic culture Judaism is denied its claim to speak to all humanity about issues of universal concern. What is left is the residue of folk culture. For instance, certain food in certain places is regarded as "Jewish," meaning a Jewish ethnic specialty. At one time bagels were a Jewish food. But if we know how to bake bagels, we do not know anything about how Judaism, the religion, views God or virtue or salvation.

WHY DISTINGUISH SECULAR JEWISHNESS FROM RELIGIOUS JUDAISM?

When people confuse an ethnic group with a religious community, they take random, individual opinion as a definitive fact for the beliefs of the faith. Then they see Judaism is the sum total of the opinions held by individual Jews—a mass of confusion and contradiction. The confusion emerges when we consider statements such as, "But I'm Jewish and I don't believe that," or "I'm Jewish and I'm not religious at all." Both statements speak for perfectly commonplace ethnic Jews, but they tell us nothing whatsoever about Judaism, either as represented in its official writings and teachings, or as practiced by those who claim to meet God in those writings and teachings.

The ethnic group and the religion shape the life of each other, but the fate of Judaism as a religion is not the same as the fate of the Jews as a group. If the Jews as a group grow few in numbers, the life of the religion, Judaism, may yet flourish among those that practice it. The self-segregationist Orthodox Judaisms we met in Chapter 28 certainly take that view. And if the Jews as a group grow numerous and influential but do not practice the religion, Judaism (or any other religion), or practice a religion other than Judaism, then the religion, Judaism, will lose its voice, even while the Jews as a group flourish.

The upshot is simple. A book (that is, a set of religious ideas, divorced from a social entity) is not a Judaism, but the opinions on any given subject of every individual Jew also do not add up to a Judaism. In many chapters we have seen why, to have a community of Judaism—a Judaic religious system, not just a book or a personal opinion—we require a group of Jews who together set forth a way of life, a worldview, and a theory of who and what they are. We have seen that many of the great debates among Judaisms focus upon the definition of the word *Israel,* meaning not the nation-state, the state of Israel of our own day, but the people, Israel, of which scripture speaks. That is not a question of the here and now but an issue of what it means to form the people descended from the saints and prophets of that "kingdom of priests and holy people" that God calls into being at Sinai, that defines itself within the Torah. This matter of "what is 'Israel,' " and "who is a 'Jew,' meaning, who belongs to 'Israel' " has occupied our attention, much as it is a center of ongoing contemporary debate among Judaisms and among Jews.

We therefore distinguish Jews' opinions as individuals from the system of Judaism as a coherent statement—way of life, worldview, theory of the social entity "Israel." We cannot define Judaism if we identify the history of the Jews with the history of Judaism, just as we cannot define Judaism if we regard the faith as a set of ideas quite divorced from the life of the people who hold those ideas. We have to define our terms and make sure we know precisely that about which, when we study the religion, Judaism, we are concerned. All those who practice the religion, Judaism, by definition fall into the ethnic group, the Jews, but not all members of the ethnic group practice Judaism. The upshot may be simply stated: *All Judaists—those who practice the religion, Judaism—are Jews, but not all Jews are Judaists.*

That formulation conveys the paradox that is central to Judaism. Here is a religion that addresses all humanity with a message of what God wants of all creation but that is identified with a particular ethnic group, the Jews. The universality of its focus, the religion's concern for the entire history and destiny of the human race and its message of salvation—these are framed in terms that involve a specific group of people. But how else is narrative going to serve, unless it tells the story of a particular group of people? Chapter 1 has shown us what is at stake in the medium of tale telling: the possibility of conveying the message that Adam and Israel represent the possibilities of humanity.

JUDAISM'S NARRATIVE:
THE STORY OF GOD

That is the cost of choosing to make the religion's statement through a tale. What is the reward? Just as Judaism draws on scripture to tell the story of Israel and its relationship to God and obligations to him, so the story extends to God as well. Theological doctrine takes the form of narrative because only through narrative can the statement be made.

How else say, God wept with Israel and for Israel? Here is the story of how God subjects himself to the analogies of the mortal king, matching in mourning the motifs of ordinary lamentation. Once more we see how scripture becomes a collection of established facts, stories of what happened; sages then build their propositions on the foundation of scripture's narratives:

Pesiqta deRab Kahana XV:III

Bar Qappara opened discourse by citing the following verse: "In that day the Lord God of hosts called to weeping and mourning, to baldness and girding with sackcloth; [and behold, joy and gladness, slaying oxen and killing sheep, eating meat and drinking wine. 'Let us eat and drink for tomorrow we die.' The Lord of hosts has revealed himself in my ears: 'Surely this iniquity will not be forgiven you until you die,' says the Lord of hosts]" (Is. 15:12–14).

"Said the Holy One, blessed be He, to the ministering angels, 'When a mortal king mourns, what does he do?'

"They said to him, 'He puts sack over his door.'

"He said to them, 'I too shall do that. "I will clothe the heavens with blackness [and make sackcloth for their covering]" (Is. 50:3).'

"He further asked them, 'When a mortal king mourns, what does he do?'

"They said to him, 'He extinguishes the torches.'

"He said to them, 'I too shall do that. "The sun and moon will become black [and the stars stop shining]" (Joel 4:15).'

"He further asked them, "When a mortal king mourns, what does he do?'

"They said to him, 'He goes barefooted.'

"He said to them, 'I too shall do that. "The Lord in the whirlwind and in the storm will be his way and the clouds [the dust of his feet]" (Nahum 1:3).'

"He further asked them, 'When a mortal king mourns, what does he do?'

"They said to him, 'He sits in silence.'

"He said to them, 'I too shall do that. "He will sit alone and keep silence because he has laid it upon himself" (Lam. 3:28).'

"He further asked them, 'When a mortal king mourns, what does he do?'

"They said to him, 'He overturns the beds.'

"He said to them, 'I too shall do that. "I beheld to the seats of thrones [having been overturned, now] were placed right side up" (Dan. 7:9).'

"He further asked them, 'When a mortal king mourns, what does he do?'

"They said to him, 'He tears his [royal] purple garment.'

"He said to them, 'I too shall do that. "The Lord has done that which he devised, he tore his word" (Lam. 2:17).'

"He further asked them, 'When a mortal king mourns, what does he do?'

"They said to him, 'He sits and laments.'

"He said to them, 'I too shall do that. "How lonely sits the city [that was full of people! How like a widow has she become, she that was great among the nations! She that was a princess among the cities has become a vassal. She weeps bitterly in the night, tears on her cheeks, among all her lovers she has none to comfort her; all her friends have dealt treacherously with her, they have become her enemies]" (Lamentations 1:1–2).'"

What is important in this story is the manner in which through narrative it shows that God takes on the traits of mortal kings; he wishes to be perceived in ways that correspond to the ways of man. The demonstration is detailed and systematic, and the explanation, in context, compelling. The match of king to the King of the world once more rests on the fundamental conviction of a perfect match, a world we can understand by appeal to governing rules and illuminating analogies.

We end at the point at which we began: Religion is experience, image, and story before it is anything else, after it is everything else, in Father Greeley's words. In telling the story of the people, Israel, Judaism was able to say, with remarkably enduring power, what it wished to say about God. The temptation to ethnicize the story represents a small price to pay for the power to make such a statement.

Glossary

Adon Olam "Lord of the World," hymn containing dogmas of divine unity, timelessness, providence.

aggadah lit., telling, narration. Generally, lore, theology, fable, biblical exegesis, ethics.

Ahavah love. *Ahavah rabbah:* great love; first words of prayer preceding *Shema.*

Alenu "It is incumbent on us": first word of prayer cited in "Going Forth."

aliyah going up, e.g., ascent to Jerusalem for a pilgrim festival. In contemporary usage, migration to the Land of Israel.

Am haares lit.: people of the land; Rabbinic usage: boor, unlearned, not a disciple of the sages.

Amidah lit., standing. The main section of obligatory prayers morning, afternoon, and evening, containing eighteen benedictions: (1) God of the fathers; (2) praise of God's power; (3) holiness; (4) prayer for knowledge; (5) prayer for repentance; (6) prayer for forgiveness; (7) prayer for redemption; (8) prayer for healing the sick; (9) blessing of agricultural produce; (10) prayer for in-gathering of dispersed Israel; (11) prayer for righteous judgment; (12) prayer for punishment of wicked and heretics; (13) prayer for reward of pious; (14) prayer for rebuilding Jerusalem; (15) prayer for restoration of house of David; (16) prayer for acceptance of prayers; (17) prayer of thanks; (18) prayer for restoration of Temple service; (19) prayer for peace.

Amora rabbinical teacher in Palestine and Babylonia in talmudic times (ca. 200–500 C.E.).

Apikoros Hebrew for Epicurus; generally: belief in hedonism.

archetype original pattern or model

Ashkenaz (pl. *im*) European Jews, those who follow the customs originating in medieval German Judaism.

Ashré "Happy are they," Psalm 145; read in morning and afternoon worship.

Assimilation taking on the cultural traits of a culture different from the one in which a person is born.

Av, Ninth of Day of mourning for destruction of Jerusalem Temple in 586 B.C.E. and 70 C.E.

B.C.E. before the common era; used in place of B.C.

Baal Shem Tov (ca. 1700–1760) "Master of the Good Name," founder of Hasidism.

bar mitzvah (pl. *mitzvot*) ceremony at which a thirteen-year-old boy becomes an adult member of Jewish community; an adult male Jew who is obligated to carry out the commandments.

bat mitzvah adult female Jew who is obligated to carry out commandments; marked by ceremony as for *bar mitzvah.*

Berakhah "benediction," blessing or praise.

Bet Am "house of people," early word for synagogue.

Bet Din court of law judging civil, criminal, religious cases according to *Halakhah.*

Bet Midrash house of study.

Bimah place from which worship is led in synagogue.

Birkat HaMazon blessing for food; Grace after Meals.

Brit milah covenant of circumcision; removal of penis foreskin on eighth day after birth.

C.E. common era; used instead of A.D.

canon officially recognized set of holy books.

Central Conference of American Rabbis association of Reform rabbis.

code an organized system of rules and laws.

Cohen/Kohen priest.

Conservative Judaism religious movement, reacting against early Reform, that attempts to adapt Jewish law to modern life on the basis of principles of change inherent in traditional laws.

credo confession of faith.

creed a formula or accepted system of religious belief.

cult a system of religious worship, a mode of serving God, not to be confused with another use of the word *cult* for an unconventional religious group.

dayyan judge in Jewish court.

Decalogue "Ten Words"; the Ten Commandments (Hebrew: *Aseret HaDibrot*).

Derekh Eretz lit., "the way of the land"; normal custom, correct conduct; good manners, etiquette.

Diaspora the settlement of Jews outside of the Land of Israel; the dispersion of the people of Israel in many countries.

dichotomy division into two parts.

dietary laws pertaining to animal food; pious Jews may eat only fish that have fins and scales, animals that part the hoof and chew the cud (e.g., sheep, cows, but not camels, pigs). Animals must be ritually slaughtered (Hebrew: *shehitah*) by a humane method accompanied by blessing of thanks. Jews may not eat shellfish, worms, snails, flesh torn from a living animal, and the like. Any mixture of meat and milk is forbidden; after eating meat, one may not eat dairy products for a period of time (one to six hours, depending on custom). Fish are neutral (*pareve*). See *kosher.*

dogma beliefs that the faithful are expected to affirm.

dynamic system a religious system that develops and changes over time.

El, Elohim God, divinity.

Emancipation providing for Jews political rights that were denied them in medieval and early modern Europe; including the Jews within the political community of the nation state.

erev evening, sunset, beginning of a holy day.

eschatology theory of the end of time, death, judgment, the world to come, messianic era, resurrection of the dead.

etrog citron, one of four species carried into the synagogue on *Sukkot,* from Leviticus 23:40, *"fruit of a goodly tree."*

exegesis critical explanation of scripture or other holy books.

exilarch head of the exile (Aramaic *Resh Galuta*; head of the Jewish community in Babylonia in Talmudic and medieval times.

gaon eminence, excellency; title of head of Babylonian academies; later on, distinguished Talmudic scholar.

Gedaliah, fast of third day of autumn month of *Tishré,* commemorating assassination of Gedaliah (II Kings 25, Jeremiah 40:1).

Geiger, Abraham (1870–1874) early reformer in Germany who produced modern prayerbook and wanted Judaism to become a world religion.

Gemara completion; comments and discussions of Mishnah. Mishnah + *Gemara* = Talmud.

get bill of divorce, required to dissolve Jewish marriage.

golus Ashkenazic pronunciation of *Galut:* exile; life in the Diaspora; discrimination, humiliation.

Hadassah U.S. women's Zionist organization.

Halakhah "the way things are done," from *halakh:* go; more broadly, the prescriptive Judaic legal tradition.

Haskalah Jewish Enlightenment, eighteenth-century movement of rationalists.

Habdalah the rite that at sundown at the end of the Sabbath or Festival marks the separation of the holy time of the Sabbath or festival to the secular or profane time of the everyday week; see Kiddush.

Hebrew Union College (Jewish Institute of Religion) founded in Cincinnati in 1875; center for training Reform rabbis, teachers with campuses in Los Angeles, Cincinnati, New York City, and Jerusalem.

heder room; elementary school for early education.

hiddush novella; new point, insight, given as a comment on classical text. Often ingenious, sometimes hair splitting.

Hillel first-century Pharisaic leader who taught, "Do not unto others what you would not have them do unto you."

Hillul HaShem profanation of God's name; doing something to bring disrepute on Jews, Judaism—particularly among non-Jews.

Hillul Shabbat profanation of the Sabbath.

Hol HaMoed intermediate days of festivals of Passover, *Sukkot.*

Holocaust the mass murder of more than 5 million Jews in Europe by Germany and its allies from 1933, when the German National Socialist Workers Party ("Nazis") came to power, to 1945, when the Allies vanquished Germany.

Huppah marriage canopy, under which the ceremony takes place.

inculcate instill.

Jehovah transliteration of Divine name, based on misunderstanding of Hebrew letters YHWH. Jews did not pronounce name of God, referred to the deity simply as *Adonai,* Lord. Translators took the vowels of *Adonai* and added them to the consonants *JHVH;* hence JeHoVaH.

Jewish Theological Seminary founded in 1888 a center for training conservative rabbis, teachers in New York, Los Angeles, and Jerusalem.

Judah the Prince head of Palestinian Jewish community ca. 200 C.E. who promulgated Mishnah.

Kabbalah lit., "tradition"; later, the mystical Jewish tradition.

Kaddish doxology said at end of principal sections of Jewish service; praise of God with congregational response, "May his great name be praised eternally." Eschatological emphasis; hope for speedy advent of Messiah. Also recited by mourners.

Karaites eighth- to twelfth-century Middle Eastern Jewish sect that rejected the Oral Torah and lived by the Written Torah alone.

kehillah Jewish community.

Kenesset Israel "assembly of Israel"; Jewish people as a whole.

Keriat Shema recital of *Shema.*

Ketubah marriage contract specifying obligations of husband to wife.

Ketubim writings; biblical books of Psalms, Proverbs, and so on.

kibbutz galuyyot gathering together of the exiles; eschatological hope that all Israel will be restored to land. Now applied to migration of Jewish communities to the state of Israel.

kibbutz collective settlement in state of Israel, where property is held in common.

Kiddush HaShem "sanctification of the name of God." Applies to conduct of Jews among non-Jews that brings esteem on Jews, Judaism. In medieval times, martyrdom.

Kiddush sanctification, generally of wine, in proclamation of Sabbath, festival.

Kol Nidré "All vows"; prayer opening *Yom Kippur* evening service declaring that all vows made rashly during the year and not carried out are null and void.

kosher lit., fit, proper; applies to anything suitable for use according to Jewish law.

Lag BeOmer thirty-third day in seven-week period of counting the *omer*, or sheaf cut at harvest, from second day of Passover to Pentecost (Leviticus 23:15). Day of celebration for scholars.

Lamed Vav thirty-six men of humble vocation who are not recognized but by whose merit the world exists; they bring salvation in crisis.

liturgy religiously prescribed prayers

lulab palm branch used on *Sukkot*.

Maariv evening service.

Magen David Shield of David; six-pointed star that became distinctive Jewish symbol after the seventeenth century.

Mah Nishtannah "Wherein is this night different from all others?" Opening words of four questions asked by child at Passover *seder*.

Mahzor prayer book for New Year and Day of Atonement.

Malkhuyyot sovereignties, section of New Year Additional Service devoted to theme of God's sovereignty.

Maoz Tsur "Fortress, Rock of My Salvation"; Hanukkah hymn.

maror bitter herbs, consumed at Passover *Seder* in remembrance of the bitter life of slaves.

mashgiah supervisor of rituals, particularly ritual slaughter; must be expert in laws, pious and God-fearing. Ignorant man, motivated by financial gain, cannot supervise religious rites.

maskil enlightened man, follower of *Haskalah* (Enlightenment).

masorah tradition.

matzah unleavened bread, used for Passover.

mazzal tov good luck.

mazzal lit., constellation, star.

megillah scroll; usually, scroll of Esther, read at Purim.

Melavveh Malkah accompanying the Queen; the Sabbath meal held at end of holy day to prolong Sabbath celebration.

menorah candelabrum; nine-branched *menorah* is used at *Hanukkah;* seven-branched *menorah* was used in ancient Temple.

Messiah eschatological king to rule in end of time.

mezuzah parchment containing first two paragraphs of *Shema,* rolled tightly and placed in case, attached to doorposts of home.

Midrash exegesis of Scripture; also applied to collections of such exegeses.

miqveh ritual bath for immersion to wash away impurity; baptism.

minhah afternoon prayers.

minyan "ten"; number needed for quorum for worship.

Mishnah code of law promulgated by Judah the Prince (ca. 200 C.E.); in six parts concerning agricultural laws, festival and Sabbath law, family and personal status, torts, damages, and civil law, laws pertaining to the sanctuary and rules of ritual cleanness.

mitnaged "opponent"; opposition to Hasidism on the part of rationalists, Talmudists.

mitzvah "commandments." Technical sense: scriptural or Rabbinic injunctions; later, also used in sense of good deed; every human activity may represent an act of obedience to divine will.

Moed festival.

mohel ritual circumciser.

Mosaic what pertains to Moses or to the writings attributed to him, such as Mosaic law.

Musaf additional service on Sabbath and festivals, commemorating additional offering in Temple times.

musar lit., chastisement; instruction in right behavior; movement in modern Judaism emphasizing study and practice of ethical traditions, founded by Israel Salanter (1810–1883).

mystic someone who experiences a direct encounter with God's presence.

myth religious truth set forth in narrative form.

nasi prince.

navi prophet.

neder vow.

Neilah closing service at end of *Yom Kippur,* at nightfall when fast ends.

niggun melody, traditional tune for prayer.

Olam Hazeh, Olam Haba this world, the world to come.

omer sheaf cut in barley harvest.

Oneg Shabbat Sabbath delight.

Orthodoxy traditional Judaism; belief in historical event of revelation at Sinai of Oral and Written Torah, in binding character of Torah, and in authority of Torah sages to interpret Torah.

paradigm example, pattern.

Passover (Hebrew: *Pesah*) festival commemorating Exodus from Egypt, in spring month of *Nisan* (April).

peot "corners"; Leviticus 19:27 forbids removing hair at corners of head, meaning not to cut earlocks.

peshat literal meaning of scripture; distinct from *derash,* or homily.

Pharisee (from Hebrew *Parush*) separatist; party in ancient Judaism teaching Oral Torah revealed at Sinai along with Written Torah, preserved among prophets and sages down to the Pharisaic party; espoused prophetic ideals and translated them to everyday life of Jewry through legislation. Distinctive beliefs, according to Josephus: (1) immortality of the soul; (2) existence of angels; (3) divine providence; (4) freedom of will; (5) resurrection of the dead; (6) Oral Torah.

philosophy rational investigation of truths concerning being, ethics, conduct, knowledge.

pilpul dialectical reasoning in study of oral law.

piyyut synagogue poetry.

pogroms race riots against the Jews, involving looting, destruction of property, violence against persons, and murder; common in nineteenth-century Russia and twentieth-century Germany; a foretaste of the Holocaust.

profane secular, not sanctified; not to be confused with "profane" as in "profanity."

Purim festival commemorating deliverance of Persian Jews from extermination in fifth-century B.C.E., as related in the Scroll of Esther; takes place on the 14th of *Adar,* generally in March.

rabbi "my master"; title for teacher of Oral Torah.

Rabbinical Assembly association of Conservative rabbis in the United States.

Rabbinical Council association of Orthodox rabbis in United States.

Rashi a name for R. Solomon Isaac (1040–1105), from Rabbi Shelomo Yitzhak, hence *Rashi.* He was the writer of the most widely consulted of all commentaries on the Bible and Talmud.

rationalism belief that reason governs opinion, serves as a reliable source of knowledge.

Raba fourth-century Talmudic master, head of the Babylonian school at Mahoza.

recondite hidden, concealed.

reconstructionism movement to develop modern, naturalist theology for Judaism, founded by Mordecai M. Kaplan (1881–1983). Emphasizes Jewish peoplehood, sees Judaism as natural outgrowth of Jewish people's efforts to ensure their survival and answer basic human questions.

Reform religious movement advocating change of tradition to conform to conditions of modern life. Holds *Halakhah* to be human creation, subject to judgment of man; sees Judaism as historical religious experience of Jewish people.

Rosh Hashanah New Year, first day of Tishré (September).

rosh yeshivah head of Talmudic academy.

Sabbateanism Movement of followers of Sabbatai Zevi, messianic leader who became an apostate. Followers believed this apostasy was part of divine plan.

Sabbatai Zevi (1626–1676) Kabbalist who made mystical revelations and announced himself as Messiah in the Smyrna (Turkey) synagogue in 1665; went to Constantinople to claim his kingdom from sultan; was imprisoned and converted to Islam.

Sadducees sect of Temple priests and sympathizers who stressed the Written Torah and the right of the priesthood to interpret it against the Pharisaic claim that the Oral Torah held by them was the only means of interpretation. Rejected belief in resurrection of the dead, immortality of soul, angels, divine providence.

salvific having to do with salvation.

Sanhedrin Jewish legislative-administrative agency in Temple times.

secular everyday affairs, not sanctified.

Seder order; Passover home service.

Sefer Torah Scroll of Torah.

Selihot penitential prayers, recited before New Year.

semikhah laying on of hands; ordination.

Sephardi (pl. m) descendants of Spanish Jewry, generally in Mediterranean countries.

Shaharit morning service; dawn.

shalom peace.

Shammai colleague of Hillel, first-century Pharisaic sage.

Shabuot feast of weeks; Pentecost; commemorates giving of Torah at Mt. Sinai.

shehitah ritual slaughter; consists in cutting through both windpipe and gullet by means of sharp knife, examining to see both have been cut through.

Shekhinah presence of God in world.

Shema proclamation of unity of God: Deuteronomy 6:4–9, 11:13–21, Numbers 15:37–41.

Shemini Atzeret eighth day of solemn assembly (Numbers 30:35); last day of *Sukkot*. This is a holy day in itself.

Sheva Berakhot Seven Blessings recited at wedding ceremony.

Shiva seven days of mourning following burial of close relative.

shofar ram's horn, sounded during high holy day period, from a month before New Year until the end of *Yom Kippur*.

Shoferot *Shofar* verses concerning revelation, read in the New Year Additional Service.

shohet ritual slaughterer.

Shulhan Arukh prepared table; code of Jewish law by Joseph Karo, published 1565; authoritative for orthodox Jewry.

Siddur Jewish prayer book for all days except holy days.

simhah celebration.

Simhat Torah rejoicing of law; second day of *Shemini Atzeret,* on which the Torah-reading cycle is completed; celebrated with song and dance.

Sukkah booth, tabernacle.

Sukkot autumn harvest festival, ending high holy day season.

synagogue Greek translation of Hebrew *bet hakeneset* (house of assembly). Place of Jewish prayer, study, assembly.

taboo any prohibition based on religious concerns.

takkanah decree, ordinance issued by Rabbinic authority.

tallit prayer shawl consisting of four-cornered cloth with fringes (Numbers 15:38), worn by adult males in morning service.

Talmid Hakham disciple of the wise.

Talmud Torah study of Torah; education.

Talmud Mishnah plus commentary on the Mishnah produced in Rabbinical academies from ca. 200 to 500 C.E. (called *Gemara*) form the Talmud. Two Talmuds were produced—one in Palestine, the other in Babylonia. From 500 C.E. onward, the Babylonian Talmud was the primary source for Judaic law and theology.

Tanakh Hebrew Bible; formed of Torah, Nebi'im, Ketubim, Pentateuch, Prophets, Writings; hence, TaNaKH.

tanna one who studies and teaches; a rabbinical master mentioned in Mishnah is called a *Tanna.*

Tannaite an authority of the Mishnah or of the same period as the Mishnah, up to ca. 200 C.E.

Tefillin phylacteries worn by adult males in morning service, based on Exodus 13:1, 11, Deuteronomy 6:4-9, 11:13–21. These passages are written on parchment, placed in leather cases, and worn on the left arm and forehead.

Tehillim psalms.

teqiah sounding of *shofar* on New Year.

tenet opinion, principle, doctrine

teref, terefah lit.: torn; generally: unkosher food.

theology systematic statement of religious faith in proportionate and coherent presentation.

Torah lit., revelation. At first, the Five Books of Moses; then scriptures as a whole; then the whole corpus of revelation, both written and oral, taught by Pharisaic Judaism. Talmud Torah: study of Torah. Standing by itself, Torah can mean "study," the act of learning and discussion of the tradition.

Tosafot novellae on the Talmud, additions generally to the commentary of Rashi. The Tosafists, authorities who produced the *Tosafot,* flourished during the twelfth and thirteenth centuries in northern France.

Tosefta supplements to the Mishnah.

tractate a subdivision of the Mishnah. The Mishnah is divided into six divisions that in turn are divided into tractates, each with its own topic. A tractate, then, is a topical exposition of the Mishnah. Commentaries to the Mishnah, the Tosefta and the two Talmuds then select Mishnah-tractates for close reading and amplification.

transcendent what goes beyond the ordinary limits of this world.

tzedakah righteousness; used for charity, philanthropy.

Tzidduk HaDin justification of the judgment; prayer of dying man.

tzitzit fringes of *tallit.*

virtuoso a person who has special knowledge or skill; an expert; a specialist.

Wissenschaft des Judentums science of Judaism; scientific study using scholarly methods of philology, history, and philosophy of Jewish religion, literature and history; founded in nineteenth-century Germany.

yahrzeit anniversary of a relative's death.

Yahweh see **Jehovah.**

Yamim Noraim Days of Awe; *Rosh Hashanah* plus the intervening days and *Yom Kippur,* ten days in all.

Yeshiva (pl. *ot*) "session"; talmudic academy.

Yetzer HaRa, Yetzer Tov evil inclination, good inclination.

Yigdal hymn that contains the thirteen principles of faith formulated by Maimonides; sung at the end of synagogue worship as the creed of Judaism.

Yiddish Jewish language of Eastern Europe, now used in United States, Israel, Argentina, and Mexico, in addition to vernacular; originally a Judeo-German dialect with large number of Hebrew and Slavic words.

Yom Kippur Day of Atonement; fast day for penitence.

Zaddik righteous man; in Hasidism, intermediary, master of Hasidic circle.

Zikhronot remembrances, prayers on theme of God's remembering his mercy, covenant, in New Year Additional Service.

Zionism movement to secure Jewish state in Palestine, founded in 1897 by Theodor Herzl.

Zohar medieval Kabbalistic (mystical) book, completed by the fourteenth century in Spain; mystical commentary on biblical passages; stories of mystical life of the *Tanna* Simeon bar Yohai.

Index

A

Abraham, 11
Adam
  commandments assigned
    to, 10–11
  parallel with Israel, 8–9, 52,
    129
Adon Olam, 293
Adonai, 295
adultery, 81
African-American civil rights
  movement, 263
ages of Judaism, 17–24
aggadah, 293
agricultural rules, 51
agriculture, as principal
  occupation, 58
Agudath Israel, 244–45, 254
Ahad HaAm, 231, 232
Ahavah, 293
Alenu, 126–28, 293
aliyah, 293
altruism, 19
Am haares, 293
American Judaism of
  Holocaust and
  Redemption, 255–63,
  273–74, 276
Amidah, 113, 293
Amora, 293
Amos, 5
The Ancient City, 229
androgyneity, and Israel,
  83–88
anti-Semitism, 22–23, 26–27,
  184, 202–3, 228–30,
  238–39, 258–59. *See also*
  Zionism
Apikoros, 293
apostates, 257
Appointed Times, 51, 53, 54
Aqiba, 96
Aramaic, 66
archaeology, 234
archetype, 293
Aseret HaDibrot, 294
Ashkenazim, 293
Ashré, 293
assimilation, 272, 293
Auschwitz, 256
Austria-Hungary, 201
Av, Ninth of, 293

B

Baal Shem Tov, 246, 293
Babylon, Israel in exile in, 17
Babylonian Talmud. *See* Bavli
Bar Kokhba, 18, 91–93, 96
bar mitzvah, 140, 159–60, 293
bat mitzvah, 140, 159–60, 293
Bavli (Talmud of Babylonia),
  20
B.C.E., 293
behavior, in religion, 14
belief, 14
Ben Kosiba, 18
Berakhah, 293
Berger, David, 252
Berit milah, 156–59
"Besht," 246
Bet Am, 293
Bet Din, 293
Bet Midrash, 293
betrothals, 81
Bimah, 293
Birkat HaMazon, 293
birth rites, 156–59
Book of the Pious, 178–80
Breuer, Isaac, 215
Brit milah, 294
burial rites, 140, 160–61

C

calendar, Judaic, 138–39
Canada, 259
canon, 294
caste systems, breakdown of,
  200–203
C.E., 294
Central Conference of
  American Rabbis, 205–6,
  222, 294
change, as reform, 199, 207–8,
  214, 223, 226
charity, Jewish, 273–74
Christianity
  and Israel, 31–32, 100,
    101–2, 197
  and Judaism today, 28–29,
    257
  messianic crisis and, 93–94
  and Pharisees, 31–32
  predominance of, 21–22,
    25–26
  rise of, in Rome, 29, 30

Chronicles, 6
chronology, of events in
  Judaism, xxiii–xxx
circumcision. *See* Berit milah
civil law, 51, 53
classical Judaism. *See* Rabbinic
  Judaism
cleanness/uncleanness, 33, 55
code, 294
Cohen, 294
commandments, God's, 10–12,
  90, 116, 135–36
community
  relating Midrash to, 66
  and religion, xx–xxi, 14
  social entity of, 57–58
confession of sin, 154–55
Conservative Judaism, 220–27,
  294
  demography, in U.S.,
    270–71
  as third Judaism in moder-
    nity, 199, 202, 207
Constantine, 29
converts, to Judaism, 103,
  279–81
Coulange, Fustel de, 229
covenantal nomism, 184–85
creation, 114–16, 130, 131,
  148, 154
credo, 294
creed, xx, 294
criminal law, 51
Cronbach, Abraham, 209–10
cult
  conduct of, in Mishnah,
    51, 52–53
  cultic purity, in Mishnah,
    51, 55
  defined, 294
  system of, 32–34
cultural Judaism, 268
cultural Zionism, 232

D

Damages, 55–56
Daniel, 6
dates, table of, in Judaism,
  xxiii–xxx
David, 5, 35, 233–34
Day of Atonement (Yom
  Kippur), 139, 153–55, 271